ACCOUNTING THOUGHT AND PRACTICE THROUGH THE YEARS

Edited by Richard P. Brief

A Garland Series

CHAMBERS ON ACCOUNTING

Volume II: Accounting Practice and Education

R. J. Chambers and G. W. Dean, editors

Garland Publishing, Inc.
New York and London
1986

For a complete list of Garland's publications in accounting,
please see the final pages of this volume.

The papers in this volume are reprinted with the permission of the
journals, editors, and publishers listed in the table of contents.

Library of Congress Cataloging-in-Publications Data

Chambers, R. J. (Raymond J.), 1917–
Accounting practice and education.

(Chambers on accounting ; v. 2) (Accounting thought
and practice through the years)
Reprint of works originally published 1949–1982.
1. Accounting. 2. Accounting—Study and teaching.
I. Dean, G. W. II. Title. III. Series: Chambers, R. J.
(Raymond J.), 1917–   . Chambers on accounting ; v. 2.
IV. Series: Accounting thought and practice through the
years.
HF5603.6.C46   vol. 2   [HF5629]   657 s   86-9896
ISBN 0-8240-7859-4   [657]

Design by Bonnie Goldsmith

The volumes in this series are printed on
acid-free, 250-year-life paper.

Printed in the United States of America

CONTENTS

PREFACE

These papers deal variously with some aspects of practice, pedagogy, and prescription. The foundations of practical expertise and of confidence in the wisdom of a profession are laid in the course of professional education and training. Rules of practice and habits of thought then learned strongly influence what is passed on to the next generation. If the colleges and universities inculcate respect for disciplined thought as the foundation of serviceable practice, graduates might acquire the habit of submitting established and proposed rules to scrutiny in the light of their experienced or prospective consequences; alternatively they might look to the universities for appraisal of existing practices and for the exploratory development of better practices. These things are characteristic of fields of inquiry and practice that have an established inquisitive and critical tradition. If, on the other hand, the colleges and universities provide instruction that is largely traditional and doctrinaire, the next generation of practitioners (and, indeed, teachers) can scarcely be expected to be inventive themselves, to tolerate criticism of prevalent practice, or to be sympathetic towards innovative proposals.

In the mid-twentieth century accounting had no critical tradition. There had been some notable critics—Paton, Hatfield, Canning, Sweeney, and MacNeal. But the strictures and suggestions of few count for little against the many who have been indoctrinated in the conventional wisdom. The general textbook literature was already being augmented by recommendations of the professional bodies. Both lent their weight to what was regarded as accepted practice, notwithstanding the increasing evidence of flaws in the basic ideas on which it was based. All alleged deficiencies were considered as minor blemishes, to be overcome by some variant of commonly used rules. The upshot was the corpus of overlapping rules, two or more for almost every item found in periodical financial statements, that has become the common lore of accounting.

The double-entry process gave accounting the appearance of being systematic, but the multiplicity of permissible rules made the appearance a delusion. The increasingly discursive nature of textbooks and the growing periodical literature appeared to provide justifications for the rules. But often they were ad hoc justifications, offered without regard for the internal consistency of periodical summaries or for the usefulness of those summaries in practical business affairs. That the profession should uphold such a style of practice, and that its academic arm should perpetuate it, seemed to be demeaning to both. Many of the papers in this volume are critical; some were intended to be stridently critical, for the attention of the many is not likely otherwise to be drawn from their perennial preoccupation with the minutiae of business or, in academia, with the bland exposition of what is respectable. Whatever might be offered in their place, traditional practice and pedagogy deserved close examination.

The sixties and seventies were marked by increasing disquiet, among governmental and regulatory authorities, with corporate accounting practices that yielded misleading information and masked actual or potential financial distress. In well-publicized cases, actions alleging negligence and misrepresentation resulted in heavy damages awards against auditors. Leaders of professional organizations had for some time been of the view that the number of alternative permissible accounting rules should be reduced. The conjunction of these things gave impetus to the setting of accounting standards by boards or committees sponsored or endorsed by professional bodies. The papers written since the early seventies are concerned mainly with a number of aspects of standard-setting. Among the most important is the necessity of a well-formed notion of the function of periodical accounts. The prevalent superabundance of potentially conflicting rules and prescriptions is the legacy of a past undisciplined by acknowledgement of the relevance to choice and action of dated factual information. If that were acknowledged, few and quite general standards would be sufficient guidance to skilled professionals to secure the fitness to function of the products of the accounting process.

R.J. Chambers
G.W. Dean
December 1985

THE TRAINING OF ACCOUNTANTS

TRAINING OR EDUCATION?

The spirit of innovation which appears to invest almost every aspect of living to-day has left unmistakeable marks on our systems of education. It could be said that the invasion of utilitarianism (on which is based so many of our modern practices) has even perverted our notions of education completely, leaving in its stead "training", and in the minds of the young a desire for "training" rather than for "education". Let me clarify the distinction I wish to draw.

The type of intellectual exercise most eagerly sought to-day is training for the purpose of following a selected vocation. The student is concerned more with the acquisition of a few formulae, cut and dried dogmas or rules of thumb fit for immediate practical application, than with the development of an outlook on life, an underlying code or philosophy by which his approach to vocational and personal problems may be guided. There has been, even among so-called "educators", a tendency to mistake the shadow for the substance in

1

training their protegees, with the result that the latter go out to face the problems of business or profession armed only with the limited range of remedies their "practical" studies have brought before them. This, of course, is to the very great detriment of both teachers and taught.

The mental discipline which seems to me to be most useful and practical (though the philosophers may scorn the suggestion) is just that which has so roundly been condemned as "theoretical" and "impractical" and "academic" by so-called practical hard-headed men of affairs. This generalisation I make without specification of any particular vocational objective. For, whatever individuals hope to do in life they must do with, or to, or in competition with, or through, other people. All who aspire to responsibility in any society, therefore, need some theory of society, some philosophy of the place and function of power, skill and knowledge in modern societies and some idea of the evolution of modern social (including business) and political institutions. These may be acquired only through the study of subjects such as modern and ancient history, philosophy, literature, the theory of law and government, anthropology, economics and related subjects.

But why are these subjects so lightly regarded as basic education for a life in business, public administration or in the professions? Mainly, I think, it is due to the absence of a theory of education among the practising managers and public officials, who, and the professional bodies which, regulate entry into responsible positions in their respective fields. The above subjects *seem* to be too remote from practical affairs to be of real consequence. As a result, many of to-day's graduates and those leaving the higher educational institutions have insufficient breadth of view and inadequate theoretical concepts to meet successfully to-day's multitudinous complex problems.

Education may be considered as a process by which the innate qualities of the student are drawn out and developed, and by which the student's mind is enriched both because of the experience suffered and because of the knowledge gained. Teaching to be really educational should, therefore, aim to provide such stimuli for the student that he goes forward seeking an understanding of the principles of his subject rather than sitting back smug in the knowledge that he "swatted" the correct material for his examination.

STATUS OF THE ACCOUNTANCY PROFESSION.

Those who have had the patience to labour through the above comments may well wonder what all this has to do with the training of accountants. In my opinion the present accountancy syllabi suffer from the defects implied by the above comments and the consequences are apparent in the composition of the profession to-day. Attention was drawn at the Annual General Meeting recently in Sydney to the fact that accountancy is hardly recognised as a profession in America and the extent to which it is conceded a professional status, except among accountants, in Australia appears to be in doubt.

It seems to me that this is a direct consequence of the type of service accountants give or are equipped to give, and indirectly of the type of people we accountants are. It would be too much to expect recognition as professional people when it is a common jibe that "adolescents with little ability in any particular direction may find employment as accountants," and that "the ranks of accountants are filled by people who have no chance, by reason of intellectual limitations, of excelling in any other field". We should, I think cease worrying about status and recognition by the business, professional, or general community and concentrate on delivering the goods—recognition will come if we deserve it. It is my thesis that accountants in Australia have never earned the right to recognition as a potent force in the business world: our inter-Institute differences have shown us a disunited series of groups interested in status, membership and similar things rather than service to the business community and to the profession itself.

INTELLECTUAL CONDITION OF THE PROFESSION.

Lest it be said "criticism is easy, proof less so" I would like to give some facts to support these contentions. In the first place, one of the common objects of professional institutions, including institutes of accountants, is the advancement of the knowledge of the subject of their profession. This involves three separate things,

Training of Accountants—continued.

to my mind : reading, thinking, writing. In each, accountants as a group are lagging seriously.

Though some of the Institutes provide quite good library facilities, some registrars must be disappointed with the extent to which the libraries are used. An examination of the lending section of one such library revealed that only the standard texts, strictly utilitarian reading, were used to any great extent. I was greatly disappointed to find that hardly any of the hundreds of Sydney metropolitan members found the time or inclination to venture into the closely allied subjects of economics, statistics, finance or management. The extent to which magazine articles are read is a matter I have not tried to determine, but the fact that scarcely any correspondence takes place on the subject-matter of such articles may be taken as some indication of lack of active interest. Or does it mean lack of thought?

Which brings me to the second deficiency mentioned above. Australian accountants seem to be singularly credulous. How few really thoughtful people there are among us! How few have courage enough to tackle the dogmas and the practices which modern accounting has thoughtlessly inherited from a more leisurely past! One needs only to scan the pages of *The Australian Accountant* to see how few of the members of the Commonwealth Institute are assuming the responsibility of advancing the frontiers of accounting knowledge. The rest of us, ostrich-like, bury our heads in our daily problems and resolutely refuse to believe that there are any theoretical problems or unbeaten paths in accounting. And even those of us who are taking an interest in the recent developments in accounting theory, stemming largely from America, are adopting too receptive an attitude, in my opinion. Can we expect recognition if we shirk the obligation to clarify our theories, to replace blind acceptance of accounting practices with a critical, inquiring approach to the problems of those we serve? The professions of law and medicine oblige their members to keep up with developments in their fields ; until some such discipline is imposed on accountants from within or without as is imposed on lawyers and doctors, I fear it will be worse

than useless to continue to deplore our status.

In writing we are quite as resourceless as in thinking. Unquestionably it is useless to write unless prior thinking has given rise to new concepts or to a new understanding of relationships between concepts. Our failure to build up a substantial literature is perhaps only a reflection of lack of critical or constructive ability. I cannot but deplore the nebulous character of the concepts purveyed in some of the standard texts used by accounting students ; the fact that of the first fifteen "cost" bulletins of the Australasian Institute of Cost Accountants only *five* were the work of individual accountants ; and the fact that so few of us recognise that accountants as such must perpetuate themselves and that a sound step in the direction of professional eugenics is the provision of a worthwhile literature for accountants in training and in practice.

WANTED—A THEORY OF TRAINING OR OF EDUCATION.

The indifference to which I allude in the above broadside seems to me to pervade the educational standards of the institutes. One of the purposes of the institutes is to provide guidance for training institutions and to establish standards for admission to the various ranks of membership provided. The opportunity to select for admission only people who would be a credit to the institutes appears to me to have been forgone by the educational committees of the institutes. I was very interested to read in the March issue of *The Australian Accountant*, Mr. Keown's suggestions for revision of the syllabus of the Institute. But piece-meal alteration of the syllabus will only be effectively carried out if :

(*a*) there is an underlying educational theory by reference to which each subject in the syllabus may be justified, and each subject may be placed in its most satisfactory position in the course of study.

(*b*) a worthwhile course is established as an ideal towards which each small alteration may contribute.

I hope opinions will vary regarding the content and scope of a "worthwhile course", for only if there are divergent

3

Training of Accountants—continued.

opinions, a "clash of minds", may we expect a carefully constructed and educationally justifiable course to emerge. It should be clear therefore that I expect no immediate general agreement with the proposals set forth below: I shall be disappointed both by passivity and by violent agreement because this note shall then appear to have failed to stimulate the criticism which precedes creation or reconstruction.

Criteria for a Professional Course.

To the best of my knowledge, the educational committees of the Institutes have never made public, except in brief references in annual reports, the educational theories upon which course structures have been based. It may be, of course, that there are no such theories recognised by the committees, and it may be that there has been no cause to parade the educational bases of accounting courses. The criteria which I propose to set down therefore will not have been considered in their explicit form by accountants generally before; and they consequently deserve close attention.

FIRSTLY: If accountants are to be accorded similar professional status to that enjoyed by University graduates in vocational subjects, *the course of study must resemble in admission qualifications, in structure and in scope, other University courses.* This requirement is not to be taken as a device for restricting the field to be covered; though it certainly will restrict entry to those with a recognised level of general education and an aptitude for, or keen interest in, intensive vocational study. Regarding structure, it might be said that degree courses commonly require continued study in each of a restricted number of broad fields, so that the fields of study most nearly related to accounting studies should be considered at least. "Scope" suggests the inculcation of a wide general approach or outlook rather than too narrow and specialised a form of training; a broad appreciation of the function, social significance and potential developments of accounting certainly cannot be acquired under to-day's courses and tuition.

SECONDLY: *Provision must be made to give a satisfactory grounding in scientific methods as a basis for work in the main* fields of study, mentioned in the previous paragraph. As I have suggested earlier, far too much is taken for granted by accounting students to-day; too much confidence is placed in the dogmas of the textbooks and too little in the exercise of reason —and all because of the type of training sanctioned by the profession. We must learn to evaluate textbook rules and concepts for ourselves, discounting the prestige of writers and speakers, and exercising independent thought on all matters pertinent to the profession. Scientific method should of course form the basis for proceeding to useful generalisations or uniformities throughout the entire course of study.

THIRDLY: *A vocational course should combine the theory of and applied aspects of the main subjects in expedient proportions.* The importance of this feature cannot be too strongly emphasised. If accountancy is to be anything better than a trade, it must involve more than a routine trade skill. Accounting courses at present place high premiums on specific "trade" skill, i.e. the ability to balance books, compile balance sheets, draw cheques satisfactorily etc.—theory occupies a very subordinate place, because firstly the importance of theory has scarcely been recognised and, secondly because there is little theory underlying the courses as they are at present. A widening of the scope of training will inevitably increase the theory necessary in a well balanced course.

General Direction of Improvement.

The proposals submitted under this section will perhaps be met with considerable suspicion by many older, experienced accountants who will claim that the "old ways" of teaching are the best ways; they will also doubtless be met with alarm and even opposition from many teaching bodies because of the costliness of longer courses and the consequent scaling down of the number of original enrollees. It is, however, a matter for the members of the profession to decide; we will succumb to the vested interests if we have no pride in the development of worthwhile standards of competence, and we will set infinite store by the opinion of the "die hards" if we have no concept of the impact of social and economic change on the place and functions

Training of Accountants—continued.

of accounting and accountants in the business world of to-day and to-morrow.

In present courses there seem to be five major omissions which I shall deal with in detail. They are:

(a) Economic Theory.

(b) Relationships between accounting theory and economic theory.

(c) Management, and the place of accounting in management.

(d) Elementary Actuarial Studies.

(e) History of the development of accounting theory and practice.

It is not suggested that one full course should be required in each of these; (a) and (b) in conjunction appear to warrant two papers, though of itself (b) is not a major subject; (c) and (e) are in my opinion worthy of one paper each, at least.

(a) *Economic Theory*:

Unquestionably accounting is the technique developed and used universally for the measurement of significant economic phenomena. This being the case it seems highly irregular that the training of accountants should cover so little of economic theory. That part of the field of financial economics which, in the Commonwealth Institute's syllabus, is entitled "Banking, Finance and Foreign Exchange", is surely inadequate for the student who is to spend his lifetime in the midst of every variety of economic circumstance. A wide treatment of economic theory is essential to an understanding of the place and limitations of accounting procedures. The Economics Department of the Sydney University permits undergraduates to specialise in accounting in their programme for the degree of Bachelor of Economics, but concurrently the full sequence of four economics subjects must be taken. I think something more rigorous than the present smattering of economics should be required of all accounting students, not because it would serve as a restricting device, but because it would engender greater respect for the skill of the accountant and the status of his profession.

(b) *Accounting Theory and Economic Theory*:

The relationship between the two fields of study, accounting and economics, has been the subject of much vapid comment, but little constructive thought. It is admitted that students cannot be expected to explore the more difficult aspects of accounting theory, but it is believed some attempt should be made to indicate the fruitfulness of a greater understanding between accountants and economists. The approach of each is, of course, based on rather different premises; the line that should be taken, I believe, is that one field is really complementary to the other, that each can throw valuable light on the problems of the other, and that for effective administration of business the findings of each should be accepted within the field it purports to cover. The impact of each on the other would result in considerable clarification of the basic assumptions of much economic and business theory.

(c) *Management*:

It should not be necessary to point out that the accountants qualifying through Institute examinations fall within either of two main vocational groups; those who are engaged or who hope to engage in practice as professional accountants, and those who are engaged in accounting or administrative work in commerce and industry. Apostles of specialisation would probably argue for special courses to cover the immediate vocational needs of the two groups. However, in providing only one syllabus for both groups, I believe educational committees have acted wisely, for, every case of specialisation introduces new problems of integrating the specialists, whereas a sound general training for all students ensures wider dissemination of knowledge of the nature of the problems of those who for various reasons specialise in post-training years. General training which ignores the immediate environment of every accountant, however, does not come within what I describe as a "*sound general training*".

Every accountant, whether in business or in practice, is continually surrounded with forms of organised activity and problems of management. I do not know whether it is true in fact that accountants, by training or by the nature of their work, develop an attitude which is inimical to harmonious relationships with other technical people in specific business situations. But I do know that many people trained in other technologies *feel* that way about accoun-

5

tants. It could be argued that too great a preoccupation with figures does predispose people to adopt an unrealistic attitude towards the practical issues which the figures only imperfectly describe; but it is not my aim to amplify that matter just now.

A sound accounting syllabus should recognise that many professional accountants become directors of companies; that quite a number of commercial accountants become directors or managers of the enterprises they serve; and that all who progress no further than the middle executive level are constantly in contact with other specialists in a service capacity which they are only qualified to fill if they acknowledge explicitly the limitations of their techniques and the importance of the *facts* which they endeavour to record. Recognition of these things should take the form of some managerial studies in formal training for accountants, firstly, so that a narrow technological bias may be corrected, and secondly, so that accounting may be set in its true perspective in the field of business.

The Accountancy Diploma Course of the Sydney Technical College requires studies in "Personnel in Commerce", "Business Administration and Organisation" and "Business Economics" in its final year; the Melbourne College also requires study in Management in the fourth year. For their potential corrective effects, such wider studies should, I believe, be included in all accounting training for responsible positions in commerce and industry.

(d) *Actuarial Studies:*

The recognition of the need for an elementary knowledge of statistical procedures should lead to like recognition of the value of an elementary knowledge of the bases of actuarial practice. I feel that few accountants take much interest in, or are greatly concerned with, the theory underlying calculations relating to sinking funds, depreciation rates, annuities and perpetuities, largely because of the failure of their training to inspire any regard for the relevance of these calculations to business practice. The growing interest in superannuation systems, self-insurance and similar matters seems to justify much greater attention to actuarial studies from accountants than appears to have been given in the past. But not only it is a matter of immediate practical consequence, it is a field which would repay close attention by accountants because of the greater variety of techniques or concepts it would provide for the prospective theorists in accounting.

(e) *Development of Accounting Theory and Practice:*

In previous sections there have been set down recommendations by which accounting can be set in its true business or managerial environment. I think it is also important that students in any subject should understand the processes by which present theories and practices were developed. The doctrinaire approach of many tutors and teachers in formal training institutions tends more often to stifle the initiative of trainees, than to encourage them to undertake the great intellectual adventure which is open to all who keep before them the concept of development and potential growth in the art, science or technology to which they are allied.

It is contrary to all experience to continue in the belief that the accounting forms and concepts deemed adequate to-day will remain adequate for future purposes. Students who are not required to study formally the growth of accounting practices and theories, and the economic and business facts which have played a part in moulding them, are in danger of overlooking the possibility of improvement. Accountants, and all people occupying positions of responsibility, are continuously meeting novel combinations of factors already experienced, and situations involving altogether new factors; the very novelty of these situations demands an imaginative approach rather than uncritical applications of outmoded procedures taught in dogmatic fashion, without the perspective which a study in derivation and development could give.

POSSIBLE DELETIONS FROM EXISTING SYLLABUS.

The five suggestions just outlined may be regarded independently of what follows. In themselves they would add substantially to the content and rigor of the course. But even if none was adopted, within the present course structure there is, I think, room for improvement.

Training of Accountants—continued.

Vocational training, it will be agreed, must take into account the probable subsequent occupational environment of trainees. No professional man pretends to be able to go through his professional life without making full and frequent use of handbooks, reference books, indices and other aids. It seems, however, that accounting trainees are obliged to take the view that they are learning for all time, for the accounting and auditing subjects require rather an elaborate knowledge of the special accounting procedures of many different types of business undertaking, including banks and insurance companies. (This generalisation is not explicitly supported by the Commonwealth Institute's Syllabus; but the contents of the recommended textbooks lend it plenty of implied support. This seems an appropriate point to suggest that authors, instead of mingling their material, might in future consider offering basic training material in one part and applications of basic principles, *for reference* by people in professional practice, in an entirely separate part of their works. For special accounting systems and audit programmes this is particularly pertinent.

It is recognised by examiners and educational committees that *every* type of business cannot be covered. Why then bother to cover *any* special application? If it is for the purpose of lending breadth to the course, surely there are many better ways of doing it than by elaborating special types of bookkeeping problems!

Another direction in which the present syllabus could be changed is by the inclusion of auditing in the accounting subjects. When all is said and done, there is little in auditing that is not either a matter of accounting or of law; why then the special subject? It may be urged of course that auditing is an important, if not the most important, part of a public accountant's practice. That may be so, but the same things which concern accountants as auditors, concern accountants in commercial undertakings; to use the term "Auditing" as a separate division of course material is only defensible in respect of specific auditing techniques. There may be sufficient of such material to justify a single course, but not two courses. I am thus in agreement with Mr. Keown (*The Australian Accountant*, March 1948, p. 68) regarding the status of auditing as a separate subject; with his suggestions for altering the content of the legal subjects I also fully agree.

REFORM IN GENERAL.

Throughout this paper I have endeavoured to keep in mind:

(a) the desirability of a wider training and a more selective training for accountants, as a basis for a broader outlook on business and community life than narrow specialisation bestows.

(b) the practical difficulties which confront the introduction of subjects radically different from the main line of study into any course of vocational training.

There are other subjects which could profitably be considered as the basis for a broad general education for accountants, but many of them may be regarded as beyond the immediate interest of an examining body for admission to a specific profession. However, it is considered at least necessary that preliminary qualifications should include secondary education to matriculation standard, *without* nominating any special matriculation subject. There will be ample specialisation to follow, without putting the trainee-accountant in blinkers before he commences his qualifying studies.

PROPOSAL.

No delusions are entertained that within a short period many sweeping changes can be introduced into the syllabi of accounting institutes. While there is a plurality of institutes there will be competition for membership, and so long as training remains to a large extent in the hands of private tutors they will be able to call the tune. However, in the hope that some of the burdens under which the profession labours may at some future time be removed, the following outline of a course of professional study is offered. The subjects are listed as study sequences within selected fields, not as they might be required for defining intermediate and final stages.

Accounting and Auditing:

(a) Intermediate Accounting and Auditing.

7

Training of Accountants—continued.

    (*b*) Business Statistics.
    (*c*) Advanced Accounting.
    (*d*) Auditing and Investigations.
    (*e*) History of Accounting Theory and Practice.

Law :

    (*a*) Commercial Law (including Bankruptcy).
    (*b*) Company Law.
    (*c*) Taxation Law.

Economics and Business :

    (*a*) Scientific Method in Business.
    (*b*) General and Descriptive Economics.
    (*c*) Financial Economics.
    (*d*) Business Organisation and Management.

No attempt has been made to specify the degree of intensity of study in the above fields for the proposal is an expression of a long-term objective, rather than a plan for immediate implementation.

AGAIN—TRAINING OR EDUCATION?

Accountants comprise one group in a very large class of people who are closely concerned, in their day to day activities, with relationships between many different social groups. These relationships are not just a matter of debit and credit or pounds shilling and pence; they involve the hopes, opportunities and aspirations of sentient human beings. The ability of the accountant to add something worthwhile to social situations will depend on the quality of his thinking and the range of concepts within his reach. The above outline, though still strictly vocational, attempts to provide for the development of critical thinking by the requirement of study and application of scientific method and of some historical study. It adds to the accountant's range of concepts by obliging him to embark on some study of managerial problems. But much more can be done to increase his effectiveness as a contributor to social progress. Post-graduate study of such subjects as political theory, social philosophy, and managerial theory and practice would be an ideal way of rounding out the education of accountants. The Institutes should provide opportunities for such studies should the new generation of accountants develop a taste for creative thinking on the social and business problems of their day.

Meanwhile, as it is so difficult to arouse interest in Institute activities even of an immediately practical nature, I expect little reaction to these radical proposals for post-graduate work. Those who do think in terms of true professional status and expansion of the field of business knowledge and theory should remember that no movement of the type they suggest is initially a mass movement; it depends for its origin, impetus, and often for its fruition, on the effort of the critical, imaginative minority. That being the case, it is certain that the accountancy profession, as many other professions, will never be able to claim that the bulk of its members have been so educated that they have developed a philosophy of their place in society and the social function of their technology, unless a revolution in the profession, much far far-reaching than the above proposals, takes place.

Those who take an active and hopeful interest in the progress of the profession, and have its advancement at heart need no spurring; the remainder of the profession should consider the words of Francis Bacon:

I hold every man a debtor to his profession; from the which as men of course do seek to receive countenance and profit, so ought they to endeavour themselves by way of amends to be a help and ornament thereunto.

THE SPICE OF ACCOUNTING

Variety of mere nothings gives more pleasure than uniformity of something.
—RICHTER.

The extent to which the form and content of financial statements are discussed in recent and current periodicals and books may easily be taken as a measure of rapidly growing acceptance of the need for a clear and unequivocal public statement of business facts. The conclusion, however, seems to be contradicted, sharply contradicted, by the facts. There may be growing acceptance, but its growth is scarcely measurable in some respects, even if we examine the practices current during a period as long as ten years. It is the writer's purpose here to illustrate this contention from the "stock" notations in the published statements of a sample of fifty companies, large and small, whose securities are listed on one or more of the Australian Stock Exchanges. (It should be pointed out that this is only part of a wider study, the final conclusions of which may differ in some respects from the present tentative conclusions.)

IS UNIFORMITY A DESIRABLE OBJECTIVE?

For the purpose of gaining some general idea of the changes in balance sheet presentation, a list was made of the various ways in which the different assets and their bases of valuation were described. It is granted that of all assets, the item "Stock in Trade" was likely to show the greatest variety of bases of valuation, and that the case made out here is stronger than if we were to take all the items in the assets side of the balance sheet together. But the writer was not at all prepared for the bewildering array of descriptions derived from the sample of fifty. It seemed at first glance that the only generalization possible was that uniformity in accounting, or rather in the presentation of accounting statements, was not highly regarded amongst those responsible for published statements.

It seems that no case has been made out, by the Institutes and individuals who proclaim the virtues of a standard terminology, with sufficient strength or cogency to influence the general body of accountants to adopt recommended forms and terms. And, it is submitted, no change of a general and noticeable character can be expected until accountants generally *are* persuaded of the real importance of uniformity. The fact that accountants are in reality subject to the directions of managers and boards of directors in these matters is not overlooked; but, unless accountants are convinced, they will have little in the way of argument or personal conviction to offer to their managers or boards as justification for a change to newer and better methods of presentation.

There are many reasons why uniformity in technical details (such as stock valuation notations) as between companies should be widely adopted. Firstly, uniformity aids shareholders and investors, particularly those who have interests in a number of different undertakings; the present variety must be very confusing, so confusing, perhaps, that the whole purpose of giving a valuation notation is defeated. To know that stock is valued on a few widely accepted bases is better than having to decide on the effect of some of the vague and almost meaningless phrases now used. Secondly, it would aid all those who assist investors, for it would remove the need for much of the speculation which must take place about stock values and fixed asset values.

Thirdly, it would aid creditors and bankers, for these groups are concerned even to a greater degree than investors

10

and shareholders in the liquidity of businesses, of vastly more business undertakings than individual investors; and in appraising the financial situation, stock may be a most important item.

Fourthly, it would give to all outside interested parties — the general public, the consumer, the worker, governmental authorities — more obvious evidence than they have yet had that there is a definite, recognized procedure among accountants, a form that is correct, a terminology that is widely accepted. The profession can well afford to take great pains to have this view established; otherwise it will lack cohesion, and hence social influence and strength as a profession.

THE TABLE

A glance at the table will show how heterogeneous in this one respect of stock valuation notations is Australian practice. Thirty different notations are distinguished, and the variety is even greater, as may be gathered from the notations in parentheses (A4) and the use of "etc." (e.g. A5, B5). It may be objected, of course, that this list really contains relatively few different bases or methods of valuation that, although the words vary, many items don't differ at all in meaning. That would have to be proved. But granting that is so; published statements are important not only for what lies behind them but also, and perhaps more so, for the impressions they create in the minds of people who have no access to the figures and facts behind the balance sheet. And their impressions must be gained from bald words and figures.

The different notations are listed in full so that the meaningless phrases and the unnecessary variety may be seen most readily. It is suggested that very little knowledge can be gained about the stock valuation methods of these companies in spite of these notations.

Meaningless Phrases

In the first place, the tag "as certified by . . ." conveys nothing at all to outsiders; they can know little of the competence (to value the stock) of the office or officers mentioned in the notation. The phrase is quite superfluous unless an outside expert valuer has done the job.

The second type of phrase is much more serious, however. The "open end" notation (e.g., cost or under) sets an upper limit to the valuation basis, but who knows what the lower limit may be?

In 1948 the cases described like this total eighteen (groups A4, A5, A6, C6, D5), compared with sixteen (groups A2, A3, A4, A5, B6, B11) in 1938—no improvement at all, in spite of all the work done by the Institutes and individuals to promote better reporting in that interval.

The third quite useless term is "at valuation." However much it may be qualified by other phrases, it says nothing about objective tests of value at all, though admittedly the figures may have been quite objectively determined. The important thing, as far as outside parties are concerned, is to say so, if some objective basis, such as cost or market price has been used.

On these counts and because two companies give no stock notation, we may say that in 1948, thirty of these fifty companies told outsiders nothing about their stock valuation methods except that they were conservative. How conservative no one outside could tell.

Unnecessary Variety

The previous paragraph has dismissed the whole of class C and most of classes A and D in the table. Let us examine class B.

These notations all carry slightly different shades of meaning, but I doubt very much whether such shades of meaning are intended. It is extremely likely that "Cost or Market" (B1) means "Lower of cost or market," but it need not necessarily do so. The adjectives "current" (B3) and "fair" (B4) complicate the descriptions. One might ask "What other market value than current market value would be used for this purpose?" and "What is fair, in any case?"

11

The Spice of Accounting—continued

Class B really includes two types of notation, one referring mainly to market price or value and the other to replacement price or value. As there seems to be no precision in so many other respects, one may be excused for assuming that replacement means market price in at least some of these cases. But the recommendations of the Chartered Institute and the company represented by D6 in the table clearly envisage three possible bases of valuation: cost, market and replacement value, each with a definite meaning and each required to be stated to define with any precision the limits of the stock valuation.

SUMMARY

We may say that of these fifty notations, in only those companies represented by A1 are stock values objectively determined, and in those cases the notation has a more precise meaning than in all the other cases.

If we ignore the defects imputed to conservative valuations, we may say that only groups A1, B2 and D6 (twelve cases out of fifty) comply with the requirement of clear and meaningful expression in financial statements. Or to put it another way, the only acceptable notations are:

Cost Price,

Market Price,

Lower of Cost or Market, or

Lowest of Cost, Market and Replacement Values—

and only the former two can claim to be rigorously objective and consistent.

Changes in the Period

As appears from the table, there were relatively few changes in notation or basis during the period. There were eighteen changes in all over the ten years, four of them occurring in 1948. The greatest movement was into group A4, an open-end group.

More significant than the movements in the data as a whole, however, is the effect unplanned or capricious changes may have on the meaning of the accounts of individual companies.

Here are the changes one company made, taken not from the balance sheet but from the directors' report each year.

1938-42: "Stock valuations do not exceed cost or replacement price, which ever is the lower."

1943: "Stock in trade has been listed at or below cost."

1944: Similar to 1942.

1945: "Stock has been listed at values not in excess of cost price, market selling price or replacement value, whichever is the lowest."

1946-48: No mention of stock valuation basis.

Unless one is prepared to ignore these notations entirely, the task of interpreting the statements to which they refer is an unenviable one.

Multiple changes occurred in only this and two other cases of the fifty examined.

A change to the best method of presentation ought to be planned, so that the inconsistency made inevitable by change can be worked out of the accounts in the shortest possible period.

Time and Place . . .

We may well agree with Dr. Johnson's statement that "The great source of pleasure is variety." But who reads balance sheets for pleasure?

Uniformity in technical details is as important in business as in science; accountants should recognize its importance even if only by analogy with the needs of accounting procedures.

Variety may be the spice of life, but surely people expect to find their spice in other places than published financial statements! We may take our pleasure in "variety of mere nothings," but we could derive considerable professional satisfaction, perhaps even an improvement in status, from a greater measure of "uniformity of something."

The Spice of Accounting—continued

Stock Valuation Notations in Balance Sheets of Fifty Australian Companies, 1938 and 1948

BASIS		1938	1948
Cost—			
A1	Cost ..	6	5
A2	Cost or depreciated cost ..	1	–
A3	Cost less amounts written down ..	1	–.
A4	Cost or under (or lower, or less, at or below cost, at and under cost)	9	12
A5	Cost or under as certified by, etc.	3	3
A6	At or below cost, less depreciation	–	1
		— 20	— 21
Cost and Market—			
B1	Cost or market	1	1
B2	Lower of cost or market ..	5	6
B3	Cost or current market value, which ever is lower	1	1
B4	Cost or fair market value, which ever is the lesser	–	1
B5	Cost price or market value as certified by, etc. ..	1	1
B6	Not exceeding lower of cost or market ..	1	–
B7	Lower of cost or market replacement price	1	–
B8	Cost or replacement value, which ever is lower..	3	2
B9	Cost or replacement as certified by, etc.	1	1
B10	Cost and/or replacement values ..	1	1
B11	Cost, replacement value or under	1	–
		— 16	— 14
Valuation—			
C1	Valuation ..	7	5
C2	Valuation as per certified stock sheets ..	1	1
C3	Valuation made by, etc. .. '	1	1
C4	Valuation after providing for possible obsolescence of stocks ..	1	–
C5	Valuation after providing for diminution in value of stocks ..	–	1
C6	Valuation not exceeding cost	–	1
		— 10	— 9
Other Bases—			
D1	Fair market value ..	1	–
D2	As certified	1	1
D3	Cost and valuation	1	1
D4	Lower of cost or valuation	1	–
D5	Not exceeding cost, market or replacement value ..	–	1
D6	Cost, market, or replacement value, which ever is least	–	1
D7	No notation	–	2
		— 4	— 6
	TOTAL ..	50	50

13

EDUCATIONAL POLICY

A SUGGESTION

THE general body of members of a professional association may well lose interest in the requirements for entry once they have been admitted. The ordinary demands on many a practitioner's time may be so heavy that he has not the opportunity even to consider whether his juniors are obtaining a useful training for their vocation, much less to consider what is the best training. This latter question is, nevertheless, a live one, in spite of the lack of publicity given to the views of those who frame educational policies for the accountancy profession.

The profession is not lacking· in members who question the adequacy of existing syllabi to produce capable, knowledgeable and thoughtful recruits. But their questioning seems to be ineffectual for the want of adequate discussion in the official journals. Knowledge of the educational policies of professional associations is also of critical importance to those who have assumed the role of teachers; for, unless they have been acquainted with the principles underlying the changes and prospective changes in the syllabi of the associations, they have no way of planning to meet those changes, and no way of testing their own ideas on the education of accountants. The number of teachers and research workers in the colleges and universities is increasing, and it is not improbable that some of them will find the existing syllabi of the professional bodies to be much less than they believe to be necessary. Ideally there should be some means for constant and continuous consultation between the education committees of the associations and the teaching profession—not so much for the purpose of ensuring that educational institutions conform with the requirements of the professional institutions, as for the purpose of advancing the level of education and competence of those who seek to enter the profession.

Possible sources of policy

In the absence of explicit statements of educational policy, one can only speculate upon the kinds of criteria which are adopted by the education committees. There seem to be at least three distinct sources from which the contents and changes in the accountancy curriculum may arise.

Firstly, the course may be dictated by what it has long been customary to require. This is the least justifiable reason for any programme of study. Tradition is a valuable thing for some purposes, but to pay too great a respect to the decisions of our professional forbears implies disregard for the changes which have occurred in the content of the subject and in the environment in which it is practised. The changes in both have been considerable.

Secondly, the course may be influenced by practical needs, by the growing requirement of particular skills. This has an obvious rationale.

15

But it has also some defects. A course which overemphasises particular skills may leave in the mind of the student no clear idea of the general basis of the subject, no concept of unity or relationship between different parts of the subject matter, and no general concepts to which he may have recourse in novel situations. Further, no curriculum can possibly cover all the special types of enterprise for which variations from the general pattern of accounting are necessary. Those which come to be included cannot necessarily be considered as typical or as the most important; they are quite possibly those which have attracted attention among accountants about the time of their introduction, or those which have particularly concerned those members of the profession who have a controlling influence on the syllabus.

Thirdly, the course may be designed to give effect to certain concepts of professional education and competence. What these concepts may be will appear at a later stage, but it seems to be incontestable that all changes in the subject-matter required to be studied should, in some way, contribute to the development of a syllabus which inculcates a wide understanding as well as a particular expertise. The profession is well acquainted with piecemeal changes in the curriculum, but many of those changes suggest that expedience, or the feeling of having to do something different, here and now, has exercised a greater influence than prolonged reflection on what is necessary or desirable from the general viewpoint of the profession.

There may be sources other than these three, but they appear to be the principal ones. No single source of ideas may be considered to be the sole justification for any of the observed changes in the syllabi. A decision to change a syllabus is likely to be based on all three, but much greater weight appears to have been attached to the first and second than to the third. This was to be expected. The development of courses of study must follow the de-

velopment of subject matter. As the writers on bookkeeping and accounting have, until relatively recent years, been concerned predominantly with practical procedures, practical procedures were all that could be made the subject of examination. The reaction of examiners, confronted with the task of designing a syllabus which would appear to be a stiff enough test for entry to a profession, can be imagined. The absence of theoretical and analytical material, and the belief that accounting is essentially a set of definite and unquestionable procedures, would have obliged them to fill out the course with specific types of accounting—enough types to provide a respectable array of "subjects". Vestiges of the necessity to fill out the course still remain. The consequence has been that students find little more in the whole subject than rules and technicalities; and some of those who have undertaken other studies in which the derivation, refinement and relating of concepts play a very large part, have been heard to deplore the lack of intellectual content in accounting as a subject.

To depend on variety when there was little depth was good enough in its time. But now variety may well be replaced. There is a large and growing literature devoted to the discussion of accounting ideas, and techniques may well bow to it.

Professional skill and competence

To give effect to the third criterion of educational policy, it is necessary to consider what kinds of competence it is desirable to develop.

The most obvious is specific skill in dealing with accounts and accounting statements. This is essentially a trade skill, similar to the manual or mental skills which are the substrata of other professions. A round and thorough knowledge of it is necessary, for much of the work of accountants consists in keeping books of account or examining the books of account which others have kept.

The second is a capacity for making intelligent use of the products of accounting, for the purpose of discovering the cause or causes of conditions represented in accounting summaries, and for the purpose of suggesting future courses of action. Such a capacity for analysis and reflection is one of the qualities which distinguishes professional competence from trade skill. What is contemplated is more than acquaintance with the techniques of financial statement analysis, cost analysis and budgeting. These techniques are simply means of putting existing information into special forms or relationships; to interpret the result requires much greater familiarity with the problems of business finance and business administration than present syllabi envisage.

Coupled with, and perhaps even anterior to this capacity, is the ability to think clearly and to reason cogently. The pervasive, doctrinaire approach to the subject, amply illustrated by the pedestrian quality of much of its literature, cannot be expected to generate inquisitiveness or conviction. It has often been said that accounting is a logical method and that the study of accounting is thus a training in logical method. This is too much. The assertion recognises by implication the desirability of the capacity for careful inquiry and thought, but it also implies, quite wrongly, that formal arrangement, classification and consistency are sufficient evidence of the use of logical processes. If a system of classification is uninformative (as it well may be), or if consistency involves the misrepresentation of reality (as it well may do), the evidence of logicality is lacking; the appearance of logicality is superficial and illusory. In addition to the need for a reasoned approach to practical problems, clarity and incisiveness of thought are necessary for fruitful study of the literature of accounting. False analogies, undisclosed premises and questionable argument are frequently encountered; but the infrequency with which these flaws are challenged is suggestive of a greater respect for the views of writers, and a poorer regard for the value of independent thought, than is warranted.

Intellectual and historical perspective should also be developed. The practices of the profession should not be thought to have reached the end of their development. Growth will inevitably be stunted while students are taught there is only one possible way of measuring income, or capital, or cost. They should be exposed to some of the ideas of others than accountants who have studied the same phenomena. The lack of such an experience is probably the reason for the barrenness of joint discussions between accountants and economists on problems which are of mutual interest, problems of business behaviour and policy. The subject "money and banking" or "monetary theory and policy" appears to have been introduced with the intention that some subject other than straight accounting and law should be included in the curriculum. But, as a subject, it seems to be more decorative than relevant. Its content does not confront the student with other ways of looking at the conceptual content of words he uses in his studies in accounting. It takes him to an entirely different field, a field the particular features of which are far removed from the market place in which he will do most of his business. It would be much more to the point to require a study of the theories of value and distribution, for they concern themselves with a range of concepts and phenomena many of which are the daily preoccupation of accountants. To see accounting concepts and economic concepts in juxtaposition would bring under examination the utility of ideas which are now so widely accepted as incontrovertible.

And why historical perspective? Is it not sufficient to know what contemporary ideas and practices are? A knowledge of the history of an idea or practice is another tool for the constructive. Many practices in business, as elsewhere, develop to meet specific sets of circumstances; some of them

17

survive in spite of the disappearance of the initiating circumstances. To know their origins would enable students and practitioners to test the present value of long established practices. History is a corrective for the feeling that everything that can be done has been done. It provides avenues for speculation and grounds for criticism and synthesis which may serve accounting in much the same way as a laboratory serves the physical sciences.

Finally, it seems to be desirable to develop a knowledge of, and an interest in, the accounts which reflect the general state of the economy, and in the relationships between accountants and the community at large. By his training, the accountant is more familiar with accounting statements than the lay public. Is it not proper that he should pay some attention to the government accounts and the social accounts as part of his professional responsibility? And is it not proper that he shall ask, for example, whether those for whose benefit accounts are published are being fairly and reasonably treated? A study of the assumptions underlying the publication of financial statements and of the role of communications in business would provide some guides to professional action and some further tests of present practices.

In general, the curriculum should develop breadth of vision and understanding. This it will be able to do if it incorporates some studies which serve to portray accounting in its historical setting and in its contemporary business environment, and if it includes some studies at greater depth, even if this means fewer superficial studies of particular sorts of accounts. Rather than a lot of slim sandwiches, a few "dagwoods" would seem to be the appropriate diet.

It is not suggested that the capacities and interests mentioned in this section are the only qualities which a course of study should generate. They represent a concept of professional skill and competence which may be used as a starting point; discussion among members of the profession may lead to the recognition of other significant characteristics.

The suggestion

Several additional types of study would need to be incorporated in the syllabus if the abovementioned qualities are to be fostered. Accounting theory, governmental and social accounting, business finance, and the history of accounting practice and thought, deserve more attention than they now receive. In many respects the available literature is inadequate to cover all these fields; but, assuming there were an adequate literature, how would these studies be introduced? There does not seem to be any great objection to increasing the number of papers for which a student must prepare; many professional examinations involve more papers than the professional examinations in accounting. But the increase need not be great. Some of the suggested subjects could be accommodated within the present framework, simply by dropping some of the special cases or uncommon forms of accounting; others seem to require sufficient study to justify a full paper.

The following outline may serve to indicate the relationships between the different subjects and stages in a course which may meet the foregoing requirements:

Stage 1 A. Elementary accounting and auditing
B. Commercial law
C. Introduction to the theory of accounting.

Stage 2 A. Corporate accounting
B. Company law
C. Business organisation and finance.

Stage 3 A. Advanced accounting and auditing
B. Taxation law and practice
C. History and theory of accounting.

In each stage, it will be noticed, there are three general divisions; or, to put it another way, through all three stages there run three strands—one technical, one legal, and one which, for want of a better term, may be called theoretical. It does not seem to be necessary to justify the A's and B's in each stage or to elaborate upon their contents. The following comments will attempt to show that the C's will provide for the development of knowledge and attitudes towards the technical and legal parts of the curriculum which are now lacking.

In the first place, two general observations may be made. The technical subjects deal, in the main, with accounting as it is practised. Neither the text-books nor the examination syllabi seem to contemplate the need for students to understand the general purpose and function of accounting, or the possibility of devising different methods of accounting from those commonly adopted. For this reason, it is unlikely that more than a few students will exhibit an enterprising and critical attitude towards their subject, to the detriment of its growth. Secondly, the legal subjects deal, in the main, with the law as it exists. There is no attempt to demonstrate that law is an evolving thing, or that the law at any time is a crystallisation of what, at a certain point of time and against the background of a specific economic and social environment, seemed to be the general desire of certain legislators. If the study of law leaves the impression that the law is a neat, final and unalterable code, it can only have a restrictive effect. If the law is dealt with, on the other hand, as a growing and constantly changing codification of currently acceptable customs, students will be encouraged to think about what the law ought to be, and to seek for the answers in the prevailing social or economic framework. The three subjects C, comprising the third strand in the course, are designed to overcome the limitation of interest and vision which arises from formal studies of existing practice and law.

Now, for some particulars.

The third sequence

The first of the C subjects would concern itself with the functions of accounting in different types of organisation, and with the development of a set of ideas about the accounting process and the concepts which the accounting process may attempt to quantify. These ideas will not necessarily be identical with the ideas underlying the accepted practices by which things are represented in accounts. It seems, in fact, to be desirable to demonstrate that it is not possible to quantify some very useful concepts, and that approximations or alternative concepts have been adopted. The first stage is not too early to encourage a questioning and critical attitude, for to know its limitations from the beginning is to know one of the most important things about an art. Even if it is not necessary, at this stage, to consider exhaustively all the possible concepts of income, or capital, or cost, or what have you, some contrasting concepts should be studied.

The second C subject would be devoted to a study principally of business finance and the functions of the accountant in business organisations. Accounting is concerned entirely with the delineation of the financial facts of different organisations. It seems strange, therefore, that no provision is made for the study of business finance in existing syllabi. For the purpose of making entries in company accounts, students are required to know some of the characteristics of some of the instruments of corporate finance. But why does a given company adopt its particular method of financing operations? and in what cases is a large equity to be preferred to a large funded debt? and why do companies make bonus issues? and what criteria are to be adopted when deciding whether new capital shall be raised in one way rather than in another? and when is a company undercapitalised? and when overcapitalised? None of the questions is adequately answered in the prescribed texts. How, then, can the accountant understand the reason for the entries he is required to make in the books of account about these things? and, how can he advise

19

when his advice is sought as, we are told, it so often is? An accountant with varied experience may be able to draw upon experience, but students should surely be expected to know why things are done, as well as how the consequential book entries are made. Intelligent analysis of financial statements depends on an understanding of many of these features of business, and to study the subject concurrently with company accounting and company law would provide an ideal mixture of law and business practice.

The third in the sequence of C subjects may be devoted to a study of the major changes in business conditions which have given rise to changes in accounting, or which have stimulated speculation about possible changes in accounting methods. It would be appropriate, for example, to consider such things as the practice of conservatism and its decline from favour, the background of certain legal decisions which have influenced accounting method and thought, and the pressure which has been brought to bear on the practice of accounting by creditors, investors and workers or their representatives, and through the efforts of the profession itself. There seems to be no reason why the student should not be introduced to controversial questions, such as the adequacy of conventional accounting information for the purposes of outside supporters and management. It is quite possible to teach and to examine on such matters without committing the examining body to support one side or another of such controversies. To require some such study seems to be desirable, for controversy provides tests of existing methods and ideas which should be welcomed in a live and vigorous profession. Opportunity should also exist for a survey of changing fashions in concepts and of the development of accounting theory. The entity, the proprietorship and the fund concepts of accounting, depreciation, income, bases of classification, matching, objectivity, and many similar and related notions deserve more attention and more rigorous study than they are now spared.

This sequence of theoretical and environmental studies would oblige students to recognise that there is more in the subject than figure work. It would make possible more penetrating examinations in the technical subjects, and the discursive treatment it requires would force examinees to acquire some proficiency in discussing issues and in prose composition — the need for some discipline which will promote proficiency in these respects is notorious.

Some criticisms

The whole suggestion may be dismissed because of its novelty or the difficulty of implementing it or for other reasons. Two such criticisms seem to warrant notice.

Firstly, there are no convenient text books which serve up this kind of material in an appropriate mix and dose. This is true, and it does mean that the introduction of such a programme would be difficult in the immediate future. But there is an abundance of material in periodicals and in books other than those on the prescribed list. Is it asking too much of prospective entrants to a profession to expect them to read more widely than a limited list of handy text books? If it is desired to raise the general level of understanding, and "grubbing" for the appropriate material seems to be too great a task for students (because, for example, the sources are few and inaccessible), it is not impossible to have articles and extracts reprinted for the benefit of students.

In any event, this outline is not to be considered as a recipe which may be tried immediately; it represents a goal to the accomplishment of which future changes in the syllabi may be geared.

The second major line of criticism is more fundamental. This third strand of subject matter may be deemed by some to be too theoretical, too far removed from the everyday problems of accountants. But is it? Is any discipline which makes one think twice, when about to follow an established procedure, too theoretical? Is any course which grapples with the very foundations of an art removed from everyday realities? Is any study which fills in the background, or furthers understanding of the reasons underlying a practice, useless or inconsequential? It is too much to hope that, once launched on their careers, young accountants will develop powers of discrimination and broader knowledge of their particular subject and related fields. Each will have quite a restricted environment in which marginal problems will arise only occasionally, too infrequently for him to acquire from experience the breadth of view and expertness which critical situations demand. If facility in dealing with ideas is not inculcated during the years of training, it is improbable that it will be acquired subsequently, except by the few who are curious by nature. In any case, the amount of material or the number of examinations in the suggested third sequence would amount to no more than about one-fifth to one-quarter of the whole curriculum, and this does not seem to be too much theoretical and environmental study, however abstract it may be.

Options

Suggestions for the inclusion of new material, representative of large areas of practice, may give rise to the feeling that there are some directions in which a degree of specialised instruction may be required. One of the more obvious arises from the potential distinction between the knowledge and skill required of public and of administrative accountants. Would it be wise to permit candidates to choose between studies in auditing and studies in costing, according to the type of work in which they expect to engage? Another group which may merit special consideration includes those who are in

government or semi-government employment. Would it be reasonable to permit such candidates to take special examinations in government accounting and public finance instead of the analogous subjects in the ordinary curriculum?

It seems to be preferable to avoid options of this kind. It is true that particular vocations within the profession may require special knowledge; to the extent that this is so, a general course may well incorporate an introductory or comparative treatment of the distinguishing features of the main fields. If each category of accountants is made familiar with the different problems and viewpoints of other categories in the course of professional training, there will be greater possibility of speculation by each about the merits of the systems and ideas used by others; this may benefit all categories if it leads to reasoned cross-comparisons. As for the development of skill in each of the distinct fields, it seems to be quite sufficient to rely on the school of experience. Outside the trades there can be few courses of study which equip the student to do more than handle ideas with skill; that it does just that is high commendation for a professional course of study.

Consequences

What may be the consequences of the introduction of the suggestions here put forward? Nothing but advantageous as far as those who complete such a course are concerned. But it may mean that the number of persons qualifying each year may fall somewhat. If this may happen, the profession is confronted with a dilemma; it must decide whether it is desirable to have fewer qualified persons of greater competence, or more of less competence; fewer with greater understanding and insight, or more with technical competence only. It may become necessary to recognise a skill in bookkeeping beyond the limits of which many who now qualify as accountants may not rise. If this is necessary in the interest of the pro-

21

gress and vitality of the profession it seems to be the obvious course to follow.

. . . . .

Whatever merits or faults the main proposal of this note may have, a point mentioned at the beginning stands clear. Educational policy and standards need to be developed deliberately, with an explicit and widely known purpose. Changes in syllabi which are fathered in obscurity make the task of educational bodies difficult, particularly if they are in the form of piecemeal variations which do not seem to conform with recognisable and acceptable objectives. Differences and potential differences between the requirements of examining bodies, both here and overseas, suggest the desirability of greater discussion of educational problems and policies. Progress on a broad front will not be achieved without common knowledge of what is considered to be an ideal professional education, and to this notion of an ideal the official bodies and individual members of the profession may all contribute facets.

22

CONVENTIONS: DOCTRINES AND COMMONSENSE

It has become almost habitual in antipodean expositions of accounting to offer some treatment of the so-called conventions and doctrines of accounting, and to regard these as the foundations or the theory on which accounting rests. The formal treatment and amplification of conventions and doctrines appears to have been introduced to the non-periodical literature in GOLDBERG's *Accounting Principles*,[1] published in 1946 as part of the post war reconstruction training scheme. Subsequently they appeared in FITZGERALD's *Analysis and Interpretation of Financial and Operating Statements*,[2] in YORSTON, SMYTH AND BROWN's *Advanced Accounting*,[3] in CARTER's *Advanced Accounts*,[4] in MATHEW's *Accounting for Economists*[5] and in CARRINGTON AND BATTERSBY's *Accounting*[6].

In the first of these publications only four conventions (entity, continuity, accounting period and monetary conventions) and four doctrines (conservatism, consistency, disclosure and materiality) were presented. These were derived, as was the use of the terms "convention" and "doctrine" in respect of them, from GILMAN's *Accounting Concepts of Profit*.[7] FITZGERALD did not produce the list completely, particularly in respect of doctrines. In his list of conventions he excluded the entity convention, substituted for the monetary convention as it was treated by GILMAN and GOLDBERG a constant money value convention, added an historical record convention and retained the continuity (going concern) and period conventions. YORSTON, SMYTH AND BROWN (1947) retained the original list of conventions and doctrines, but in 1949 added to the list of conventions. The entity, continuity and period conventions were retained: the monetary convention was interpreted in much the same way as GILMAN and GOLDBERG had interpreted it, though there were references to changes in the significance of the monetary unit; the historical record convention was retained following FITZGERALD. Two new items were added, the accounting equation convention and the recognition of law; but these were dropped in the 1963 edition. The new *Carter* presented the entity, continuity and period conventions following GILMAN, the historical record and constant money value conventions following FITZGERALD, the equities or algebraic convention following the accounting equation convention of YORSTON, SMYTH AND BROWN, a new "arithmetic" convention, and omitted the recognition of law convention of the then current edition of YORSTON, SMYTH AND BROWN.

The matching of costs with incomes was added to the list of doctrines.

MATHEWS noticed the entity, valuation, period, continuity and constant money value conventions, all of which he described as assumptions, and the doctrines of conservation, consistency and disclosure. CARRINGTON AND BATTERSBY gave the largest list yet published: seven conventions—entity, valuation, period, continuity, constant money value, historical cost (following FITZGERALD of 1956), and recognition of law; and seven doctrines—conservatism, consistency, disclosure and materiality, all well established, and comparability, objectivity and economy, all introduced for the first time as doctrines. The 1963 edition of FITZGERALD appears to abandon the older structure altogether. It treats, as assumptions, the five imperatives of the "C" postulates of MOONITZ,[8] which, for the purpose of relating them to the established denotations, may be described as continuity, constant money value, consistency, disclosure and objectivity assumptions.

In all, the texts mentioned refer to ten named conventions and eight named doctrines, and in quite a few cases the connotations differ as between texts.

The Emphasis on Practices

In the light of these differences it seems timely to inquire what is meant by conventions and doctrines and what we have in their substance. It is instructive to go back to GILMAN who, after a brief consideration of the meanings ascribed in several standard dictionaries, conveys the sense in which he understands these words and the ways in which he is prepared to use them. The characteristics of conventions are that they are propositions which are "based upon general agreement" and are "more or less arbitrarily established" (*op. cit.*, p. 184). From the illustrations he gives, these propositions are descriptive of practices. FITZGERALD speaks of conventions as practices in a similar manner: "a convention of accounting is a practice generally followed . . . more often than not based on an implicit general understanding" (*op. cit.*, 1956 edition, p. 8). As for doctrines, after considering these as propositions "taught by some persons" and as "a body or system of principles or tenets", GILMAN concludes that a break with the implications of these dictionary phrases "would be a matter of considerable convenience"—a conclusion which is, to say the least, quite arbitrary. He chooses to use "doctrine" as "referring to a general statement of accounting or reporting policy" (*op. cit.*, pp. 186, 187). FITZGERALD does not find it necessary to break so obviously with the common usage of the language: "an accounting doctrine is a belief that a given practice should be followed . . . a dogma inculcated by teachers of accounting, textbook writers or authoritative associations of accountants" (*loc. cit.*).

Now it is a matter of fact that systematic studies of the ideas implicit in accounting practices have not a very long history. PATON's explicit statements[9] of forty years ago were not developed or even adopted by other writers, and it was not until the mid- and late-thirties that interest re-awakened. One would not wish, therefore, in any way to minimise the difficulties of any person wishing to give a systematic account of accounting, accounting ideas and accounting practices. Nevertheless a few simple analogies will suggest that the form which has been taken by the texts cited, and in particular the emphasis on practices, is a form peculiar to accounting and should give rise to some doubts about its merits.

The practice of medicine involves such processes as diagnosis, prescription, surgery, and therapeutic care. But there are principles of medicine which are in no way dependent on practice; they are embodied in knowledge of the human organism and of the organisms and inorganic substances which affect it. The practice of law involves such processes as pleading and the assessment of evidence. But there are principles of law which are in no way dependent on practice; they are embodied in knowledge of the legally recognised relationships between persons. The practice of engineering involves such processes as designing and construction. But there are principles of engineering which are in no way dependent on practice; they are embodied in knowledge of the stresses which develop in and which may be sustained by structural materials and of the way in which materials may be combined. Examples can be multiplied. But in each case the principles are independent of practice. One may know the principles without ever having in mind the operations of diagnosis, pleading or building. One may expound the principles without reference of any kind to these operations. Truly there may be conventions in the practice of diagnosis, pleading or building; but these are peripheral and incidental, as the mere fact that they vary from place to place suggests. The heart of the matter is always something more substantial than the conventional forms with which practice is embellished or restrained; it subsists in the realities with which a particular kind of practice is concerned.

It seems to be quite otherwise in accounting. It appears to have become accepted that the ideas embodied in the conventions and doctrines of accounting constitute the fundamental or basic ideas for the field. The warrant for this inference is the fact that no other categories of ideas or of knowledge are put forward by

the exponents of accounting as fundamental or basic to it. The conventions and doctrines are not peripheral or incidental elements of practice: they are all there is. All we have as fundamental or basic is thus a set of propositions which are more or less arbitrarily established, or which are plain dogmas. There is no body of ideas or knowledge by reference to which we can judge whether or not these propositions are preferable to others; we must simply accept them.

This position is surely offensive to any inquisitive mind. And in any case it conflicts with common sense. For if there is a set of bodily conditions and disturbances which exercise the mind of a physician quite independently of the "conventional" bedside manners he adopts, surely there is an analogous set of conditions which exercise the mind of an accountant (as accountant and not as business adviser) independently of conventions.

At this point the reader may interpose the suggestion that perhaps GILMAN and his successors have simply made an unfortunate choice in the designations they have given to certain groups of ideas. But this choice was made quite deliberately, by GILMAN at least. Nevertheless we will examine the suggestion. Examination is not easy, however, for in many of the expositions there is no clearly identifiable proposition which unequivocally states what the author(s) mean.[10]

Some Conventions Examined

Consider first a convention which appears in all the quoted sources—the period convention. YORSTON, SMYTH AND BROWN assert that "necessity requires that in most cases [the] life [of the business enterprise] be divided into chapters known as accounting periods" (1963, p. 12). Now, in the first place, the everyday and commonsense usage of the term "convention" implies some kind of agreement, and in an earlier paragraph it was noted that GILMAN and FITZGERALD countenance the notion of agreement. One might expect therefore that the statement of a convention would begin in some such manner as "Accountants are agreed that . . ." But the proposition quoted has not this form. It says "necessity requires that . . ." If we are told simply that accountants agree to do a certain thing, and if we know that accountants in fact agree, the proposition could not be further questioned. It would be a statement of fact and not a convention. When, however, the statement says "necessity requires that . . .", we are bound to ask the nature of necessity, and what there is in the nature of necessity which requires that accounting periods be recognised. Necessity is said to be the mother of invention. May we then read "The mother of invention requires that . . ."? The resulting proposition may seem ludicrous, but it tells us no less than the quoted proposition. If there is anything which requires periodical accounting, then periodical accounting is a consequence of that thing.

And if there is such a thing, it is surely preferable to know it than simply to be assured that its consequence is a convention. The writer believes that the necessity of periodical accounting stems from a number of environmental factors, statements about which will lead to a conclusion of the form "If such and such ends are to be served, accounting statements will be prepared periodically". The necessity of periodical accounting becomes a reasoned conclusion, a status which is much superior to that of a mere convention.[11] Furthermore, most of the texts cited refer to periods of equal or fixed length. Good reasons may be offered for periods of variable length in some cases; and indeed some firms summarise results and plan operations for unequal periods. A convention which refers to periods of equal length states too much to be considered as a general rule without qualification.

Consider next the accounting equation convention. CARTER does not state this convention in any clearly discernible propositional form. But the treatment given to it (*op. cit., pp.* 4-5) has the form of an argument from certain premises and definitions. As we have just previously observed, the conclusion from a line of argument can in no sense be described as a convention. To do so simply results in the devaluation of it; for a conclusion based on argument from acceptable premises, that is from premises which conform with experience, is a far superior foundation of practice than something agreed upon more or less arbitrarily.

The recognition of law convention may be objected to, as a convention, on rather different grounds. We are told that "records and reports should give recognition to the legal position of the parties to whom the accounts refer (CARRINGTON AND BATTERSBY, p. 44). Are we to understand that accountants simply agree to abide by this proposition and is it a more or less arbitrarily established proposition? Neither. Common sense suggests that the laws relating to the keeping of accounts are part of the environment of accounting. We do not consider all the elements of our environment to be simply conventions. We consider them as data, the facts of life. But, further, the authors go on to say that "it is frequently necessary to frame accounts in a manner that does not precisely display the legal position." And indeed every consolidated statement is a statement which does not display a legal position. Clearly, then, we are being told that accountants agree to give recognition to legal positions, and apparently they also agree not to recognise legal positions. What do they agree upon? If they agree upon both then neither can be considered as a convention.

This leads us to another curiosity. *Carter* includes, as we have noted, the constant money value convention and the arithmetic convention. The former, we are told "assumes that the purchasing power of money remains constant, which is not, of course, a fact" (p. 4). In respect of the arithmetic convention we are told that "all the accountant's figure work is done by means of

arithmetic; it is an obvious fact, and so is entitled to be known as a Convention" (p. 5). Here we have two propositions designated conventions one of which is a statement of fact and the other of which is contrary to a statement of fact. Quite apart from our objections to describing any statement of fact as a convention, what useful meaning can be ascribed to the term "convention" when it is used to describe such obviously different statements?

But, consider more closely the constant money value convention. The sense of it may be conveyed in the form: accountants agree that, in the accounting process, changes in the purchasing power of money shall be ignored. Now if accounting were no more than a recreation, an end in itself as far as accountants are concerned, one could not perhaps cavil at anything they agree to do. But, if it were not obvious, there are countless statements in the literature to the effect that accounting is not a mere game for the delectation of accountants, that it and its products are "utilitarian in character" and "indispensable to modern business and finance."[12] As the usefulness of the information produced is a usefulness to other parties, it seems obvious that what accountants agree to do is not a matter of indifference—to themselves or to any one else. Accountants are presumably no different from any other reasonable persons in attending to their own affairs. In budgeting their expenditures they do not think of the prices of bread, and cheese, and wine, in terms other than the prices they know to be relevant at the time. If they buy or sell a second hand car they do not expect the sum initially paid for it to be relevant to themselves or to the seller or buyer. Yet, in respect of the information they supply to other people they agree, in effect, that other people do not need, or shall not have, the up to date information which they themselves would require. They themselves need to adjust their affairs to the immediate facts of life, but apparently other people need only to adjust themselves to the facts as they existed weeks, months or years ago. Ethically and logically, this is a most curious position to adopt. It requires more than mere convention to justify accounting on the basis of this notion. If there are reasons underlying the constant money value proposition we are entitled to be told of them, in which case the proposition is a conclusion, not a convention. In fact, if usefulness is a criterion, common sense suggests that the reasons for accepting the proposition cannot be other than slight, if there are any reasons at all.

Sources of Confusion

It appears then that the term "convention" is applied to statements of fact, to statements contrary to fact, to conclusions from argument and to propositions of other kinds. Looseness of this kind can only mean that what is designated as a convention is itself quite arbitrarily determined. Without pure rote learning and indoctrination one cannot know what "accounting convention" means. For all its technical appearance, it apparently means nothing of a uniform kind which common sense would suggest we might expect of a term used in a technical context, even if it is also a term in everyday usage.

The doctrines are no less confusing and confused. Consistency in accounting is strictly a quality deducible from features of the world at large: its necessity stems from the fact that all judging and choosing, and therefore all action, involves comparisons, and the fact that valid comparisons can be made only of statements which are consistent or are derived by consistent principles. Disclosure means nothing more than informing, and that is the very essence of accounting. To give an account is to disclose. Accounting implies disclosure; nothing more need be said. And generally nothing more is said except by way of giving illustrations. Materiality is nothing more than an informed sense of proportion. In every day affairs we are quite accustomed to the kind of discrimination that is entailed. It therefore seems scarcely necessary to have an accounting doctrine to tell us to use our common sense. If the idea is extended to discrimination as between methods rather than as between results, it may acquire greater significance; YORSTON, SMYTH AND BROWN make brief allusion to such an extension (1963, p. 17) but generally the illustrations given of its application relate to formal features of aggregative statements rather than to the quality of the information they convey.

All of this may be confusing enough. But the failure to state what authors mean by the conventions and doctrines they treat leads to greater confusion in the treatment. Only a few examples will be given. YORSTON, SMYTH AND BROWN, dealing with the continuity convention, state:

> From the accountant's point of view, since the enterprise is to be kept continuously alive for the greatest length of time, financial and accounting policies automatically dictate that everything done is to be directed towards maintaining such continuity of activity; in other words, a policy will be undertaken conducive to nourishing the business for as long as possible (p. 12).

It is difficult to see by what line of reasoning such a conclusion can be reached. Surely it is the concern of managers or owners to keep a business going, or to decide whether it shall be continued or abandoned. The only role accounting and accountants can play subsists in supplying managers or owners with information on which their own judgment may and accounting policies automatically dictate nothing; they themselves are dictated by or chosen because of circumstance and managerial preference. The only conceivable accounting "policy" is a policy of providing comprehensive and relevant information.

Again, we are told that the accounting period convention "necessitates accruing and deferring items of income and expense" (idem, p. 13). There is no such implication. Entities which keep accounts on a cash

basis also account periodically. It is true that if one does not account periodically the question of accruing and deferring items does not arise; but that is altogether different from the cited statement.

In a discussion of disclosure we are told:

> If the basis of valuation of each asset is stated, persons reading the report are in a position to form their own opinions of the true meaning and significance of the report (Carter, p. 7).

But what sort of a position are they in? This statement implies that the report has not, in and of itself, a true meaning and significance; or it implies that "true meaning and significance" is only a matter of opinion. Disclosure surely means very little that is useful if the true meaning and significance of reports are not apparent and are only matters of opinion. In any case how may the true meaning and significance be deduced from the stated figures and the stated valuation bases? Suppose that a company shows its commodity stocks at £10,000 and states that they are valued at "cost or lower", which is a very commonly stated basis. If the true meaning and significance of this valuation is not £10,000—and the quoted passage implies that this is so—how much better off is the reader for knowing that the valuation basis is "cost or lower"? No better off whatever. The value shown may be cost, £1 less than cost, or £1 million less than cost: but the user has no means whatever of knowing. How then can he form any opinion about the true meaning and significance of the statement or the report in which it appears? No skilled accountant could do it; yet accountants are quite prepared to assert that persons generally can do it. If the quoted example is a fair illustration of what the doctrine of disclosure means then it is an almost worthless doctrine.

Although no reference is made here to the periodical literature or to the English and American literature, it would be misleading not to point out that the kinds of confusion to which we refer occur also in that literature. Brief illustration may be given by reference to the continuity convention. Generally the meaning attributed to the idea is continuity of the accounting entity. But continuity is variously interpreted. Some speak of the enterprise remaining in operation indefinitely,[13] some of it having "a life expectancy greater than that of any asset which it now owns",[14] some simply of it having a continuous life in commercial circle,[15] to continuity of proprietorship,[16] and MAY refers to continuity of the accounting process.[17] Here is a series of quite diverse ideas masquerading as one; or at least having only one name. One wonders what respect would be accorded to physicians who had only one term for all diseases, or to lawyers who had only one term for all crimes. To make one term serve for many concepts may be useful when all the separate concepts have been identified and labelled; but not when a general term is used sometimes to convey only one idea and sometimes to convey only one other idea. One other aspect of the

27

matter is the explicit exclusion of the possibility that there may be any form of accounting for non-continuing entities. In many expositions the possibility is admitted, but it is brushed aside. Not even accountants treat continuing and non-continuing entities alike; so, if there is a convention to cover one type, in the interest of consistency and completeness there should also be a convention for the other type.[18] By implication a great deal of accounting is just ignored.

Oversights and Omissions

The conventions and doctrines, whatever they do assert, leave an enormous number of questions unanswered. They do not tell us why accounting exists at all. They do not say why it is necessary to conceive a business to be distinct from its owner(s). They do not give any rules or tests by which we may distinguish an accounting entity. They do not say why accounting is necessarily historical and not also anticipatory. They give no adequate reason for the preparation of two summaries, or for the form these take. They give no criteria by which the proper length of an accounting period may be determined in any particular circumstance. They do not tell us why some entities account on a cash basis and others account on an accrual basis. They do not tell us how to decide what is relevant information. They do not tell us how we may choose from among the multitude of valuation bases the basis which is appropriate in any particular undertaking.

In the whole range of discussions of conventions and doctrines generally, there is no body of factual knowledge which is put forward as the foundations upon which practices are to be based. There is much talk, in accounting as in other areas, about knowing why as well as knowing how. But it is no advance in a man's knowledge if he asks why accounting summaries are prepared periodically, and receives the reply that it is an accounting convention; nor, if he asks why follow the same methods from year to year, and is told that it is an accounting doctrine. If on the other hand one asks a surgeon why he makes an incision laterally or longitudinally he will explain his action in terms of the nature of the tissues, of the location of the blood vessels or the nerves and of the nature and location of the organ he seeks. If one asks an engineer why he goes to the trouble to get structural steel in special shapes rather than flat or round sections, he will explain his action in terms of the improved resistance to stresses which special shapes possess. The actions of these people are made understandable by reference to the qualities of the things they work with. Knowing why in accounting can rest on no other basis than the qualities of the things accountants work with.

Necessary Fundamental Knowledge

What are these things? They are all observable and it is a relatively easy matter to make sensible and useful statements about them. It is not so easy to weave those statements together so that they provide a comprehensive foundation for accounting rules.[19] We are content here to list some of them briefly.

It is an observable fact that people seek to have accounting information so that their actions are the better informed. Therefore we should understand the limitations of people which oblige them to seek such information. We should understand how people make choices and the part which habits, beliefs and verifiable knowledge play in the process. We should understand the part which valuation, estimation and measurement play, and the roles of experience and judgment in the selection of actions.

It is an observable fact that accounting is concerned with the economic aspects of actions. We should understand, therefore, something about the nature of the goods and services men seek to possess, of the processes by which they are transferred and of the media of exchange by which their transfer is facilitated. We should understand the different kinds of contexts in which actions are, or are to be, taken; and the different kinds of institutions for which accounting systems may be required.

It is an observable fact that accounting information bears on the actions of people in their relations with others. Therefore, we should understand the nature of co-operative systems, whether they are maintained voluntarily or contractually. We should understand something of the inducements and rewards of co-operation, of the nature of organisations and of the relationships between people in organisations, and between organisations themselves.

It is an observable fact that the processes of accounting involve the manipulation of numerical symbols. We should know, therefore, something of the ways in which such symbols may be arranged and related so that they do no violence to the real events and things they are used to represent. We should know something of the nature of information processing methods and the problems of minimising losses of information in the translation of events to symbols and symbols to events.

It is an observable fact that accounting implies communicating. Therefore, we should know something of the nature of communication processes, of the interferences which may arise when human interests are affected by what is communicated, and of the rectifiers which it may be necessary to build into a communication system to overcome these interferences.

Sufficient examples have been given to suggest strongly that there is an extensive range of knowledge, of facts and principles, which underlie the practice of accounting. We can ignore them if we choose; we can be quite content with the vague notions which are described as conventions and doctrines. But to do so is to ignore the observable facts to which we have drawn attention, or to deny that they have anything to do with the case. In the name of common sense we can do neither. Intelligent persons in their relationships with the external world do not seek to resolve their problems by insisting that the world conform with their own image of it. When they find that the world cannot be made to conform, they are obliged to adapt themselves to a world, of which they then have a better understanding. The brute facts of life cannot be met by conventionally accepted or arbitrarily adopted rules. If accountants are taught to think otherwise so much the worse will it be for their future.

One cannot help believing that accounting must shake itself free of the very terms "convention" and "doctrine". They have hindered and obfuscated inquiry long enough, and as long as they survive they can do nothing but create the impression that accounting is a maverick among the professions and among the fields of knowledge. There can be no reason but self-destruction behind persistence in accepting arbitrary and dogmatic and authoritarian propositions which are formulated without regard for the realities of experience in the world at large.

In the place of the customary framework we must seek to establish a body of propositions which represent the context or the environment of accounting and to deduce from these in a rigorous, common sense manner, even in a scientific manner, the principles and rules to which accounting should conform. In their personal behaviour accountants act in just such a way, as do

all reasonable people: in their professional behaviour and in formulating their own principles, they cannot surely be satisfied to do less.

1) Technical Publication No. 21, Department of Labour and National Service, Industrial Training Division, Melbourne.

2) Butterworth & Co. (Australia) Ltd., 1947.

3) Law Book Co. of Australasia Pty. Ltd., 1947.

4) Curtis A. Reid, ed., Sir Isaac Pitman & Sons Ltd., 1956.

5) F. W. Cheshire, Melbourne, 1962.

6) Whitcomb and Tombs Limited, 1963.

7) The Ronald Press Company, New York, 1939.

8. MAURICE MOONITZ, *The Basic Postulates of Accounting*, Accounting Research Study No. 1, American Institute of Certified Public Accountants, New York, 1961.

9) W. A. PATON, "Assumptions of the Accountant", *Administration* June 1921, pp. 1-17; and *Accounting Theory*, New York, The Ronald Press Company, 1922. In the former, eleven assumptions are given only five of which appear among the conventions and doctrines of Australasian writers.

10) T .K. COWAN's exposition "Notes of Accounting Theory", *The Accountants' Journal*, June 1957, is a refreshing exception. Each of his propositions is clearly identified by the introductory "that . . . etc. . . ."

11) For a demonstration of the argument, see R. J. CHAMBERS, "Detail for a Blueprint", *The Accounting Review*, April 1957, pp. 209-210.

12) YORSTON, SMYTH AND BROWN, *1957 Ed.*, p. 1 and CARTER, p. 1.

13) e.g., CARMAN G. BLOUGH, "Accounting Principles and their Application", *CPA Handbook*, Vol. 2, New York, American Institute of Certified Public Accountants, 1956, p. 13.

14) SMITH AND ASHBURNE, *Financial and Administrative Accounting*, New York, McGraw-Hill Book Company Inc., 1960, p. 50.

15) e.g., PATON AND LITTLETON, *An Introduction to Corporate Accounting Standards*, American Accounting Association, 1940, p. 9.

16) *op. cit.*, p. 81.

17) G. O. MAY, *Financial Accounting*, New York, The Macmillan Company, 1943, p. 49.

18) M. MOONITZ, (*op. cit.*) is the only author known to the writer who specifically provides for both possibilities.

19) An attempt is made in the author's *Towards a General Theory of Accounting*, Australian Society of Accountants, 1961.

29

Professional Education*

Before examining the specific proposals of the Report, we consider, as did Professor Vatter, the objectives of a programme of professional education. "Professional competence", says the Report, "comes from the possession of knowledge about the professional field. Thus the accountant's competence is based on his knowledge of business situations and business measurements and in his ability to apply this accumulated experience to problems in any particular business". Perhaps elision is permissible in a document addressed to the informed, and perhaps, therefore, one should not expect this statement by way of orientation to embrace what will be obvious as soon as it is mentioned. But it is curious that "business situations and business measurements" are mentioned as if they constitute the "professional field" and no reference is made to the very feature which distinguishes accounting, namely **monetary** aspects of business situations and **monetary** measurements.

The omission may be trivial if it were not for the fact that the less precise and the more abstract the definition of the field, the more diffuse and the less pointed will be the efforts to promote professional competence. It is not easy to point to any specific part of the Findings and Recommendations to demonstrate this, because most of the "right" words occur in the suggested programme. But the very vagueness of the descriptions at many points leaves the impression that the financial or economic aspects of business situations are a rather fuzzy core of the programme.

We would like to amplify the objectives of a programme of professional education in a way that provides a justification for "wider" studies than studies of technical detail, and that suggests how wide they should be. We seek broadly a good professional man. The first

31

* From a paper titled "Professional Education and the Vatter Report", presented at a Conference of the Australasian Association of University Teachers of Accounting, Melbourne, May 1965. The report, **Survey of Accountancy Education in Australia,** was commissioned jointly by the Australian Society of Accountants, The Institute of Chartered Accountants in Australia and The Australasian Institute of Cost Accountants. The survey was conducted by Professor W.J. Vatter in 1964. The proposals referred to in the text are proposals made in the report.

requirement shall be that he is technically expert in a limited field. By expert we mean that he shall be fully aware of all the purely technical elements of the **general** practice and the specific application of the existing level of technical knowledge in his chosen field. We do not expect him to be master of the technical elements of **general** practice and the specific application of the existing level of technical knowledge in his chosen field. We do not expect him to be master of the technical elements of **specialized** practice in his field. Only some will aspire, and only some will be competent, to practice as specialists within the limited field of a profession. The second requirement shall be that his conception of his professional task is tempered by an understanding of and a sympathy with the environment of that task. At its simplest, this means an understanding of the place of the expert and the function of his task in the immediate environment. At its broadest, it means a wide understanding of the elements of the culture of his society, and an openmindedness which will admit the influence, on his outlook and his practice, of shifts in the customs, institutions and general values of his society. If there is any ethical element in the practice of a profession it rests on this understanding and sympathy, not on technical competence alone. We do not believe that this "tempering" is achieved, at the basic educational stage, by the mere addition of some seasoning to the educational mix. A profession, limited though its task, is practised in an environment whole. The professional requires, then, not an introduction to other professions to broaden his understanding and engage his sympathy, but an orientation to the environment whole as an integral part of the introduction to his own profession.

Given these requirements it will be clear why we said the Vatter Report uses the "right" words. Specialized knowledge within a limited field is part of the immediate environment of practice; a prescription of any kind could scarcely omit reference to special topics of a highly technical kind. And the subject matters of psychology, sociology, political science, economics and so on are elements of the wider environment of practice; reference to them likewise can scarcely be omitted. What we challenge is the method by which these topics or cognate fields shall be introduced, and the extent to which they shall be introduced, into a programme of professional education.

The Proposed Programme

There are a number of difficulties about attempting to appraise the proposed programme of study. The first is the lack of any indication as to the manner in which it may be implemented. If we disregard many of the realities and constraints it is possible to devise and perhaps to justify almost any programme of study. Part II of the Report has a deal to say about the role of universities and technical colleges in professional education; but there is no comment to the effect that preparation by way of correspondence courses should be abandoned, an oddity in view of the large proportion of the sample which proceeded to qualification in this way. The proposed programme differs to such an extent from the existing professional syllabi that some uniformity would be expected by the professional organizations; and it differs so much from the existing style of courses in universities and colleges that it would be beyond implementation in the foreseeable future even if its desirability were granted. To mention only the problems of the universities, their objectives have always exceeded mere preparation for professional practice and within the limits of their existing regulations and educational philosophies the introduction of the additional material suggested in the report would be impossible – at least in some places. The flexibility of the American undergraduate credit system is not generally available within the Australian system; nor in some quarters is it believed that it should be.

A second difficulty is the absence of any indication of the extent of the material to be covered in each phase of the programme. One element of this is the time which it is considered should be devoted to each section. The outline is laid out in years. But what is meant by a year of, say, social science? One hour per week, or five, or what, and for how many weeks? If this were known it would be possible to think for ourselves just how much ground could be covered; it would provide some idea of the intensity or variety which the proposal contemplates. Again, are we to suppose that each of the subdivisions in any year should share equally the time involved in a year's work? are the social science, economic analysis and basic accounting units of the first year to be equivalent in study hours or work load? And again, are we to suppose that a year's work involves the same time or work load in successive years? are the accounting units in each year, for example, to be

33

considered as equal burdens? These may all seem to be trivial questions.
But as we are given no idea, by reference to a list of topics or a set of
texts for example, of what is implied by the outline, we are forced to
ask for some other indication of the dimensions of the programme.

Suppose, for the purpose of discussion, that the plan is something
akin to the usual university undergraduate course; and that to each
division of the programme for any year there is allotted three to four
hours of class work and twice that amount of reading, learning and
exercising time. One is given seriously to wonder how much Psychology-
Sociology-Political Science can be done in that time, and with what
effect, in the light of the fact that relatively little of any one of
these fields can be covered in a **full** first year course for each subject
singly in university programmes at present. The same applies to the
tripartite "Economic analysis" and to other divisions. Truly, subjects
can be cut down or blown up to any size one wishes; but the miniscule
proportions to which the programme reduces wide-ranging fields of study
is likely to do little to encourage the respect of candidates for
disciplined thinking, intensive or extensive. It is more likely to
produce dilettantes than professionals; in others it may well induce
ridicule rather than respect.

When one comes to details there are grave difficulties still. To
take the Social Science unit, one would like to know what materials are
contemplated which would give "an understanding of how these fields
relate to business activities". For even if, in the end, different
educational institutions choose to use different materials, in the
beginning it would help to know in which direction to turn. It is
demonstrable that, even in the universities, the concurrent study of
economics and accounting has done little to establish in the minds of
students the character of the relationship between the two. The present
writer knows of nothing in the social science field which will serve the
stipulated function of giving an understanding of relationships at the
first stage level of study. This is not to say it cannot be done. But
it is not done; for the very reason that most of the writers in other
fields write, as do accountants, for their professional fellows, as an
introduction to their own professions, not to establish relationships
with other fields. Some acquaintance with the literatures of related
areas leaves no doubt that conclusions which may be quite significant for

students of accounting may be drawn; but they have not been explicitly drawn and they leave no clear ideas, for beginners, about the manner in which accounting methods "relate to the economic and statistical notions of analysis, and what implications there are between accounting and the social sciences generally".

Why a four-year programme to qualification has been chosen is not easy to understand, unless it is somehow analogous to the American undergraduate programme; or perhaps, allowing for the difference between Australian and American secondary education, it is analogous to the undergraduate plus professional programmes offered in some American colleges. Again, if for comparison we take the present professional syllabi, the switch to such a large proportion – one-half – of non-accounting units requires to be supported by argument. And again, the relegation of some matters to the advanced stage seems to require more support than is given; it may well be supposed, for example, that public auditing, system design and such matters have more bearing on professional competence of a general kind than studies in marketing and production problems.

35

Looking at the four-year qualification programme as a whole, it seems to have been designed specifically with the processes of management in mind. But this seems to be an unfortunate bias in view of the important function accounting plays in influencing the relationships between owners and managers, lenders and borrowers, buyers and sellers of securities. Overemphasis on management and internal accountability may well mean underemphasis or neglect of external accountability; the result may be intellectual dependence on the views of management instead of the intellectual independence which may be expected of the professional impulse. Because of the rapidity of change in the affairs of any firm, the role of the auditor is of particular importance as assuring the reliability of information not open to inspection by others. Little enough attention is paid as it is to this authenticating function; but to relegate its study to the post-qualification stage removes a significant element of the general apparatus of discovery and the general practice of the profession.

Scope of the Programme

But turn, now, to the scope of the programme; if we telescope the description in the Report, we have the following list of specific things to be studied over a four-year period: psychology, sociology, political science (all to an extent not indicated); statistical and mathematical analysis, through to time series, index numbers, regression and correlation, probability and statistical estimation, tests of hypotheses and statistical inference; micro- and macro-economics to a level beyond the "typical" first course in economics; measurement and communications (concepts and their application) in accounting; machine and computer work; business institutions and business decisions (an intensive view); business law and finance and financial institutions; business organization and management; quality and price policies, channels and methods of distribution; plant location and layout; inventory control, quality control; operations research, linear programming and mathematical models (some preliminary ideas); taxation and financial mathematics; organization theory "in relation to the overall management area"; financial management; and the ordinary basic accounting material plus "the conceptual and logical basis of financial statements" and "adjustments for changing price levels", (to mention just two additions to the present curriculum). And all this in two full-time years and two part-time years of study! There must be serious doubt whether the world will ever see the product of putting a matriculant through this programme in the stipulated time.

At the risk of digressing, but because it has some features in common with the Vatter proposals, we mention another set of observations on the future training and education of accountants. As you may know, there is at present in progress in the United States an inquiry into the common body of knowledge necessary for certified public accountants. One of the submissions to the inquiry has already been given publicity[1]. Its authors make the following suggestions. ". . . the accountant's education . . . certainly should include economics, history, political science, psychology, natural science, physical science and a foreign language . . . . The accountant's formal university-level education must include such courses as psychology, anthropology, sociology, political

1. Submission to the Commission on the Common Body of Knowledge for CPAs, by the Committee on the Education of an Accountant, of the College of Measurements of The Institute of Management Sciences, **The Journal of Accountancy,** December 1964, pp.79–83.

science, and organization theory . . . . `operations research´ must
become the concern of accountants . . . . the accountant [should] be
thoroughly grounded in linear algebra, with special emphasis on the
theory of matrices and determinants . . . . a working facility with the
fundamentals of integral and differential calculus is desirable . . . .
the accountant of the future must be thoroughly grounded in [electronic
data processing] techniques . . . . Accountants need a background in
statistics that emphasizes the mathematical theory of probability and
sampling theory . . . . He needs to be intimately acquainted with the
finance function, the production function and the marketing function.
The accountant must concern himself with all problems of management. He
must comprehend the total environment of the business, including the
legal, regulatory, cultural, political and social environments in which
it operates, as well as the internal forces in the organization".

One wonders how seriously readers are expected to take this
prescription, and how such a paragon could be produced (if at all) in
anything like the six years of undergraduate and graduate work which the
submission stipulates.

Rather than analyze these detailed proposals, we will in the sequel
look at the whole problem from another angle which appears to offer an
alternative solution to the basic problem of what should be taught and
learned.

Some General Views of Professional Education

There can be no question that the growth in knowledge and the growth
in the complexity of social organization impose increasing burdens on us
all. We cannot be adequately equipped to deal with our environment
unless we know something of what is going on out there, and something of
a more or less contemporary kind. It follows that educational programmes
will necessarily be different from those of a less complex age. And as
new knowledge reaches the point where it is not simply the "heresy" of
its discoverer, but has become part of the general framework of
knowledge, educational programmes should take cognizance of the fact.
However, this does not entail that educational programmes designed to
produce the experts in any one field should be crammed with what is the
proper business of other kinds of experts. One cannot turn back the
clock. Specialization has always been the way in which men have sought

to cope with complexity; it is folly to suppose that the process can be halted by attempts to annexe incipient new specialisms; the more one imposes on an entrant to an expert profession the less expert will he become.

Many proposals for giving a new look to curricula appear to overlook these points. The age of the encyclopaedist is past in any event, and there never was an educational programme for producing an encyclopaedist. The type of educational programme we have been considering we do not believe to be the type which will produce at once the competent expert and the sympathetic and comprehending professional. Instead of an infusion such programmes are mixes. They take so much of so many ingredients, ingredients often specially prepared for other purposes, and mix them in a selected order, in the expectation that the result is digestible and wholesome. There is a danger that it may produce what Pope described as

> The bookful blockhead ignorantly read
> With loads of learned lumber in his head.

It seems curious that little notice has been taken of some of the observations of a number of people who have concerned themselves with the broad problems arising from the vast expansion of knowledge and the growing complexity of affairs of this century.

Some forty years ago Whitehead[2] was already concerned with the rate of progress in knowledge and the professionalization of knowledge. He granted that "effective knowledge is professionalised knowledge, supported by a restricted acquaintance with useful subjects subservient to it". But professionalism in knowledge "produces minds in a groove. Each profession makes progress, but it is progress in its own groove. Now to be mentally in a groove is to live in contemplating a given set of abstractions . . . . But there is no groove of abstractions which is adequate for the comprehension of human life". Whitehead sees the tendency to professionalism in knowledge as a great danger in society at large; " . . . the specialised functions of the community are performed better and more progressively, but the generalised direction lacks vision. The progressiveness in detail only adds to the danger by the

---

2. **Science and the Modern World** (1926). The quotations are from Chapter XIII, "Requisition for Social Progress", of the 1938 Pelican edition.

feebleness of coordination". Wisdom being "the fruit of balanced development .... the make-weight which balances the thoroughness of the specialist intellectual training should be of a radically different kind from purely intellectual analytical knowledge .... [it should] strengthen habits of concrete appreciation of the individual facts in their full interplay of [diverse] emergent values .... There should be some analysis even here, but only just enough to illustrate the way of thinking in diverse spheres".

The dilemma - specialization only or specialization plus balanced development - is a difficult one to face. Specialization is a relatively easy way for those who practise it, as teachers or as professional experts. It is inevitable, but its dangers may only be mitigated by a different device than the mere accretion of additional specialisms or specialist abstractions to those of any professionalized field.

Ortega y Gasset approaches much the same problem from a different direction, from an examination of the function of the university in a world of professional specialization[3]. Ortega concludes that the university's teaching comprises three functions, the transmission of culture, the teaching of the professions, and scientific research and the training of new scientists (p.48). It is the combination of the first and second which gives the good professional man, of competence and sympathy as we suggested earlier. It is the combination of the first and third which produces the good professional teacher as we shall consider him later.

Ortega is impatient with the "fabulous profusion" of studies characteristic of university programmes. "It is impossible even for the better than ordinary student to come anywhere near real success in learning what the university professes to teach him" (p.49). "Instead of teaching what **ought** to be taught, according to some Utopian desire, we must teach only what **can** be taught; that is **what can be learned**". What is suggested is that we are too prone to believe that the capacity of students is more or less infinite, or perfectly plastic, that we can cram any quantity of subject matter into a programme and that it will **ipso facto** produce a better graduate than a smaller quantity. Ortega

39

---

3. Jose Ortega y Gasset, **Mission of the University**, London, Lund Humphries, 1946.

protests. We must rather take the limitations of students consciously as a datum. We must then select from all existent knowledge what appears "strictly necessary for the life of the man who is now a student", and this must be pruned to "what the student can really learn with thoroughness and understanding". Only thus can we avoid the cant, the humbug, the pretentiousness, the delusions of grandeur, which would strike at the integrity of educational institutions.

This is not to be understood as setting a low standard upon what can be taught and what can be learned. It is natural that really novel discoveries must pass through a stage in which, although their merit as new knowledge is recognized by the vanguard of scientists, their application to professional life and their incorporation in programmes of study is delayed. Ways of teaching must be modified, new ways must be learned; but the delay between discovery and exposure of students to new discoveries should be as short as possible. But of that more later.

It will be important for the sequel to understand what Ortega means by culture. He means the "repertory of the active convictions" of an age as to the nature of the natural and the social environments and as to the prevailing hierarchy of the values of the age. Explaining this, he says: "Naturally any age presents very disparate systems of convictions. Some are a drossy residue of other times. But there is always a system of live ideas which represents the superior level of the age, a system which is essentially characteristic of its times; and this system is the culture of the age. He who lives at a lower level, on archaic ideas, condemns himself to a lower life, more difficult, toilsome, unrefined . . . . The man who lives on a plane beneath the enlightened level of his time is condemned, relatively, to the life of an infra-man . . . . It is a life crippled, wrecked, false . . . . he is swindling himself out of his own life" (pp. 65-67).

If we accept Ortega's tri-functional idea of the university and the natural limitations of men, as students or teachers, we are more or less bound to his view that science must be distinguished from practice, that the university does not, except in few cases, produce scientists (in any field), and that curricula of the general kind should not be geared to the requirements of the scientist as such (in any field). The design of such a curriculum calls for clear apprehension of the core of a professional specialism and a capacity for syntheses and systematizations which contribute to the general understanding of the relationship of specialisms to life beyond the "groove". This requires "a kind of scientific genius which hitherto has existed only as an observation; the genius for integration" (p. 72).

Jacques Barzun[4] more recently finds cause for disquiet in the tendency for the mystique of science to invade, even to overwhelm, the common understanding. Like Whitehead and Ortega he recognizes the productivity of specialization and the pervading scientific component of contemporary culture. But, like them, he deplores the disparity between the veneration for science of the common man and his lack of understanding of what science is. He attributes this in part to the increasing divergence between technical and vernacular vocabularies. Even specialists in related fields "decline to speak the same language even when they can" (p. 11). Specialization leads to esotericism; science moves further and further from the possibility of it being an "object of contemplation" to laymen. And as we are all laymen beyond the limits of our own specialism, we are increasingly unable to bring to bear on our many-valued and many-sided actions the fruits of the processes of science. "The rampant specialism, an arbitrary and purely social evil, is not recognized for the crabbed guild spirit that it is, and few are bold enough to say that carving out a small domain and exhausting its soil affords as much chance for protected irresponsibility as for scientific thoroughness" (p. 27). The solution to the problem of recognizing specialization and tempering its effects does not lie in exposing men to a variety of specialisms as such, but in cultivating an understanding of the many facets of living as a whole at the same time as professional competence is developing. If, because of his wide influence and his involvement in problems having many of the elements of living as a whole, we regard the ideal professional as a "universal man", we may take up Barzun's prescription: "A universal man should approach within himself the universality of all men. Though he cannot take in all possible conclusions, his mind should be open, at least temporarily, to all modes of use, from the analysis of the scientist to the synthesis of

41

---

4. **Science: The Glorious Entertainment**, London, Secker & Warburg, 1964.

the historian, from the art of the poet or musician to the study of primitive man's superstitions, and thence upward to the intuitions of mystics and religious men" (p. 299); or, as he puts it succinctly, "one mind in many modes".

Education for Professional Accounting

Now what has all this to do with a professional programme in accounting? Very much, we believe.

In the first place, the importance of deciding the scope of the specialism itself is undeniable. Without such a decision it is impossible to know what must be regarded as bearing on professional competence as an expert; and what may therefore be regarded as tempering the judgement. In the second place, as a principle of economy, we may select from the field of practice those elements which can best be learned in the course of an educational programme, leaving aside those elements which, because of their specificity to particular environments of individual experience and practice, can best be learned through experience. Those elements which can best be learned are general in character; for the object of the educational process is to fit a man for meeting many situations which are not replicates of the particular past experiences of teachers, book-writers or practitioners or their clients. In the third place, as a principle emerging from the objective of training professional men, we may select from the field of knowledge, those elements which are of general importance for all professional specialists in accounting. There will thus be excluded such highly specialized elements as are of interest, or of application, in narrow fields, however important they may be in those fields. Techniques and ideas peculiarly relevant to the research workers and "scientists" of the specialism would thus be excluded; for the object is to give students the best of the product of scientific inquiry, not to make of them scientists as such.

What is the residue from this filtering process? The first filter removes matters which are not strictly of the same class. If, for example, we decide that accounting has a function which relates to economic behaviour, the decision commits us to concern with economic concepts and magnitudes; if by force of circumstance physical concepts and magnitudes must be resorted to, it will be only because they have some bearing on economic concepts and magnitudes. The point should be

42

emphasized that the scope of the function is a matter for decision, and
if necessary from time to time a change in the decision. The example
just given is given as example only, not as a full description of the
function. But whatever decision is reached it will of necessity be
conditioned by, if not absolutely determined by, the carefully considered
needs of users of the products of accounting. The second filter excludes
all purely mechanical operations, the form and style of which are matters
of taste and vary from place to place. It lets pass all matters of
general principle; such for example, as the implications of the
separation of the producer from the user of the products of accounting,
or the implications of the differences between discovery and evaluation
of what is discovered, or the implications of the specialist, and
therefore necessarily, abstract nature of the product. Matters of this
kind have hitherto attracted little attention, but we believe they are
very much at the heart of general practice. The third filter excludes
advanced technical specialisms whether they be of the highly
mathematical, or methodological, or highly legalistic kind.

43

The filtrate is the necessary common body of specialist knowledge
relevant to the general practice of accounting as a specialism. But
already the illustrations of the previous paragraph suggest the direction
in which educational processes for the profession should move. They
should move, it seems, in the direction of intensified study of facets of
accounting which are already acknowledged, but the implications of which
are not so readily acknowledged. To clarify the view we hold, we list
the components of what seems to be the necessary foundation of specialist
practice.

(a) **A knowledge of the methods of empirical inquiry generally, and
some familiarity with their application in some of the sciences.** The
practice of accounting consists in "finding out" some of the facts of
one's environment; it is thus essentially a method of empirical inquiry.
There is a descriptive literature of many of the sciences which expounds
their methods and illustrates the results of the applications of those
methods. It is not necessary to study these methods (including the
mathematical and statistical devices employed) intensively. But some
descriptive study of the ways in which others go about the business of
"finding out" has long been the habit of those who wish to engage in the
same business; it is no less appropriate in accounting. At the same time

such study may contribute to sympathy, in the environment of practice, with other specialists whose modes of thought are conditioned by the sciences. And lastly it contributes to the awareness of fields beyond one's specialism, fields which have contributed materially to the general culture of one's time.

(b) **A knowledge of the history of the development of science, with particular reference to the methods of discovery used and to changes in concepts and beliefs through time.** This is a necessary antidote to fixity of beliefs in set ways of solving problems, and of beliefs as to matters of "fact". If, as is commonly said, accounting records and statements in series represent financial history, then apprehension of the variability of knowledge and of the variability of the present significance of past facts is a necessary qualification. Some study of the development of accounting in parallel with developments in other fields would be instructive. In any case, a sense of history also contributes to an understanding of the culture of one's time.

(c) **A knowledge of the perceptual, cognitive and affective limitations of individuals; of their ends and modes of pursuing ends.** We do not require a general study of individual psychology, but sufficient insight to comprehend the advantages of cooperation, the gains and losses from conflict, and the role of the division of labour (or specialization) in human affairs. All of these matters are directly pertinent to the practice of accounting and to the design of accounting systems and statements which are to serve as interpersonal messages, for accounting as it is commonly practised is a form of the division of labour and its products have a bearing on cooperation and conflict between those it serves.

(d) **A knowledge of the relationship of knowledge as experience, knowledge as new information, and of expectations, to action.** It is necessary to distinguish the knowable from the unknown and unknowable; to distinguish information from hypothesis; to consider the nature of evidence and the dependability of statements. All this as part of the process of sharpening the powers of discrimination; but more specifically because, as expert, the accountant is caught in the midst of such diverse kinds of proposition in the course of his duties. Failure to distinguish the objective from the subjective, the knowable from the unknowable, fact from prediction, puts his technical task beyond discovery and prevents understanding of the way in which these contraries influence action.

(e) **A knowledge of the legal and social processes by which interpersonal relationships are established and maintained and modified.** We do not mean a lawyer's knowledge of law, a sociologist's knowledge of sociology, nor any other such thing. We mean rather a sufficient insight into the appropriate special fields to regard legal, social, organizational, economic and other processes as ways in which living is structured under interdependence. This would include some knowledge of the roles of groups; of individuals in groups; of associations, corporations and government; of experts. And its value lies in the fact that the accountant is involved both in micro-social processes as an expert, and in macro-social processes as a citizen.

(f) **A knowledge of the nature of systems and of the role of communication in systems.** Firms, organizations generally, economies as a whole, are examples of systems. Some systems are externally regulated; some are self-regulating; some are exceedingly simple; some exceedingly complex. In some systems the linkages or means of communication are physical; in others verbal and numerical. Accountants are involved both as parts of systems and as operators of sub-systems. They have no role otherwise and their role is only discoverable and understandable in the context of some system. The contents of accounting records and statements constitute systems which are linked to and descriptive of the systems which are accounting entities. The notion is pervasive and its use enables the interconnections between the elements to be readily apprehended.

(g) **A knowledge of market and price formation processes and of the nature and role of money in those processes.** Again a specialist knowledge is not requisite; but a reasonably satisfactory working knowledge is. For, on the one hand, accounting is intimately concerned with money prices; and on the other hand, those who use its products are intimately involved in adaptive processes carried on through the medium of money in markets. If the accountant fails to understand that pricing and production and financial policies are not unilaterally determinable, he is unable to discriminate between the relevant and the irrelevant.

(h) **A knowledge of the theory and methods of clasification, measurement and calculation.** This is perhaps a subdivision of (d); it is distinguished here for its quantitative element. Of what is knowable,

45

only some things are measurable. It is of importance to distinguish what
is measurable, to know the conditions under which measurement is possible
and calculation is necessary, both in general and in relation to monetary
magnitudes specifically. This involves logical rather than mathematical
exercises. For general practice of the specialism it seems unnecessary
to proceed to advanced mathematics, not the least reason being the
crudity of anticipatory magnitudes and the imperfections of markets as
sources of measures.

It will be apparent that this list has two features. Every item has
a specific relation to the actual practice of accounting as a general
expertise. And every item has also a wider aspect which contributes to
awareness of or sensitivity to the general characteristics of living, in
large or small groups as occasion demands, to the "height of the times",
to use Ortega´s phrase. The variety of subject matters included in the
Vatter prescription and others occurs here too; but in integrated
fashion, not as a mere mixture; and in a limited but perceptibly relevant
way.

But there is a further point. Being integrated with what we believe
to be necessary professional education, the treatment does not depend on
the availability of general texts in the related fields or on the
"servicing" of studies by experts in those fields. It depends rather on
the actual interweaving of the appropriate propositions or findings of
experts in other fields with the technical features of accounting as and
when they become necessary. The task is entirely in the hands of the
teachers of accounting as such. They alone have the particular
orientation necessary to select from the findings of logicians,
scientists, pychologists, economists and others, those which are
pertinent to accounting. They have it in their hands to make the study
of accounting a routine, clerical, technical exercise or a rich
experience, full of the verisimilitude of practical living in a complex,
differentiated society.

Yet another point. Studies organized on this pattern do not fall
back on the seemingly lame notion that there is a thing called liberal
arts to which a certain percentage of time should be devoted, for
"broadening" or "cultural" purposes. These effects are built in. We
believe it is as possible to make the study of accounting a liberal study
as it is to make the study of philosophy or history or literature a

narrow and technical and limiting experience. But not without some
costs.

The costs, it seems, are the paid labours of teachers and
researchers. The problem of giving a professional education to the
general practitioners of a specialism is linked closely with the problem
of producing the teachers and researchers behind such an education; but
they are not the same problem. The link subsists in the fact that, if
teaching is to be at the topmost level available at the time and within
what is capable of being learned, teachers have a necessarily
discriminatory role. They must know more than they can teach. It is
their business ideally to know what is the utmost level of presently
available knowledge in their fields; otherwise there is no way of
considering what at any time can be learned. And it is their business to
translate the findings of the researchers into forms which are relevant
to the world in which general practitioners will practice, which are
assimilable into the existing framework of doctrine but advance its
level, and forms in which those findings are capable of being learned.
Teachers are the organizers, the integrators of the new and the old, the
matchers of the essentially technical with the necessary elements of
adjoining fields of study. If there is any distinction between teaching
and research it subsists in this: that the researcher's role is
analytical, exploratory, critical, destructive and constructive, whereas
the teacher's role is discriminatory and integrative, pedagogical,
illuminative and in a sense emotive.

It is fashionable these days to speak of interdisciplinary studies,
to feel that the narrow boundaries of subject matters should not be too
highly respected; and to believe that the way out of the dilemma of
producing either the generally informed non-expert or the narrowly
informed expert is to require some study by students of things beyond
their lines of specialism. That is the source of the suggestions which
involve mere additions to the curriculum. It entails the belief that
somehow or other students will be able to see as a whole the several
things served to them in discrete parcels. We believe this is a baseless
and forlorn expectation. There is abundant evidence to the effect that
what does not become an integral part of one's educational experience and
of one's practical expertness is soon forgotten; and that the integration
of diverse matter is beyond many teachers, and **a fortiori** beyond

47

students. What the situation demands is interdisciplinary work by teachers, leading to a richly interconnected curriculum tightly related to a professional objective, however diverse its contents may seem superficially. Against "the mental dryrot" of "inert ideas", Whitehead enunciated two educational commandments: "Do not teach too many subjects" and "What you teach, teach thoroughly". "The result of teaching small parts of a large number of subjects is the passive reception of disconnected ideas, not illumined by any spark of vitality. Let the main ideas . . . be few and important, and let them be thrown into every combination possible"[5].

48

These observations are perhaps rambling. Their purport however is simple enough to state. A new philosophy of education in accounting is called for by the recognition of the complexity of modern commercial affairs, the vast growth in technical knowledge, and the necessity of producing experts who are technically proficient and who have a wide-ranging sense of the realities within the framework of which they practice. Major changes have occurred in the teaching of English and Mathematics in our time, in response to major appraisals of the available knowledge and of the functions of educational experience in these fields. A similar change is necessary in respect of accounting. To attempt to cover in a curriculum the diverse applications of accounting method found in practice seems simple in the abstract, but its effect is to limit the understanding and to place precedent above reason. It goes no distance towards meeting the objective of producing practitioners who will confront the unusual and the novel with the utmost understanding of broad principles and of the conditioning forces which will or should influence the choices made under circumstances not previously experienced.

For too long accounting has been cut off from the stream of advancing ideas in other fields of inquiry. But the deficiencies of present programmes will not be made good merely by adding here and there an annexe from other disciplines. The relevant findings of those disciplines must be absorbed into contemporary ways of thinking about and teaching accounting. The vague belief that other disciplines have "some" relation to accounting or "some" usefulness is not enough.

_____

5. Alfred North Whitehead, "The Aims of Education" (1916), in **The Aims of Education**, Mentor Books, 1957.

We have been concerned here primarily with the task and the general content of a professional education programme. We believe that the basic ideas which we have suggested may be made the framework on which the technical features of accounting may be superimposed progressively; and that the whole may be taught and learned effectively, because it is linked systematically to understandable elements of the environment, in a three year university programme. Whatever may be the divisions and subdivisions of the material in any given programme, the development of professional skill, understanding and responsibility will be impeded unless the study of the subject is loosed from the shackles of long-standing habit and geared to the demonstrable features of other forms of empirical inquiry. The myths, the fictions, the unsystematic nature of present doctrines, we have gone on accepting, largely we believe because of the long divorcement of accounting from other fields. Ill-considered accretions will only compound the present confusion; a major reconstruction, one could hope, would do much to eliminate the illogical, the patently irrelevant, and the obfuscating features of doctrine and practice.

49

A Matter of Principle

IT SEEMS to be time to try to find our way out of the wood. We have been worried for a long time. We have tried to assuage our worries and uncertainties by pointed attacks on critical contemporary problems, as in the *Accounting Research Bulletins* of the American Institute and similar exercises by other professional groups. We have tried to tidy up the untidiness made apparent by frauds, indictments for negligence, and similar commercial disorders. Also, we have on occasion mounted massive offensives against what have seemed to be serious threats to our self-respect; as examples there are the Institute-Stock Exchange cooperation in the early 'thirties and the Study Group on business income in the early 'fifties. But almost continually the smaller sources of worry have been so many, so varied and so insistent that we have become almost insensitive to the larger. In trying to avoid the trees we have become so preoccupied that the wood has been forgotten. It seems necessary to retrace our steps, perhaps a few, perhaps many, before we are again able to proceed with a sense of direction and confidence.

Observations such as these may very well represent the feeling which inspired the Accounting Principles Board to approve the preparation of the "Inventory of Generally Accepted Accounting Principles for Business Enterprises," *ARS No. 7*. No indication of the sentiment of the Board is given in the prefaces. Indeed the author

suggests in another place that the study had its origin in a context apart from reflection on confusion.[1] Be that as it may, its appearance as *ARS No. 7* suggests that the necessity of retracing steps may have arisen from the inconclusive and cacophonous reception of earlier studies.

The remarks which follow require some basic justification. They would be pointless if the propositions of the "Inventory" were stated categorically only. Many must have long wished for an inventory of generally accepted accounting principles; for whether one wishes to adopt, to rebut, or even simply to think about these principles, it would be useful to know what they are. But the Inventory is not a simple listing. A great deal of *ARS No. 7* is devoted to justification of the listed propositions and to the rebuttal of objections to them. The study is argumentative. As such it invites cross-argument in a way which would not be open if it had been simply a descriptive list. It invites cross-argument because both the justifications and the rebuttals seem to be incomplete and inconclusive. In what follows, therefore, we do not consider whether the list is complete,

[1] Paul Grady, "Inventory of Generally Accepted Accounting Principles in the United States of America," THE ACCOUNTING REVIEW, Jan. 1965, p. 21.

51

though we do consider the characteristics of principles in general. Rather we are primarily concerned with the arguments on which it is sought to establish the propriety of the principles listed.

Professional Responsibility

The first of the arguments deserving attention occurs at the very outset, where the limitations in scope of the inquiry are given. It is not easy for another to identify specifically the limits set, or to know unequivocally the weight attached to parts of a line of argument. This is merely the consequence of the shades of interpretation which may be put upon any written statement.

Dealing with the responsibility of the CPA for the accounting principles followed by a client corporation, the author writes: ". . . we are not referring to legal responsibility, which would rest upon determination by the courts, but rather to his professional responsibility as reflected in the Code of Ethics and other technical literature . . . " (pp. 15–16).

Whether or not the Study deals with legal responsibilities, there is a presumption that at least the legal responsibilities of CPAs are to be recognized by them. But the phrase "which would rest upon determination by the courts" seems to imply that until the courts have ruled, and only insofar as the courts have ruled, is the law effective. Nor does the quotation or its context make clear whether the legal responsibilities referred to are those arising from statutes or those arising out of litigated cases of alleged negligence or fraud or other misdemeanors. In the framing of principles it seems quite proper to exclude from discussion the case law on negligence and such matters, for this is clearly at the lower fringe of behavior. It does not seem proper, however, to exclude from the discussion any statute law which is pertinent.

If on any matter there is a stated law, or regulation in pursuance of a statute, such a statement is, prima facie, the law. Legal responsibility rests upon determination by the courts only where the statute or regulation is in dispute; it does not so rest of necessity. The law is written for the general regulation of the relationships of all members of a society, whether or not they are also members of other groups which have views on matters treated in statutes. If the law imposes obligations on any class of persons, it does so regardless of the obligations which members of that class may impose upon themselves. But the law does not in principle countenance the self-imposition of obligations on the members of a class among themselves which is inconsistent with the general law; oppressive or minatory combinations of members of a class, for example, may be broken up. Nor does the law countenance the imposition on persons beyond a given class by members of that class, of burdens additional to the general burdens of the law.

It seems, therefore, that insofar as the law is superior in effect, as representing the will of a whole society, no discussion of the responsibilities of CPAs which neglects or passes over statutorily imposed duties can be complete. Now the law does indeed lay specific responsibilities on CPAs. The Securities Act and the Securities Exchange Act regulate the affairs and the reporting on the affairs of certain corporations "in the public interest and for the protection of investors." There can strictly be no rule of practice that fails to conform with this statutory principle. It may happen that, on the occasion of a dispute, the courts are required to interpret the principle; but the principle is in any case stated as a rule of general behavior.

If a given class of persons wishes to enjoin on its members a higher "morality" or ethic than that of the general law, that is to some extent the concern of its members. But no such class may enjoin on its members a lower "morality" than that of the general law, for to do so would "outlaw" its members. No code of ethics is complete which does not fully satisfy the law. If a professional body enjoins on its members a specific behavior, it cannot but be a behavior which is equal to or superior to the behavior which reasonable lay persons would interpret the statute as enjoining. In the present case, a code of ethics for CPAs could enjoin a behavior no less, and ideally even more, "in the public interest and for the protection of investors" than the lay person would suppose. It is curious, however, that the Study makes no reference to this phrase which is, if anything, the keynote of the basic securities legislation.

Generally Accepted Principles

The phrase quoted from the statute seems in fact to have been largely ignored since it was written into the law. Instead of drawing out the implications or meaning of the statutory principle, professional attention is commonly drawn to "generally accepted accounting principles." We will attempt to show later that these principles are contrary to the purport of the statutory principle. But for the moment we concern ourselves solely with the status of generally accepted principles in an ethical context. Under what circumstances are generally accepted practices invoked or relied upon as a test? There is a range of problems in other kinds of professional practice—medicine, law, engineering—in which the same phrase is invoked. This range is on the fringe where competence is questioned or incompetence is alleged; where, in medicine for example, a practitioner appears to have failed to take precautions or appears to have failed to exercise an adequate level of professional skill to the detriment of a patient; or where, in

engineering, a practitioner has specified or used materials of inadequate quality or other specification. In such marginal cases the law steps in. At this point it is open to the accused to plead, in defence, adherence to generally accepted practices.

At the opposite end of the scale there are also marginal practices. But it is certain that no person acting on the basis of the general practices of his profession plus his own special or extraordinary knowledge or skill would be accused of violating generally accepted practice if he were, say, to perform a unique operation, the first of its kind. In so doing he puts himself beyond what is generally accepted; but he does not endanger his reputation, even if he fails, provided that in all other respects he acts with the greatest care. Only by exceeding the general standard is a profession promoted: at the upper fringe of practice, adherence to generally accepted practice would impede the progress of the science and art. That a given behavior exceeds the level of generally accepted practice does not invoke social wrath and censure.

Only at the lower margin of practice then does the violation of a general standard become of importance, professionally and socially. But not with the object of lowering the standard to a new level. The test at this margin is not even what is good *average* practice. It is almost certain that indictment would be secured only if the behavior in question were clearly below the *minimum* standard of practice. The minimum is not, of course, a point on a scale, easily determinable either by individual practitioners or by jurists on the evidence of practitioners. But there are minima; practitioners are occasionally indicted; and the test of minima is the evidence of what is generally accepted practice in the context of the knowledge of the time. Anything at all above the minimum will pass the test; but that does not make the minimum the ideal of professional per-

53

formance. If professional pronouncements are made they would tend, in keeping with an advancing ethic, always to be well up the scale of skill and competence, and to change as knowledge in the field of expertise changes, not only as other external changes occur.

The status of generally accepted practices in accounting seems to be in marked contrast. Whereas the phrase is invoked in other fields only at the point where professionally or socially unacceptable behavior is alleged, in accounting it is almost the touchstone of respectable practice. The phrase tends in other fields to be used as the defence of the incompetent, never as the ideal of the competent. It would almost seem that, by using the phrase, professional pronouncements would be advertising a mediocrity their originators would not wish to imply. In any case it seems that any statement purporting to have an ethical or idealistic foundation should claim much more than mere general acceptance.

Quite apart from these observations there should be some discomfort from the fact that the origin of the phrase "generally accepted accounting principles" can be traced to a point of time when in fact *general* acceptance was not required to be the criterion of use. The proposals resulting from the discussions of the early thirties included a provision that each company should register with the stock exchange its own practices.[2] The possibility of uniformity was denied; and by implication the generality of acceptance was not considered as a test of the propriety of a practice. The possibility of uniformity is still being denied, notwithstanding that the use of the phrase "generally accepted" strongly suggests uniformity. Something quite similar in a different field suggests what has happened.

... all the great mechanical brains, translating machines, learning machines, chess-playing ma-

chines, perceiving machines, etc., accounts of which fill our press, owe their 'reality' to a failure to use the subjunctive mood. The game is played as follows: First, it is asserted that except for trivial engineering details, a program for a machine is equivalent to a machine. The flow chart for a program is equated to a program. And finally, the statement that a flow chart could be written for a nonexistent program for a nonexistent machine establishes the existence of the machine. In just this way Uttley's "Conditioned Reflex Machine," Rosenblatt's "Perceptron," Simon, Shaw and Newell's "General Problem Solver," and many other nonexistent devices have been named in the literature and are referred to as though they existed.[3]

In brief, the appropriate formulation of statements about generally accepted accounting principles would be something like: If there were a body of generally accepted accounting principles, then ... (for example, readers of accounting statements would be able to rely on their contents, their comparability, and so on). Stated in this way, the proposition may have induced a search for these principles. The omission of the subjunctive enabled the phrase to be adopted without the search.

It is in fact curious that in the present Study no attempt is made to provide any kind of empirical evidence to support what are said to be generally accepted principles. It seems not unreasonable to suppose that investors, whose protection is the object of the legislation, would interpret generally accepted as accepted generally, that is, accepted by the great majority of companies or the great majority of accountants. Authoritarian statements are quite different; they may, but need not be generally accepted; many outmoded statutes fall into this category. It seems quite pointless to say that a principle can be

[2] See Bishop Carleton Hunt (ed.), *Twenty-Five Years of Accounting Responsibility, 1911-1936* (American Institute Publishing Co. Inc.), Vol. 1, pp. 112ff. The proposal was not adopted.
[3] Mortimer Taube, *Computers and Common Sense* (Columbia University Press, 1961), pp. 59-60.

"generally accepted even if not generally followed" (p. 51). The difficulty of determining whether a generally accepted principle is being followed lies in the fact that many of the principles assert two contradictory things at once. Thus: "fixed assets should be carried at cost . . . in the historical amounts, unless such cost is no longer meaningful" (Principle C-2). In other words, fixed assets should be carried at cost or not at cost; which, because it includes all possibilities, cannot be infringed, provides no guidance, and cannot therefore be regarded as a principle. The corresponding objective is similarly contradictory: "Account for the assets . . . in a meaningful manner. . . . It should be understood that financial position or balance sheet statements do not purport to show either present values of assets to the enterprise or values which might be realized on liquidation" (Objective C). For the protection of investors, the very things that are meaningful are the things excluded by the last sentence. The objective thus seems to be "to account meaningfully unmeaningfully."

The Character of Principles

One of the more serious omissions of all statements on accounting principles is adequate preliminary discussion of the manner in which "principles" is to be interpreted. There is a tendency to suppose that we can get along quite well without exercises in definition. In no other field having any pretension to rigor of thought or development is this presumption entertained. A nail or a screw is a definitely shaped piece of metal; a carpenter does not use any old piece of metal for the purposes for which nails or screws are used. Likewise in the process of thought we can make little progress without shaping the materials, the ideas, we use. There is also a tendency to suppose that, if we must shape our ideas, references to dictionaries will yield

adequate definitions. This too is mistaken. Dictionaries seldom go further than giving commonly accepted and acceptable alternative words and phrases for a given word, substitute symbols; and generally the alternative or substitute symbols are those in lay use—they are not adequate for specialist use. A novice in the study of physics might be helped by what he finds under "atom" or "neutron" in a dictionary; a physicist would have no use for such a source. To choose from a series of possible lay usages one which will serve for the development of a technical field is to bind technical development to lack of precision, or to a precision that is good enough for lay use only. To suppose that lexicographers know all the uses to which a term may be put in all technical fields is to suppose they are omniscient.

Likewise, the interpretation given in dictionaries to "principle" is inadequate of itself. For better guidance it seems useful to resort to interpretations found to be serviceable in technical, generally in scientific, discourse. Even in such fields the nature of postulates, principles, laws, and rules is not entirely beyond dispute. But it is possible to make a distinction between postulates, principles, and laws on the one hand, and rules and descriptions of practices on the other.

In empirical science all have to do with some observable phenomena. Principles are statements of a general nature about classes of events or occurrences in the abstract. But they are no less useful because they are abstract. In the field of optics there is a principle of the rectilinear propagation of light in a medium of uniform density. But in fact a medium of uniform density is an abstraction, and so is a straight line. "A straight line has no width, no depth, no wiggles and no ends. There are no straight lines. We have ideas about these non-existent impossibilities; we even draw pictures of them. But they

55

do not exist."[4] All principles are of this general abstractive kind. They are conceptual. They represent a grasp of the general form of certain regularities, without specification of what will or might happen in the case of any particular phenomenon of the class with which they deal. They emerge from observation and contemplation of some aspect of the universe of experience. Their usefulness subsists in their capacity, as premises, to inform actions of great variety in contexts of which the phenomena they describe are a part.

In this sense principles are not usefully described as generally acceptable or generally accepted. The test for their use by any person or class of persons is whether or not they are consistent with "the nature of things." Each can make the test anew for himself; that others agree with him may be satisfying, psychologically; but the usefulness of such principles is not a function of general agreement or acceptance.

Statements of the second class referred to above are characteristically different from principles. Rules and statements of practice are normative or positive statements descriptive of desired or actual responses to particular problems. If we wish to formulate rules of behavior which are consistent with the nature of things, as that nature is conceived and expressed in principles arising from observation and contemplation, we will do so with those principles in mind. What we do is take a principle as a major premise, a particular circumstance or objective as a minor premise and deduce a consequence, which even though expressed in the indicative mood, is a rule of behavior.[5] In choosing minor premises, of course, we necessarily have to decide the circumstances in which principles are applicable and the extent to which they are applicable; but this is nothing more than the application of more or less common sense discrimination.

We do not have to do this, however, if we simply wish to formulate rules of behavior—only if we wish to formulate rules of behavior that are consistent with the nature of things. Rules that are not consistent with the nature of things can be formulated, and they can be imposed on others and enforced among the group which sponsors them if the sponsoring group is able to surround its operations with an effective mystique. But however consistently such rules are applied, they are not the better for this kind of consistency. Experience constantly informs us that to act on beliefs that are inconsistent with the nature of things is to court disgrace and disaster. King Canute tried it, but we seem constantly to have to relearn it.

If we have no principles that are representative of our understanding of the nature of things, it is common wisdom (based upon nothing more substantial than the gregarious instinct) to seek support in numbers, to base our rules of behavior on general acceptance. It is no less common wisdom to base our rules of behavior on general acceptance even when we have identified and endorsed principles representing our understanding of the nature of things. But in this latter case there is more than mere agreement or general acceptance to support the rules we adopt. Thus, although general acceptance of rules of behavior (or practices) may be a necessary condition of lay respect for a given expertise, it is by no means a sufficient condition. Much of the confusion about the criterion of general acceptance may, it seems, be traced to failure to distinguish between conditions which are necessary and conditions which are both necessary and sufficient.

[4] Billy E. Goetz, "The Usefulness of the Impossible," in William L. Schaaf (ed.), *Our Mathematical Heritage* (New York: Collier Books, 1963), p. 187.
[5] See Bertrand Russell, *An Inquiry into Meaning and Truth* (Penguin Books), pp. 24–25.

Something like the distinction we have drawn is built into the report of the Special Committee on Research Program, reproduced at p. x of *ARS No. 7*. But the distinction is blurred at the point where "principles" is introduced. It seems reasonable to say that "the principles . . . should serve as a framework of reference for the solution of detailed problems." But this does not entirely clarify the question of the nature of principles. It could be interpreted as saying that general rules should serve, just as easily as saying that principles (in the more fundamental sense) should serve, for the solution of detailed problems. And it is apparent that the former interpretation is the one most commonly adopted. The Study points out that in some of the Institute-Stock Exchange correspondence of the 1930s "practices" and "principles" were used interchangeably (p. 49). But the glossing over of the difference in that correspondence provides no valid ground for persisting in the manner of a generation ago. Yet this is done in the Study. The substantive part of the Inventory is presented in the form of directives or rules: "the objectives" and the "principles" are all cast in the form of imperatives. We are left with no statements which are the product of contemplating the nature of things, no principles at all in this sense.

It seems therefore that the so-called generally accepted principles of accounting are strictly nothing more than generally accepted rules of behavior, at the best. This conclusion is supported by a number of features of the Study.

Authoritative Support

The rules are ostensibly founded to a material extent on the authority of persons rather than on the authority of reason. The author accepts an earlier description of accepted accounting principles as "those principles having substantial authoritative support back of them" (p. 16). The sources from which substantial authoritative support may be inferred are business practices, views of the stock exchange, regulatory prescriptions including those of the Securities and Exchange Commission, opinions of practising and academic CPAs, and published opinions of the AAA and the AICPA (pp. 52–53).

No evidence is adduced to show that any one of these sources has formed its opinions on the basis of analysis of the nature of things. We are not suggesting at this point that the views of the sources were not formed on the basis of analysis; we merely point out that "authority" appears to be taken as sufficient warrant for the designation of a practice as a generally accepted practice.

But even here there are difficulties. "Whether a given principle or practice has authoritative support is both a question of fact and a matter of judgment" (p. 16). The judgment referred to is the individual practitioner's judgment. In fact then, what comes to be done or accepted in any particular case is a matter of an individual judgment; and no person using the resulting statements may have any assurance that the practices used are endorsed or followed by other business firms whose statements he may consult in forming his opinions, or followed by the profession. The lay user of such statements, of course, may not be expected to know that the choice of practices is left to individual judgment, the more so since the auditor's opinion includes references to generally accepted principles and to consistency, both of which tend to give assurance of a useful degree of uniformity. Such terms therefore give an impression of the adoption of practices the justification of which is beyond individual judgment, whereas the initiated know that there is no such justification.

In effect, the dependence on authority,

57

the authority of persons or groups of persons, is completely eroded in practice by the permissive exercise of judgment. It would be quite different if the views of all the persons or classes of persons converged on a specific given set of practices. But the Study makes abundantly clear, as we shall presently see, that there is little in the way of convergence, and the authorities are therefore authorities for little in the nature of guidance.

Authoritative support is not the only foundation on which the propositions of the Inventory purport to be based. There are some conceptual foundations which approach the kind of thing we would designate as principles. But even these are not entirely consistent with the nature of things.

Accountability

We are told that accounting information has a function in relation to the "fiduciary accountabilities" of management. There is no discussion of accountabilities of any other kind.

In the first place there is some confusion about the accountability referred to. It is said that "the separation of ownership from management of the business entity is a primary factor in imposing *on the entity* the fiduciary accountabilities to its stockholders" (p. 26, emphasis added). At a later point reference is made to the fiduciary accountabilities *of management* (p. 57). As fiduciary accountabilities are the basis on which the generally accepted accounting principles are "set forth" (p. 26), it seems that no distinction as between accountabilities of the entity and of management has any bearing on the sequel. Yet it is a matter of importance to know who is being held accountable. It seems undeniable that the business entity ("an organization of persons and properties," p. 26) cannot be held accountable, and that in fact it is the management of such

an entity which is accountable.

Now the relationships of managers "to stockholders, creditors, government, and others having bona fide interests" (p. 57) can scarcely *all* be described as fiduciary relationships, without warping the meaning of fiduciary. None of these relationships is a fiduciary relationship in the customary sense. It is no doubt reasonable to say that directors and managers occupy positions of trust, in the sense that others trust them. But not in the sense that they are trustees. They are appointed or engaged contractually, under the charter or rules of a business firm and under specific contract within such rules, to assume business risks on behalf of equityholders; and to negotiate with creditors, other groups and governments, when necessary, on a contractual basis. They often have contractual rights of indemnity. They are not committed to the preservation of a capital sum held in trust (notwithstanding the use of "corpus" in Principle B-2), and no action can lie against them, in the absence of fraud and such offences against the general law, for the recovery of any part of the sum contributed by equityholders which is lost in the course of business. Their relationship with equityholders we see as one of *agency*, not as one of trusteeship; and their relationship with all other parties is one of contract, as contracting agent of the corporation proximately (in the case of a corporation) or as contracting agent for the equityholders (both in the cases of corporate and non-corporate business enterprises). We venture to speculate that the notion of a fiduciary relationship is in fact a vestigial remnant of the form of trust, which in the days before the recognition of corporate rights in real property was the only device available legally for the holding of titles in real property for the use and benefit of a large group of persons.

The object of these observations is not to clarify a simple verbal point. It is to strike at the root of what seems to be an error in conception. If the accountability of management is seen as a fiduciary accountability in the usual sense, it will lend support to the idea that management is accountable in respect of the sums of money "entrusted" by equityholders, and a balance sheet showing aggregate outlays from such sums may be held to be justified; the initial costs of assets will be acceptable as balance sheet figures (as in Principle C-2). But, in the first place, not even the proponents of the cost basis hold that balance sheets shall show ↑ initial ˝costs without deductions (Principle C-2). Nor in the second place do they hold to the cost basis for all assets (p. 258). In both respects the fiduciary notion is not in fact respected, though it is held *as a rule* for durable assets: the inconsistency should be regarded as fatal. In the third place, if management is held accountable, not simply in the fiduciary sense but for the exercise of all powers and the use of all assets under its control at any time, it follows that it cannot be held accountable at any time if the money sums which designate assets are not money sums which correspond in the best possible way with the money equivalents of those assets at that time. We hold that this is the only realistic way in which accountability may be viewed, and that it clearly points in a different direction from the initial price or cost basis. To hold management accountable in sums of money spent under conditions no longer prevailing, and in all likelihood spent by persons who are no longer managers, and sums which have no logical or discoverable relationship to a present monetary equivalent, is to fly in the face of the nature of things and to make accountability a ludicrous notion.

Consistency

Another conceptual foundation is consistency of practices from year to year. There is a strong presumption that financial statements drawn in conformity with generally accepted principles applied on a basis consistent with that of a previous year can, and will, present fairly the financial position and results of operations of an entity (p. 31).

Now, at first glance, consistency commends itself as a principle which might enable us to devise rules which will result in comparable information for successive periods for a given firm. If rules were devised to secure comparability of such information, their consistent application would be a valuable rule of behavior. But in fact the practices of accounting as they are represented in the Study were not devised with this object in mind; they are themselves virtually inconsistent, and the consistent application of mutually inconsistent rules cannot yield comparable results. We demonstrate the point.

The Study devotes no attention to the elucidation of "financial position" and "results." There is no definition of financial position or of income, though there is some discursive but inconclusive discussion of the latter in the section on the Terminology Bulletins of the AICPA. Perhaps it was supposed that these terms are so generally used and understood that no definition is required. But the acreage devoted in the literature to argument about income and the absolute neglect of financial position should suggest that this supposition is unwarranted. If these terms had a specified meaning we could consider what steps should be taken to quantify them, and we could grasp what we are expected to be able to compare and what therefore is the precise object of consistency of application of rules. We are left without such help, and consistency seems therefore to be unconnected with practical necessity. (One may lie, or talk nonsense, consistently; is consistency then a virtue?)

It is demonstrable that the result of applying generally accepted accounting

59

principles does not give financial position as it is understood by merchants or financiers in the market place, or even as it is understood by laymen. Let any man ask himself or another what is his financial position. He will not for a moment think of giving what he paid for his house and land, his securities and other assets. Ordinary knowledge of personal transactions in markets informs him that if he wants things other than what he holds (and that is one of the reasons for wanting to know financial position), he must think of what he could get on the market for some of the things he holds. This is "in the nature of things." Financial position is a position of an entity in relation financially to the rest of the community at a point of time. Past transactions may have left the entity in possession of certain physical things at a point of time; but it is the resale prices of those things, not the things themselves, which determines the relationship, financially, of the entity to the rest of the community.

Consider also now the idea of income. The idea has no meaning other than that, by virtue of some event or events during an interval, an entity has improved its relationship financially with the rest of the community during that interval. Now if, for the sake of consistency, income is calculated by setting off against contemporary revenues the measure of contemporary costs given by the Lifo method, there remains in the balance sheet a series of residues which are increasingly less contemporary as time passes. The balance sheet represents financial position less and less fairly at each successive balancing date. In fact therefore, generally accepted practices, of which Lifo, is one, are found to lead to internal inconsistencies in any period, the income account being more or less contemporary in our example, the balance sheet becoming increasingly outdated; and the comparison of inconsistent

statements over successive periods cannot but be deceptive.

Insofar then as consistency is held to be a basic principle it is found, like the notion of fiduciary accountability, to be applied as long as it is wanted; as long, that is, as it serves to lend support to practices which otherwise have no standing by reference to the nature of things.

Diversity

The next presumption we consider appears to have some foundation in contemplation of the nature of things. It is that "diversity in accounting [is inevitable, or tolerable, or permissible] among independent entities" (p. 32). But here again the critical objective of analysis of observable things is bypassed, the objective of finding the essential uniformity among diversity. The "overwhelming" arguments against "a minority view which urges uniformity in accounting" (pp. 32–33) appear to be entirely without foundation.

We are told that "judgment and estimates play a substantial role in accounting on an accrual basis . . . and . . . when there is diffusion in decision-making, a necessity in the free enterprise system, there is bound to be diversity in the accounting results" (p. 33). But we are not told precisely how far judgment and estimates play a role. Does judgment extend to the concepts which shall be quantified or only to the quantification of stipulated concepts? The difference is significant. Every different method of accounting entails a different concept of income and financial position. If every pharmacist were to have his own concept of poison, and every lawyer his own concept of crime, there would be not only diversity but chaos; yet these and other groups of persons could claim the necessity of judgment no less than accountants. As for the application of judgment and estimates to the quantification of specified concepts, accounting is in this respect no different from the exact sciences. It is freely admitted in the sciences that there is an element of judgment in every measurement process. Measurements are only approximations, their accuracy depending on the variables of the object, the context, the instruments, and the observer. The judgment and estimate argument is no argument for diversity; for if there is any skill in the practice of accounting the divergences arising from different measurements of the same property will be nominal only.

As for "diffusion in decision-making," this is the very circumstance which makes uniformity of rules obligatory. Within firms, manuals of rules and procedures are written with the object of ensuring that different persons doing similar things do them in a similar way, so that, wherever in an organization action must be taken on the result, the result is always interpretable in the same way. People acting at different points in a firm could not act in a coordinated manner if their informational premises were at variance. For even greater reasons, if the decision-making is really diffuse, if the users of the information are both internal and external to the firm, uniformity of information is imperative; negotiations between one firm and another or choices of external parties as between contracts with alternative firms, cannot be seriously considered unless the information produced by all firms is equally interpretable.

We are told, further (p. 34), that uniformity would require detailed manuals covering every conceivable rule for all firms. It is questionable whether any advocate of uniformity has ever contemplated any such suggestion. Uniformity in principle and in effect is what has been advocated. Advocates of uniformity have in mind uniformity of "principles" in the "framework of reference" sense in which "principle" is used in the report of the Special Committee; not in the sense of rules or directives in which sense "principles" is commonly used in the Study. We are told, too (p. 35), that "recognition of the concept of diversity in accounting among independent entities . . . in no way imperils the objective" of narrowing the areas of difference and improving the comparability of financial statements. On the contrary, the stated concept and the stated objective are flat contradictories as conceptual foundations.

Much of the discussion of the matter over a long period has been confused by the idea that business firms are independent (p. 35). It is a matter of direct observation that they are not; they are all interdependent. They are interdependent in the money market; for when money or credit is scarce, what some firms get others do not. They are interdependent in the commodities, the labor and the finished goods markets for the same reason. They are creditors of one another, investors in one another, suppliers to one another. They are all interlinked by market processes, and none can intelligibly communicate or negotiate with another unless the symbols they all use are equally interpretable, as symbols, at a given point of time. This is why uniformity is in principle imperative. Not only that. Investors, whose benefit has been at the heart of legislation and regulation in respect of financial information, cannot and do not think of firms or corporations independently. They consider them comparatively. Indeed, all forms of choice are fundamentally based on comparison; but comparison is pointless if the methods used themselves are capable of producing greatly divergent results and aggregates from the same data.

What the diversity argument entirely overlooks is that, although different firms have different operations, all persons interested in the financial characteristics of firms are interested in the same things,

61

such as solvency, rate of return, and so on. At the same time, all interested persons are so interested because they have alternative opportunities of lending or investing. They cannot choose sensibly unless the financial statements, which yield such information for different opportunities, are comparable; and they will only be comparable if they are based on uniform rules. It is the common concern with money outcomes that makes common rules necessary. This is in the nature of things. A free enterprise society which condones anarchy in its communications system will not long remain rational or free.

The Consequences of Diversity

Consider now the alternatives explicitly indicated in Chapter 10.

It should be clear that if there are two methods of assigning a monetary quantity to one asset, and three methods of assigning a monetary quantity to another asset, and that if each method yields a different monetary quantity, there are in total six methods of finding the income of a firm and its financial position at the close of an income period, and six different results of applying those methods. In the following we limit the variants to major classes. We presume that each of the methods listed in Chapter 10 is a true variant, yielding a different result from each other method listed in its class; otherwise there would have been no point in its separate inclusion. Further we regard every such method as a legitimate method; being described as generally accepted, we are entitled to suppose that each is *acceptable to all accountants* regardless of the selection of particular methods to suit the circumstances of particular accounting entities. The results of our exploration will therefore indicate the methods of accounting which are embraced by "generally accepted accounting principles." They do not give the number of methods available to any singular firm or

corporation. They do give the number of methods to which any reader of two or more sets of financial statements may be subjected.

(a) Revenue (p. 373). There are at least four methods: recognition at time of sale, and subsequent recognition of cash discount; recognition at time of sale and immediate recognition of cash discount; recognition at time of collection; recognition on completion of product.

(b) Pension payment charges (p. 374). There are apparently at least four different methods each of which will yield different magnitudes in any period.

(c) Taxes (pp. 374–5). Disregarding allocation alternatives, there are apparently eight methods each of which will yield a different magnitude in a given period.

(d) Depreciation. There are at least two basic sums on which a depreciation charge may be calculated, cost (three permissible methods) or an appraised value (p. 377). Whichever is adopted, there are at least six methods of calculation, each giving different magnitudes for the charge. Whichever of the methods is applied to the basic sum chosen, there are three ways at least of obtaining the aggregate for a class of depreciable assets—composite, group or individual calculations. There are thus $4 \times 6 \times 3$ ways of finding the amount to be shown for any aggregate set of depreciable assets.

(e) Inventory. There are five named cost methods: Fifo, Lifo, average cost, base stock, standard cost. We omit the many possible combinations of these for any given inventory. In respect of each, cost may or may not include "overheads." There are thus at least 5×2 methods. The suggestion of "combinations" entails that each of these methods may be applied to the whole inventory, to groups or to individual items. There are thus at least $5 \times 2 \times 3$ cost methods. There are two named market methods, replacement cost and net realizable value. Further, there is the method of the lowest of cost, replacement cost, and net realizable value; this will in any year provide a magnitude potentially different from any of the straight cost or straight market methods. The number of potentially different magnitudes is thus the number of cost methods multiplied by the number (3) of the alternatives, for under this formula no reader of the statement will know which of the three in any given period is the lowest. There are then $5 \times 2 \times 3 \times 3$ methods of this kind. The total number of methods is therefore 30 cost methods, 2 market methods, and 90 cost or market methods; total, 122 methods.

(f) Miscellaneous. There are five classes of items in respect of each of which there are two possibilities (pp. 376–7). There are thus $2 \times 2 \times 2 \times 2 \times 2$ ways of representing these items in any set of accounting statements, 32 ways in all.

There are also many ways of treating other individual items found in financial statements (pp. 378–9). But we disregard these. It should be clear that "generally accepted accounting principles," in respect of the items specifically considered above, countenance (a) 4, (b) 4, (c) 8, (d) 72, (e) 122, (f) 32, methods; or for any financial statements in which these may all occur—over 30 million possibilities!

Now the Study warns against making such "astronomical" calculations.[6] To do so "would be useless because it would merely confirm that accounting is not an exact science" (p. 379). We disagree. The purport of the exercise is not to indicate that an astronomical range of possibilities is open to any specific business or to say that an astronomical array of results could be obtained for any specific business. Its object is to show that, as the range is so vast and the results may be so divergent, any user of the resulting statements cannot know what precise set of methods has been used and cannot therefore know with what

provisos he must accept any of the financial statements of different companies he may wish to consult at a given time to inform his choices.

Defences of Diversity

Attention is drawn to the observations which are adduced in support of the diversity which is disclosed. It is said that "the basic concept of 'diversity in accounting among independent entities' is fully supported by the variety of methods" (p. 380). The circularity of this should be obvious. We start with a basic concept, which one may suppose to be one of the premises on which accounting is based; it permits diversity; we then find diversity and believe it supports the concept!

The Institute-Stock Exchange correspondence is cited as authority for the view that "if the significant practices were adequately disclosed and consistently followed, the effect of differing methods on periodic income would soon be unimportant, although there might be considerable difference in balance sheet items carried forward to future periods" (p. 380). The correspondence appears to give no reason at all for this hope. It is in fact impossible to justify; for if the significance of differences in income calculations becomes unimportant the significance of differences in balance sheets would at the same time become unimportant. There could only be a divergence in the degree of significance of the differences if the rules for calculating the one were substantially at odds with the propriety of the other. The divergence which has in fact arisen has been due to just that—disregard for financial position and, in consequence, a notion of income which is of even more bewildering complexion than it was thirty years ago.

---

[6] We do not know whether this warning was induced by some earlier exercises of ours: see R. J. Chambers, "Financial Information and the Securities Market," mimeographed in 1963, published in *Abacus*, I, 1 (1965).

We are told that adherence to "consistency and disclosure standards" permits comparability from year to year for the same entity. In fact it does no such thing. If it did there would be no point in the suggestion that financial statements in dollars of current purchasing power would improve comparability (p. 382). The figures which appear in contemporary financial statements are mixtures of measures taken in scales of monetary units having different purchasing powers at different times. People may in practice compare them, but this does not mean they are comparable. In no other discipline is this disregard of a basic mathematical rule tolerated.

As for "comparability between entities," we are told that investors have the protection of a "qualitative standard of comparison" (p. 381). What this is is not at all clear; it can mean very little if there are literally millions of sets of rules for deriving financial statements. It is almost certain that if the difference in the ultimate effect on income or financial position of the adoption of either of two rules were immaterial, there would be or there would have been no cause for adding an alternative rule to the first one used. It is therefore almost certain that every rule which has survived has survived because its use made a material difference to the result at some time or for some firm. It seems odd therefore that rules which were adopted because of the material effects they procured are now held to be justifiable, yielding results which satisfy a qualitative standard of comparability. It would be useful to know what this means and how this standard is set, particularly as methods of accounting are at the discretion of "the management and directors of each enterprise." It would also be useful to know how "the leading financial and business executives and financial analysts" can "fully understand the value of the qualitative standard of comparability" (p. 381). It is far more likely that,

where there are millions of sets of possible rules, they are simply unable to differentiate between them, much less understand them.

Finally some words on the view of Mr. Justice Holmes which has been widely quoted in support of variety and the status quo in accounting. The words of the learned jurist are, with respect, far too laconic to do justice to the problem that confronts us. In practice affairs, as in the law, logic and good sense are only in apparent conflict if one regards them as two distinct and contradictory manifestations of mind. Good sense surely is seeing things as they really are; if we see things as they are, we are able to apply to them the disciplined thought (logic) which enables us to reach conclusions consistent with them. Good sense and logic seem to be complementary, not contradictory, manifestations of mind. The mind that longs for certainty and repose can achieve it at little cost—by inventing a simplified world in which the problems of the real world have no counterpart; a world, for example, in which numbers can be added regardless of their individual significances; a world in which changes in prices or price levels are non-existent or wholly without significance; a world in which all business firms are independent of one another; and so on. To imagine that the world is like this is to elevate fiction above good sense; this gives the illusory certainty which is the butt of the remarks of Justice Holmes. This is the illusory certainty which has given rise to, and comfort from, the whole idea of "generally accepted accounting principles." If there were in fact a set of such principles there would be uniformity. It is only because no accounting principles *are* generally accepted that there is diversity and hence the need, psychologically not logically, to defend diversity and to challenge uniformity.

We have not attempted to lay out the

system of ideas we would substitute for the arguments put forward in the Study. This has been done elsewhere.[7] Our object has merely been to join issue with the argumentative sections of the Study. Some final words on the propositions which are represented as generally accepted principles, and which we accept as fair representations. Accounting has for too long suffered from overdoses of weasel-words. Attention has been explicitly drawn to a long list of them by Kohler.[8] A variety nevertheless occurs in the stated principles: proper (A-1), proper (A-2), appropriate (A-3), proper (A-4), misused, arbitrarily (A-5), misleading (A-7), properly (C-1), meaningful (C-2), appropriate (C-3), ordinarily (C-4), applicable (E-1), meaningful (E-2), appropriate (E-3). Similar words occur in many places in the argument as well. The reader may well ask himself what each of these means in its context; he will not find it easy to give a generally accepted answer. And he will not therefore quite know to what he is supposed to assent.

The Study is unquestionably valuable. It makes very clear the massive difficulties with which the users of financial statements have to contend—which brings us full circle to an observation made earlier in this paper. We suggested that the law

does not countenance the laying of burdens, additional to legally stipulated burdens, by one class on another. And we suggested that an important element of the law in the present context is that it provides for the publication of information "in the public interest and for the protection of investors." As all choices involve comparisons it seems beyond argument that the multiplicity of available methods will defeat every serious attempt to choose as between companies or to choose between the continuation and the liquidation of specific companies on the basis of published information. The burden of discovery imposed on the public and the investor seems unconscionable; it is far from the ideal, of disclosure of the facts upon which the general public and the investor can act to protect themselves. The Inventory, at least by implication, makes it abundantly clear that great changes are necessary to put contemporary practices on the footing of the requirements of the statutory principle, and even greater changes to establish practice on the ethical footing which we have suggested is ideally more solid and dependable than a statutory specification.

[7] *Accounting, Evaluation and Economic Behavior* (Prentice-Hall, Inc., 1966).
[8] Eric L. Kohler, *A Dictionary for Accountants* (Prentice-Hall, Inc., 1963), p. vii.

65

Prospective Adventures in Accounting Ideas

I OWE my title in part to Alfred North Whitehead's *Adventures of Ideas* of some thirty years ago; indeed I owe more than the title. But the switch in its form is significant. Whitehead recounted the vicissitudes of some of the great ideas that have modified the course of man's knowledge and thought, which, indeed, have modified his whole history. I am more concerned with our personal involvements in the process. The adventures I allude to are the intellectual opportunities that lie open to us, rather than what happens to our ideas. The two, of course, are not wholly separable. "A great society," said Whitehead, "is a society in which its men of business think greatly of their functions." If we think greatly of our functions our ideas will themselves persist or contain the seeds of even greater ideas of the future.

We cannot profitably look back over the thousands of years which Whitehead spanned. Almost the whole of the development of accounting ideas as they are today relevant has occurred within the lifetime of the Association; and in that development members of the Association have played a prominent and honored part. Without belittling the record or the massive endeavors of many we cannot here name, we can usefully look at a few ideas, a few cases in which men have thought greatly of accounting.

Looking Backwards

These fifty years have seen quite a few potentially fruitful ideas, with wide implications, brought to notice, noticed scarcely at all and almost abandoned. In 1922 Paton set down what he saw as the accountant's postulates or assumptions. This was an adventurous exercise, novel in the literature. At the same time he roundly criticized some of them. This too was rather bold. But though the intervening years have provided outstanding illustrations of the inadequacy of these assumptions, substantially the same assumptions underlie today's accounting. Sweeney, impelled as it seems by respect for some obvious facts of experience and for some of the basic mathematical verities, and MacNeal, impelled as it seems by a strong sense of the ethos of accounting, launched spirited attacks on some of the inherent illogicalities of extant practices. But although there has been abundant

241

68

evidence of the validity of their criticisms, there has been little response. The enterprise of Paton and Littleton on accounting standards foreshadowed a great possibility, that accounting could become a real language of business finance instead of a mass of only vaguely understood and only vaguely understandable symbols. But the shadow has since been taken for the substance and twenty-five years later we still have the confusion of tongues which plagued the construction of the Tower of Babel.

At the heart of each of these ventures lies a seminal idea, waiting to be taken up, worked over, polished, applied, tested. We cannot know why we do what we do unless we are aware of our assumptions; we know scarcely more about them than when Paton first essayed to state them; indeed I think we understand them less clearly. We cannot improve our technique unless our professional "nerves" are sensitive to the observations of such as Sweeney and MacNeal; they seem to have touched quite different nerves. We cannot talk to one another, let alone talk to the business world in the manner entailed by that magnificent word "disclosure," unless we have a standardized vocabulary and syntax. But Paton and Littleton's exercise was followed by no serious polishing, application, or testing; and even to speak of uniformity in accounting is today still anathema to many.

These men were opening the casements on some new vistas. They were on the brink of something new, something uncertain and therefore something exciting to the adventurous. I do not know whether they felt the excitement or exhilaration of say Balboa when he gazed on the Pacific, or of Archimedes as he raced towel-clad down the street, or of Roentgen as he pored over his apparatus and X-ray pictures for days without thought of food. But certain it is that there was not much

excitement about the possibilities they hinted at—the possibility of an increasingly useful accounting on the one hand, and the possibility of increasingly mature study of it on the other.

It may appear to be unseemly to talk of the subjective feelings, the emotions, of men whose labors are in the realm of ideas; a kind of abstract, bloodless and bodiless realm, as it is commonly thought. But the extent to which we *feel* there is something transcendental about what we do or could do, something universal or path breaking or elemental or liberating, determines the success with which we do it. Excitement, exhilaration heightens our capacities for apprehension, so that we see things we would not otherwise see—possibilities and difficulties both. The more we see the more extensive and intensive does our understanding become. The more we see the more we are able to see. We see old things in new settings. Because we see the world differently, we see a new world. But new worlds are only for the adventurous.

From Symbol to Myth

Accountants, as such, necessarily lead symbolic lives. They receive symbolic messages, digest them in a symbolism of their own, and transmit other symbolic messages. Some accountants, those who write about or talk about or teach accounting (this includes a great number of practitioners as well as teachers and theorists), are drawn even further into the morass of symbolism. They talk about what accounting is, what accountants do, and to whom and why—all in symbolic terms.

Now like the use of fire, the use of symbols can give us greatly increased power to do things, things in the real world. But like the misuse of fire, the misuse of symbols is fraught with the danger of losing what we have. We face the gravest danger of taking the symbol for the substance, of losing our apprehension of what is real, the advanced form of which, of course, is psychosis. Professional psychosis! A rather shocking thought. But I use no idle metaphor, for this elevation of the symbolic above the real has happened on an alarming scale.

We frequently tell ourselves that market prices at any time are unrepresentative, unrealiable guides to "true values" or "real values" (whatever those symbols may mean), when in the hard cold world of business in which our symbols are somehow supposed to be useful, market prices are the very things that influence the behaviors of the firms about which we account. We have told ourselves that movements in prices and in the purchasing power of money are irrelevant in accounting, when in fact they are so relevant in business that businessmen spend much time and ingenuity taking steps to profit by or to avoid losing by them. Some of us talk about firms replacing assets with identical assets, and on that ground argue for the use of replacement costs; but replacing durable assets with identical assets is a thing firms never do. Some of us talk about going concerns as going on doing what they are doing; but no firm ever does just that. We talk about money being a common denominator, but then promptly disregard the fact that money amounts held or spent at different times denominate nothing in common that is of any present use.

We say that "historical cost" data are relevant to present behavior and serve up the result of manipulating them to managers and investors, when we wouldn't dare give our wives household expense checks adequate for 1956 prices. Many of us say that the value of an object to its owner is its cost (meaning its price); which is patently false, for otherwise the owner would surely have preferred to have the money which gives him greater freedom of choice. You well know that the literature and

practice of accounting abound with such statements and operations as these. And you well know that the stated antithesis in each case holds in the world of business and commerce. How we can expect the rational businessman or investor, of whom we often speak, to act sensibly on the basis of reports derived on such plainly unreal principles is difficult to understand.

If we must lead symbolic lives, and if we make any pretensions to produce useful information, our symbols must have some immediate and apprehensible connection with the things symbolized. Rather than struggle to do this, we seem to have contemplated our umbilicus, to have invented entities of a kind which do not exist, performing operations in a world we have invented of a kind that does not exist. We have then told ourselves, and sometimes others, that in accounting this or that is the proper, or appropriate, or useful, or meaningful, or satisfactory, or best thing to do —and almost always with a host of caveats which nullify what we have said. We make these epithets serve as reasons because there are no reasons or none we care to expose. (Have you ever noticed how many useless and unnecessary adjectives and adverbs befog the literature? If they were excised there would be room for quite a few more articles in the journals. The Preface to recent editions of Kohler's *Dictionary* should be prescribed reading.)

In effect we have built a wall around ourselves. Inside the wall we do what is proper *in accounting*. When in Rome we do what Rome does. The erection of any wall is, of course, the way to security, personal security. Wall-building is after the manner of fearful people, those who want to hold what they have. Some, like the Romans, have built physical walls. Some, like the psychotics, have built walls of ideas. Some build intellectual walls. But all wall-building spells the end of adventure. Protected by walls, people have no longer to use

69

their wits; their wits get rusty, for they think they have solved the problem of security. One of two things, however, may bring about a change. People beyond the walls may be anxious to conquer them, to breach them—think of Rome, think of the Maginot Line. The once walled-in are then the losers. Alternatively there may still be a few adventurous souls within the walls who will not be constrained. They are prepared to take the risk for the sake of the new possibilities they envisage. Columbus was one such adventurer; and Spain, once walled in by beliefs about the Atlantic, became much the richer. History forgets the unadventurous; it remembers the adventurous, and the course of history is changed by them. The questions confronting us today are whether we are going to isolate ourselves to the point where we become flabby, to use Hatfield's epithet, and open to destruction, or whether from within we are to encourage and undertake adventure.

What walls, then, have we built, and with what materials? What impediments are there now to adventures in accounting ideas? But before I attempt to answer these questions I would like to assure you that wall-building is not peculiar to accounting. It has occurred over and over again in the history of ideas, even in what we now call the exact sciences. Its origin lies in something basic in human nature, perhaps the desire for security, the wish to enjoy the good life, a life made good by what seems to be the very efficacy of the ideas held at any time. There is absolutely no good reason to be shamefaced about accounting if for long periods we observe no major transformation in its theory or practice; for accountants are also people. They are just as desirous of the good life as others, and just as prone to seek freedom from doubt by belief in the perfection of present modes and belief in the wisdom of their intellectual forbears.

Nevertheless, we may well be made to look foolish yet, if the walls are breached from outside because we have trusted in them too blindly. What walls, then?

EXCLUSIVISM

The first I shall describe as exclusivism. Many of us believe that accounting is not like other subjects of inquiry and fields of practice; that it is not capable of being analyzed by the same methods as other fields of knowledge; that it is not a science and cannot be brought under laws and principles of the kind which give order and intelligibility to other fields of knowledge. Every such notion limits our vision; it *makes* our field of interest an isolated field. It cuts us off from the very experiences of business that alone give meaning to our professional existences. And it cuts us off from the benefits we might have from contemplating other modes of inquiry.

If we were conscious of these effects, we would ask on what authority this notion of exclusiveness is asserted—for it is only asserted, never proved. Is it true, or reasonable to suppose, that there can be a form of mentality, of intellection, peculiar to accounting? If the answer is yes, we must accept the consequences—namely that anything accountants do, the product of that intellection, cannot ever be grasped by the ordinary run of intelligent people. In saying "cannot ever be grasped" I am merely stating the logical consequence of the assertion of different forms of mentality. Now, of course, there are some who assert that accountants must educate the rest of the world to understand what their statements say. But it is also a logical consequence of the assertion of different forms of mentality that we *cannot ever teach* others to understand; for to teach others we must begin with the assumption that our modes of thinking are the same. In short, if we hold this view we are bound forever to talk only to ourselves about our own mental constructions—and clearly clients do not pay accountants to do just that. We become nothing but mystics.

If the answer is no, there is not a peculiar form of intellection, we must accept the consequences of that—namely that the same mental procedures, and the generation of broad principles and general laws, apply equally in accounting and in every other field of human inquiry; and that the statements we produce should be understandable to intelligent people without any indoctrination on our part.

In case you suppose I overpaint this exclusivism consider just a few examples. We have almost fled from the use of the term "principle" in the sense in which it is used in other fields of rigorous discourse. We have cut the meaning of "objectivity" down to a size that suits us, regardless of its meaning in other fields of discourse and in the ordinary everyday world. We speak of "measurement" and produce measurements in ways that are quite inconsistent with other usages and forms of careful measurement. We speak of "financial position" with reference to something no ordinary intelligent person would think of as his financial position. We include as assets and liabilities things which no ordinary intelligent person would think of as assets and liabilities. And, on a more general level, hardly ever do we find in the literature any reference to analogous procedures in other fields of thought and practice. And this, in spite of the fact that analogies have produced many of the great leaps in human thought; and in spite of the fact that we argue freely from what we call "models," which are after all only invented analogies. So much for exclusivism.

Mistaken Identification

A second type of wall-building material or principle I shall describe as the principle of mistaken identification. The basis of this principle is in flat contradiction of the principle of exclusivism: nevertheless we seem to be able to hold these two contradictory positions at the same time— and this is an indication of professional schizophrenia. Let me develop the idea by several examples.

There is a great tendency to identify theory and practice. The tendency finds expression in many ways. It is said explicitly by some that theory is the rationalization of practice, that theory must be based on practice. A great deal of what is called research—and research is properly the handmaiden of theory—consists in looking at what is done by accountants, disregarding the actual or potential consequences in the outside world of what is done. A great deal of the textbook literature presents what is called theory, but what is really no more than descriptions of practice.

Now, in the normal practice of a profession in any age, there is necessarily a great deal which must be taken as accepted or acceptable among practitioners. If it were not so there could be no common understandings among them on professional matters and no basis for contractual arrangements among their principals or clients. However, notwithstanding this stability, there has been, in all fields marked by clear signs of technical progress, a concurrent questioning of the nature of things among those who may properly be described as theorists. These people are not concerned with making better things today. That is a technician's job. They are concerned with reaching better understandings of the nature of things. It is a happy circumstance when they reach this better understanding, for it paves the way for practitioners and technicians to produce better everyday commodities or services. The theorists see a new world, the practitioners exploit it. Both have their adventures.

But if theory and practice are closely identified—by theorists *or* practitioners—

71

it is very unlikely that any such happy circumstance will occur. Something else will occur however. Both will identify themselves with the same causes, the same doctrines. As against the rest of the world (given, for example, the tendency to exclusivism) they will reinforce one another's beliefs in those doctrines. They will build defenses against opposing doctrines. These are well-known features of group behavior. They will together build bigger walls. But if the foundations are shaky, and no one is paying any attention to the foundations, the bigger the wall the more resounding the crash.

Instead of making any such identification, it should be recognized that practitioners and theorists have complementary functions. Both are concerned with the same materials, the same devices, the same end products; but in different ways, against different frameworks. The practitioner's framework is the immediate urgency of a single client's problems, which he must resolve in the manner commonly accepted in his field given the state of the art. The theorist's or researcher's problem is to see the field whole, without regard for immediate clients, but with high regard for the relationship of the field to all contiguous fields and to the whole enterprise of human discovery. *If theorists adopt the same reference framework as practitioners, the immediate solution of immediate problems, they no longer act as theorists.* But if theorists assert, as some do assert, that they are unconcerned with immediate problems or practical problems, they forfeit the right to be considered as theorists —dreamers perhaps, but not theorists. The challenges lie out there in the real world in the first place, not in our heads.

Another illustration of the principle of mistaken identification is the identification of teaching and learning. These appear to occur at the same place and time, but the appearance is deceptive. The practicing profession wants recruits; it wants them in a hurry and in many cases it wants them already equipped to earn an honest dollar. That is to say they must be equipped to carry on the normal practices of the profession at the time. This is an understandable expectation in some ways. But no one ever expects a new automobile, a new secretary, or a new wife to perform up to expectations without a running-in period. On the other hand, the teachers often have quite varied notions of their task. Some go along wholeheartedly with the idea that they should produce graduates fully equipped for normal practice, and that is all they try to do. Some on the other hand think practice is less important than "a sound theoretical foundation" for practice. They justify this on the ground that they are educating, not training; a quite legitimate justification in most people's minds. What very often happens, of course, is that their students get just another kind of indoctrination, in somebody's theory. There are others who think an educational process is different; it means throwing a whole lot of theories and practices at students and saying "Take your pick." This at least has the effect of not closing the mind; it also has the effect of not helping the emergent intellect to discriminate.

But it seems to me that students graduating under the hands of any of these types of programs are handicapped in one way or another from the start. They are being sent out into a world where they will be leaders in twenty years more or less; but in that time it will be a different world. How are they equipped to meet that? Those who have learned normal practice will be badly equipped unless they have managed to hold back the advancement of their profession to the level it had reached when they graduated. Those indoctrinated with someone's theory will be no better off unless that theory has stood the test of intervening changes in the world outside. Those who were thrown the lot are likely to flounder and vacillate until they find thinking too hard, then settle down to the conventional wisdom—which, as you may remember, Galbraith pictured as always being behind the times.

There is an alternative to all these policies which lays a foundation alike for good researchers, good teachers and good practitioners, ten, twenty, thirty years from now. That method is to inculcate the idea that the world of experience, not just accounting experience, is the perennial source of useful insights, indeed the only source of tests of our mere beliefs and opinions; and to show how observation of that world will lead to thoroughly valid sets of accounting ideas now, and as long through his life as the graduate takes with him the idea that the observable world is the matrix of his life. The graduate then will go on learning as the changes in the world teach him. He will never be out of date. He will not "learn by experience" as this phrase is commonly used in contrast to academic learning. He will learn by the "intellectual content of experience," as Dewey in *Experience and Education* described it.

> . . . experiences in order to be educative must lead out into an expanding world of subject-matter, a subject-matter of facts or information and ideas. This condition is satisfied only as the educator views teaching and learning as a continuous process of reconstruction of experience. This condition in turn can be satisfied only as the educator has a long look ahead and views every present experience as a moving force in influencing what future experiences will be.

This type of teaching is teaching-*for*-learning.

I wonder how many students have gone out without an atom of sense of the adventures they may have in continually reconstructing experience as the facts of the real world impinge on them and their art. Many, I fear, have been walled in, from

graduation; with no sense of where their foundations lie, but knowing only the current dogma of their time.

But the point I am making here is that it is a mistake to identify teaching with learning a curriculum. Teach techniques we must, otherwise students will not even know what we are talking about if we question those techniques. But the teacher should also, as it seems to me, be *the bridge* between what is past and present and what is to come. At the very least he should know and present the very best of what is being done in the laboratories and the studies of the researchers, for there is a distinct probability that some of it, heresy today, will become orthodox and accepted in practice in the students' lifetimes. Failure to do this only promotes wall-building.

I would like to give further examples— of the identification at important points of accounting with management, of accounting with economics, of accounting with anticipatory calculation. In all these cases some have failed to see that the two things are neither in conflict nor identical, but complementary. If we fail in apprehension we move further from the real into the symbolic world we have substituted for the real.

PREMATURE DISMASSAL

The third material or principle in wall-building I shall describe as the principle of premature dismassal. We all tend to simplify our problems in some respects: the only way we can cope with complex problems is to cut them down to a size we can manage. The trouble is we often do this all too thoughtlessly, so that we cut out of the picture we have of the world and our part in it some quite vital elements. And this is a grave distortion of reality. Again some examples.

In the mid-twenties Hatfield, a very adventurous soul who many times championed the cause of direct observation,

73

straight thinking, and exact expression, observed that everyone would agree with the importance of the balance sheet as a product of accounting. I wonder what Hatfield would say today. In the last thirty years the balance sheet has been so run down in the eyes of accountants that it can be described merely as a footnote to the income account. How is the mighty fallen! There is no time here to trace the downfall of the balance sheet. But it began when accountants realized that the balance sheets and income statements they were drawing up didn't make sense in the outside world. They chose to have "better" income statements and to give up worrying about the balance sheet. Yet in the world outside it is as demonstrable as ever that statements of financial position are necessary to the users of financial information. Instead of seeing the two statements as complementary, and facing the challenge of really making them consistent, one of them was just dismissed, regardless of the needs of the outside world.

At the same time as this was happening it appeared that some practices, by which it was attempted to show assets at something like current values, had been used wantonly. Instead of seeing how wanton misuse could be curbed without doing violence to the quite proper use of the same idea, the whole notion of asset revaluation upwards was banished, and we took in its place the cost doctrine. Now presumably one of the uses of accounting information is to help people and business firms to be better off than they are now. But the application of the historical cost doctrine will never tell us how well off we are now; nor for the same reason could it tell us how well off we were last year; and for the same reason it could not allow us to discover how much better off we are as a result of last year's business, which in the case of business firms is income! Instead of seeing that both original prices and intervening changes in prices are complementary pieces of information in the derivation of the present actual position, we just dismissed one of them outright. Again that is cutting the world's business back to a size which is the *proper* size *in accounting*.

My third example of premature dismissal is quite different. There are many practitioners who conscientiously believe that research can only properly be done by those actively engaged, or who have long been actively engaged, in practice. There are also very many academics who believe that properly to carry out research one must keep intimate contact with practices. Both dismiss the possibility that "outsiders," those who are not so intimately familiar, can see what the problems of accounting are. The history of many ideas of course proves this to be quite a false position, quite apart from the necessary subjectivity of the views of anyone closely involved in a thing he is also observing. If we take the more or less traditional origins of some famous physical discoveries, we will note that Archimedes did not discover his displacement principle as a professional bather; nor Newton the gravitational principle as a professional dropping-apple watcher. Nor was Galileo a professional rubbish dropper from the tower of Pisa, nor Einstein a professional time-keeper or clock-watcher. And to take some examples of the opposite sort from chemistry, Priestley and Dalton, two of the founders of modern chemistry were, respectively, a cleric and a meteorologist professionally. None of this proves that professional practitioners cannot conduct research, or should not. All it does is serve as warning against the dismissal of other kinds of experience, and particularly of independent observation, as qualifications for research activity. In a very real sense, the independent observer can be the auditor of professional practice, and just as valuable to the professional practitioner as the professional auditor should be to the manager and the investor. As in the other examples, what are so often seen as alternatives may be much more realistically seen as complementaries.

There are other examples of this principle of premature dismissal. But I turn now to the mortar that binds the bricks together in this wall which encompasses accounting.

Dogmatism

If two things are complementary it is highly probable that their methods and styles should be different. I have contended that accounting practice and accounting theory are complementary in as much as they take place, or should take place, against different settings. I am now to propose that dogmatism is necessary in the one, but thoroughly stifling in the other.

There can be no objection to the dogmatic statement by practitioners, or their official exponents of the professional view, that inventories *should* be valued in such and such a way; that marketable securities *should* be valued in such and such a way; and so on. (There are, of course, grave objections to statements which are both dogmatic and self-contradictory, as when more ways than one of doing a specific thing are promulgated. I have dealt elsewhere with this, and am not concerned with it here.) The continual assertion of such statements is one way in which younger practitioners come to learn the present state of normal practice at any time. It also has the effect of holding practitioners, who might otherwise deviate under pressure from clients, to a firm line (if, that is to say, there is a firm line). It also makes clear to observers, such as theorists and other users of financial statements, what the rules are supposed to be.

But there is the strongest objection to value-loaded, dogmatic expression in a theoretical literature. Like all dogmas, statements in the imperative mood have the effect of stifling discussion, of closing an issue by making a judgment. This is quite inconsistent with the ethics of inquiry, of research, and of the reporting of conclusions in other fields. Not only that; history demonstrates repeatedly that dogmatic systems will survive only if they are supported by authoritative measures that effectively cut off their subjects from intercourse with the world at large. Indeed it is one of the objects of dogma to make adherents independent of the facts of the world at large, to close their eyes to the facts. The ideology of Nazism could only be sustained by the constant assertion of statements that were demonstrably false and by the elimination of all who could make contrary assertions and of all whose very existence was evidence of the truth of contrary assertions.

Notice that dogma can only survive if it is backed up by force. Now theorists, of course, have no political power to back up dogmatic assertions, to make them effective in practice. They have, at least they *can* have, only the power which their apprehension of the facts of the world and the rigor of their logic gives them. But if theorists, upon whom the world depends for the discovery of error and the testing of ideas, become so debilitated that they see no logical errors, see no divergences between dogma and common sense observation, they will make no contribution to the advancement of understanding or of practice.

Take a small cluster of illustrations involving two notions, the cost doctrine and the accrual principle. Suppose a firm buys two identical machines from two different suppliers at the same time but at different prices, $400 and $500. In practice the accounts for these two machines will open with these two money magnitudes, and the charges for their use will forever afterwards

75

be different. Now an independent observer, say a theorist, will surely apprehend that for every practical purpose the two machines are the same; the contribution each makes to end products is the same, and if both produce the same end products the prices of those products will be the same. Yet accounting practices imply that the contribution each machine makes to end products is different! Isn't there ground for some uneasiness in this contradiction? Now suppose there is subsequently a rise in the price of such machines due to an increased demand for their products. Every unit of service output of those machines will then produce a greater inflow of cash than previously; as we say colloquially, every unit of service output is more valuable to the firm. But we will find in practice that the charge for each unit of service output is no different from the charge before the rise in the price of the machines. Another contradiction. Now under the accrual principle we take notice of changes in the machines through use long before the amounts of those changes become finally discovered, long before we get their scrap value in cash. But under the cost principle we *refuse* to take notice of the rise in prices of the machines on the ground that the distance to discovery of the effects, which again is the point where we get the scrap value in cash, is remote. Put briefly, there is one event in the future which determines both things; its futurity stops us from taking account of one change, but doesn't stop us from taking account of the other. The conclusion of an independent observer of all this must surely be that the cost doctrine yields numbers which do not, subsequently to purchase, tally with the facts as they are pertinent to managers; that the accrual principle is both held and denied at the same time and that the two principles are mutually contradictory or inconsistent.

I am well aware that some people are relaxing their allegiance to the cost doctrine. But they are still hanging on to it as even the latest official statements attest; witness the idea of supplementary statements. But as someone has said, "To move forward clinging to the past is like dragging a ball and chain."

As I have said, the role of the theorist is not just to observe practices, to rationalize them, and to parrot the conventional wisdom; it is to observe their effects in the world at large, to collect evidence of their effects, and to judge them on the weight of evidence. But he will not do this as long as he is walled in by what is done *in accounting*. The proof of a pudding is not in the cooking, but in the eating. If he gets out beyond the wall, he will find that many things dogmatically asserted and passionately believed are just not so. And that, of course, is the beginning of pure adventure, for he cannot just push the facts aside, and yet he runs the risk of appearing foolish, of being described as heretical and a lot of other things besides. If, however, he thinks greatly of his subject, he will enjoy the risk for the improvement his observations promise.

THE WAY AHEAD

Once we grasp the futility of accepting dogmatic statements a whole new universe opens for exploration. As long as men accepted the dogma of the sanctity of the human skin, they were unable to benefit from the knowledge which enlivened the anatomical work of Vesalius and the art of Leonardo and Michelangelo. As long as men conceived the objects about them as being of the essences of earth, air, fire, and water, after the manner of Aristotle, they were unable to benefit from the knowledge to which the dawn of the age of empiricism gave birth. As long as men accepted the postulates of Euclidean geometry they were unable to benefit from the insights which the geometries of Bolyai, Lobatchevsky, and Riemann have given the world. These examples are mixed: some relate to the consequences of patient observation; some relate to sheer invention; but none of them would have emerged from mere observation of normal practice at the time.

But besides the possibility of new ideas emerging from observation of the practice and the consequences of the practice of an art, is the fact that only observation of the consequences provides any test of the usefulness or failings of the art. Who, then, sits off, *independently*, and examines the consequences of accounting as it is practiced? Not managers, nor investors, nor creditors. None of them is independent. Neither are practitioners independent of their practices, for they practice them. In fact no one does this independent assessing if theorists and researchers do not do it. No one marshals the evidence for or against any practice by reference to its *actual* consequences if theorists and researchers do not. Compared with the volume of mere opinion and dogma which fill the so-called theoretical literature of the past fifty years, the amount of actual evidence, the empirical evidence, is pitifully small. Yet the amount of evidence there is, in those fifty years of commercial history, of the inadequacy of many accounting practices I believe to be enormous and much of it is a matter of publicly accessible record.

Let me illustrate the method of observation by reference to astronomy. Astronomy has many things in common with the study of accounting. The observables of astronomy are remote and not manipulable by astronomers in the way chemicals are manipulable by chemists. The observables in the study of the consequences of accounting practices are remote; they are the actions and interactions of business people, and these are not manipulable by theorists; we can only observe. Both astronomy and accounting are concerned with problems of measurement, and in both cases because measurements are or are believed to be of guidance to others than astronomers or accountants themselves. How then are astronomers, or accountants, to test the beliefs that are held, by reference to the observable facts of experience? for to do so is the only assurance that those beliefs are not merely myths. The only way is by working out the logical consequences of those beliefs and seeing whether over time the consequences turn out to be as they were expected. Time is the crucible—and perhaps in accounting also space. Time is necessary because it takes some time for the consequences of fallacious devices to become apparent. As for space, we can test the consequences of beliefs if we find them held also in other countries that otherwise have different conditions.

By observing and testing, however, I do not mean taking the actual financial statements of firms and demonstrating what they would have looked like if they had been prepared on some different basis. That only proves that some alternative can be used; it does not prove that a hypothetical alternative would be more efficacious in the practical world of business. The proof I would seek is proof from the actual devices used and the actual observed consequences. It is the same in kind as Copernicus accepted as evidence of the defects in the Ptolemaic system of astronomy—the divergence over time of what was expected from what was actually experienced.

Observation is also the beginning of the construction of a set of ideas which shall be a firm foundation for a practically useful system of accounting. In this case we are not looking for tests of an existing rule, but for uniformities which might yield useful generalizations. The theorists' conclusions are thus not of the form "I believe . . . " or "I recommend . . . " or "We should do

78

this or that." They are of the form "If A, then B." The whole fraternity of researchers and theorists is then able to see clearly the assumptions, presuppositions, and data on which the conclusion rests. They can then themselves test every step of the argument, every piece of factual evidence, every generalization. Attempts may be made to test the concurrence of A and B. Inquiries may be made to discover whether the conditional proposition is consistent with other propositions so far accepted within the literature, or accepted in the associated field of experience, or accepted in the literature or practice of any analogous field. If and as the evidence mounts, the validity of the conclusion becomes accepted, the more so if the evidence is shown to be "real world" evidence.

There is enough evidence of this kind ready to hand to demonstrate the folly of many things now asserted as practical rules and used in practice; I am convinced that one of the major reasons why fallacious rules persist is that the theorists of the game have not known how to marshal it; for practical men, the practitioners, cannot long hold to rules which on "real world" evidence are shown to be inconsistent with their ethos, the reason for their existence.

Whitehead reminds us that "The history of ideas is a history of mistakes. But through all mistakes it is also the history of the gradual purification of conduct." The instrument of this purification he speaks of as a "noble discontent" which is provoked by "the gradual emergence into prominence of a sense of criticism founded upon appreciations of beauty, and of intellectual distinction, and of duty." If we value dogma above duty, rationalization above reality, bovine placidity above intellectual distinction, we shall never experience that noble discontent, the sense of the possibility of intellectual adventure.

I have been striking out in many directions, looking at the past and present to see into the future. I would like to stress, that all my suggestions have a common source: a passionate belief in the value of knowledge, in the capacity of knowledge to free us from the influence of dogma, in the capacity of knowledge to free us from the conceits and deceits of others. And when I say us, I do not mean just theorists, or just practitioners; I mean us as ordinary intelligent men in the street as well, and all other ordinary intelligent men in the street.

One of the basic tenets of free societies is that every man shall be able to choose for himself what he shall do within the law with the things secured to him by the law. This is a great and valuable freedom; its possession is one of the things in which free societies take great pride. To choose for himself *knowledgeably* is what the laws governing the sales of goods and the sales of securities try to ensure to every individual. There is not a law for the wise and a law for fools. The law requires the facts to be stated as they are known at the time any statement is made about goods or securities, leaving the consumer free, knowledgeably free, to make his choices. The law has imposed a great responsibility on accountants to assist in this process—to free the millions of investors in corporate securities from being misled by the wishful thinking, and even in some cases the twisted thinking, of those who have the use of investors' money. Quite apart from the legal situation there is a similar responsibility that accountants assume as specialists, even in the ordinary course of business—to free the hundreds of thousands of managers from being misled by their underlings and from being misled by their own optimisms. The basic question we must ask of ourselves is, therefore, whether we are going to help all these parties to be knowledgeably free. If the statements we prepare or publish or permit to be published contain old elements of the past that have no present relevance or if they embody expectations of the future that are always and inevitably subjective or if they are prepared on the basis of dogma we impose, the managers and investors of this world will never be knowledgeably free. As long as our practices have these elements, they prevent the users of financial information from having the constitutional right to choose knowledgeably, which the institutions of a free society are expected to uphold and enforce. It is our business to discover the facts as they unfold themselves, to report them as they are, not to confuse the picture by telling only part of the facts (as when we use historical costs) or by including things which are not facts (as when we use our own estimates of future things which may never happen).

At a meeting of this Association (under its earlier style) some 43 years ago, Hatfield said "Let us boldly raise the question whether accounting, the late claimant for recognition as a profession, is not entitled to some respect, or must it consort with crystal-gazing . . . . and palmreading?" I wonder what Hatfield would think today, to see how far some would have us go in the direction of crystal-gazing. I leave you to think about what I am referring to.

There are some among us who think little of Hatfield's "houn' dog." His coat has been allowed to become shabby; he has become a psychotic. Some seers sound as though they await his early demise. But count me not among them. I am only anxious to prevent this psychosis from developing to the point where he must be "put away" in the public interest.

79

Audit Under Audit*

The world is full of specialists of one kind or another, the function of each of which is to perform a set task with skill. We do not expect specialists to be skilful in a wide range of things; we have become very tolerant of the failure of specialists in respect of matters other than those in which they specialize. But the extent to which we expect them to be expert in their chosen field is indicated by our willingness to pay for their time and advice on a scale higher than we are prepared to pay for the services of the non-expert. Society at large even accords the expert a higher social standing and to groups of experts the right of self regulation or self-government within their field of specialism.

This right of self government is valued by groups of experts as a token of the confidence of a general community in the level of knowledge and the degree of integrity which they demonstrate. But it is a right which, like all rights, is subject to recall or restriction if the demonstrated knowledge and integrity fail to meet the demands of the community. The community may for long periods let alone its valued institutions - its constitution, its financial system, its educational system, its professions; but every now and then it finds them inadequate, and makes appropriate noises. Specialists, experts and institutions have no inherent right to be left alone; they earn it by continually keeping up with the demands the community makes of them. What is more, they cannot protect themselves from the force of opinion merely by making public noises in return. Apologetics and pleas are not enough. Not all the wealth of the few and the power it gave could stem the factory reforms of England or the introduction of the anti trust legislation or the securities regulation legislation of this country.

If now, from time to time, the audited financial statements of corporations attract the critical attention of bankers, financial analysts, regulatory officials, and even academics, we must consider this as the audit of accounting, and, more closely the audit of auditing by

---

*   Beta Alpha Psi, Lambda Chapter (University of California at Berkeley), Address, San Francisco, January 1967.

the community. Now the AUDITED know that if they want a clean report they must do something about the representations they make in their statements. Likewise if the AUDITORS are the AUDITED, they likewise must do something about the demands made by the community.

The common reaction to criticism in the past has been to protest the difficulties under which the accountant and auditor works; it is said that the financial statements are, after all, the representations of management; and it is said that the accountant´s task is to provide information for other purposes as well as those for which, for the moment, they are under criticism. These protestations, which fill the editorial pages of professional journals and sometimes the speeches of professionals within their own circles, are quite useless as devices for stemming the tide of criticism. They may assuage the anxieties of rank and file members of the profession; they may lead those members to suppose that others will answer for them; at best they are no better than whistling in the dark, to keep up courage. For, as it seems to me, it is the business of professionals to be concerned with the substance of criticism, to be concerned individually and constantly with the effectiveness with which they play their roles - not to accept for relief the opiate of injured tones and phrases. Anything which dulls the sensitivity to criticism of the professional does him and his expertise potential damage.

The alternative to indulgence in such tranquillizing is to face the facts; discover the difficulties and remove the causes of criticism. Maybe that is easier said than done; but it is also one of the characteristics of the professional that he has passed the point where trivial problems interest him. He relishes the hard problems for they are the only ones which put him on his mettle. He will not even take comfort in the "easier said than done" evasion. I want briefly to see what could be done about the three sorts of excuses mentioned earlier which may be offered in response to criticism.

The first was "the difficulties under which the accountant and auditor works". These find their most telling form in the assertion that accounting and auditing involves a great deal of judgement and a keen apprehension of the various effects which the use of different accounting procedures may have on "interested parties". It seems to me that most assertions with respect to judgement assert too much; and most of the statements by auditors by implication assert too little. We are told for example, that the determination of the amounts at which depreciation, inventory charges and balances, and so on will be shown in accounts are matters of judgement. But so is driving a car. When driving a car, however, there are certain impelling constraints, certain things one just does not do, judgement or no judgement. I seriously wonder whether there is anything which the traditional literature and practice of accounting forbids - excluding of course outright dishonesty. There is, for example, no generally held notion of the function of the balance sheet and income statement taken together; for the implication of traditional accounting based on initial purchase prices of assets is that the income statement should be up to date while the balance sheet may be as out of date as the oldest remaining asset or equity. To speak of exercising judgment when there is no positive notion that the balance sheet should represent something which is presently significant - or up to date - is to play fast and loose with the very meaning of judgement. The multiplicity of permissible rules having divergent effects makes the whole of the exercise almost free of judgement. But suppose we allow the choice of some combination of accounting methods to be taken by the accountants or managers of a firm. What then is the auditor to do? has he any "judgement" superior to that of the officers of the firm? any point of view or source of wisdom which makes or could make his judgement more reliable? Not unless there is a fixed principle or principles beyond the realm of judgement, in other words a definite function which the two financial statements taken together perform. In the absence of any such principles auditors must in most cases merely accept what is offered as the "best judgement" of the firm's officers.

The problem of exercising judgements over the vast range of possible, acceptable alternatives is not a problem which has been forced on the accounting and auditing profession by the community. We ourselves have put ourselves in this predicament either by inventing new rules, or accepting the suggestions of others without choosing as between old and new rules, or accepting what our teachers and professional superiors have simply handed on to us. It is up to us to extricate ourselves from this position, not to plead our own invented difficulties when the community attacks our product.

I have elsewhere demonstrated that the number of possible representations of the net income and financial position of a firm exceeds a million – and the demonstration has not yet been demolished. If there are so many possible rules we may as well admit there are no rules, for no person can knowledgeably say what particular combination any firm has adopted in any year, and no person can therefore say what the significance of the numbers appearing in any financial statement is. We cannot expect the community, our auditors, long to put up with this state of affairs.

The second type of excuse I mentioned was that the financial statements are, after all, the representations of management. The issue cannot be dodged in this way if we have any sense of professional skill and pride in that skill. If the auditing profession has any notions of what constitutes satisfactory financial reporting it is the business of the profession to make it known so that there is clear guidance for clients as to what will pass without qualification. Preventive medicine and preventive maintenance are much better than patching and making shift when things go wrong. But have you ever seen a positive statement as to what constitutes the ideal to which every set of financial statements should be a close approximation? To determine this ideal is not the function of management. Managers engage scientists – why? because they do not know enough about science themselves. They engage engineers, physicians, statisticians for the same reasons. And when they engage these people they do not **tell them** how they should practise science or engineering or medicine or statistics. Managers engage accountants, and auditors to check them – why? Because they need to know how a company is making out against the rest of the world, and presumably because accountants and auditors are experts at doing this or discovering whether it has been done well.

Now here is the crux of the problem. The managers need to know how their companies are making out against the rest of the community in order to decide whether to change their modes of operation. If they are at all concerned with efficiency they will want the discovery system to be as acute as possible, they would want every measure of what they have done validated by reference to the market's present assessment of what they have done. This means that every measure of assets will be a present market price and every measure of equities a present measure of an obligation. They should not want the signals to be confused by their own opinions of what things are worth - and they should not expect their accountants or auditors to take much notice of those opinions. But, on the other hand, the very statements which should represent how their firms have made out against the rest of the community will be used by others, investors and financiers, to judge the performances of managers. Managers thus have a vested interest in the information which flows from the processes of accounting and under the scrutiny of auditors.

I am by no means suggesting that managers in general deliberately try to circumvent the scrutiny of the investors and creditors by feeding into the financial records estimates and values which are self serving. But anyone with half an eye to the history of commerce will know that there have been many such managers. And the tendency to self protection is very strong in any case; so that if managers could believe that they can reconcile what is in the best interest of stockholders with the protection of their own interest, it should not be expected that they would pass up the opportunity. And the opportunity is wide open because there is no statement of the ideal to which financial statements should conform.

It is the very possibility that managers may distort the representations of a firm's position and results - whether for personal or altruistic motives is immaterial - that the statutorily recognized function of auditors was instituted. The law seeks to forestall even the temptation to biased statement. But the foresight which is embodied in such laws seems not to have been sensed by the profession. It does not seem to have anticipated the consequence either of the law or of the propensities which the law sought to curb. And as Whitehead observed "Where there is no anticipation, change has to wait upon chance, and peters out amid neglect". The opportunity to take a firm stand on the ideals of the Securities Acts was passed, and the state of the art has become so varied that it would be impossible to say it has any ideal form of expression. As I shall presently observe, if it is to survive it seems to me the profession must find answers to this problem too; it cannot merely protest the difficulties it faces.

My third type of excuse was the difficulty said to be experienced in meeting at one time the demands of many different users of accounting information. The view prevails that because there are many users there must be many kinds of ways of looking at the same firm at a given time, hence many different but feasible and allowable methods of accounting. This is supported from a different direction by the view that because there are many kinds of enterprise there must be particular and different ways of representing results and financial position, presumably one for each kind of enterprise. But these views are both confused. Consider the first: different users means necessarily different information. The fact that there are different classes of equity holders does not entail different qualities of information at all. No one has yet demonstrated that balance sheet and income statement information is irrelevant to bondholders and other creditors. Different classes of equity holders may be **primarily** interested in one facet of the financial facts rather than another; but which facets will come under close scrutiny by any class depends entirely on what the results and position in any year turn out to be. And the design of the system of accounting is clearly anterior to discovering the results and position for any year. What is generally overlooked is that the financial statements are the only integral representation of results and position for a firm as a whole, and every investor, bondholder and junior-creditor must make his own inferences from the statements as a whole. Further, as their several interests may conflict, it is fair to none of them to give a slant to the representation which is biased in favor of one, for the bias may rebound. It is a simple exercise to show this – an exercise you may undertake at leisure.

As for different enterprises requiring different accounting, it seems to be overlooked that the object of publication is to enable financial contributors to do the best for themselves **whatever** firms they may wish to invest in. They need to compare, and they can only compare the substantive features of firms if the representations are not distorted by mere differences in accounting methods.

My object has been to show that if we look at the rationalizations offered when financial statements and their auditors come under scrutiny, we find that the difficulties complained of by accountants and auditors

86

are of their own making, or have arisen because of failure to express an
ideal to which the statements should conform.

The public audit to which the profession is exposed is likely to
lead, and has led, to public comment of a critical kind, in my opinion,
because the profession has lacked an adequate **internal audit.** I hope you
don't tire of my analogy. But it is the business of a profession which
seeks to retain its right to self-government to maintain not merely an
etiquette, but an ideal notion of its technical ends. This ideal must be
informed by something better than the incomplete thinking and
rationalizing which I have been illustrating. We need to accept a more
thorough-going and well-developed theory of the place of accounting and
auditing in the functioning of an industrial society than the patchwork
now accepted. Let me offer some more words of Whitehead. By a
profession he understands

> "an avocation whose activities are subjected to theoretical
> analysis, and are modified by theoretical conclusions derived
> from that analaysis. This analysis has regard to the **purpose** of
> the avocation and to the adaptation of the activities for the
> attainment of those **purposes.** Such criticism must be founded
> upon some understanding of the natures of the things involved in
> those activities, so that the results of action can be foreseen.
> Thus foresight based upon theory and theory based upon
> understanding of the nature of things, are essential to a
> profession".

Now who is to establish this complex of foresight, theory and
understanding which is the underpinning of a profession. Who are its
internal auditors? For the answer to this I turn to one of the great
educationists and educational administratoru of this country. Robert
Hutchens deals with the relationship of profession and university thus:

> It is hard to master the intellectual content of a profession
> while one is practising it. The demands of active professional
> life are not favorable to study and reflection. On the other
> hand, universities are not well adapted to teaching the tricks of
> trades ... The great problem of the university is the problem of
> purpose.

Notice that this is the concern with purpose which Whitehead saw as the object of analysis underlying a professional avocation. And as it seems, the function of the university is to develop the complex of theory and understanding which serves as the touchstone for professional expertise and the basis of professional foresight. If accounting and auditing are under criticism clearly there remains much to be done at the level of study and reflection on purpose.

Now some will no doubt object, claiming that we are well supplied already with that theory and understanding. I would just like to parade some of the evidence to the effect that this is not so.

In the standard audit report it is said that the balance sheet and statements of income and surplus present fairly the financial position and results of operations. How often have you seen an analysis and exposition of what is meant by "financial position"? Everyone with a reasonable knowledge of the alternatives dealt with in any textbook will know that any given selection of alternatives will give a position which can be vastly different from the result of another selection. Under existing practice financial position is just an empty phrase. Balance sheets certainly do not give the financial positions of firms at the dates they bear.

If you look closely at the standard audit report you will find that it makes much of accounting statements, accounting records, auditing standards and accounting principles. All these are references to how the accounting and auditing has been done. Nowhere does it expressly say that the statements about particular assets and equities and so on have been authenticated by tests other than the assertions of management and the entries in the records. Yet in the nature of things it is far more important for receivers of the statements to know that the monetary amounts assigned to particular items are realistic, independently authenticated and contemporary than to know that the bookkeeping is impeccable.

I have looked in vain in the literature for recognition of the idea that the users of financial information want to be informed of present facts, and of the function of the auditor as the specialist who authenticates the statements. When people acquire equities in firms they are not acquiring equities in financial statement symbols; they acquire equities in identifiable things and rights; and the securities law seeks

to inform them of the extent of the goods and rights which underlie their
security holdings. If auditors have any respect for that law and for
fair dealing between buyers and sellers of securities and between
security holders and management, the symbols they accept as representing
a firm must have some hard core, something other than amounts of money
spent long ago, long before the incumbent managers and many of the
present shareholders became associated with a company, and something
other than the necessarily vague and potentially biased estimates of
future inflows. To keep the picture up to date requires the continual
discovery of the new magnitudes which represent assets, and the continual
authentication of those discoveries. Has it ever occurred to you that
one of the now well established audit rules is directed to such a process
of discovery: the observation or physical testing of inventories. But
has it ever occurred to you that this is directed to discovering present
physical magnitudes whereas the auditor's task is strictly only to do
this for the purpose of discovering present monetary equivalents?
There's not a line in the text books on this point.

    It is a curious thing that in this day and age we are bombarded by
the evidence of man's insatiable desire to know the latest so that he may
act with the least delay in a knowledgeable way. From the ass-borne
courier to Telstar, from handwritten and mentally calculated messages to
the telex and the computer we have come a long way; but not in the
audited messages which we convey to managers and companies convey to
investors. We do not seem to sense that the role of investors is to
choose the more efficient companies as the firms which survive and to
choose the less efficient for liquidation, and that the auditor's role in
this process is crucial. We do not seem to sense that in permitting
reporting practices which materially deviate from the ideal of
continuously contemporary information we are putting a brake on the
growth in industrial efficiency, that we are interfering with the process
of free and informed competition which so often we claim to be a way of
life.

    If auditors were mere technicians they would have been jolted out of
this state of misapprehension long since. But the professional mystique
preserves them from the common disciplines. Only their own sense of what
is practically sound and ethically justified, only their sense of

dedication to an ideal of public duty, will preserve them from public censure.

I speak tonight mainly to a group which hopefully still has the idealism of the relatively unstructured. This is the spirit which it seems should persist in the professional, and indeed it is the spirit which should enliven the professional school. Each generation is in fact the auditor of the previous generation, probing, testing what it passes on. And each generation of auditors is the auditor of its predecessors, probing and testing what it has accepted as doctrine. Similarly, the professional schools have a role as the auditors of their respective professions; they are the institutions by which the community at large seeks continuously to prevent its practices, and its views of the nature of things, from becoming ossified, doctrinaire, effete, useless. If there is public and official criticism as audit passes under audit, there is ample evidence of work yet to be done, ample opportunity for the exercise of that fore-sight based on theory and theory based on understanding of the nature of things which keeps a profession alive and free from externally imposed constraint. I like to believe that those who have labored to establish the public accounting profession can and will trust the idealism of the new generation to whom they pass on the torch, or the green ink pen as the case may be. As Aldous Huxley has observed "The survival of democracy depends on the ability of large numbers of people to make realistic choices in the light of adequate information". We may say the same about economic progress. It is the auditor's function to see that the light of adequate information is shed. In a world in which the powerful may hold power by withholding light, it is a significant function. In a world in which there is so much interdependence it is a function which provides the counterweight to power or the diffusion of power. If this is understood it might yet happen that in response to the purport of the Securities Act - "Let there be light", we may say "And there was light".

NEW PATHWAYS IN ACCOUNTING THOUGHT AND ACTION*

To many it may seem that there is little new that can be said about accounting. In the past such a view has been held in respect of other arts and sciences. But no sooner have men come to the conclusion that at last they knew all than some new idea or ideas have opened up entirely new ways of looking at things; and the reorganisation of old knowledge and the alignment with it of new knowledge have begun all over again. There is no reason to suppose that accounting may not undergo changes such as the change in mechanics which resulted in Newton's mechanics becoming regarded as a special case of Einstein's mechanics, or such as the changes in biological science which followed the discovery of micro-organisms.

We hold that there is much that is new to be said about accounting. Many seem to think that the foundations of accounting are well established. We hold, on the contrary, that they are yet to be established. Many seem certain that present accounting practices, being the product of long use and experience, yield quite satisfactory and useful information. We hold, on the contrary, that they yield information which is far from satisfactory and which, in many important respects, is useless. Many seem to think that new levels of sophistication have been reached by the association of accounting with managerial decision-making. We hold, on the contrary, that the association is as yet merely verbal and that much of what is described as accounting for decision-making is quite unlinked with any decision process. Many seem to think that the computer is the most significant thing that has happened to accounting for a long time. We hold, on the contrary that the computer is a moron, and that it has little to do with the kernel of accounting.

These views may seem presumptuous. But they are not idle. They may seem to imply that our professional ancestors have done very little. They imply no such thing. At different stages in the history of other arts and sciences men have avowed that they were only able to see so far because they have stood on the shoulders of giants. It is not likely to be otherwise in accounting. But we have fewer ancestors in accounting. After all, the only history of accounting ideas that has counted towards what we now know and use is no longer than five generations, and in many respects no longer than two generations. Contrast this with some facets of the history of science. For two thousand years, until LAVOISIER, men of science believed that water was the generator or source of all matter. For almost the same interval, until COPERNICUS, the earth was believed to be the immobile centre of the universe. For fourteen hundred years, until KEPLER, the motions of the planets were believed to be basically circular. The history of science is full of such examples. But the men of science were neither dullards, nor idle, during these long intervals. They observed, they thought, they experimented —all three perhaps rather crudely by modern standards. But then they did not have the advantages of modern standards. And indeed, without the accumulation of their observations, without the benefit of their inconsistencies and failures, modern standards would not be what they are. Those who propounded what is now believed could not have done so.

There are good reasons why for a long time accounting ideas and practices have lacked a systematic foundation. Workers with metals have used heat for thousands of years without having any systematic knowledge of heat as such. They have handed down processes which were known to produce specific effects because the effects were apparent. Accounting, however, is not something which produces observable and nearly consistent effects. The commercial environment is volatile, so that it is never possible to conduct controlled experiments which would show up the advantages or deficiencies of different modes of accounting. The knowledge produced by any actual accounting system becomes combined with all kinds of other knowledge of those who may be supposed to act upon it, and with mere beliefs and hopes as well. It is impossible then to tell whether the consequences of any action, based on such a mixture, are due to factual knowledge, or beliefs, or hopes, or chance. Opinions about alternative methods of accounting likewise are the product of factual knowledge, beliefs and hopes, even though they are given the appearance of being based on factual knowledge more often, and to a greater extent, than they deserve. It is a difficult task to unravel the threads of fact, hope and unsupported belief, particularly when men, all men, tend to cling tenaciously to the hand-me-down recipes of their instructors, in business, profession or college. It is more difficult still if we fail to take advantage of the hindsight we may have from the failures and successes of men in other fields of disciplined intellectual endeavour.

If we seek new pathways in accounting thought and action, we have much to learn from other fields. The newness which concerns me is not a complete novelty in ways of thinking. It is the application of tested ways of thinking about other things, ways which, until recently, have not been tried in the field of accounting. This is where the newness lies. Doubtless many currently held ideas about accounting are legitimate and fruitful ideas. But many other such views are inconsistent and some are demonstrably false. To make progress we need to examine them systematically; to eliminate the false, the self-contradictory and the anomalous; to endeavour to set up a system of ideas which is observably realistic and logically coherent.

Evolution or Conscious Construction?

We may take either of two views of the development of accounting thought and practice. We may suppose that there is some evolutionary process by which what now is done is best because what has survived. Or we may suppose that what now is done is a consequence of a mixture of insight, precedent and dogma.

If we take the former view we will be little concerned with systematic analysis. No amount of analysis will upset our conviction that incompetent methods, ideas, principles will have been cast off in the process of growth.

This view has notable defects. The advancement of knowledge is not an evolutionary process. Unquestionably each generation, each century, each millenium is the inheritor of the products of preceding periods. But mere inheritance proves nothing about the quality of the knowledge transmitted. Taking a long view of the growth of knowledge in most fields, we will find that some novel ideas survive for long periods eventually to be discarded; that some after being discarded are later reinstated, if not in the field in which they originated then in some other field; that some ideas which engage their promoters for lifetimes of work yield nothing enduring; that others are extraordinarily fruitful. We find that ideas sometimes lie dormant, almost forgotten, often completely forgotten, until some fortuitous set of circumstances makes their exploitation possible. We find that many ideas arise from the mere chance that some person is confronted with what then seems to him an anomaly worth further investigation. The strong accidental element—the coincidence of persons and circumstances—in the history of thought casts grave doubt over the notion of evolutionary development.[1]

Again, if we take a long view, how are we to know whether the ideas we now hold will not shortly become the dinosaurs and the brontosauruses of thought and practice, swept away without progeny because they are unfitted to the environment of the moment? There is no virtue in holding on to rules which the accidents of history have thrust upon us.

The alternative view is to regard the development of the subject as something which may have occurred in accidental fashion, and to apply to each phase of it the critical analysis of informed common sense. Consider an example. We all take stock of our personal finances now and then, when we are thinking of buying a new house or a share in a business or of taking an extended vacation. When we do this we would not dream of adding up the initial purchase prices of the house and land, the shares or bonds and the car we already own. We would try to find out their market prices. Yet when we take stock of the position of a business we merely add up the initial purchase prices of assets (less some formally calculated depreciation, in some cases) and resolutely refuse to take notice of market prices. What we find quite sensible for ourselves we find quite ridiculous for business. Why? Some will say, because business firms are to be treated as going concerns. But when we make such calculations for our personal affairs it is not because we contemplate bankruptcy. We view ourselves as going concerns, going to do the same as before or something we judge to be better, depending on what we find out our positions to be. The only difference between persons and business firms is that business firms must take stock of their positions more often, because changes in customers' preferences, technical processes and the degree of competition force them to consider changes in their asset holdings more frequently. This makes up to date knowledge of their positions even more crucial than for persons. Yet the historical cost basis of traditional accounting ignores this, in defiance of common sense. We shall look at the matter again presently from another angle. Even at this point, however, it should be apparent that there is something curious if not absurd about the processes we adopt or the way they have come down to us, something needing conscious analysis and reconstruction.

Verbal Analysis or Observation?

There have been ages in which the pursuit of knowledge has been hampered by metaphysical beliefs about what is good or proper or permissible. Until the time of LEONARDO DA VINCI and MICHELANGELO, for example, dissection of human corpses was forbidden by the church, and these men, who wished to know more of the structure of the body for the advancement of their arts, were forced to be grave robbers and dissectors, illicitly and nocturnally. When factual knowledge is either forbidden or believed to be unattainable, men turn their ingenuity to purely verbal and logical analysis of the views of their masters, those they esteem to have been the intellectual giants of their fields. This was the mode of medieval scholasticism. Learned men spent lifetimes in disputation, interpretation and comment on the works of wisdom of "authorities".

But these are, and were found to be, sterile exercises. As LEONARDO said "All our knowledge has its origin in our perceptions". He had scant respect for authorities as such, preferring the full and complete observation of nature. Since his time, observation has been regarded as the prerequisite of scientific inquiry and the test of scientific conclusions.

There can be little doubt that accounting at present is closer to the mode of the scholastics than to the mode of inference from observation. For years the touchstone of accounting propositions and practices has been the dicta of authorities. Sometimes they have been legal authorities, as in the case of the distinctive rules for valuing current and fixed assets; sometimes they have been accounting authorities whose names have been lost but whose dicta have survived. In recent years we have come to accept statements by professional bodies or their committees as authorities. But it is noticeable that hardly ever is any "authoritative" statement backed up by a demonstration of its consequences and by argument to the effect that these consequences conform with what is required of accounting.

Consider again the traditional practice of recording assets and representing them thereafter at cost less depreciation. Suppose a firm buys three pieces of machinery: A for $1,000 in 1955; B for $1,000 in 1960 and C for $1,000 in 1964. The total of these outlays would appear in the balance sheet of 1965 as the cost of these assets. There will be shown as deductions from this total (assuming each piece has an expected life of 20 years) the sum of $500 (A), $250 (B), and $50 (C); in all $800. The balance will be $2,200. Superficially this seems sensible. But a closer examination will surely show it to be rather absurd. It is well known that $1,000 in 1955 and $1,000 in 1964 did not mean the same thing. None of us personally would think that $1,000 was the same for any personal purpose in those two years. The New Zealand consumers' goods price index (base $1958 = 100$) rose from 91 to 115 in that interval. If over any period of years we are to add different sums of money spent in different years we should at least recognise that equal sums have not equal meanings.

We may give them subscripts to distinguish them. The total outlays would then appear to be $\$(1,000_{55} + 1,000_{60} + 1,000_{64})$. Once this is done it is clear that the sum is not $3,000_{65}$. It is not 3,000 dollars of any particular year; and in representing the total as $3,000 the cardinal error of adding unlike things will have been made. If, at the end of 1965, the firm had also $1,000 in cash, this amount is strictly $1,000_{65}$. But it makes no sense to add $1,000_{65}$ to $2,200 of unknown but mixed vintage; a second example of adding unlike things. Further there will have been deducted (in respect of asset A, for example) 50_{56}, 50_{57}, 50_{58} . . . 50_{65} from $1,000_{55}$, so that the depreciated value, $500, means nothing that we can readily grasp. This is a third example of the same kind of error, this time

subtracting unlike things. It is impossible to conceive that a balance sheet which is the resultant of such repeated fallacious addition and subtraction can mean anything sensible in 1965.

It may seem that this misrepresents the traditional and authoritatively endorsed accounting for such items. It is said that accounting for fixed assets subsists in writing off a proportionate part of the cost each year. Taking this view, in each year, in respect of asset A, the amounts written off through the income account were: in 1956, 50_{55}; in 1957, 50_{55} . . . in 1965, 50_{55}. In this case the asset balance will be 500_{55} in 1965. But then the charges made in the income accounts of successive years will have committed the same error as before. For the current revenues and outlays of 1965 will be in $_{65}$ while the depreciation charges will be 50_{55}, 50_{60} and 50_{64}. Further, the balances in the balance sheet will include cash $1,000_{65}$, asset A (net) 500_{55}, asset B 750_{60} and asset C 950_{64}; and to add these, as is done in balance sheets, is an example of the same fallacy.

It is thus demonstrated that the traditional practice, however simple and sensible it may seem on the surface, involves arithmetical fallacies at numerous points. These fallacies will never become apparent if we merely take the dogma of authorities for granted. The advancement of knowledge depends on finding out what is observed and observable as matters which have a clear impact on human action. In accounting it is useless merely to observe what accountants do; it is necessary to show that the results of what they do have a clear connection with the kinds of action people take and with the attainment of the ends they pursue. It is easy to say people do act upon financial statements; but if it is shown that the very processes used in deriving those statements are fallacious, then it follows that the actions of users are misdirected by the information given in the statements.

Accounting and its products can be of little use unless all of the changes which take place in the financial position or condition of a firm are fully represented as they occur, so that the contemporary position at any time, in terms of current prices, is continuously discoverable. Only such a continuously contemporary accounting can arm managers and investors to meet the possibilities they foresee or the exigencies which external circumstances impose on them.[2]

Facts, Opinions and Judgments

Some things are matters of opinion, others are matters of fact. Whether a face, a figure, or a flower is beautiful, is a matter of opinion. As it is said "Beauty is in the eye of the beholder". But before any opinion can be expressed there must be some face, figure or flower in contemplation; a present or recollected fact or set of factual configurations which give rise to the opinion. If, however, an opinion is to be formed about something which cannot be brought directly to the inspection, there is the possibility that a representation made by some intermediary may serve. There is also the possibility that the intermediary may distort the original by the way in which he represents it. The tricks of perspective used by cameramen can make what is naturally beautiful in the eye of a direct beholder seem ludicrous or abhorrent to the beholder of a photograph.

The relation of accounting to the users of accounting statements is the relation of a representation of the financial characteristics of a firm to persons who must form an opinion about those characteristics of the firm. No manager of or investor in a firm can have the whole of the firm before him for direct observation. He must rely on a representation of it, or a successive series of representations. The opinions to be formed of the firm will be of no avail to managers or investors unless the representations are factual. And if they are factual they will be of equal value to all who must form opinions of the firm—managers, investors, creditors, trustees for secured creditors, potential investors and creditors and all.

The necessity of such a factual foundation for opinions seems to have been quite lost to sight by accountants. Of this there are several clear strands of evidence.

First, there is a relatively recently developed notion to the effect that different users of information need different kinds of information, for they have different points of view. Certainly different persons may have different points of view. But this applies as between different shareholders just as much as between, say, a shareholder and a creditor. Some shareholders may become disposed to sell, others to buy, others to hold, when they become aware of a company's results and position. No accountant can possibly tell which shareholders will do which. Clearly a seller, if he had any say in the matter, would want the best possible "face" presented by the company, while a buyer (who is a shareholder already) would want the worst possible "face" presented, if each is to make the best of his bargains. If the accountant has any latitude in the "view" he will present, there is no way in which he can determine which shareholders to favour at any time. The same applies to the juxtaposition of, say, shareholders and creditors. Suppose there were published a "shareholders' financial statement" and a "creditors' financial statement", both on different principles, for that surely is what "different kinds of information" must mean. A shareholder who was also a debenture-holder would be in a quandary. He would not know which to believe, particularly if both statements have an auditor's report to the effect that a true and fair view was given. The problems raised by the notion in question are insoluble. They do not even arise if it is understood that users of financial statements want factual statements. They are pseudo-problems and should be seen to be absurdities.

Second, there is the view that accountants, and auditors, are entitled to accept the opinions of man-

agement on the values placed on various classes of assets. Now it may be a fact that managers hold the opinions that they say they hold. Notice, however, that the audit report appended to financial statements does not say anything in affirmation of the managers' holding of such opinions. It purports to assert something about the representation of the results and position of the company, not something about the managers' opinions about the results and position of the company. The opinions managers hold are personal to them. They may be optimistic or pessimistic. But optimism and pessimism alike are attitudes towards the future and should have no bearing whatever on what has passed nor on the representation of what has passed. No one would take seriously the claim by a manager that his firm had sold $100,000 worth of goods when in fact he got only $70,000 for them. There is equally no good reason for taking a manager's opinion on the value of inventories and other assets *unless*, of course, his opinion coincides with some independently ascertained values or prices. It is the accountant's and auditor's business to find out whether or not there are such coincidences. If there are, if the representations are based directly or indirectly on present market prices, then it is reasonable to regard them as facts, and not manager's opinions. There is another side to this question. The financial statements are indications of how the management of a firm has been able to make out against the market places in which the firm operated. To allow managers to influence the score-keeping process is surely curious when their performance against the firm's markets is one of the things on which the users of financial statements would like to have facts on which to form their own opinions.

Third, there is the view that the audit report is after all only an opinion, and that all the auditor is required to do is to assert whether the view given of the results and the state of affairs of the company is a true and fair view in his opinion. There seems to have arisen some confusion over the significance of the audit requirement. The auditor is not called upon to say anything about his opinion of the company. He is required only to say something about the relationship of the representations to the facts. Users of financial statements want an assurance that the representations are fair representations of facts. Given the facts they will form their opinions. The emphasis given to opinion either has stemmed from, or has lent weight to, the view that the individual monetary representations of *specific* items in accounting statement are only opinions. On this matter many have spoken simultaneously with two voices. While asserting the influence of opinion and judgment they have, at the same time, upheld the notions of objectivity and of independence on the auditor's part. But worse still, we are now being told by many that financial statements should have more components of the nature of opinions and less in the nature of objective statements of fact. Nearly all proposals which involve taking account of the possibilities of the future rather than of the actualities of the past are of this kind.

The counting of cash, the custody of negotiable documents, the physical counting of inventories, the inspection of plant, the examination of title deeds, and so on, are all steps designed to secure that at least some elements of the components of financial statements are matters of fact and not of opinion. No one supposes that, if a check of physical inventories disagrees with the perpetual inventory, one or both of the figures is a matter of opinion; an attempt is made to discover which is factual. Yet, when it comes to putting a monetary measure on such inventories the same recourse on what is factual at the time is generally forgone. The most obvious case is the use of initial purchase price for marketable securities when there is a discoverable market price. Accountants and auditors are in no doubt at all that the goods physically possessed at one time are not necessarily those physically possessed at another. Why they are not equally sure that the *prices* of goods possessed at one time are not necessarily the prices which should be applied to the same goods at another time is hard to see; especially when their real knowledge and expertise is supposed to lie in the direction of monetary, not physical, calculation and representation.

In saying all this I am not saying there is no place for opinion or judgment. I am only saying that the accountant—like the artist, the pianist, the engineer, the surgeon—can have opinions in the practice of his art only within limits. The limits are imposed by knowledge of the media with which he works and the ideal function his product performs. If he disregards these he is no more skilful, for all his opinions, than a mere layman. He must know that people need factual statements as indicators of progress; and when the facts are hard to get he must perforce exercise his judgment about what he will consider as best approximations.

If he is an auditor he must exercise his judgment about the steps others have taken to get at the facts. He is not called upon to say whether the results and the position of a firm are true and fair; he is required to say whether they are truly and fairly *represented* by the statements. He will never see this as his task if he supposes there are many true and fair views, all matters of opinion.

Wholes and Their Parts

In the ordinary course of living we deal with most things as wholes. We deal with automobiles, business firms, accounting systems as wholes. For most purposes this concern with wholes is sufficient. However, if we hold out to be expert in any matter we need a much more exact knowledge, otherwise we are prone to take superficial appearances for substantial reality. For about two thousand years men classified the inert substances with which they were familiar on the basis of appearances—as earths, liquids and airs, or as metals, salts,

acids and bases. Modern chemistry differs from pre-eighteenth century chemistry because the practice of thinking of things only as wholes was abandoned, and wholes were understood in terms of their constituents and the ways in which they combined. There seems good reason to suppose that accounting may make similar distinctive advances if attention were directed to the understanding of wholes in terms of the constituents.

We have all heard of going concerns, and the valuation of assets on a going concern basis. But hardly anywhere is there a discussion of what "going" means. We think generally of a going concern as a whole, but without consideration of its processes. We distinguish going concern values from values under forced liquidation, but without considering the processes by which forced liquidation is avoided.

Consider this. We are told that durable assets should be valued on a going concern basis, and that that basis is cost, or initial purchase price. Now from time to time a going concern must change its asset holdings. To think of the possibilities managers must know what its holdings are in cash or the equivalent of cash, that is to say cash and the resale prices of its non-cash holdings. Initial price is quite irrelevant. A going concern may borrow on the collateral security of its assets. To think of the possible extent of such borrowings managers must know the resale prices of its assets. Initial price is quite irrelevant. A going concern will seek to insure itself against the loss or destruction of its assets. The direct amount of any such loss is the resale price of the asset. Initial price is quite irrelevant. A going concern will seek to secure itself against illiquidity; but if illiquidity threatens, it will keep the resale prices of its several assets under notice so that any necessary sale of assets involves the least expected sacrifice. Initial price is quite irrelevant. Instances of these component elements of "going" could be multiplied. In no case is the initial purchase price or cost basis of valuation relevant. The view that it is relevant can be upheld only if we think of "going" as a whole process and disregard the constituent elements of it.

Consider an example from quite a different phase of accounting. For a long time accountants have been accustomed to regard unit product cost as a significant figure. Again, notice it is a whole. But how significant is it? Its components are a measured and priced amount of labour and materials (suppose they are directly measured). They include a proportionate part of direct supervisory costs (what part depends on the total of all other actual or expected operations under the same supervisory unit, so that it is not unique to the product). In addition there is a proportionate part of an amount spent, perhaps long ago, on the plant or machinery used (what part depends on the depreciation period and formula adopted, so that it is not unique to the product.) Also included is a proportionate part of indirect supervisory and managerial costs (what part depends on the total of all operations of the firm and the formula adopted for allocating these costs, so that it is not unique to the product). Moreover, there may be other allocations or subdivisions of those mentioned. The addition of these several components cannot possibly give a figure which is significant for the product or any decision in respect of it. The view that a total unit cost is relevant can be upheld only if we fail to consider the dubious quality of its constituents.

For a third example we allude to decision-making. The phrase is so commonly used without elaboration that there can be little doubt that its users think of it as a whole. But no one "just decides". Deciding is difficult; we often prefer to avoid it. There are several distinct components of a decision. First there are at least two possible courses from which a choice is to be made. Second, there are different expected pay-offs, to be calculated for each course by time intervals and discounted to present values. Third, there are different judgments about the relationship between the present values and the timing of pay-offs. One may prefer to lower present value if there are other valued elements in the timing of pay-offs. Fourth there is a stake, either common to the possible courses of action, or different as between them, in which case there will be further judgments about the source or the employment of the difference between the stakes. There may be other such elements. We can understand the process and the role of accounting in it only if we spell out its constituents. Every reference to choice, expectation and judgment in the preceding sentences implies managerial choice, expectation or judgment. Apart from the mere arithmetical processes of formally calculating pay-offs, the major role of accounting is to provide contemporary measures of the cash equivalents of assets, so that the choice of assets making up any particular stake in any actual situation requiring decision or choice is simplified.

The purport of these examples is simply to suggest that close analysis will yield insights which the superficial recognition of wholes will never give. We have scarcely begun the task of examining analytically the concepts and processes we employ or could employ.

Experience, Education and Research

Some may say, in response to the points that have been made, that a long tried and accepted form of accounting must have proved its worth in the world of business. But of course some said the same of the horse and buggy, which only goes to show that our experiences may confirm our prejudices. But we can also learn from experience, or rather from reflecting on our experiences. We learn from our experiences if, on reflection, we find confirmation or contradiction of the views we hold in the consequences of holding them.

Now all of our experiences of getting and spending money converge on two simple ideas. We can always acquire things we want but do not have up to the full extent of the sum of money we have and the prices we can get for the nonmonetary things we

have. And, the extent to which we judge ourselves to be better off financially from time to time is given by the changes in the purchasing power of the sum of money we hold and the contemporary prices of the nonmonetary things we hold as between two points of time. There is nothing in all our experience of getting and handling money and goods which contradicts these propositions. Yet, the accounting that is presently done for firms large and small contradicts them both. There is nothing in all our experience which leads us to believe that by adding quantities of unlike things we can get a total which has a sensible meaning. Yet accounting makes no attempt to reduce the unlike dollars spent over years by firms to a common and contemporary likeness.

We cannot pause here to inquire why practices which are contrary to all experience of a commercial or financial kind should have persisted.[3] We see their persistence merely as a roadblock in the path of progress, and are more concerned with their removal than their explanation. Their removal and the substitution of practices which accord more closely with experience may be expedited if we each will critically question the propriety of the rules we employ, and submit them to the test of our own personal experiences. After all, some other person or persons will use the results. If we, too, are persons, and not automata, what is common sense to us in our own dealings is very likely to appear to be common sense to others in theirs. No doubt many are afraid to use their common sense, otherwise we would have had changes before this. This suggests a second way of expediting improvement.

You may know that it has become a habit in recent years to present in the early stages of textbooks, college and university courses, what are called the conventions of accounting. These conventions are almost entirely inconsistent with the facts of financial and commercial dealings and many of them are self-contradictory.[4] Perhaps it is because they are so incomprehensible that they have some mystic hold over their expositors, and hence over the students to whom they are expounded and who subsequently become practitioners. We could well do with less of this mysticism and with more of the realities instead; less servility in the face of doctrinaire teaching and more courageous common sense.

There seems to be a view abroad that advanced education should be directed to giving a greater number of snippets of knowledge—a course in psychology, a course in mathematics, a course in statistics, a course in high-speed morons—in the hope that this will "broaden" the outlook and comprehension of accountants. But snippets of knowledge will not advance understanding and wisdom. What is much more to the point is an intensive analysis of the bits and pieces of accounting on the one hand and a careful study of how, in intimate detail, these and their products fit into the deliberative processes of those who use them. Students, and practitioners too, need to consider the immediate and less immediate effects of following out the rules

on managers, bankers, investors, trustees, other accountants, and, in a wider framework still, their effects on
the distribution of the command of the community's
resources between the more efficient and the less
efficient users of capital. There have been quite a few
"new looks" at accounting education in recent years.
But almost all seem to be directed to the production of
starry eyed encyclopedists rather than to the production
of well disciplined experts able to spot logical and
practical flaws because of their intensive study of what
has been done and is being done, and their comprehension of the effects of these things on individuals, industries and the economy as a whole.

The only comprehensive way in which the managers and investors and public men of a community
may keep under observation the shifts in efficiency of
firms is by recourse to financial statements which represent, with the least possible fuzziness, the results and
standing of firms. Accounting done on the varied and
often irrelevant bases described in most textbooks will
not yield financial statements which are comparable as
between firms. We would not tolerate clocks and
watches, speedometers, foot rules and similar devices
which yield inconsistent indications. There is equally
no reason why we should tolerate accounting rules or
systems which produce figures which are not comparable. There seems to be good ground for believing that
the inadequacies of accounting in this respect have
much to do with the general efficiency of industry.
Educational programmes which have no provision for
analysing these consequences in depth are unlikely to
produce the consciousness of defects which is the pre-
cursor to progress.

There is a third direction in which improvement may
be expedited: by research. Research is a relatively new
thing to accounting, and there can be little doubt that
its character is poorly understood. I take but one example of this. It has become the thing to establish
research committees. Numerous associations in different
countries have done this, and I would not wish to
belittle the good intentions of the promoters of these
committees nor the labours, often prodigious, of those
who compose them. Nevertheless by the standards of
other fields of enquiry, much, if not most, of the work
of these people is misdirected. You have never heard
of the committee to discover the laws of gravitation, or
of the committee to develop the periodic table of the
elements, or of the committee to establish the circulation of the blood, or of the committee to transmute
nitrogen into oxygen. But you have heard of NEWTON
and MENDELEEF and HARVEY and, perhaps especially,
of RUTHERFORD. You could name scores of such names,
honoured in the annals of human inquiry for their
researches. Why individual names? Because research is
a painstaking and individual affair. Researchers are men
who see anomalies—real world events and things which
do not fit into the accepted frameworks of thinking of
their time. They are puzzled, individually puzzled. They
are impelled to ask why the facts do not fit the ideas

men hold. They are not concerned to brush anomalies
aside, not content to go along with generally accepted
principles. They are concerned to inquire diligently into
the characteristics of the anomalies they observe, to
assure themselves that their apprehensions are not in
error, and if necessary to propose reconstructions of the
ideas men hold. Only individuals can bring to bear
the concentrated attention over long periods, on the
facts they observe and on the then accepted ideas of their
peers — attention which yields new insights, new
knowledge. In our time you will hear of committees to
finance research of one kind or another; but the in-
dividualistic character of research remains. Committees
may evaluate; it has never been shown that they can
originate.

There is no reason to believe that accounting is
different in this respect from anything else. The expert
accounting community may do much to help in the
direction of encouraging individual initiative. But it
will do so only if it is realised that the pursuit of
knowledge is an open-ended exercise, and that the
fruits of research are, in their nature, likely to be dis-
ruptive of established ways of thinking. If we take
seriously, instead of trying to rationalise, the observable
defects of traditional modes of accounting and of thinking about accounting, we shall welcome this disruption,
for it is the sign of vitality in any field.

To Progress or to Dream?

There have not been lacking, in the history of accounting, people who exposed what they believed to be
errors in conception and practice. It is just one month
short of forty years since HATFIELD pointed out to the
American Institute of Accountants that in argument and
practice accountants are "illogical, inconsistent and vacil-
lating"; that they "rely on reiteration in lieu of argument"; that the vagrant usage of different terms for
significant conceptions constitutes "the chief defect in
accounting". Much the same could be said today. In
1929 CANNING pointed out that accountants have no
clear concept of income, or of financial position. Much
the same could be said today. In 1936, after some ten or
so years of study of the problem, SWEENEY pointed out
the folly of treating all dollars as the same through time.
The practice persists. In 1939, MACNEAL treated at
length the misleading character of the products of
traditional accounting practices. The same practices are
still with us. And there have been other critics before
and since.

There have also been dreamers. Some are convinced that all accounting is good accounting; that if
there are faults they are due to the naughtiness of some
accountants (or some managers), not to flaws in accounting. Some are convinced that there's nothing wrong with
accounting; that there is only something wrong with
what people expect of it; and that this can be cured
by re-educating the commercial community. However,
it is noticeable that they have never been able to get
such a re-education process started. Some do not worry

about present defects: they look into their crystal balls and see the "accountant of the future" all decked out with knowledge of computers, linear programming, communication theory, higher mathematics and total information systems to his fingertips.

But flights of fancy are only escapist. What the dreamers fail to see is that ostensible defects will be removed only by assiduous re-examination of present thought and practice, by taking them apart and re-shaping their component ideas so that they conform with the way in which business is done and the need for factual information of those who do business. It is possible to delimit the accounting process, and to define asset, equity, financial position, income, cost and so on in a much more rigorous way than is generally done. It is possible to link into a coherent system the many concepts necessary for the full development of the subject—to link financial accounting, cost accounting, auditing as between themselves and to link them with the processes of appraisal, evaluation and choice of managers and financial supporters of firms. Nevertheless, at almost every step the traditional definitions and the vague ideas of linkages must be abandoned or substantially modified. There is nothing new in this. Many advances in other fields have necessitated the development of a whole set of new meanings for old terms, a new language in effect. The result may seem strange. However, its test

will lie in whether or not the resulting system of ideas is more fruitful in practical terms, and logically more coherent (more understandable) than the system it purports to replace.

The reconstruction of ideas on the basis of our unfolding experiences, the reconstruction of ideas through modifications in educational patterns, and the reconstruction of ideas through the work of researchers—all may converge on the improvement of thought and practice. By this stage in the twentieth century there have been enough disturbing experiences, and there is enough consciousness of the necessity of better education, and enough recognition of the need for research, to provide an excellent springboard for diving into the 'seventies. Only timidity or overriding respect for the habits of the past stand in the way of notable advances. The looseness, illogicality and irrelevance of much accounting is obvious to many, and is on the way to becoming notorious. The only question is whether the profession wishes to take a positive part in the advancement of practice and thought, or whether it prefers to wait until circumstances and pressures from beyond its ranks force improvement on it. That is a question the profession will have to ask and answer for itself in the near future, and almost certainly before the end of the next decade.

FOOTNOTES

(1) See for example W. I. B. BEVERIDGE, *The Art of Scientific Investigation*, New York, Random House, 1957, Ch. III and Appendix. R. TATON, *Reason and Chance in Scientific Discovery*, New York, Science Editions, 1962.

(2) The grounds for such an accounting and the method of deriving such accounting statements are dealt with at length in the author's *Accounting, Evaluation and Economic Behaviour* (Prentice Hall, 1966).

(3) A brief survey is given in *Accounting, Evaluation and Economic Behaviour*, Ch. 14.

(4) An examination of some of them was made in R. J. CHAMBERS' "Conventions, Doctrines and Common Sense", *The Accountants' Journal*, February 1964.

99

Consolidated Statements Are Not Really Necessary

THE question, to which the title of this note is the answer, has long since ceased to be asked. Consolidated statements have become part of the paraphernalia of accounting and reporting. But they seem to be the wrong solution to the problem from which they arose.

The problem is this. A company, A, which controls another, B, may direct B to buy from A or sell to A any goods at any prices it fixes. A may oblige B to lend to or borrow from A any sums it wishes on any terms it wishes. A may secure that B declares dividends in any amounts it wishes, or that it declares no dividends (within the constraints of the general law on dividends and of contracts with outsiders). In consequence of these things the financial position of B at any time and its results for any preceding intervals are at the discretion of A. Further A could have paid to original owners of B any consideration it deemed fit, either greater or less, by large or small amounts, than the market prices of the net assets acquired; and after the acquisition of B it could acquire new shares of B for any consideration it deemed fit.

The legal balance sheet of a holding company would show among the assets its shares in subsidiaries, but this would give no clue as to the nature of the assets of subsidiaries, whatever the basis used for valuing those assets. Any person relying on the legal balance sheet would not know whether the assets represented by the investment in the subsidiaries were real estate, or cash, or intangibles or what combination of these. It seemed reasonable, therefore, to give to shareholders in holding companies some idea of the ultimate investments of the subsidiaries in legal rights and tangible goods; and we accept the merit of this.

One solution, still legally available, is to give the separate balance sheets and profit and loss accounts of subsidiaries as annexures to the financial statements of the holding company as such. But this is cumbersome, particularly for a company with many subsidiaries. It also imposes severe burdens on the patience and ingenuity of any person who wishes to trace the assets which in some sense are represented by the shareholdings of the holding company in the subsidiaries.

The solution preferred by many is the preparation of consolidated statements which eliminate inter-company security holdings and inter-company transactions and the profits therefrom. We contend that this is a solution which confuses some things and does not elucidate others.

First, assets and equities (liabilities and shareholders' rights in assets) can only have a sensible meaning in relation to some legal entity which can own properties and incur obligations. The only such entities of this kind are natural persons and corporations. A holding company and its subsidiaries, as a complex, is not an entity of this kind. To suppose it is, is to depend on a fiction; and to depend on a fiction seems to invite confusion.

Second, for the above reason consolidated balance sheets and consolidated profit and loss accounts are not balance sheets and profit and loss accounts in any ordinary sense of those terms. To use the same words of the two different kinds of statements—of a legal entity and of a non-legal entity — is again to invite confusion. The use of the same words predisposes readers to make the same kinds of inferences from consolidated statements as from the proper statements of a legally competent entity; but such inferences are strictly illegitimate.

101

These two points have to do with the basic nature of the entity reported upon and the general significance of any statements embodied in such reports. But the greatest difficulties have to do with the specific significances of statements embodied in balance sheets and profit and loss accounts.

We have argued at length elsewhere that only if financial statements are in contemporary terms are they of any use to shareholders and creditors, either as indicators of past performance, or of present financial position, or of the possibilities of future growth or adaptation.[1] By statements in contemporary terms we mean statements in which assets are represented at current prices or the best possible approximation thereto. The case for doing this is not argued here. We will merely assert what seems to be self-evident: that rates of return, measures of solvency and measures of the relative interests of shareholders and creditors in the assets of a firm, are useless as guides unless they are based on prices ruling at or about the time at which financial statements are prepared.

Suppose that such a system of continuously contemporary accounting were in general use. Whatever assets were represented as those of a subsidiary company in its own accounts would be represented at their contemporary prices. Liabilities would be of known amount. The difference between the aggregate of the measures of the assets and the aggregate amount of the liabilities would be the measure of the shareholders' equity in the assets. [For simplicity we assume a wholly owned subsidiary having only one class of shares.] Only if this difference — the measure of net assets — is used in calculations relating to the financial position and results of the company will the results of the calculations be significant. No calculation using par values of the shares or the prices paid for them in the past will yield significant figures. Clearly, then, in the balance sheet of the holding company, the amount to be shown as the amount *then* invested in the shares of subsidiaries will be the amount of the net assets of the subsidiaries, which will be the same as the sum of the net assets shown on the faces of the balance sheets of the subsidiaries.

Now we have already accepted the merit of giving shareholders in holding companies some idea of the composition of the assets and equities of subsidiaries. This is readily achieved by giving, as annexures to the financial statements of the holding company, simple aggregative statements of the assets and liabilities and profit and loss account items of all the subsidiaries. These statements would be in the same general form as those of the holding company; and, for the purpose of disclosing what the statutes regard as necessary, they would contain aggregates of the specific items required by the statutes to be disclosed by holding companies as companies.

Where for any good reason it is deemed desirable to distinguish subsidiaries which are to some extent dissimilar, separate aggregate figures for the two classes could be given in the same form in separate columns. The two classes of subsidiaries referred to would generally be (i) those operating in the same country and under the same disclosure rules as the holding company, and (ii) those operating in other countries which permit the use of different accounting principles and those operating in countries whose fiscal policies or economic conditions may interfere with the holding company's rights to repatriate dividends or capital.

In the annexures, the aggregate equities would be subdivided into equities of the holding company and of outsiders, and these would be further broken down into obligations on current account, long-term liabilities, and equities arising from shareholdings. To the extent that any of these are assets of the holding company they would appear, identical in amount, in the balance sheet of the holding company. If, for any reason peculiar to class (ii) subsidiaries of the previous paragraph, the figures carried into the holding company's balance sheet were different from those

1. R. J. Chambers, *Accounting Evaluation and Economic Behavior*, Englewood Cliffs, Prentice-Hall, Inc., 1966, *passim*.

shown in the annexures, the difference would require to be explained. Where some subsidiaries earned profits and others made losses, the aggregate amounts of profits and losses would be shown, for the annexures are simply summarizations of the several statements of subsidiaries without any set-offs.

In the above brief outline we have omitted reference to many of the problems which the consolidation solution raises. Some of them simply disappear under the proposed alternative. But some indication of the reason for their disappearance may be warranted.

There is no necessity to eliminate inter-company profits. If assets are valued at a year's end at contemporary market prices, any over- or under-pricing (by reference to market prices) of inter-company sales will simply inflate the profits of one and deflate the profits of another company. However biased the inter-company pricing, its effects wash out at the end of the period; the valuation rule, current market prices, itself washes out intra-group profits. If, of course, the inter-company transactions have left one company better off than it might have been but for an "artificial" transfer price, that is merely the consequence of the transaction. It would be false to the facts to say or imply afterwards (as is implied by elimination on consolidation) that the actual transfer price was not the price.

There is no problem of splitting transactions to eliminate that part of the profit on an inter-company transaction which constitutes the holding company's proportion where there is a minority interest in a subsidiary. In consolidation accounting this is a highly artificial exercise, and its effect is false to the legal consequences of such transactions.

There is no problem of the continuous inflation of values as one company sells merchandise to another down a line of subsidiaries or as one company sells securities to another up the line. Assets are always brought to contemporary market prices at a year's end; and as the measure of equities is the measure of net assets, the measure of equities is also reduced at the year's end, if during any year shares have been issued for greater nominal amounts than the market prices of the assets acquired.

The consolidation solution has given rise to debate about the possibility of showing which subsidiaries have made profits and which have made losses. The debate is almost pointless as long as it is permissible to carry assets (of any company in a complex) at cost; for as between any two companies in a complex the amount charged by one to another may be quite arbitrary. But if current market prices are used at the year's end and the contents of the annexures are simple aggregations of the figures of subsidiaries, the amounts of profits *and* losses will be shown. This seems to be quite sufficient. For at the least it puts readers of the statements on notice of these amounts so that they can demand any elucidation they require; and to insist upon greater detail, as a matter of course, may well lead to obscuring the vision of readers rather than to their enlightenment.

It must be apparent that, as long as companies are permitted to use any one of the vast range of asset valuation methods now current, and insofar as companies within a complex employ different methods, the exercise of consolidation is a purely arithmetical one. There is, for example, no clear meaning that can be given to the sum of amounts for inventories for one company on an average-cost basis and for another on a lower-of-cost-and-market basis; the addition of such amounts is illegitimate. Whether or not any accountant or auditor confronted with such aggregates feels any uneasiness, or the obligation to make any adjustment or notation to bring such diverse magnitudes to a common footing, is not known. But the question is not raised as a significant issue in the literature.

The problem does not arise in the suggested alternative. For its basis is the valuation of assets at something approaching contemporary prices; and in principle contemporary prices are always aggregable and a clear meaning can be assigned to the aggregate. This problem is at least one of the problems which should exer-

103

cise the judgment of auditors of parent companies and consolidated statements. But if accounting were required to yield statements embodying contemporary prices of assets, all auditors could be expected to exercise similar kinds of judgment on the extent to which the figures represented the contemporary facts. One of the difficulties, and quite possibly most of the difficulties, which are commonly discussed under the caption, the auditor and the group concept, would disappear.

The suggestion that consolidated statements be abandoned in favour of aggregative annexures in the nature of explanatory notes may not be easy to accept. Consolidated statements have been accepted for about sixty years, notwithstanding the fact that their justification has required quite a deal of verbal gymnastics. In the same way so many other devices which are now questioned have arrived. The present writer has been as guilty as anyone else in perpetuating the acceptance of the consolidation solution. But it now seems that the alternative is much more easy to defend on logical and practical grounds, and that the result is far more comprehensible and realistic than the product of the consolidation process.

104

"Horizons for a Profession"*

Horizons for a Profession bears as its sub-title "The Common Body of
Knowledge for Certified Public Accountants". The Commission through
which the report was prepared has the same terms in its title. In the
letter of transmittal it is said that "it became evident that it would be
futile to attempt to compile a specific inventory as of a specific point
of time". Hence "we hopefully project guidelines into the challenging
future".

The report seems to play fast and loose with time. The letter says:
"Had such a report been presented ten years ago, how obsolete it would be
today". We seem to be invited to accept the conclusions of the report as
for a timeless future. If a report presented ten years ago would be
obsolete today, there seems to be no reason to suppose that a report
presented today will not be obsolete ten years hence. There is indeed no
way at all of overcoming the obsolescence of ideas. To attempt to do so
by projecting into an unspecified future is "futile" unless we first
attempt to find what is the specific inventory today.

The letter lays the responsibility on named groups of people "to
translate this study into positive action". Presumably now. Projecting
guidelines into the future, presumably also means projecting from now.
But as every ameliorative action depends on doing something different
from and better than what is now done, the antecedent step to any such
action is unquestionably to discover what is done now, to analyse its
shortcomings, and to state specifically what may be done to remove them.
This way of proceeding is not a prescription for any particular
discipline; it is a universal. But it is extraordinary to find no
attempt whatever to proceed from what is presently discoverable about
what knowledge is now required and where in practice it is inadequate.
If it is not inadequate in some specific identified ways, there can be no
way whatever of deciding whether the prescription of the report meets
those inadequacies.

---

* R.H. Roy and J.H. MacNeil, Horizons for a Profession, American
  Institute of Certified Public Accountants, 1967. From a note
  transmitted to The Director of Examinations, American Institute
  of Certified Public Accountants, August, 1968.

Research. The adequacy of the report may perhaps best be tested at the highest points it reaches. The key to advances in knowledge lies in the competence of its researchers. Research demands a special chapter.

Here we are told: "Accounting is a man-made art and accounting research must be in the realm of ideas, not in the realm of nature, as in medicine and engineering". This distinction is at best misleading, at worst quite false. Medicine and engineering and other applied arts have their foundations in observable phenomena: so also should accounting, and any other man-made art - using "art" as the authors have used it, of a class of formal exercises or endeavors related to some form of substantive behavior. But the researchers in medicine and engineering convert their apperceptions of observed phenomena into conceptions, which are ideas. I imagine any researcher in medicine or engineering would be quite affronted by the suggestion that he dealt with "things" not with ideas.

The paragraph continues: "Thus, the `truth´ in inventory valuation has never been discovered, nor will any `solution´ be found through research and discovery; there is no `unknown´ to be sought, nor any likelihood that the brain of some budding genius will suddenly provide the long awaited key to unlock the mystery". This must surely sound the death-knell for the hopes of many, if not for research altogether. Given that density, tensile strength and coefficient of expansion are three properties of a metal, presumably there is in engineering some way of deciding which must be used with reference to a particular problem. If there is not, we should entrust no problem to engineers, for they will be likely to tell us a ship will float merely by consideration of the coefficient of expansion of the metal used in its hull. The inventory problem is no different. But if the authors would dismiss such obviously pertinent problems as inventory valuation with the remark that no amount of research will resolve them, one might expect that they would say what problems could be solved by research. They mention none. In fact they go on to refer favorably to journals which carry articles which attempt to solve such problems as inventory valuation! Which says something either against the superficiality of the above quotation or against the superficiality of examination of the cited journals.

The paragraph continues: "Accounting research must be philosophical or methodological, must revolve around such questions as fairness, utility, relevance, equity, questions to which there are no `right´ answers". Why must accounting research revolve around such questions? We are given no reason. If there are no `right´ answers to such questions, they are certainly not the kinds of question worth asking, worth researching. I have not yet heard that any researcher has wasted his time trying to discover whether an atom of iron is green. But if accounting research **must** revolve around these questions to which there is no right answer, what use can possibly be made of the mathematics which the authors are so keen to foist on accountants and researchers? If there is no `right´ answer, no discussion is possible of degrees of error, no possible use can be made of statistics or probability theory or any other of the mathematical devices the report refers to!

We are told that "most of the research conducted under sponsorship of the professional societies and the firms deals with the intractable problems faced by accountants". We are floored again: if the problems are intractable, research is hopeless, futile. Again: "The instability of the unit of measurement creates problems to which there are no easy or single answers". This first of all misstates the problem: the unit of measurement has been a dollar for a long time; so it is not the unit that is unstable, but some feature of it. Then it goes on to say there are no easy or single answers, where the "are" is used in the present continuous sense. Researchers presumably should give up trying to find a single answer or an ideal one.

Expression. At what might be thought the most trivial level the report might be judged on its literary quality. A reader of the report might think this a less than trivial test for the quality of written and oral English is repeatedly stated to be of importance.

In any case the report is liberally spiced with ambiguous statements, cliches, non-sequiturs and grammatical solecisms. Only two will be noted. Repeatedly "methodology" is misused. In its strict usage – and strict usage should, we suppose, be respected by any document which goes on to deal with inquiry and research – methodology means the study of methods of inquiry as such, not to ways or methods of doing things. The authors use it in the latter sense: they speak of audit methodology, the numerous methodologies of accounting, quantitative methodologies, recurrent methodologies, meaning mathematical devices; there are scores of such uses. Not once have I found it used in the strict sense.

Repeated reference is made to "conceptual understanding". Is there any kind of understanding which is not conceptual? Or is conceptual introduced to distinguish the understanding of the real world by recourse to concepts from the understanding of concepts as such (whatever that may mean)? Infelicities abound; there might well be expected to be few in a document that speaks of the "style and cadence as well as content" of communications.

Non-accounting. The most noticeable feature of the exercise is the extent to which it branches out into matters which are not now considered to be the special province of accountants generally and which, in the light of the inevitable nature of specialization, may be considered to be even less the province of accountants in the future. A professional specialism usually becomes much more self-conscious as it develops; the looseness of the basic knowledge is brought under closer examination; new devices, sometimes borrowed sometimes invented, are brought to bear on **its** problems. By contrast, a vast amount of **Horizons** is directed not to the problems of accounting as such, but to the problems of accountants' clients, of business management, and so on.

The effect is twofold. One is left with the impression that there is no hard core of accounting, the content and methods of which need reexamination for the purpose of producing better specialists. And the diverse directions in which novices are expected to be trained gives the impression that accounting is just a thin slice of stuff to be served up with so much "dressing" that its presence is unnoticed.

Opinions may differ on what is meant by a common body of knowledge for CPAs. But it is almost certain that the same body of knowledge paraded in **Horizons** could be said to be necessary for every other kind of business school graduate besides CPAs.

The observations on accounting knowledge are superficial in the extreme. Apart from some brief observations about concepts and induction and deduction, there is no indication of what it is that entitles a body of propositions to be regarded as a body of knowledge. If a body of knowledge apposite to CPA's is to be distinguished, it might be expected that all peripheral studies would be tightly and logically related to the specific core of accounting. There is no such demonstration. In every case the only relationship suggested is the exiguous similarity, in what are often trifling respects, between accounting and other operations.

Accountants "deal with" formal organizations; they **should** know something about them – but the most crucial features for accountants are not even mentioned (they are the effects of technical specialization on internal communication). Accountants "deal with" numbers; they **should** know more about "quantitative methodologies" – but no reference is made to the peculiar problems of handling numbers of money units through time, except by the briefest allusion. Accountants "deal with" firms; they **should** know more microeconomics – but there is no reference to the sense in which this knowledge has any direct bearing on accounting.

On accounting specifically the impression is given that all is well – an impression which anyone familiar with the field should strenuously deny. It is said that the beginning CPA should know what is meant by the expression "generally accepted accounting principles", whereas numbers of knowledgeable accountants have asserted that they know of no such things. The observations on almost every one of the conceptions current among accountants – measurement, asset, periodicity, timeliness, objectivity, for example – gloss over the extent of the debate which surrounds them. There is no significant reference to the uniformity – diversity debate.

* * * * * * *

It is not likely that an inquiry will be undertaken of the same kind for a long time. But I believe it would be tragic if too much notice were taken of the suggestions **Horizons** contains. Accountants are already more apt to venture into neighboring territory than to sharpen up their own tools. To do so seems to me to be selling out their own proper business at a heavy discount.

The Linked Logics of Practice and Pedagogy*

I am concerned with the dissonance amongst accountants. It may be detected from the utterances of practitioners on teachers and teaching; from the utterances of teachers on practitioners and practice; and from the utterances of practitioners *as* practitioners and of teachers *as* teachers. Both classes, as it seems to me, have paid inadequate attention to some of the ineluctable circumstances and demands of their callings. Certainly some members of both classes are presently anxious about the prevailing relationship between teaching and practice. But anxiety is not enough. Without some deliberate analysis of the situation, anxiety will demand relief: and it may take the form, as it has done in the past, of diffuse effort in unrelated directions, leaving confusion worse confounded.

There are superficial signs of an *entente* between educational and professional people and organizations. The inhabitants of the city's towers are looking more than ever before for the products of the ivied towers. At least some teaching institutions, if not most, have felt they should give the city what it seems to want; in general, more of its own kind. But, in both cases, it is doubtful whether the wants are well-grounded. And, notwithstanding these superficial signs, there is still evidence of an uneasiness on both sides, amounting almost to disdain, which will, if it continues, establish nothing more than an artificial or transient bond; as if the product of the universities, graduates or ideas, were merely articles of commerce.

PREVAILING DISSONANCE

The impression of dissonance and disdain must be substantiated, if I am not to be put off by allegations to the effect that trifling differences are being over-emphasized.

Anyone who has paid attention to the writing of professional accountants will have noticed the almost total absence of references to the work of teachers and scholars. The subjects on which practitioners write are dealt with, often repeatedly and at length, by

teachers, sometimes in professional journals themselves, but more often in books and academic journals. But to read the articles of practitioners one would suppose either that there is not an academic literature at all, or that it is beneath notice. There is not much difference between disregard and contempt. Few, if any, practitioners are aware of the books and articles you and your colleagues have written, even in the recent past; or if some are aware, it is only vaguely; few are moved.

Practitioners are not entirely to blame for this; which brings me to the attitudes of academics. The same kind of example, the literary kind, can be given. Few academics write about the kinds of things practitioners do. They may write much about what they think practitioners do or ought to do, or about what practitioners individually or "by sample" say they do. But there are few studies of what practitioners actually do, notwithstanding the wealth of material available. On the other hand the number of articles loaded with polysyllabic persiflage and pedantry is large. On both counts practitioners are unlikely to find the work of academics interesting or instructive even if they know of its existence.

Another kind of indicator of the leaning of teachers away from practice and practices lies in the descriptions given by some of this task as they see it. It is not at all odd to hear: "We are not concerned with the details of practice; we are concerned to teach basic concepts and principles, with training the mind, with broadening the outlook" — and other such noble sentiments. It is held that this view is "in the interest of the intellectual development of the individual and the good of society" — whatever this means, for seldom is any attempt made to show how teaching in the manner so vaguely described will lead to the end envisaged. There is no avowed interest here in producing skilled and competent persons, able to assume leadership in a specified profession. The attitude shows no concern, indeed it shows some disdain, for the anxieties of a profession which, by the very actions of its members, shows that it wants the most competent people the teaching institutions can produce.

*Based on a paper presented at the Annual Conference of the Australian Association of University Teachers of Accounting, Newcastle, August 1968.

111

There is a contrasting type of attitude which may attract the passive disdain of practitioners. Teachers may be so anxious to please practitioners or so anxious to avoid criticism that they write and teach only the "conventional wisdom" which, as Galbraith observed, is always long out of date. Practitioners would certainly find the products of this formula comfortable, easy to live with — recruits who could parrot the words, phrases and rules which are familiar to eye and ear; addresses and articles which have a pure ritualistic function, to confirm beliefs in the rightness of what was learned ten, twenty, thirty years before. But neither the recruits nor the speeches and articles of their teachers would be worth any other notice by practitioners, certainly not the notice which presages leadership; for there is nothing in what the one learns and the other teaches that is not already old hat to the practitioner.

But we have said nothing yet about dissonance among teachers. There are few subjects on which teachers have so many divergent views as accounting. There are some who, misunderstanding the nature of the academic enterprise, see in this diversity a sign of vitality. There are others who see it as the effervescence of immaturity — not yet worth bottling. This is unfortunate; for while practitioners judge it thus they are unlikely to accept academic work as a guide to the advancement of the profession. But even if teachers contemplate their own bailiwick, diversity is unfortunate. If there is a common subject matter and if there is a common respect for the modes of discovery, demonstration and argument which workers in other disciplines respect, it is just not possible that there could be so many divergent doctrines as there now are.

THE COURSE OF LEARNING

It is commonly said that learning is a life-long process. There would be less agreement about what "learning" means in this context. To some, no doubt, it means the accumulation of factual knowledge; to others it may mean increasing the systematic understanding of the relationships between things; to some it may mean growth in general wisdom; some may think of learning as all of these things.

A child learns many things before school age: the names of persons and things — elementary exercises in the art of discriminating and classifying; the relationships between some persons, between some things and between some events — elementary exercises in causal and sequential relations. Primarily he wants to know what things are and how they can be used, in some sense or another. It would be foolish to try to tell him he was learning to discriminate, to classify and to sense causal and other relationships. But it is important that teachers recognize that this is, in fact, what is occurring.

In school some of this learning is formalized and extended. The child learns many more facts. If the teaching is well done the facts will be systematically arranged, so that the grasp of some will make easier the grasp of others. He learns something of the symbolic arts, language and arithmetic; something of the social arts, getting along with superiors, equals and inferiors; something of the use of tools and instruments. These are learned not merely from the descriptions of his teachers; they are learned the better by observing and doing himself — writing, computation, play and team sports, manual and experimental work. He learns that doing things in some ways will and in other ways will not produce results he expected or has been led to expect. He learns that there are easier, harder and useless ways of going about some things, particularly those things which have to do with physical objects. But at the same time he learns that some things can be done in many ways, no one of which can be said to be right or wrong because "tastes" differ. This applies to such things as literary expression, music, and the graphic arts, to forms of human interaction generally. We may distinguish the two differently structured kinds of learning we have just juxtaposed as formal-scientific and social-dramatic.

The general learning of elementary school continues into higher school. The child learns more facts, more of the art of discriminating and classifying, and more of causal relations. He learns how to draw conclusions himself from facts he is given or observes. He learns even by making mistakes. The effect of all of this school learning is to overlay the natural or instructive capacities and drives with something of the culture of the society in which he is to live. We speak of intellectual and social discipline; we mean that the child learns of the constraints he is expected to live within or work within if he is to live amicably among his fellows or work knowledgeably at a chosen task.

In technical school and university, studies become specialized. There are still facts to learn and skills to acquire and relationships to apprehend. But the student is approaching the age when he will have to face the world of affairs, where there are many more things related in much more complex ways than he has so far understood. The tasks and problems which he faces in his tertiary education begin to approach, in style and scope, the tasks and problems he will face as a technologist, a specialist, a professional in just a few years. From the tertiary stage he will emerge either as a specialist, skilful in a chosen, restricted art; or as an analyst and constructor, knowing a particular art and what it has to do with the world's affairs, and skilful in moulding that art to the complexities of scientific, economic, social or cultural realities. The tertiary educational institutions are expected to provide the kinds of learning experience which will serve these two kinds of person. There seems to be little doubt that that is what students expect; and little doubt that the institutions attempt to provide it.

But no school or university can hope to cope with the variety of experiences which a man will meet in his commercial or professional life. Whatever his understanding when he graduates, it is generally expected that it will grow as his knowledge and skill are confronted with more varied and more complex situations. However, growth in understanding is not inevitable. We must distinguish between advanced understanding and adroitness in problem-solving.

Because in the world of affairs there are no clear divisions similar to those of academic "subjects", there are few problems which may be resolved solely on the grounds of one kind of academic specialism. There are more compromise solutions than uniquely determinate solutions. We are always to some extent free to exercise tastes, free to weigh up or evaluate differently the several features of any problem or any solution to it. We are commonly short of time to find out all the facts pertinent to a problem, and to work out all the relationships between them. We are not even competent to deal with matters of which we have no specialist knowledge; we must choose whether to seek specialist advice or to try to get along with our lay knowledge. There are at least three kinds of reaction to complexity.

One may choose the role of problem-solver, simply. Even though he understands only moderately the field of knowledge he professes, he may be highly regarded among his associates. His reputation may depend much more on his apprehension of the state of the "polygon of personal forces and strategies" in problem situations, than on his understanding of his specialism and its function. A person adept at making "political" decisions, which will please or appease most people, or rock fewest boats, is not likely to acquire greater understanding of his professed specialism; for, by compromise at an early stage of any dispute, he will avoid placing his professional ideals and principles under rigorous test. He is unable to distinguish between what is a matter of principle and what is merely expedient.

A second kind of reaction is to fall back on the learned doctrine, or to avoid complexities by formulating rules which ignore them. The effect of both is to cut off the opportunity of learning from experience. For to learn by experience means to reconstruct one's knowledge in the light of new events, to see things differently as newly experienced events shift the weight of evidence from favouring old beliefs to the support of new beliefs.

A third kind of reaction is to attempt to face complexity, to use it to advance one's understanding. But a man will only advance his understanding of his technical or professional field, on passing from the hands of his teachers, if he has been shown clearly how his teachers and others have distinguished what is right from what is wrong. What is relevant from what is irrelevant, what is necessarily true from what is contingently true. He will only be able to carry on, in business life, the reshaping of his knowledge, if in his university years he has been shown clearly how the things he has been taught depend on things he can observe himself. In short, he must learn how to learn. Learning for himself entails the same kind of discriminating and classifying as he began to learn at an early age. But unless his higher education has brought explicitly to his notice the way in which generally useful notions emerge from particular instances, and the way in which choices are made between any two or more notions about the same object or event, his subsequent acts of discrimination and classification are likely to be short-sighted, or pedantic, and in both cases restrictive.

Certainly in university and in professional life he will (or should) meet problems which are more complex than in junior schooling. And he will (or should) find that specific problems are solved by the weighing up of many different kinds of potential consequence. But the necessity of compromise in specific situations does not mean that there is less need for sharp distinctions and clear apprehensions at the prior stage of reflection. We use our understanding to reflect upon problem situations before we turn our hands to meeting them. The more complex they are the greater the need for a clear sense of the principles their solutions depend on. And the greater the need for sufficient self-consistent principles to cover systematically the range of phenomena which do or may constitute such situations. For the grasp of complexity, only the most discriminating analysis of the diverse forms of experience will suffice.

Discriminating analysis does not mean footloose fantasy. To dream, to make believe, to suppose things to be otherwise than they are, is the fashion of children at play. The discipline of practical affairs leaves us much less freedom; we must take the world as we find it and do with it what we can. Intellectual discipline is not less constrained but more so. Whereas in any practical circumstance we may adopt what is or seems expedient, in the course of disciplined reflection expedience is the last resort. We seek to understand generalized situations, to derive general principles which will serve, as major premises, in any chain of reasoning about specific instances of a given class of situations. The incidental or contingent elements of specific instances are set aside. If in subsequent experience we meet particular circumstances, it is open to us to join major premises (the general rules of recurrent behaviour) with minor premises (the specific elements of those circumstances) and to deduce the action which, while conforming with general principles, is appropriate to the particular circumstances we are in.

Given the understanding of this relationship of the general principle to the specific act, one may hope, throughout his professional life, to go on learning whether or not the general principles he has espoused conform with the general character of experience, and to react positively to this learning rather than, in the manner of children at play, to brush aside the realities. Learning from experience can mean nothing more nor less fundamental than this. We must work within two kinds of boundary — the factual and the intellectually satisfying, or the logical. The exercise of the mature imagination is thus properly directed, not to the circumvention of problems by inventing a world in which they do not exist, but in the discovery of complete and consistent ways of resolving them.

This brief outline of the course of learning suggests several things.

THE OBJECT OF LEARNING

To begin at the end, the object of advanced learning and of professional experience is surely the one object: to advance the world's work by bringing to it, as well as technical expertise, a more intensive and sympathetic understanding of the relationship between one thing and others. Formal learning experiences should telescope the period which it takes to absorb a basic understanding of those relationships, thus extending the amount of time, out of a man's lifetime, which he can devote to the application of his learned skill and understanding, and to the advancement of both in the interest of his profession. There is no conflict between academia and the city in terms of ends.

Even this proposition, which seems innocuous enough, may give rise to dissent. Some will say that no amount of classroom tuition can be a substitute for real-world experience. This is confusing the part with the whole — on two scores. We did not suggest that the classroom can provide the distillate of all experience; only that it can provide the essence of some experiences, in concentrated form because it excludes in greater or lesser degree the contingent and peripheral components of those experiences. The classroom and the world are, in terms of ends, complementaries not substitutes. On the other hand the observation in question seems to presume that the real-world experience of any one man is superior to what can be conveyed in a classroom. Certainly in its totality a man's experience is richer than a classroom diet can be. But in respect of any particular subject matter the classroom diet can be far richer than one man's life-time experiences. For it is the proper function of the teacher to garner and digest the best of the experiences and ideas of many men. That some may do the garnering and digesting inefficiently is no argument against the principle.

Some will say that the function of the university is not to serve as a substitute for some part of practical experience, but to develop the mind by submitting it to an academic discipline or disciplines. This is an example of unnecessary discrimination, pedantry, hairsplitting. If "developing the mind" is anything but a cliché it means developing the capacity to identify the

connections between the substances of experience, the better to be able to choose wisely and deal swiftly. One who knows, or knows how to discover, the relationship between antecedents and consequents, between causes and effects, is the better able to choose wisely and to deal swiftly. If "discipline" means anything but jargon, it means the disciplined study of some objects or events, some real-world things. Certainly in the disciplined study of objects and events it may be necessary to resort to simplified examples. It may be necessary to contrive or to imagine that other things remain constant while one thing is examined. But observer, student and teacher alike are deluded if the simple or simplified instance is made or appears to be unreal. We study one thing at a time intensely the better to understand the real-world occurrence of it in varied forms and combinations. This is an eminently practical end, quite consistent, as we have said, with the ends of practitioners.

A second point which emerges from our outline of the course of learning is the role of exercises in the attainment of understanding. Again there is no necessary conflict between the work of the classroom and the work of the practitioner. But again there may be some dissents.

It is not uncommon to hear accountants complain that recruits are unable to handle what to them are the simplest kinds of practical exercise. Flaws in the mode of academic teaching may be responsible for this, in part; we return to the question presently. But the expectation that a recent graduate should be able to carry out any simple exercise places much too great a burden on the teaching institutions. There are numerous ways of doing many tasks in practice; the way in which a given practitioner (or his client) does a given job is to a large extent idiosyncratic, contingent upon a variety of facts, beliefs, expectations and past and present circumstances. For *all* practitioners (a graduate may come into the service of *any* one) the variety is enormous; no classroom tuition could cover it. And it is unnecessary. Many of the things a recruit may be said to be unable to do, can be picked up in a short space of time, task-by-task, by the very doing. It certainly "costs" the practitioner something to give this instruction or direction in detail; but there are few jobs under the sun which can be undertaken by a man fresh from the classroom without costs of this kind, the costs of becoming familiar with the specific environment and character of specific acts.

But there may be flaws in the mode of teaching. There is at least some ground for believing that "techniques" are losing favour among some teachers. Some belabour the formula: we are more concerned with concepts and principles than with techniques of bookkeeping. One should not put too strong an emphasis on the priority suggested in such statements. But it does indicate a difference in emphasis by comparison with the style of tuition which concentrates on bookkeeping and statement preparation exercises. The flight from techniques however may go too far. One may suppose it has arisen from the belief that there are opportunities in the business world for two classes of people, those who think and those who do. This is a gross over-simplification. There may well be a class of people who do in a routine fashion, without much thought. The other class is the class of those who *do* with understanding, and who therefore should be able to construct the routines which others will follow. But notice, they are doers too.

It is highly improbable that anyone can understand a technical art without doing. A budding surgeon may learn about scalpels, saws and sutures; but he will not go far unless he learns how to manipulate them. When he can manipulate them without intense concentration he is able to give his attention to the real object of his work. We cannot learn to drive a car from a handbook. We must take the wheel, get accustomed to the kinaesthetic and external signals which doing one thing or another produces. When we can take in all these signals and respond to them without self-consciousness, we can give the greater attention to what is crucial, or to attaining the maximum efficiency and safety in driving. Similarly a budding accountant must learn to perform the common operations of his art, skilfully to the point of routine, but not as mere routine. Such elementary operations as double entry bookkeeping and aggregation arise from universal commercial realities; they must be done with an apprehension of what is real about them, not because they are traditional or habitual. I know of no textbook which shows clearly what may and what may not properly be aggregated in accounting: I do not therefore find it odd that so much false and misleading aggregation occurs in practice.

The flight from techniques may also have arisen from the belief that the university must produce men who will be researchers and teachers, knowing much about concepts and principles but little concerned with technique. This too is muddled. Advances in knowledge do not come from the bulk of the university's graduates. They come from very few. And often long after the few have mastered the established knowledge and technique of their undergraduate, and even their postgraduate, years. It seems inept to adopt a position geared to the few for the teaching of the many.

In any case it seems inept to adopt such a position for many or few. Ideally, techniques are the expression of principles, and principles are the fruit of observation and experience. It seems folly to concentrate on principles and concepts as such when their function is to link specific kinds of acts with empirical circumstance. This kind of isolation, I feel sure, has given rise to the veneration of such unreal conceptions as "book value", "historical cost", "cost less depreciation" and so on, all terms which have no counterpart in any present market place, which the market place can get along very well without, and which accountants could get along better without. The only effective way of avoiding the land of Jabberwocky, of avoiding conceptions which have no real counterpart, of avoiding the error of supposing that in a given discipline a particular real phenomenon may be conceived in quite different ways, is by forcing attention on the relationship of principles to the techniques by which they are expressed in a manner consistent with real-world usage and circumstance.

FACT, SYMBOL AND FEEDBACK

The ends of practitioners and teachers may be alike; both practitioners and students may best learn by doing; between these lies the heart of the matter. I presume that it is proper to distinguish what is right from what is wrong, and that it is possible to establish what is right and what is wrong. If you find the dichotomy "right-wrong" distasteful, you are at liberty to substitute "best-inferior". I shall take it for granted that professional men want to do what is best, and that teachers want to convey the best of present knowledge to their students. But in translating the wish into the deed I believe both have failed. As for practitioners, the evidence lies in the disquiet and dissatisfaction within and beyond the profession with what is presently done, and the diversity of practices employed. As for academics, the evidence lies in the extraordinary diversity of views one will find at the core of the teaching on any dozen campuses. Is it possible that the logic of both practitioners and teachers has failed them? I think it is.

If we wish to discover whether any act will procure an end we seek, and if we have no exact knowledge of the outcome, we may try it and see. We can test any simple act by reference to its tangible or observable consequences. This is the procedure of the laboratory: but it is also what we do in many cases within our ordinary experience. Let us undertake a simple "thought-experiment" of this kind.

Suppose that on January 1 you had just $500 of your own money. This constitutes your capacity to buy any goods on sale; it constitutes your relationship, as far as property goes, with the rest of the community. Suppose that you bought a parcel of shares with the whole sum, and that at June 30 those shares were being bought and sold at around $1000, and that nothing had happened to the purchasing power of money in the interval. You would be confident that at June 30 you were $500 better off than at January 1, and that your relationship with the rest of the community at June 30 is represented by $1000, not $500. You could put your confident belief to a test, by going out and selling the shares. But there is no need to do that because the market's buying price is quoted. No ordinary mortal, and no accountant holding shares in his own right, would think otherwise than I have sug-

115

gested. Nor would he think he was still as well off at June 30 as he was at January 1 if the quoted price of the shares at June 30 was $300. When we think about our own shares the proximity of the scrip and the market price list prevent us from blunders about our relationship with the rest of the community and the gain or loss we have made. If you decide to hold the shares after June 30, and the price subsequently goes up or down, this movement has nothing to do with what happened to your relationship with the rest of the community *up to* June 30. What happens to your relationship after June 30 depends on your decision at June 30 to go on holding the shares. Now, if you were to ask an orthodox accountant — one who follows the customary procedures of accountants, and the customary doctrine of the textbooks — to draw up some accounts of your affairs he would draw them up in a way which would tell a different story. He would show that you were just as well off at June 30 as at January 1, and that you had made no profit at all. If you are wise you will disbelieve and dismiss what he says; for it has nothing to do with what you know has happened and nothing to do with the actions you may then take. If you were wise you should also dispense with his services; for if he has not been able to tell you what has happened up to June 30 he will not be able to tell you what has happened between June 30 and December 31.

If, when dealing with their own shares (and other assets), practitioners and teachers are guided by what they observe, why do they take such unusual and obviously wrong steps in making up the accounts of others? Why, when *dealing* with assets do they take notice of contemporary market prices to ascertain where they stand and what has happened, and yet in keeping the accounts of others, in writing books and articles, and in courses of instruction, they adopt an entirely different premise? It is not an act of charity on my part, but an attempt to understand, which obliges me to suppose that the adoption of this premise — the present relevance of out-of-date prices — is an unwitting mistake. Those who continue to make it seem to be under the influence of misleading verbal habits which should long since have been exposed among accountants, for they have repeatedly been exposed by others. We will analyze the sources of confusion.

First: accounting is not itself a practical art, though it is related to the practical art of commercial and financial dealing. It is related to buying and selling, borrowing and lending, investing and dis-investing, using and deferring the use of money and things, and choosing or rejecting courses of action entailing the use of money and things. But accounting itself is a symbolic art. Its object is so to represent the course of events that, in the absence of real things, others may know what has happened and what is the upshot.

there should be no confusion over the "real things", referred to; anyone who has learned any accounting will know that the predominant class of acts in accounting consists of recording the prices of goods and services; and prices are real elements of commercial experience, whether we pay them or receive them or simply take notice of them. But the symbol is not the thing. We buy and sell things. We use symbols to reflect upon the possibilities or the consequences of buying and selling things. We cannot reflect upon these or any other things without the use of symbols, verbal, numerical or pictorial. As Peirce observed, "all thought is in signs". In practical affairs all thought about real things is in signs or symbols of those things. If the sign or symbol of the thing does not closely correspond with the thing, reflection cannot but be misdirected, and the action which flows from it cannot but be mistaken. In financial affairs the role of accounting is to provide a set of symbols and prices paid, received or noticed, symbols which are some of the premises of reflection on what has occurred or may be accomplished. The proper business of accounting is thus to secure that the signs correspond, as closely as possible, with prices paid, received and noticed or discovered. If we do not reflect upon what has been and what now is, we have no basis for envisaging what may be.

It is the intermediary role of accounting which is lost to sight. It is a serious loss. For it deludes people into believing that the test of whether a rule is right or wrong is to be found at the intermediate stage — what accountants do — whereas the proper test is at the reflection stage — what has the result of using the rule to do with the potential and actual actions of a buyer, seller, borrower, lender and so on.

As an intermediate function accounting suffers from three kinds of remoteness which impede the correction of its rules.

If there were a clear consequence of what is reported it could be discovered, sooner or later whether what was reported was correct and useful or not. But in the typical business there is no clear consequence. The flux of business, in which new actions and events and the consequences of old actions and events continuously overlap, prevents the observation of the consequence of deviations of the fact from the record at specific points of time. And, if every action is predicated on the contents of the formal record, the present external facts and the judgment of the actor, and as the upshot may be due to external events which the actor could not possibly know of at the time of action, it is impossible after the event to deduce the single cause or the complex of causes of the result. The mere complexity of the flux of events interferes with feedback and with perception of the quality of the rules used in accounting.

A second form of remoteness is the lapse of time between the preparation of accounting statements and the consequence of any action based on them, even if we could isolate such an action. A recipient and user of the statements will know, even if the statements were ideal, that the position and progress reported is already some distance past. He is unlikely (except in the most unusual circumstances) to suppose that the statements could have been incorrect in any sense. If he errs in action he is more likely to lay the blame on unforeseen circumstances than anything else; but, if he thinks of the financial statements at all, he is more likely to suppose that the lapse of time is inevitable and that it is only for that reason that the statements could have been a less than ideal basis for his expectations and actions. Again, the accountant will have no feedback.

A third form of remoteness is the distance between the accountant and the user, and the dispersion of users. To consider managers as users first, the accountant is not physically remote (though he may be quite remote in mental orientation). But as it is the practice of accountants to place on managers the onus of providing some important figures, there is unlikely to be any contention on the part of managers that the financial statements were faulty if they subsequently err in action. Managers are more likely to treat the preparation of periodical accounts as a necessary ritual, and to depend for managerial purposes, on other contemporary factual information accessible to them. Investors and financiers are, by contrast, quite remote. By reason of the complexity and temporal distance already mentioned they are seldom likely to attribute error in action on their part to defects in the financial information supplied them. But if they complain about the financial information (as some have done), accountants could point (as some have done) to the fact that important components of the statements were supplied by managers, or assert that the accounts are the accounts of the management, and brush the complaint aside as none of their business. Again no feedback; or in the last case mentioned, feedback ignored.

This excursion has been hypothetical. But it seems to fit very well the facts as we know them. The postulated reactions are in every case quite reasonable reactions. No blame is implied or intended. I have merely tried to show that, in the nature of things, accountants have no obvious and direct feedback which would induce them to modify their rules, as practitioners or teachers. No feedback means no learning by experience; that is the crux of the matter.

LINGUISTIC AND LOGICAL ERRORS

There are also internal flaws of the linguistic and logical kind which I believe have caused confusion. In some sense they stem from and in another sense they reinforce the effects of the remoteness we have considered.

When an accountant opens an account, say for the shares in the example used previously, and reports a balance at the end of a period in the amount of the original purchase price, he presumes one of two things. Either he treats the holding of shares as the holding of so much money, for the holding of so much money would properly be treated in the accounts in the above way. But in this case he will have reacted in a manner appropriate to something the holder of the shares no longer possesses. He will have made an unwarranted mental substitution of one real thing for another real thing. Or he treats the accounting process as being concerned with the symbol, $500 in the illustration, not with the shares themselves and their prices. He will have mistaken the symbol for the thing. If he makes a mistake of either kind it is impossible that any action dependent on the information he supplies will be consistent with the relationship of the actor to the rest of the world.

It may seem that such elementary mistakes could not be made. A few examples are cited. It has been said that money is a common denominator in terms of which diverse objects — land, plant, inventories — may be represented in common terms. This is not so. Money is a common denominator in terms of which the *prices* of diverse objects at a given time may be represented in common terms. It has been said that an asset *is* a cost; hence accounting for assets is accounting for costs. This is nonsense. It has also been said that an asset *is* a service potential. This too is nonsense. Assets may *have* costs (e.g., purchase prices) and service potentials. But to say assets *are* costs or service potentials is equivalent to saying a car *is* $3000. This kind of substitution of the symbol for the thing, reification, is one of the common causes of error in thought and exposition; and, through them, of error in action.

A second type of error in thought and discussion is of a closely related kind. It is the consideration of wholes and the oversight of components. Accountants seem to think of the products of accounting as whole summaries. In fact a financial statement is a collection of singular component statements — about the present amount of cash, receivables, payables and so on. Every singular component statement must bear the stamp of truth or usefulness in the context in which the whole statement is to be used. Otherwise aggregating them will lead nowhere. It is impossible to deduce anything from putting together the two statements: "I now hold $1000; I now hold some shares which I once bought for $500". Yet this is what many financial summaries assert.

There are more fallacies in the literature and practice of accounting than those I have mentioned here. My aim has been simply to show that the difficulties of learning by experience, by the feedback from what happens to actors when they use financial statements, are intensified by confusion of language and thought.

117

But neither of these difficulties and dangers is inescapable and both may be avoided by forcing the attention back to reality.

We have shown that the sense of reality may be caught in a "thought experiment", which isolates a particular action and the mode of its representation. But a careful examination of what accountants do will provide evidence of misapprehension, on a grand scale, even of the facts of practice. It is quite commonly held that most firms in most countries do their accounting on what is described as the historical cost basis. If it were so we might be entitled to suppose that none of the hard facts of the market has been sufficient to dislodge it. But it is just not so. In some countries very large numbers of companies have abandoned the rule in respect of some assets; as when revaluations have occurred. In respect of inventories it has *never* been a fixed rule. In some countries the rule has been set aside by statutorily approved revaluations or revalorizations. In the United States, where the publicity rules are probably tighter than anywhere else, the requirement of the cost rule is circumvented by the use of Lifo, and by other devices used as well in other countries; and the invention of the "pooling" doctrine on mergers is just another crutch to sustain the rule in spite of its weakness. Anyone who dares to suggest that the rule is generally endorsed and accepted is flying in the face of a mountain of facts. There would have been no such facts were it not that the circumstances and forces which influence commercial dealing have just had to be accommodated in accounting somehow.

All these divergences are open to observation by practitioners and teachers alike. In other fields the accumulation of anomalies is the signal for throwing out the extant doctrine or rules, and for finding an alternative which is more general in its coverage of experience (i.e., reducing the number of anomalies, and ideally removing them altogether). It seems inescapable that the beliefs both in the prevalence and in the propriety of the cost doctrine persist because of the use of verbal gymnastics which camouflage anomalies (as for example, the "flow" assumptions which support Lifo and Fifo) and because of the failure properly to categorize deviations from the cost basis as anomalies. My point, however, is that there is a form of feedback which is independent of the practices and experiences of particular firms, and which becomes apparent if we stand off and look at what is happening in accounting generally.

The upshot of my observations is that there is no conflict as to the ends sought by practitioners and teachers; that technical competence is a concomitant of understanding; but that when it comes to the means of developing the understanding — by observation and argument — there is much common ground between practitioners and teachers, most of it quicksand. That it should be so is not inevitable.

THE EMPIRICAL AND LOGICAL BEST

To demonstrate this I return to a question posed by a remark at an earlier point. I presumed that it is proper to distinguish what is right from what is wrong, and that it is possible to establish what is right and what is wrong (or what is best and what is inferior). I feel confident that both of these propositions will be hotly contested.

There is a widespread feeling that what is right (or best) in accounting is a matter of opinion. The words "opinion" and "judgment" are bandied about so freely among accountants that the ubiquity of the aforesaid feeling is not surprising. But any who hold this opinion, by the very holding of it, reject the force of experience and the power of reason, reject in fact what years of schooling were devoted to inculcating. If there is any sense in which experience of the world teaches us, it is in the direction of forming firm impressions of the empirical relations between things or between classes of things. We speak of those firm impressions as facts and of the relations as factual relations — meaning that they are not matters of opinion, but matters on which others can show us to be right or wrong. And if there is any sense in which logic extends our understanding, it is in the direction of enabling us to draw necessary conclusions from stipulated premises. If the premises are just those that have not been shown to be false, and if the process of drawing conclusions is free of flaws, we are entitled to regard the conclusions as established knowledge. We no longer regard them as mere matters of opinion.

Some will contend that at any time we do not have sufficient facts; that we do not know whether the subsequent discovery of additional facts will falsify a premise which has not yet been shown to be false; and therefore that we cannot safely draw conclusions. This is merely face-saving procrastination. No scientist yet has had, and no scientist will have, all the facts that are or will be available to his successors. But if men had not been painstaking in their observations, and bold in their conjectures and conclusions, they would never have formulated the principles and laws which enabled their successors to see more, and more clearly. We can only know what is best given the state of factual and derived knowledge at any time. Given that knowledge there is some set of principles which embraces it more perfectly than any alternative set. To teach those principles seems to be the proper aim of higher education at any time; to follow the rules which those principles imply seems to be the proper aim of the profession.

There are some who hold, however, that the proper function of the university is to expose students to many views, on the ground that they are able enough to choose for themselves what is the best. There can be no more confusing a policy than this; and there is reason to believe that this lack of vigour and definiteness lies at the root of the vacillation and inconsistency of much present day practice. In no other field are the halting and mistaken steps taken in the early stages of knowledge paraded before students, much less on an equal footing with the best of present knowledge. But, "a science which hesitates to forget its founders is lost", said Whitehead.

From the available facts and the exercise of discrimination in argument it should be possible to distinguish what is best from what is inferior. But we still find it said that this or that is best for some purposes. Particularly is it said in defence of accounting on the historical cost basis. However, I know of no demonstration to the point that those purposes are not equally well served by another or other forms of accounting which are superior in other respects. The task of finding what is best is rather like finding where to put a specially shaped piece in a jig-saw puzzle. It must fit in with the rest of the picture not just by virtue of the coincidence of one angle or one side, but at all angles and all sides and on the face of the picture too. A set of accounting rules which satisfies one or two conditions is just not good enough. Scholars need, teachers need, students need and the world needs an accounting which satisfies the greatest number of conditions simultaneously. I would welcome any demonstration to the effect that continuously contemporary accounting, as I have expounded it, does not meet this test.

+   +   +

If this paper has seemed to meander it is because the commonly held ideas I have tried to examine are vagrant, undisciplined. I can best make amends for this by stating what seems to me to emerge from my reflections on the dissonance which I noticed at the outset and the misapprehensions mentioned by the way.

I cannot share the view that no common conclusion can be reached by observant and thoughtful professionals and teachers, on the best of present knowledge, or on the best accounting practice in the present state of knowledge. It requires no more than a thorough respect for the facts of commercial life and a thorough belief in the fruits of systematic thought, both of which have been elements of learning and experience for the greater part of the lives of all of us.

I do not believe that, for the purpose, we need any more facts than are now available to us. Some stare us in the face daily in what we do or what we see done; others can be unearthed with a modicum of care and effort. To see only the facts we wish to see is a piece of folly. Teachers who indulge it will produce men ill-equipped to learn by experience; practitioners who indulge it will leave clients ill-equipped to meet their own problems; nor can take professional pride in that kind of handiwork.

I do not believe that the logic of teaching and learning differs one whit from the logic of practice. Teachers and students may seem to be concerned with broad principles; but we only learn broad principles from seeing their particular instances or applications. Practitioners may seem to be concerned with particular cases; but whether or not they consciously recognize it, they all have recourse to broad principles of some kind in the solution of particular problems. What is crucial is that the most general principles shall be consistent with the circumstances in which they are to be used; for no one can reason from unreal premises to practically fruitful conclusions.

I believe that practitioners and teachers should regard their roles as mutually dependent and mutually supporting, as are warp and woof (without double-*entendre*). So to regard teaching and practice is common in other professions which depend on advanced technical skill and knowledge. But there is no need to depend on analogy. "All knowledge of reality starts from experience and ends in it", said Einstein. The commercial world is the source of what it is proper to do in the counting house and in the classroom; it is also the only place in which conclusions reached by reflection and deduction can be tested. There is every reason therefore why practitioners and teachers and researchers alike should regard themselves as part of a common enterprise. But with different functions in some respects.

I believe that practitioners should concede or respect the right of teachers to reflect, to research, to re-examine, rather than attempt to duplicate, or outdo or supplant them. Embroiled as they are in commercial affairs, practitioners have neither the time nor the independence of their own immediate commitments to reflect upon what they and their colleagues do, to amass the facts which support significant generalizations, to test them and to formulate them as principles and systems of principles. Teachers and researchers should have both time and independence. I believe, however, that such conclusions as researchers reach should be put under the closest and most patient scrutiny by practitioners; for only under the closest scrutiny will conclusions be failed or affirmed; and only by patient scrutiny is there likely to develop that sympathy between researcher and practitioner which will secure the trial of a tentatively affirmed conclusion. To take part in this review is a proper function of professionals, and a proper involvement in the process of advancing knowledge, understanding and practice. There has, unfortunately, been too much stand-offishness on both sides hitherto.

I believe that teachers should strive for the respect of practitioners by common allegiance to the established canons of inquiry, and by deliberate choice of what is best and by deliberate rejection of the rest. If the house of learning is divided against itself it cannot stand. If it is cut off from the house of experience it will deserve to stand empty. A common logic and linked but different functions in the common pursuit of excellence in thought or practice will, I believe, quell the dissonance which now assails us.

119

Tax Allocation and Financial Reporting

Summary

This paper considers the various treatments proposed for accounting for income taxes and the consequence · of income taxes where assessable incomes and commercially calculated incomes diverge. Divergences have existed since the introduction of income taxation, but they have been given particular attention in the last twenty five years. The primary causes of divergence are provisions of the tax codes relating to depreciation and similar charges and the spreading of losses.

We contend that the doctrine of deferred tax credits is unnecessary; that it has been supported on grounds which are inconsistent with well established principles; that it disregards the disclosure provisions of the laws relating to the fair representation, year by year, of what has transpired.

We find that the deferred credit idea has obtained what popularity it has by default of argument, rather than on its merits; and that it rests mainly on the specious belief in the usefulness of annual income net of taxes as a guide to performance and prospects.

We show that income tax is not an expense like other expenses; and that, to avoid confusion, it is better to treat it as an appropriation of net profits as determined by commercial accounting principles, than to treat it as other expenses.

We claim that the deferred credit idea entails an implicit forecasting of future profits, which forecasting has long been considered improper among accountants.

And we claim that to show deferred taxes as a liability does not fairly represent financial position, that it may be detrimental to present shareholders, and that it may be inimical to future loan financing and hence also to future shareholders.

At the outset, it was our intention to cover the official statements, recommendations and cross argument of a number of countries; the United Kingdom, Canada, Australia and New Zealand as well as the United States of America. Substantially the same view, however, is expressed in the literature of these countries. It would have lengthened the analysis considerably to include the references and the particular forms of explanation or recommendation used. We have therefore chosen to limit the analysis to materials of the U.S.A., without

121

99

implying anything about the origins of the ideas discussed. Only occasional allusions are made to the laws and pronouncements of other countries. By adopting this limitation we will be able to notice the sequence of events through which the notion of deferred taxation has risen to prominence and the grounds or forms of appeal (as we think, mistaken) by which its endorsement has been justified—in one country. Given the general similarity of publicity laws and tax codes and the objects of both, the conclusions are considered to be of general application.

Disclosure Laws and Tax Laws

Laws and regulations relating to the publication of financial statements have one general object or function. It is to secure the preparation of balance sheets and income accounts which give a true and fair view of (as in the U.K. and Australia), or which fairly represent (as in the U.S.A.), the financial positions of companies and their periodical profits from time to time. The differences in the forms of words expressing the general object are not material. What is ideally required is the same. Those who do not have intimate knowledge of the affairs and operations of companies are expected to be so informed by financial statements that they may reflect upon what has happened and the effects of what has happened, and form their judgements upon past performance and future prospects in the light of that knowledge. By their nature, financial statements represent only the financial aspects and effects of what has happened. But also, by their nature, they are the only statements which can give in one form of notation the consequences of every kind of act, transaction and event. The laws and regulations, be it noted, refer only to financial positions and profits or results—both entirely pecuniary or financial notions. But they are notions unquestionably significant in the course of any reflection on the past and the future by investors, creditors, financiers and their aids and advisers.

Laws and regulations relating to the taxation of the incomes of companies have a quite different object. It is to state the rules which enable taxable income and the tax assessable on that income to be discovered. Income taxes are levied periodically, on the basis of periodical taxable income. In so far as the tax payable on the taxable income of one period is not paid until the next, the liability to pay a tax is pertinent to any consideration of the financial position of a company at the end of the former period. The amount of the tax payable, or a close approximation to it, is thus an element the disclosure of which is necessary to give a fair view of, or to fairly represent, the position at the end of each period.

The Eighth Schedule of the U.K. *Companies Act, 1948*, requires that in the profit and loss account there shall be shown 'the amount of the charge for United Kingdom income tax and other United Kingdom taxation on profits': and that, in the balance sheet or by way of note, there shall be shown 'the basis on which the amount, if any, set aside for United Kingdom income tax is computed'. There is no reference to the year, or the income of the year, in respect of which the disclosures are required. The corresponding schedules of the Australian Acts require that the profit and loss account shall show the 'provision made for payment of income tax in respect of the period of accounting'. Precisely what this means depends on which word one emphasizes. It could mean provision *made* in a given period, whatever it is based on; or it could mean the provision made in respect of the *income* of a given period. In the U.S.A. Rule 5-03 of *Regulation S-X* of the SEC, dealing with income statements, requires that 'all items of profit and loss given recognition in the accounts during the period covered by the profit and loss or income statements shall be included. Only items entering into the determination of net income or loss shall be included'. Under 'income deductions', 'provision for income and excess-profits taxes' is specifically mentioned. These requirements also seem to be ambiguous. 'Given recognition in the accounts during the period' does not mean 'occurring during the period'; the reference to 'net income or loss' makes no mention of the period; neither does the reference to the provisions for taxes.

In every case the stipulations are ambiguous. The amounts of the charges or provisions could be the amounts based on the taxable income of the year reported on; or the amounts given recognition, in the year reported on, as amounts payable in respect of income taxes without regard for the year or years covered by the amounts payable. If the ambiguity is to be removed, recourse must be had to some guiding principle other than the explicit words of the cited publicity regulations.

123

Fiscal and Policy Functions of Tax Laws

Income tax laws are primarily the means of raising public revenues by levies on taxpayers having assessable incomes. But they are also means of promoting policies which governments adopt from time to time. They have been used to encourage primary production (by special concessions, or depreciation rules or inventory valuation rules), to encourage general industrial rehabilitation or development, to encourage exports, and to encourage the discovery and development of mineral resources, among other things. These objects could otherwise be served by special imposts and bounties, levied and given under statutes other than the tax laws. But to use the provisions of the tax codes is administratively simpler and politically more palatable (for the incidence of burdens and benefits is less obvious). We do not here challenge the use of the taxation machinery for such purposes. They are mentioned against the possibility that taxes will be thought by some to be merely revenue-raising devices, the proceeds of which are spent on services consumed in common by all constituents of a community.

One consequence of the mixing of fiscal functions and policy functions in an income tax law is that the amount of taxable income of any taxpayer need not be the same as the amount of the pre-tax income calculated by applying the prevailing rules of accounting. Thus if there are discriminatory rules for calculating depreciation or valuing inventories as between different classes of taxpayer, and if the prevailing rules of accounting are followed in common by all taxpayers, there will be differences in the liability to tax of taxpayers having the same pre-tax income in any year. If the amount of this liability is deducted from the pre-tax income of any year, the net incomes will be different for taxpayers having the same pre-tax incomes.

Even in the ordinary course of events there may be differences in income calculated on the prevailing commercial rules and the assessable income of a year. Thus some revenues may be regarded by tax authorities as assessable which for commercial purposes would be regarded as prepayments, in one year, of revenues of a later year. Some expenses may be regarded commercially as charges against the revenues of one year, whereas the tax authorities may regard them as provisions against future contingencies which will be allowed as deductions from assessable income if, when, and to the extent that those contingencies become actual experiences.[1] Such divergences as these stem from administrative considerations such as the protection of the annual revenues of government, the certainty of the amount of assessable income and the probability that taxpayers will have the means of paying taxes at one time rather than at another.

These administrative considerations carry weight in most, if not all, tax systems. But, in no other sense than as specifying how the assessable income and the tax of any one year shall be determined. As the tax paid in or payable in respect of a year is an outgoing or a liability, the amount of it seems a proper subject of the disclosure laws. Further, discriminatory tax rules having policy objectives are common, and in so far as they favour some taxpayers they burden others. All taxpayers are thus affected, unequally. But, as before, in no other sense than as specifying, in part, the liability to tax, are discriminatory elements of the tax rules relevant to the disclosure laws. We have thus not found in the tax laws any principle which might resolve the problem of what should be disclosed in the financial statements of a given year when the disclosure laws are ambiguous.

One attempt, indeed, to align the disclosure laws and the tax laws provides an example of the consequences of attempting the impossible. Not long after the SEC was established, lifo was made a permissible inventory valuation method for tax purposes, provided it was also used in published statements. The effect of lifo is that if inventory prices move in one general direction over a number of years, the balance sheet figure for inventories becomes increasingly inadequate as an indication of the present consequences of past events. Financial position is increasingly misrepresented. Of course, taxpayer companies which chose the lifo method obtained the advantage of a lower immediate tax; but at a price to the users of financial statements, namely the loss of up to date inventory values in balance sheets. The intention of the *Securities Act* was defeated by the provisions of a Revenue Act.[2]

1. A long list of examples is given in *Accounting Research Study No 9*, 'Interperiod Allocation of Corporate Income Taxes' by Homer A. Black, New York, A.I.C.P.A., 1966, pp. 8-10.
2. The point is made at greater length in Chambers, 'Why Worry About Accounting?', *Proceedings* of The Fifth Accounting Forum of Hayden Stone, Incorporated in New York University Graduate School, November 1966.

The Matching Idea

Notwithstanding the ambiguity of the disclosure laws and our failure to find any principle in the tax laws which might resolve it, opinion in some quarters seems to have settled in favour of charging pre-tax profit with the amount of tax notionally attributable to that profit. The ground for this is the idea of matching revenues and expenses.

If an isolated venture is undertaken it is ordinarily not difficult to match the revenues and expenditures which it entails. But if, as is generally the case, business firms engage in a continuous series of partially overlapping ventures which share in the use of some common resources, matching by ventures or transactions is impossible. This is recognized in the general practice of accounting and in the form of statutory publicity rules. Profits and losses or results *of the year* are required to be shown; positions as at the ends of years are required to be shown. Further, income taxes are levied on *periodical* assessable incomes, not on the incomes from specific ventures. This is so notwithstanding that some kinds of specific venture or investment may attract greater or smaller concessions or allowances than others; for the concessions or allowances are against the amount of tax that would be payable but for their allowance, not against a venture income which is separately assessable.

125

Given that the revenue of a year is determinable, the question arises: what expenses may properly be set off against or matched with that revenue? The simple answer is: the expenses of the year. But this needs elaboration. In respect of taxes the question probably has a long history. We will look no further back than 1944, and we will trace the rise to its present status of 'deferred tax' accounting.[3]

---

3. The pronouncements to be considered are Accounting Research Bulletins (A.R.B.) of the Committee on Accounting Procedure of the American Institute of Certified Public Accountants, Opinions of the Accounting Principles Board of the Institute, and Accounting Series Releases (A.S.R.) of the SEC. The specific documents, in chronological order, are:

1944 *A.R.B. No 23*, 'Income Taxes', as in Chapter 10B of *A.R.B. No 43* (1953).
1945 *A.S.R. No 53*, 'Statement of the Commission's Opinion Regarding "Charges in Lieu of Income Taxes" and "Provisions for Income Taxes" in the Profit and Loss Statement'.
1952 *A.R.B. No 42*, 'Emergency Facilities—Depreciation, Amortization and Income Taxes', as in Chapter 9C of *A.R.B. No 43* (1953).
1954 *A.R.B. No 44*, 'Declining-balance Depreciation'.
1958 *A.R.B. No 44 (Revised)*, 'Declining-balance Depreciation'.
1960 *A.S.R. No 85*, 'Statement of Administration Policy Regarding Balance Sheet Treatment of Credit Equivalent to Reduction in Income Taxes'.
1962 *Opinion No 2*, 'Accounting for the "Investment Credit"'.
1963 *A.S.R. No 96*, 'Accounting for the "Investment Credit"'.
1964 *Opinion No 4 (Amending No 2)*, 'Accounting for the "Investment Credit"'.
1966 *Opinion No 10* (part), 'Tax Allocation Accounts—Discounting'.
1967 *Opinion No 11*, 'Accounting for Income Taxes'.

Accounting Research Study No 9, 'Interperiod Allocation of Corporate Income Taxes', by Homer A. Black, assisted by the Staff of the A.I.C.P.A. Accounting Research Division, was published in May 1966.

The position taken by the American Institute's Committee on Accounting Procedure seems to have become the pattern for much subsequent discussion.

> Income taxes are an expense that should be allocated, when necessary and practicable, to income and other accounts, as other expenses are allocated. What the income statement should reflect under this head, as under any other head, is the expense properly allocable to the income included in the income statement for the year.[4]

This statement glosses over several difficulties.

TAX AS EXPENSE   Taxes have some of the features of expenses. They entail the commitment and subsequently the paying out of cash, which is therefore not available for dividends or any other purpose; and they entail charges which reduce the amounts carried to equity account balances. Expenses voluntarily incurred do both of these things. However, expenses of the kind ordinarily allocated also have some functional relationship to the substantive scale and style of the operations of companies. The most significant expenses allocated between periods are depreciation and inventory costs. Whether the common methods of allocation are satisfactory or not, there *are* indicators, such as physical quantities on hand and prices, which serve as guides to allocation between or among successive years.

Income taxes on the other hand are unrelated to any such indicators. If taxes were in the nature of prices paid for services provided to all taxable entities in common by governments (public works, public health, public education, defence, and so on), and if they were levied on some basis proportionate to the benefit derived by each taxable entity, there would be grounds for treating them as expenses.[5] Every taxable entity would then be taxed. But this is not the case in respect of corporate income taxes. They do not fall equally on companies which benefit equally from publicly provided services. They fall only on those which make profits which are assessable. Certainly companies may so arrange their affairs that they attract the fewest penalties and the greatest concessions allowed under a given tax code. But neither penalties nor concessions are operative unless a company makes an assessable income. This applies even to the carry-back and carry-forward provisions for losses; they are available only to companies which at some time have made or do make assessable incomes. By reason of these circumstances and by reason of the mixed fiscal and policy functions of income taxes, income taxation can only be regarded as a form of discriminatory expropriation (the words are used descriptively, not pejoratively).

A further distinction between income taxes and expenses lies in the fact that expenses are deliberately incurred in anticipation of benefits to be obtained. Taxes are not. As we have said, they fall *after and only if* it has been discovered that an assessable income has been derived. It does not seem to be consistent with the nature of an income tax to describe it as 'an excise tax on the right to

126

---

4. *A.R.B. No 23.*
5. For an exposition of the view, see William H. Mateer, 'Tax Allocation: A Macro Approach', *The Accounting Review*, Vol. XL, No. 3, July 1965, pp. 583-6.

operate and earn income as a person or separate entity';[6] for, though 'loss' companies have the right, they pay no tax; and a tax which varies with the result of exercising a right is clearly not a tax on the right.

Only at a superficial level and by an attenuated analogy can corporate income tax be thought to be an expense.

NET INCOME EMPHASIS   The statement refers to allocation 'when necessary and practicable'. The necessity seems to arise from a common supposition about the use of reported figures. As we have noted, Rule 5-03 of *Regulation S-X* alludes to 'items entering into the determination of net income or loss'. This may be supposed to be in contemplation of investors, brokers and analysts who wish to have some convenient, inclusive indicator of the performance of a company over successive years, or of two or more companies in the same year. Income of the year or years, net of income taxes, is an obvious and ready-to-hand indicator, used in conjunction with a denominator such as paid up capital, total equity or shares outstanding. It may be regarded as indicating the combined effects of using the available opportunities for commercial dealing and for arranging affairs to minimize tax burdens.

127

However, income net of taxes represents the combined effects of those factors *plus* the incidence of the tax rates proclaimed *and* the policies (of encouragement, repression and diversion) which the government is pursuing through the tax mechanism in a given year. At best, it is an indicator of a very mixed character. Further any given company, in any given year, may not be able to take advantage of the maximum benefit from the tax rules and concessions of that year. Income net of taxes will therefore vary according as the opportunity to benefit from the tax concessions coincides with the capacity to exploit it.

No comparison of rates of income net of taxes, as between different years for the same company or as between different companies for the same year is necessarily a guide to the future potential performance of the company or companies. Net income is a compound consequence of matters which can be thought about and arranged by managers and directors, and of matters which are contingent upon discriminatory governmental policy and the discriminatory means chosen to implement it.

ALLOCATION   The statement refers to 'expense properly allocable to the income'. The matching notion in its commonly received form relates to the matching of *revenues* and expenses, periodically. The propriety of the idea rests on a presumption that there is a functional relationship between expected expenses and expected revenues, that expenses are incurred in the expectation of revenues. The annual accounts are consequently to show the extent to which expectations (of any year) have been realized in the year of accounting.

6. The ruling in *Pollock* v. *Farmers' Loan and Trust* (1895), cited by David Drinkwater and James Don Edwards, 'The Nature of Taxes and the Matching Principle', *The Accounting Review*, Vol. XL, No. 3, July 1965, at p. 580. The authors themselves conclude against allocation.

Now, as there is no necessary or functional relationship between income and income taxes, it is plainly incorrect to apply a principle which presumes there is. And as there is no other principle than matching which gives substance to the words 'properly allocable', incorrect use of the matching notion must lead to 'improper allocation'. Only assessable income is related to income taxes; and the relationship between a given assessable income and the tax it attracts is not invariant, but is fixed, *ad hoc*, annually by the revenue or tax assessment acts.

Entrenched usage of the term 'allocation' apart, there is no good reason for its use in respect even of amounts payable in one year in respect of previous years. Suppose we hold the orthodox view that accounting statements are properly and entirely historical, and that analysts would like to know how much of the tax stated to be payable at the end of a year was in respect of that year or prior years. The problem is not one of allocation, in the same sense as allocation is used of, say, depreciation charges. It is simply a problem of identification. To use allocation in these two different senses is unwarranted. It may well be said to have done some damage to straight-thinking about the disclosure of taxes assessable and taxes payable. And that in spite of a very clear statement on the matter in the following year, to which we shall next refer.

The SEC on 'Tax Savings', 1945

In 1945, confronted with the increasing frequency of 'cases involving the treatment of so called "tax savings" ', the SEC set out its views on the tax allocation problem and the general nature of accounting in *Accounting Series Release No 53*. It used as an illustration the statements of a company whose reporting treatment it deemed questionable. In effect, the company had shown as the amount of excess profits tax, the amount it would have had to pay were it not for the tax rules for amortization of certain facilities, which provided for a shorter period of amortization than the company used for its own purposes. Below the line showing net income after taxes, it had shown the amount of the difference between the amount above-mentioned and the tax actually expected to be payable, as 'reduction' in taxes, augmenting the amount transferred to earned surplus.

The Commission took the view that the amount which should have been deducted in arriving at net income after taxes was the tax estimated to be payable in respect of the year. It objected to the reasoning underlying the company's presentation; namely that the short-run 'saving' in tax entailed the future payment of higher taxes in some later years, and that the 'excess' of future years should, in those years, be charged against the 'saving' credited in the year in question to surplus. *Inter alia*, it said:

> In our opinion financial accounting is essentially historical in nature—it consists of an accounting for costs that have actually been incurred by the business and for the revenues that have been actually derived from the business . . . financial accounting is in our opinion concerned with what did happen, not with what might have happened had conditions been different. And it does not attempt to forecast

the future . . . a statement of past operations . . . is primarily an historical record of actual events, not of prophesied events . . . Nothing, in our opinion, would be more misleading than to present, in the guise of an actual earnings statement, data which, in fact, was an estimate either of expected future earnings or of the effects of subsequent conditions and transactions on prior operations . . . amounts shown should be in accordance with the historical facts and should not be altered to reflect amounts that the draftsman considers to be more 'normal' or likely to recur in future years . .'. It is not the role of the financial accountant to adjust them to eliminate the effect of unusual circumstances which actually occurred . . .

The Commission dealt also with the role of the analyst, pointing out sharply the difference in the objectives of accountants and analysts. 'The analyst begins with reports of actual operations and conditions and adjusts them to give effect to expected future changes and events in order to arrive at his estimate of future earnings.' The accountant's task is to supply those reports of actual operations. Normalization of accounting statements the Commission described as a 'misconception'. It pointed out that in *A.R.B. No 23* no effort was 'made to state the reasons why Federal income taxes must be considered as an expense in the same category as, let us say, wages'; and after discussing some differences between taxes and expenses proper, it concluded that there was 'much to be said for the position that true income taxes are in the nature of a share of profits taken by the government.'

A.R.B. No 42, Emergency Facilities, 1952

129

Notwithstanding the clarity and comprehensiveness of the Commission's statement of opinion, the American Institute clung to its original position. In November 1952 its Committee issued *A.R.B. No 42* on 'Emergency Facilities— Depreciation, Amortization, and Income Taxes.' The problem at issue was as before: the treatment of taxes where tax laws provided for a shorter amortization period than a company used for its own accounting and reporting purposes. The tax laws, under a section introduced in 1950, provided for accelerated 'relief' in respect of emergency facilities covered by 'certificates of necessity.' Paras 11 and 12 of the *Bulletin* include the following:

> In such cases, after the close of the amortization period the income taxes will exceed the amount that would be appropriate on the basis of the income reported in the statements. Accordingly the committee believes that during the amortization period [for tax purposes], where this difference is material, a charge should be made in the income statement to recognize the income tax to be paid in the future on the amount by which amortization for income-tax purposes exceeds the depreciation that would be allowable if certificates of necessity had not been issued . . . the committee believes it desirable to treat the charge as being for additional income taxes. The related credit in such cases would properly be made to an account for deferred income taxes . . . By this procedure the net income will more nearly reflect the results of a proper matching of costs and revenues.

The continuation of reference to net income and the proper matching of costs and revenues should be noted. There is no discussion in the *Bulletin* of the question: if and to what extent would the result of the proposed form of accounting yield a balance sheet which fairly represented the financial position of a company which adopted it?

A.R.B. No 44, Declining-Balance Depreciation, 1954

The American Institute's *A.R.B. No 23,* the case cited in the SEC *Release No 53,* and the American Institute's *A.R.B. No 42* related to war time conditions or emergency facilities. The tax allocation possibilities were extended beyond those limits by section 167 of the Internal Revenue Code of 1954 which provided certain tax amortization options not previously available. Depreciation on the declining balance method was allowed at up to 200 per cent of the rate permissible on the straight line method (previously it had been 150 per cent); the sum of the digits method and other reasonable methods consistently applied were also allowed as options.

130

A.R.B. No 44, of October 1954, affirmed the Committee's previous view on allocation and deferred taxes. In July 1958 this was superseded by *A.R.B. No 44 (Revised).* It seems that the previous statement was, to that time, considered to apply to specific assets or to a group of assets 'which are expected to be retired from service at about the same time', clearly a straight consequence of the war time and emergency provisions of the tax laws which related to identified assets. Tax deferment would extend only for a limited time in respect of any such asset. The Revision stated that the principle espoused by the committee applied

> also to a group of assets consisting of numerous units which may be of differing lengths of life and which are expected to be continually replaced; in this case the excess of depreciation taken for income-tax purposes during the earlier years would be followed in later years by substantial equality between the annual depreciation for income-tax purposes and that for accounting purposes, and a tax deferment would be built up during the earlier years which would tend to remain relatively constant thereafter. It applies also to a gradually expanding plant; in this case an excess of depreciation taken for income-tax purposes may exist each year during the period of expansion in which event there would be a tax deferment which might increase as long as the period of expansion continued. (Para. 4).

The deferred tax credit had thus reached its apotheosis. From its origins in emergency, it had now achieved immortality. No longer was it to be carried for specific items for limited periods (up to, say, ten years); it could go on, for an unidentified mass of assets, indefinitely. Whereas it may have represented the apprehension, however dim, of an effect which *could* have arisen in the relatively near future, it now represented the apprehension of an effect which may never arise, a deferred credit against which the debit could not be foreseen.

The fictional character of the deferred credit balance must have been sensed; for the *Bulletin* continues:

> Where it may reasonably be presumed that the accumulative difference between taxable income and financial income will continue for a long or indefinite period, it is alternatively appropriate, instead of crediting a deferred tax account, to

recognize the related tax effect as additional amortization or depreciation applicable to such assets in recognition of the loss of future deductibility for income-tax purposes. (Para. 5).

If apotheosis is not appropriate, use metamorphosis. It is difficult to see how a balance which arose because there *might* be some future liability can be transformed into an immediate charge against an asset or an immediate increase in the depreciation provision, except as an outright admission that the amount of the depreciation and the balance of the asset account, prior to this additional charge, did not fairly represent the position. If a company's financial accounting in the ordinary course of events were designed to represent fairly the investments in specified assets, no tax rule, nor any consequence at present only imaginary of a tax rule, can make the representation of investments in specified assets unfair, and therefore to be altered.

The notion that tax-deductibility is an element of the characteristics of assets seems to be quite foreign to the usual notion of assets and asset values. It surely cannot be said that tax-deductibility *attaches* to assets. For, if two companies have the same assets presumably the same tax-deductibility would attach from the outset to the assets of both. But if one of them never makes a profit, how should or can the tax-deductibility of its assets be amortized? Tax deductions only arise when, but for the deduction rules, there would be assessable incomes. They are elements of the tax calculation rules, and their amounts may be varied if other rules for the calculation of tax are varied. They relate to the mode of calculating taxes payable, not at all to intrinsic features of assets.

The *generalizing* of the rule has an obvious parallel with the introduction of lifo already mentioned. A tax rule introduced in the first place for a limited range of conditions (i.e., a discriminatory rule) is subsequently extended to cover all kinds of conditions, with specific consequences which prejudice adherence to the disclosure laws. For if such a rule interferes with the fair representation of the amount of a specific asset, or of any provision against such an asset the effect of which is to reduce the net amount of the asset which the application of accounting principles would yield, it also interferes with the fair representation of a company's position as a whole at any given date.

Statement of SEC Policy, 1960

In December 1958, the SEC gave notice of intention to prescribe the mode of treatment of the liberalized depreciation provisions of section 167 of the Internal Revenue Code of 1954. After receiving written and oral submissions, it issued in February 1960 its 'Statement of Administrative Policy Regarding Balance Sheet Treatment of Credit Equivalent to Reduction in Income Taxes' *(Accounting Series Release No 85)*. It was 'not intended to direct or establish any system of accounts or to specify the manner in which a particular item shall be recorded in the books of the reporting companies'. The intention was rather to indicate 'the Commission's views as to the presentation in financial statements filed with the Commission of the credit arising when deferred tax accounting is

131

employed'. In fact it proposed to treat as misleading or inaccurate any filed financial statement which designated as earned surplus or as part of equity capital the amount of any deferred tax credit.

The Commission had long since chosen to seek such improvement in reporting as it deemed necessary through consultation with the American Institute and other parties concerned rather than by direct exercise of its powers. In giving notice of its intention to prescribe in 1958 and in inviting submissions, it was apparently seeking to sense the prevailing opinion on deferred tax accounting. The proposed announcement, as given in the notice of intention, reproduces substantially the sense of the argument for deferred tax credit accounting as it was given in *A.R.B. No 44 (Revised)* of the American Institute committee. No reference was made to *Accounting Series Release No 53*, in which as we have shown, strong argument against such a form of accounting was put forward, and in which the Commission had said no argument had been offered in support of the Institute committee's view.

Many of the respondents to the Commission's invitation to make submissions seem to have taken the view that the Commission favoured deferred credit accounting.[7] The writer's examination of the submissions left the impression that the majority of the profession did not favour such a form of accounting; at least there was a substantial amount of opposition to it. Consistently with the disclaimer of intention noted above, the Statement of Policy made no reference to the arguments for or against, or the weight of opinion for or against, deferred tax accounting. Where it stated the sense of the Institute committee's opinions, the whole paragraph carried a footnote reference to the Bulletins issued by the Institute committee; this seems to be indicative of a desire not to take a position on a matter widely disputed. But at a number of places the Statement gives ground for supposing that the Commission endorsed and adopted deferred tax credit accounting as a proper form of accounting under the disclosure laws which it administers. To deal officially at all with the final location of an account balance implies that the balance arises from an accepted and acceptable form of accounting.

The Investment Credit

The *Revenue Act* of 1962 provided for the allowance of an 'investment credit' in respect of certain depreciating assets acquired and put into use after 1961. For assets whose expected service lives were 4 or 5 years, the base amount was to be one-third of the investment; for lives 6 or 7 years, two-thirds; for longer lives, the whole of the investment. The amount of the investment credit was to be 7 per cent of the respective base amounts. It was to be taken, in the first year in which qualified property was put into use or the first year in which

7. The material is collected in Arthur Andersen & Co., *Cases in Public Accounting Practice, SEC Policy Re: Deferred Tax Credits*, privately printed, 1961.

depreciation could be claimed for tax purposes, as a credit against the tax liability arising under other provisions of the Code. The maximum amount of the credit was not to exceed the first $25,000 of the tax liability plus one-fourth of the tax liability in excess of $25,000. The tax basis of the qualified property was to be reduced by the amount of the credit.

In every material respect these provisions seem to have the same object and effect as other forms of liberalized depreciation for tax purposes. They are part of the formula by which is determined the amount payable by taxpayers in the year of a claim for credit, that is to say, the amount of the tax for that year. They allow greater concessions in the year of claim than previously, and leave a smaller deductible balance to be claimed for tax purposes in later years. There are carry-back and carry-forward provisions for unused investment credits of the same kind as applied to losses and unused excess profits credits in the 'forties.

In December 1962, the Accounting Principles Board of the American Institute issued *Opinion No 2* on 'Accounting for the "Investment Credit" '. It considered two principal alternatives.

133

TAX REDUCTION   The allowable amount of the credit could be regarded as 'a selective reduction in taxes related to the taxable income of the year in which the credit arises'. No argument was offered *for* this view. In respect of it the Board concluded that

> the investment credit is an administrative procedure to permit the taxpayer to withhold the cash equivalent of the credit from taxes otherwise payable and that it is not an element entering into the computation of taxes related to income of the period.

It seems curious to take the Revenue Code apart and to assert that some parts of the concessions, allowances or credits it provides do, and some do not, enter into the computation of taxes related to income of the period. The Code of 1962 may differ from the Code as it was in prior years; but it is, the whole of it, the Code of 1962: and its object is to say who shall pay what, and to provide rules for computing the taxes payable in respect of periodical income. The ordinary provisions for allowances for depreciation and other things may not be described in the statutes as 'credits'; but in practical effect they are the same as the investment credit. Both permit the taxpayer to withhold the cash equivalent of taxes otherwise payable. It seems reasonable to treat the specific words used (e.g. 'credit') as the most convenient way in which the draftsman could introduce a new concession without major modifications of the words of, but in the context of, the pre-existing Code.

Even on the face of it, the provisions of the Act, outlined in the first paragraph of this section, cannot be interpreted otherwise than as stating the mode of computing taxes related to income of the period. The credit is applied in a specific period, to an amount calculated in respect of that period. A taxpayer may only claim if he has or has made qualified investments in the period. The limit to the amount of the credit is specified by reference to another amount of the period.

COST REDUCTION   The investment credit could be regarded 'as a reduction in or offset against a cost otherwise chargeable in a greater amount to future accounting periods' (*Opinion No 2*, para. 9). This view is said to be 'based upon existing accounting principles'.

Now suppose a vendor of machinery in a given year, for whatever reason (there are plausible and realistic reasons), decides to give a buyer an unusual discount on the list price. No authority has contended that the buyer should take the machine into his books at the list price on the ground that the discount is 'a reduction in or offset against a cost otherwise chargeable in a greater amount to future accounting periods'. On the contrary, such a proposal would be stoutly opposed on the ground of one of the most strongly held accounting principles— the historical principle. It is hard to see why the same principle should not apply to the investment credit: what would be 'otherwise' has surely no superiority, as fact, over what is or has been. The opinion, however, makes no reference to any specific 'existing accounting principle'.

The Board attached 'substantial weight' to the opinion that 'earnings arise from the use of facilities, not from their acquisition'. But the tax rule relates to tax concessions, which can scarcely be described as earnings in any ordinary usage of the term; nor is there any reasonable analogy. (A few lines later the Opinion refers to 'the treatment of the investment credit as income': the same objections may be taken). And the credit is provided for the year of acquisition, and presumably to encourage investment; it is not overtly related in any way to the use of facilities.

'Substantial weight' was also attached to the point that 'the ultimate realization of the credit is contingent to some degree on future developments' (*Opinion No 2*, para. 12). Now realization is generally said to occur either at the point at which cash or a claim to cash emerges, or at the point at which the amount receivable in respect of some matter is determinate. If the word can be used at all of the investment credit, then, in either of these senses, realization of the credit occurs in the year in which the claim arises; its amount is quite determinate in that year. The benefit is immediate, not ultimate.

The 'contingent future developments' alluded to are 'recapture and other provisions' of the Act. However, these provisions serve to make clear the conditions under which the credit is given, and provide sanctions against the subsequent abuse of the concession given. In any case, the propriety of the amount of a depreciation charge in the ordinary course of accounting is 'contingent' upon the amount realized when the asset is put out of service, and on the actual, not the expected, service life of the asset. Such an amount is really 'contingent', for there are no explicit conditions the fulfilment of which will secure that the price obtained and the date on which it is obtained will coincide with the expected scrap value and the expected end of life. Yet we find no reluctance to ordinary depreciation charges on the ground that the ultimate realization of the expense is contingent on future developments. If there is no ground for objection in this matter, there is even less ground for deferring recognition of the investment credit.

134

The Board concluded that 'the allowable investment credit should be reflected in net income over the productive life of acquired property and not in the year in which it is placed in service' (para. 13). It did however allow that the presentation in the income account of the amount actually payable for taxes was appropriate 'provided that a corresponding charge is made to an appropriate cost or expense (for example, to the provision for depreciation) and the treatment is adequately disclosed.' But as we observed earlier, this metamorphosis of a liability credit into an asset provision credit seems inexcusable in terms either of ordinary accounting principles or of the disclosure laws.[8]

That the opinion did not carry conviction is evident from the sequel. In January 1963, the SEC announced (*Accounting Series Release No 96*) that in view of the differences of opinion and practice prevailing, it would accept financial statements in which a method is used (a) 'which reflects the investment credit in income over the productive life of the acquired property' or (b) which defers 52 per cent of the credit (on the ground that that proportion of the credit will subsequently fall to be taxed, the tax rate being then 52 per cent). For regulated industries, where the appropriate regulations authorized or required 'flow-through to income' of the whole amount of the credit this method would be accepted. The Accounting Principles Board followed suit in *Opinion No 4 (Amending No 2)* in March 1964, finding both the full tax reduction and the full cost reduction notions acceptable bases for accounting for the investment credit.

It has long and repeatedly been said that an important objective of discussion and inquiry in accounting is the narrowing of the range of permissible practices. The ideal has been espoused by the profession and the SEC. Yet here is just another case which multiplies differences. So much for the ideal.[9] *Sic transit gloria mundi.*

Further Statements

Since 1964 there have been several further developments. *A.R.S. No 9*, 'Interperiod Allocation of Corporate Income Taxes', was published in 1966. It appears to break no new ground except in one respect. Accepting tax allocation and the treatment of the deferred credit as a liability, it proposed the discounting of the nominal amount of the liability. The suggestion was noticed in para. 6 of *A.P.B. Opinion No 10* of December 1966, but no prescription issued. A full statement on 'Accounting for Income Taxes' was issued in December 1967 as *A.P.B. Opinion*

8. The idea of loss of tax deductibility mentioned above would apply to the investment credit as well as to liberalized depreciation allowances. If it attaches to assets, it cannot attach to all assets. For the credit does not apply to assets of shorter expected life than four years nor to assets of kinds specifically excluded. And the provision does not apply to amounts of assets in respect of which the credit would exceed $25,000 plus one-fourth of the tax liability in excess of $25,000. But in this case which assets lose tax deductibility in an initial year? and why just those assets?
9. For some forceful observations on the outcome see the dissents of Maurice Moonitz and Leonard Spacek to *A.P.B. Opinion No 4*.

No 11. On the problem here discussed no new ground was broken. It was noted that 'flow-through' accounting 'has not been used widely in practice and is not supported presently to any significant extent' (para. 24). The Board concluded that 'comprehensive interperiod tax allocation is an integral part of the determination of income tax expense' to be charged against the pre-tax income of each year (para. 34). The opinion does not relate to the investment credit, in respect of which *Opinions No 2* and *No 4* are still effective. It is difficult to see why accelerated depreciation provisions and investment credit provisions of the tax code have not been considered as of the same class. Both are said to have been forms of inducement; both have their effect through immediate tax relief; and the forms of argument for and against the treatments discussed have many similar features.

We turn to consider more closely some features of the problem and the discussion of it.

136

The Contingent Nature of Tax Incidence

We stated at the outset that, because income taxes and the prescribed modes of calculating them from time to time are directed both to fiscal and policy objectives, their amounts will differ at any time from the application of the tax rate to pre-tax income as determined by recourse to commercial accounting principles. The events described show also that the tax payable in respect of any future year is not predictable. Thus, we have noticed changes in the tax code since 1944, in 1950, 1954 and 1962. In 1964 there was a change in respect of the investment credit. Whereas under the 1962 Act the investment credit was to be regarded as reducing the basis of future percentage allowances for depreciation, the 1964 Act removed this limit. In 1964, the overall rate of tax was reduced and this was to be followed by a further reduction in 1965 and later years. If, under commercial accounting principles, any company held any asset with an expected commercial life of 10 years, at no time in the 20-year interval considered would the adoption of the rates and provisions of any year have resulted in a deferred tax credit in the amount appropriate in the later years of the asset's life. The various pronouncements have permitted the use of the rates prevailing at the time of setting up the deferred credit in the accounts. But this is, in itself, recognition of the 'contingent' character of the amount, a contingency which is never mentioned but which, as the record shows, might be regarded as fatal to any attempt at 'forward matching' or deferred credit accounting.

There is a very telling footnote to *Accounting Series Release No 53* of 1945 which seems to have been disregarded or completely discounted. Adverting to the use of the term 'tax savings' with reference to the accelerated allowance of charges for tax purposes, the SEC observed:

> It seems to us that the term 'tax saving' is apt to connote some sort of standard or normal tax law and a standard or normal earnings year to which the law applies. The facts are, of course, that there has not been a static or standard or

'normal' tax law or tax status; nor has it been possible except in most unusual cases to characterize any particular fiscal year of a company as a 'normal earnings' year, from which all others are to be regarded as departures. Under such conditions, each year's tax is whatever happens to result from the application of the computation formula, provided by the tax law of that year, to the sum total of taxable transactions and tax deductions resulting from whatever business may have been done in that particular year. Moreover, the past few years during which the term and the problem of 'tax saving' appeared have clearly been unusual in nearly every respect. [The same could be said now also of every year since.] Finally if the phenomenon in question is to be described as a 'tax saving' it would seem necessary to describe as a 'tax loss' the failure to carry through a transaction which it can be said would have resulted in a 'tax saving'.

The idea of a normal tax charge, however, dies hard. So also does the idea that *net* incomes of different companies are comparable. A senior Treasury official, naming twelve classes of company which pay less than average taxes, was recently moved to remark: '. . . yet on how many of their financial statements will this fact appear? Answer: Very few.'[10]

Thus, the appearance of precision which deferred tax accounting gives is illusory, because the tax rate in any year in which a credit is set up may not be the rate effective in later years. And if it is intended by deferred tax accounting to make the net incomes of different companies in a given year comparable, or the net incomes of a given company in successive years comparable, the discriminatory tax provisions make the objective unattainable even if there were no changes in the structure of tax rates and concessions from year to year.

Accounting for the incidence of taxes 'as if' the tax laws were different from what they are at any time, and 'as if' the incidence were different from what it is, cannot be justified by reference to the historical principle or any principle which entails that financial statements are or should be factual. Nor does it seem to be consistent with the disclosure laws and regulations to report on an 'as if' basis.

Is there a Liability?

As the record has shown, there has been difference of opinion as to whether the deferred tax credit should be regarded as a liability or a category of surplus or stockholders' equity. Opinion has settled for treatment of the item as a liability. We have shown that this has resulted in an 'uncomfortable' position, leading to the suggestion that the amount be included with depreciation provisions otherwise made.

The balance sheet purports to show assets and liabilities and equities as they stand at its date. A liability at any time is an amount owed at that time to another party. It cannot reasonably be said that the amount of the deferred tax credit is

---

10. Jerome Kurtz, Tax Legislative Counsel for the U.S. Treasury Department, as reported in *The Journal of Accountancy*, Vol. 126, No. 3, September 1968, p. 68.

owed to anyone, or to the government in particular.[11] The tax code determines the amount of a liability from year to year. The mode of calculation may have some side effects in due course; but these are not in any sense present liabilities. The side effects depend on the making of taxable income in the future, and also on the persistence of the same calculation rules. To show a deferred tax credit implies a forecast that the taxpayer will in fact make such an income that the side effects fall on the company and a forecast that the tax rules will persist. It has long been held that professional accountants should not make profit forecasts. Of even greater force, perhaps, is the statute or regulation which requires that balance sheets shall fairly represent dated positions. No speculation about what the position might be at a future date can be regarded as a proper element of a statement of any present position.

It seems therefore that if the deferred tax credit is shown at all it should be shown among the surplus accounts. It has been claimed that it should be so shown, as 'restricted'. But if there is no present obligation in respect of it there seems to be no reason why it should at present be restricted. It has long been held that the annual accounts presented should have in contemplation the rights of present stockholders. If full provision is made for the tax payable in a given year, there seems to be no reason why the remainder of the year's income should not be regarded as part of the then stockholders' equity.

The anomalous character of the credit is evidenced by the debate which its treatment has generated, and by its banishment to a kind of limbo in some places.[12] But the proper treatment is not simply a matter of accounting. If it is required that the credit be shown as a liability, or in such an indeterminate way that 'for safety' readers will treat it as a liability, any reflection upon a company's position which turns on the debt to equity ratio, and any contract or indenture one of the terms of which relates to the debt to equity ratio or the amount of debt outstanding, will be affected. This point was made by numbers of respondents to the SEC's invitation of December 1958 to comment on its proposed announcement (*see* above). In the event, following upon the issue of the SEC's statement in February 1960, a proceeding was instituted by the SEC in respect of Kentucky Power Company, and its holding company. The effect of following the policy stipulated in the SEC's statement would have been to reduce the maximum level

11. 'There is, of course, no "deferred tax liability" . . .', James L. Dohr in letter to the SEC dated 6 January 1959. 'But there is no such liability. There is no creditor. Certainly, the federal government recognizes no claim against the taxpayer, and the taxpayer would react strongly if he thought it did'. Weldon Powell, 'Accounting Principles and Income-Tax Allocation', *New York Certified Public Accountant*, Vol. 29, No. 1, January 1959, pp. 25-6. Compare also: 'An amount set aside to meet future income tax is not, at the date of the balance sheet, a liability . . .' Institute of Chartered Accountants in England and Wales, *Recommendation N19*, 1958, para 9. The recommendation has been superseded, but the cited point seems timeless.

12. E.g. The U.S. Federal Power Commission in May 1958 classified 'accumulated deferred taxes on income' neither as a reserve (American usage) nor as a restricted surplus account. Even when deferred taxes are grouped with equities or liabilities, the subclassifications used suggest that they are not to be regarded in the same way as the other items in the group.

of debt financing of Kentucky and its holding company and thus potentially to force up power costs to customers. This could only be averted by agreement, by the SEC to give due weight to the existence of the accumulated credit in determining capitalization ratios in the event of future financing, and by the holding company to file supplementary financial statements dealing with the credit in the manner stipulated by the SEC. This seems to mean that the SEC would interpret the required supplementary statements differently than at their face value. The whole arrangement seems rather more complicated than the sheer commercial realities demand.

As the liberalized depreciation and other such rules leave at the disposal of taxpayers a larger amount of cash, free of any obligation or lien on the part of government, the security underlying any loan financing, in so far as uncommitted assets represent security, is surely the greater in the year of the emergence of the so-called credit. It is contrary to the admitted facts to assert otherwise, and contrary to the object of the legislation providing immediate relief. Numerous events may subsequently affect the capitalization ratios of companies; and the managements of borrowing companies must take steps against them all to avoid exceeding the limits imposed by borrowing indentures. But to cut down borrowing potential, or to make special definitions necessary to avoid this, simply on the ground of a debatable accounting entry, seems to make expectation and invention more virtuous than representation of the facts.

139

Matching What?

As we have observed, the matching idea in its original and most common form has reference to the matching of revenues and expenses or costs, and, in the case of continuing entities, the matching of these periodically. Revenues arise from the delivery of some good or service. As deliveries occur at identifiable points of time it is usually not difficult to identify the revenues of a period. Some expenses are identifiable with the parcels of goods or services delivered. Others are not; these must be identified with periods only, not with specific parcels. The whole effect of this is that the revenues of a period and the expenses of a period are to be ascertained and the aggregates of both are to be set off to obtain income.

Now taxes are in no sense based on revenues. They are based on the set-off of such parts of revenues *and* expenses as yield the assessable income. And even then the amount of the assessment is not necessarily directly related to assessable income because of concessions which may be calculable, according to the tax code, on some basis other than assessable income. Further, the effects of these concessions are not isolable from the effects of other provisions of the code; e.g. the investment credit has a prescribed and limited application to the effects of other provisions of the code. It cannot be said that concessions arise from any particular transaction. They arise from the *coincidence* of the provisions of the code relating to concessions, *and* the ascertained effect of those parts of revenues and expenses which determine assessable income, *and* the occurrence of the particular event on which the calculation of the concession is based. There

117

is no single cause of the concession, nor therefore of the tax payable. To speak of the 'tax effects of transactions'[13] is thus to misconstrue the effects of a tax law, for no transaction of itself gives rise to a tax or to a concession.

As there is no way of identifying taxes with revenues, there can be no way of matching expected taxes with expected revenues. Even though the phrase 'matching revenues and expenses' occurs in the pronouncements, it must in fact be used there in a wider sense than the literal meaning. The formula can be extended without doing violence to its meaning. As revenues augment equity and expenses diminish equity, we may speak of the matching of benefits and detriments, by periods.

140

Now, suppose there is brought into the income account of an 'initial' year a charge for 'income tax expense' in excess of the tax payable under the code in respect of that year. For this excess charge presumably there is some benefit. (We are trying to follow the line of argument for comprehensive tax allocation.) Indeed we find there is a benefit. It is the 'tax-free recovery from operations of capital invested in plant at a faster rate than . . . previously permitted' (in respect of liberalized depreciation, as stated in the SEC's notice of December 1958); or the right to 'withhold the cash equivalent of the credit from taxes otherwise payable' (in respect of the investment credit, as stated in *A.P.B. Opinion No 2*). If benefits and detriments are to be matched, the bringing in of a charge in an initial year entails the bringing in also of the benefit in that year.

We may take the nominal amount of the excess charge as the nominal amount of cash not disbursed in tax payments, for the tax allocation proposals deal only in nominal amounts. But we may add a refinement. The subsequent payments of the tax set up as a liability or deferred tax credit may extend over some years, so that the present amount of the liability should be less than the nominal amount.[14] Similarly the subsequent benefits from being able immediately to invest in new or additional assets out of the cash not disbursed in tax payments should be discounted. Indeed the present value of those benefits may exceed (or equal, or fall short of) the present value of the tax payments implied by the deferred tax credit. If we are using the matching notion in earnest, and not as some abracadabra, there is no more reason why we should not try to peer *carefully* into the future, than there is to suppose that the amount of the deferred tax credit will have to be paid in the future.

We do not suppose this refined application of anticipation would or should attract support. It is introduced simply to show that serious considerations of what is matched periodically would yield quite a different result than tax allocation as it is recommended. We are content to take the nominal effects: in which case the present excess charge would be matched by a present value of

13. The phrase has been widely used; as a particular instance *see A.P.B. Opinion No 11*.
14. Discounting was suggested as early as Thomas M. Hill, 'Some Arguments against the Inter-period Allocation of Income Taxes', *The Accounting Review*, Vol. XXXII, No. 3, July 1957, p. 360. As already noted, it was alluded to briefly in *A.P.B. Opinion No 10*, but does not appear in *Opinion No 11*.

future benefits. The debit for the one in the income account would be equal to the credit for the other; and the corresponding balances in the balance sheet would be equal. If one prefers an uncomplicated life, of course, one would simply omit both. Indeed on the ground of the historical principle, one would omit both. On no ground at all would it be proper to include only one-half of the putative effect, as the officially recommended treatment entails.[15]

The above line of argument may not be rebutted on the ground that the benefit we have alluded to is unrealistic. Everyone knows that cash now is better than cash later. Nor can it be said that Congress did not intend to confer a benefit. Taxes being what they are, a tax incentive to reinvestment will be taken by every taxpayer who can take it. On the other hand, the tax allocation procedure recommended implies that there is no equivalent or corresponding benefit whatever—which is patently false to the facts.

MATCHING IN TWO SENSES   The slip from 'the matching of revenues and expenses' to the attempt to match pre-tax commercially calculated income and income tax expense seems to have arisen from the shorthand use of 'matching' or 'the matching concept'. But two quite different kinds of matching seem to be necessary, particularly where taxes are not a direct function (e.g. percentage) of pre-tax income.

If we seek an indication of the consequences of a year's business operations, we may well match revenues and expenses. And we may, if we wish, use this pre-tax income as a guide to what may be expected, of the same kind, in the following period. But if also we wish to know what may be appropriated out of a year's pre-tax income for dividend and reinvestment purposes, we must first provide for the tax payable. Notice that the object in this latter case is to discover what may or must be done with the proceeds. The two indications mentioned thus serve quite different purposes. In the one we match revenues and expenses; in the other we match the surplus thus arising with commitments out of it. Only confusion can result if the two exercises are supposed to be the same in style and object.

The mixed and variable objects of income taxes, and the varying rates and concessions introduced in revenue acts strongly suggest that such taxes should be treated as appropriations, for they are in principle *ex*propriations. They also suggest that pre-tax income and the taxes payable in respect of any year should be used independently, and quite deliberately so, in any analysis directed to the estimating of future net income. They also suggest that all summaries published by investment services and the financial press should include earnings rates based on pre-tax income. For, if we want an indication of performance in business, pre-tax income is free of the effects of the mode of tax assessment. And, as dividends may be paid out of accumulated profits if necessary, there is

141

15. By a different route a somewhat similar conclusion seems to be reached in Wendell P. Trumbull, 'When is a Liability?', *The Accounting Review*, Vol. XXXVIII, No. 1, January 1963, at p. 51.

no good reason why income after taxes should have any direct bearing even on dividend policy. The short-cut method of using net income (after taxes) as a guide to assessments of performance and prospects is an oversimplification and potentially misleading.

Verbal Depreciation

It is of interest to note how words and phrases lose meaning in the course of time under the pressure of presumptions and circumstances. There can be no doubt of the sincerity of those who have argued for and against tax allocation. But the mere fact that there are 'sides' creates a debating situation, a political situation, in which arguments are disregarded or coloured according to the positions taken. And positions are often taken on the ground of *one* principle, not on the ground of a series of principles of equal rank.

The primary principle adopted in support of tax collection was the matching of revenues and expenses. Tax was described as an expense; no notice was taken of the difference between, say, wages (the amount of which may be deliberately increased in any year in the expectation of higher revenues) and income taxes (which may not be increased voluntarily in any year in the expectation of higher revenues). The difference may have been disregarded because of the treatment of taxes, as an allowable expense, under rate-making rules for utility companies.[16]

But rate-making and financial reporting are different in object: one is a form of policy making, the other a form of discovery. In any case, the difference in the notions of taxes and other expenses was brushed away.

In like manner 'revenues' were assimilated to 'income'. *A.R.B. No 23*, for example, refers to 'expense properly allocable to income', not to revenues, and proceeds as if such allocation were a matching of revenues and expenses. Either as a cause or a consequence of this association net income is regarded as an indicator of performance of a year. But here again pre-tax income and net income are made to seem alike as indicators, whereas fiscal discrimination and policy functions of taxes make them quite different in kind. As a consequence of these assumed or implied similarities, we find the investment credit made to seem like 'earnings' (*A.P.B. Opinion No 4*, para. 12), and we find reference to the 'flow-through to income of the investment credit benefit' (*Accounting Series Release No 96*); when in reality a reduction of taxes is not an earning, and the flow-through is to net income, not to income. The whole result looks very unlike the consequence of matching revenues and expenses.

We found a strong statement upholding the historical and factual character of accounting statements, but it seems to have lingered in limbo. *Accounting Series Release No 53* has not been withdrawn, although subsequent rulings of the SEC have not been consistent with it. This has led one writer to observe:

16. *See*, for example, Maurice Moonitz, 'Income Taxes in Financial Statements', *The Accounting Review*, Vol. XXXII, No. 2, April 1957, at pp. 175-6: *A.R.B. No 44 Revised*, para. 8.

As long as Release No 53 continues in its present form and statements are filed which contravene the release, accountants issuing compliance letters [assuring compliance with the requirements of the *Securities Act* of 1933 and of the SEC] do so with tongue in cheek with the knowledge that in this area there is a difference between theory and practice.[17]

The American Institute's committees have not taken up the point at all.

There are references to the 'significance or usefulness of the financial statements' (e.g. *A.R.B No 23*, para. 3). But there are no demonstrations to the effect that significance or usefulness is improved by showing what the present position would be if certain specific events turn out in the future to be as they are now expected. A set of statements may have usefulness or significance as factual statements or expectational statements; but no set of statements can be both at the same time. The necessity of factual information as a basis for forming expectations seems to have been confused with the forming of expectations; in the upshot the form of accounting which tax allocation implies issues in statements which are neither factual nor expectational, but some indeterminate mixture of both, and thus of no significance or usefulness as either.

143

As we have pointed out, there have been allusions to consistency with existing accounting principles; but the discernment of consistency escapes in the absence of reference to specific principles. We have seen the contingent nature of some future things emphasized and the contingent nature of others disregarded. We have seen that, whatever the deferred tax credit is, it may be treated either as a liability provision or as a valuation provision, which, in principle, are surely quite different things. Even the specific terms used are of dubious merit; for, in respect of the 'deferred tax credit', there is at the end of any given period no tax which is in fact deferred; and, in respect of the 'investment credit', it is a credit against tax otherwise payable, not a credit against an investment. It seems to have happened, as so often happens, that merely giving an idea a name has led to the belief in its existence as a thing, an entity.

There are also some modes of thinking which become habitual so that the vagueness of conclusions is not fully grasped. Throughout the whole of the pronouncements considered runs that curious word 'material'. Do this or that, if such and such is material. A guide to what is material is given in Rule 1-02 of *Regulation S-X* of course. But this in no way circumvents the exercise of judgement and the emergence of differences in the products of judgement, in the same company from time to time, or in different companies at the same time. Further, of course, every pronouncement has contained provisos, exclusions and exceptions, which require interpretive acts on the part of accountants or managers. The diversity thus permitted is itself a good reason for doubting the wisdom of allocation. Unless, of course, we are prepared forever to tolerate vagueness of prescription and vagueness of practice.

We impute no waywardness to those who have used the terms and phrases cited.

17. Louis H. Rappaport, *SEC Accounting Practice and Procedure*, The Ronald Press Company, New York 1966, p. 3.36.

But in tracing the development of arguments and justifications in retrospect we are able to see how words can lose precise meaning over time, and how conclusions may come to be based on analogies which are quite imperfect and hence misleading.

The Fundamental Questions

In his prefatory statement to *Accounting Research Study No 9*, the Director of Accounting Research observed:

> The study does not answer fundamental questions about the nature of the income tax and the validity of the concept of interperiod income tax allocation. Whether income taxes are conceptually expenses or distributions of income has not really been resolved by the profession. Similarly, whether taxes should be allocated or whether the taxes currently payable should be the income tax expense for a period has never been adequately studied (p. vii).

He expressed the hope that 'these fundamental questions will be studied by others'.

We have tried to keep to these questions in this paper, in the belief that their answers are logically prior to discussions of when, how and to what extent allocation shall be made. The author of the *Study* remarked at the outset that 'the situation grows more complicated as the intricacy of the tax law increases and the relationship between income tax payments and the components of financial statements becomes more complex'. If this is to be the case it seems well worth answering the fundamental questions, instead of proceeding 'as if' income tax were an expense and 'as if' allocation were proper in principle. If the present complexity stems from misconceptions, as we believe, only by recognizing their contrived character, and disposing of them as non-factual inventions, will we escape from the threatened morass. Adherence to the historical-factual principle and the applications of the matching principle we have suggested lead to the simple prescription that the amount of income tax arising in and payable at the end of a period is the amount to be shown in respect of that period in the statements required under the disclosure laws.

Conclusion

It may be instructive to examine at some length the provisions of the tax code relating to the carry-back and carry-forward of losses, and to those provisions of some codes which provide for complete or almost complete amortization of exploration costs and mining works in the year of expenditure. It is tempting to do so in the light of some instances, recently debated in the Australian press, of qualified audit reports of mining companies. But the circumstances and considerations here brought under review seem to be sufficiently extensive to cover the features of all such cases.

Our conclusions, then, are that

(a) income tax is not an expense of the kind to which the term 'allocation' or the process of interperiod allocation is appropriate;

(b) income tax is discriminatory, is a composite effect of governmental fiscal and policy objectives, and is not functionally related to revenues or pre-tax incomes of companies;

(c) because of (b), net income is not a basis on which business performance may be judged or extrapolated; it is a measure only of the disposable surplus of a year;

(d) comprehensive tax allocation disregards the benefit which arises from the earlier timing of tax relief, and does not therefore constitute an application of the matching principle, even less an application of the matching of revenues and costs;

(e) comprehensive tax allocation entails rejection of the historical principle and the usual meaning of realization;

(f) if comprehensive tax allocation results in the representation of the 'deferred tax' as a liability, there is no such liability at the time it is so represented, and the financial position of a company is not fairly presented in the circumstances;

145

(g) if 'deferred tax' is shown as a liability, the debt to equity relationship is misrepresented; this may adversely affect the management of finance under the terms of existing loan funds and prejudice the raising of other loan funds; both as misrepresenting the present equity from time to time and as prejudicing borrowing, the interests of present shareholders may be prejudiced;

(h) attempts to normalize disclosed net income are improper, as representing events and effects otherwise than they were or are; if it is deemed worthwhile to give investors or analysts other information than can properly be given in the framework of accounting statements, it should be given otherwise;

(i) the tax laws and the disclosure laws are not reconcilable by any form of adjustment which supposes things to be other than they are, but the tax laws do provide the basis upon which the present liability to tax of any company may be determined, and this alone is relevant to the statement of any present position as required by the disclosure laws. This is our answer to the question with which we began.

What's Wrong With Financial Statements?

QUITE a lot, to judge by the comments and criticisms of the last forty years.

The evidence that there is something wrong "somewhere" is varied. Qualified audit reports tend to suggest that "somewhere" means in the ranks of the managers and directors. The reports of official investigators suggest something similar. The extent of the litigation against professional firms, mainly but not solely in the United States, suggests that "somewhere" means in the ranks of the profession. Close examination of the doctrines of accountants and the practices of which actual financial statements are evidence suggests that "somewhere" means in the very core of the subject and its practice.

There may well be incompetent, misdirected or unfortunate managers and accountants and auditors. But we will not be able to discover which managers are incompetent and which unfortunate without reliable financial statements; and we will not be able to discover which accountants and auditors are incompetent and which unfortunate without reliable principles for preparing financial statements. We propose to answer the question at two levels — by reference both to specific practices and to the core of the subject and its practice.

Method and a Proviso

In the course of this examination we will draw on examples taken from the U.K., the U.S.A. and Australia. Many of the faults we shall illustrate occur in the reports of companies which received commendation in the 1969 list of awards by the Australian Institute of Management. To these points no reference was made in the published report of the adjudicators. Yet they seem to us far more important, more fundamental, than the matters mentioned in that report.

It has seemed to be desirable to quote specific instances. This is the only way to avoid the allegation that one has set up straw men. And it is the only way to bring attention to the meaning or lack of meaning of the constituent parts of whole financial statements. It is commonly said that one must regard these statements whole, form an impression from them whole. But if the parts are really constituents of wholes, as they are, no adequate impression of a whole can be gained from an agglutination of inadequate parts.

The use of examples from three countries is justifiable on several grounds. The general commercial, financial and legal systems of them all are similar. The practices of one have tended to become the practices of others. And even those which occur in one country only are likely to turn up in some form in another country through the osmosis of ideas expressed in the literature which they share, and through the search for permissive precedents which permissive accounting fosters. And, of course, illustrations from different places show the widespread nature of the defects we shall consider.

The use here made of the report of any company as an example is not to be taken as criticism of that company or of its directors and managers. These are all audited reports. Presumably they comply with the law and the present state of practice. The comments on the illustrations used are therefore to be regarded as critical of the present state of practice and of the law relating to published accounts.

What is expected of financial statements? — in the ordinary course of events; on the occurrence of takeover bids; by investors; by creditors; by managers?

Imagine a Jack Brabham or a Stirling Moss in a 20-lap track race. There are three elements in such a race for each competitor — distance, time, and the other competitors. Distance and clocks are not manipulable. In the end, the driver who covers the distance in the shortest time wins. In the course of the race there is competition for favoured places, places from which the average speed may be increased. Nevertheless distance and time determine the result. The outcome is determined by outsiders — those not in the race, but interested in its outcome. They have counting and timing devices of their own, and the supporters of any driver during the course of the race will properly try to see that the driver is aware of the progress of the race as non-drivers see it: laps completed, time taken, and the positions of other drivers.

147

An address delivered at the thirteenth Annual Convention of the South Australian Division of The Australian Society of Accountants.

This seems to me to provide rather a good analogy of the conduct of a business. There are managers of firms competing with others for places in the markets for factors and finished products, with specified check points, year-ends. The name of the game is competition. The object of the game is to increase a company's general command over goods and services. There are outsiders, investors and creditors, and indeed customers and workers who are interested financially in the outcome. And strictly there is only one way of finding out what the outcome is — by discovering in the market place what the company's command over resources is at the end of each year.

It would be no use Brabham, or Moss, telling the judges he won if the independent evidence showed otherwise. They would take no notice. Equally, it is no use relying on what managers say about how well they have done unless what they say tallies with independent evidence. It would be no use Brabham, or Moss, saying that he put so many gallons of gasoline in the tank, and so much pressure on the throttle in the fifth lap, and expecting that to be any evidence to outsiders of where he finished in the race. No one measures results by counting up what went into anything. Results are what come out, not what goes in.

In the case of a company what goes in, for any year, is the company's net command of resources in general at the beginning of the year. Results are the difference between this and the company's net command of resources in general at the end of the year. During the year the company's accounting could be done in any way it pleases, as far as outsiders are concerned. They are just not interested in how well it keeps its books, or whether its bookkeeping principles are good, bad or indifferent. They want to know how well it has done with what it started, and the position in which it stands as a result; and they need to know that what managers report in financial statements is supported by evidence independent of managers' hopes, fears, wishes and guesses.

Accounting as it is now done and the financial statements as they are now published do not meet these elementary commonsense tests. The primary concern of accountants is what goes in. Great care is taken to get the original entries right, especially entries recording the getting and spending of money. But hardly any care is taken to find and report the position in which a company stands at the end of each year. And if no care is taken about that, we cannot know what the results are, for results are simply the difference between two positions.

This is certain to be challenged. One of the major reforms arising from the McKesson and Robbins case of the late thirties was the requirement in the U.S.A. that auditors should attend the taking of stock. And of course stocktaking has for decades, indeed for centuries, been one way of checking on how things stand. But what is stocktaking? To find the value of a stock of anything (inventories or plant or securities) we find out how much of it there is and multiply it by a price. How much there is, when? At the time of stocktaking. What price? Under present practice: please yourself — the price paid for some things, recently or distantly; the net realizable price for some things; the replacement price for some things; the price which managers put on some things. And in a balance sheet containing reference to a variety of assets, almost all of these prices will have been used. What puzzles me is why go to all the trouble to get the physical quantity at a given date and then multiply it by a price ruling at some other date? It would be no less absurd to get the price ruling at the stocktaking date and multiply it by the quantity on hand at some other date. One might suppose that an accountant, whose main business is with money and prices, would get the price right, even if the quantity were wrong. It seems, on the contrary, that so long as the quantity is right the price doesn't matter. There are some who say, prices go up and down, so that one can't depend on the price at any set date. But so do quantities go up and down; there is no greater reason for depending on the quantity at any date. The very thing that is up to date, the quantity, does not of course appear on the balance sheet at all. Only a product, price times quantity, appears there. And no person who has not been brainwashed would suppose that a quantity at a given date would be multiplied by a price at some other date, to give a representation of the stock of things at the given date.

In the ordinary course of events everyone with any financial interest in a company needs to have information on its affairs which is complete and up to date. Further, as the financial statements are aggregative statements, the component figures must be capable of addition to give sensible, understandable aggregates. Every buyer or seller of shares, every lender or prospective lender to a company, all who advise or take part in the issuing of shares and in the buying or selling of shares need this information. No one can know what he is talking about who does not have complete and up to date information. Shareholders in companies for which take-over bids are made cannot know what they are being asked to give for what they are offered unless their information is complete and up to date.

But in the present state of the game, financial statements do not give anything like complete and up to date information. In a sense they concentrate on some of the basic raw materials, and much of the scaffolding, without any attempt to supply other necessary materials and strip the scaffolding out of the way so that readers can see what the company has built. This is what we hope to demonstrate.

Terminological confusion. What is a company's state of affairs? What is an asset, a liability, a cost, a valuation, a profit?

The phrase "state of affairs" occurs in the Companies Acts. The state of affairs of a company is required to be given as at a stated date. It is required to be given in the form of a balance sheet. The phrase "state of affairs" is not used in the captions of balance sheets, but it does occur in the auditor's report. You will look in vain in the literature for any discussion of what a state of affairs is. This seems odd when the auditor is required to make some quite definite statement about it.

The terms "financial position" and "financial condition" are sometimes used of what the balance sheet represents. But again you will find scarcely any discussion in the traditional literature of what these terms mean. Perhaps the meaning of state of affairs, or financial condition is so obvious that it calls for no discussion. But is it?

If you were asked what the state of your affairs is, I am tolerably certain that you would go about it by taking a list of all the things you own and could sell and pricing them at the price you think they would fetch, and deducting from the total the debts you owe. I am tolerably certain that that is what most people would do; and that the result is what people understand when they read any reference to state of affairs. Is there any reason why the term should mean anything else?

Business firms buy and sell; so do you and I. They borrow and lend; so do you and I. They have assets and liabilities; so do you and I. They earn incomes and spend the proceeds; so do you and I. There is nothing about them that you and I do not do or have. Including a state of affairs which changes from time to time and needs to be ascertained from time to time

Yet you know that present balance sheets do not give anything like the state of affairs described above, nothing like ordinary intelligent people mean when they use the term or understand when they read it. Nor do they give anything like financial position at a stated date as they may say they do. If a housewife goes to a store for a fry pan, it would be no use the storekeeper saying "I'm out of fry pans, why not take a colander? It's the same shape. The holes in the bottom don't matter". If people expect to find a state of affairs represented in a balance sheet, it is no less pointless to offer them something else. To assert that one thing is another is called fraud under some circumstances, and stupidity under others, and ignorance under others, and plain carelessness under others. Take your pick; all these things have been alleged of financial

statements which do not show states of affairs, of the kind we have described, at stipulated dates.

That the balance sheets of companies do not give states of affairs at the dates they bear may be due to the fuzziness of those, practitioners and teachers alike, who have written about accounting and balance sheets. They seem to have considered business firms as having continuous lives that somehow run like clockwork. There is no need to discover the state of affairs by reference to outside facts because once the clock is started it will run its course independently of what happens outside. This, of course, is nonsense. A business is not a closed system, its state cannot be determined by just what goes on inside it, or on the basis of the opinions of those inside it. It is an open system, and the only "state" which is of any consequence to those who deal with it is its state in relation to the outside world.

In more recent years the writers on accounting and balance sheets have turned to talking about accounting for decision-making. But curiously they still omit to discuss the state of a company at a point of time, the realistic statement of which alone provides a foundation for realistic decision-making.

What is this state? It is given by the relationship between the monetary equivalents of the assets possessed and the amounts of the equities in those assets. But here again there is great confusion, over what assets are and liabilities are and what monetary equivalents are. Some say that assets are costs expected to be recovered in the future. There is nothing in that statement which refers to the present significance of an asset as a repository of capacity to command goods and services generally. As a consequence assets are represented in balance sheets at cost or something based on cost, not by their present monetary equivalents at a balance date. Some say assets are service potentials, and their amounts are the present (discounted) values of what they are expected to yield. But these present values are not present monetary equivalents at all. One cannot buy bread or pay debts with what one expects to have years hence. One must have money or something presently convertible into money. To show expected values or discounted present values of assets in a statement of a present position is counting one's chickens before they are hatched.

What is that thing called "goodwill on consolidation" in consolidated balance sheets? I don't think anyone pretends it is an asset, in the sense that it has any of the properties of things like cash, receivables, plant and so on. It is described by some as the difference between the book value of a subsidiary or an interest in a subsidiary and the amount taken into the records at the date of acquisition as the net assets acquired. A company cannot buy anything with it, pay any debt with

149

it, or use it in its operations. What else can an asset be? It is more than likely that this difference is due simply to the numbers that are put in the books of account, and that the blanket figure simply or largely covers differences between what the book values of assets were before acquisition and the market values of those assets at the date of acquisition. And if, in analyzing a balance sheet, one is disposed to disregard such an intangible, it is quite likely that the amount should properly be attributed instead to some of the tangible assets.

And what are those things called leasehold rights and leasehold rentals which some have urged should be written into balance sheets? The obligation to pay rentals is not a present obligation at any date. Nor are the "leasehold rights" assets which can be sold for the amount shown to buy anything or pay any debt at a given balance date. Nor are the rentals expected to be paid out of the "leasehold rights". The whole idea of capitalizing such future obligations and rights is at odds with the notion of assets as indicative of things presently held at any date and liabilities as things presently owing at any date. We are not denying that capitalization or present value calculations are necessary in deciding whether to lease or not. Anyone making choices about anything will form his own "valuation" of what he expects it to yield; and if that valuation exceeds what he expects to be the value of any alternative use of the same outlay (its cost), he will pay its price. But all this preliminary calculating and thinking have nothing to do with the statement of how he stands at any subsequent date in relation to the rest of the community.

And what is that thing called "deferred taxation payable" which some suggest should be included in accounts where special tax allowances permit the speedier attraction of relief from tax than the expected lives of assets? This is not a present liability at any balance date. Its amount is contingent on there being future taxable profits, on the rates remaining the same and on the general rule for the special allowances remaining the same. It does not have to be met out of any present assets; if any amount does become payable it will be payable out of future assets.

And what is a profit? I'm not thinking of verbal definition here. I'm thinking of the variety of different things that affect the last line of an income statement in any annual report. Because so many different things may have so many different money amounts assigned to them according to the accounting rules chosen, and because the double entry process links the figures in balance sheets and those in income accounts, the profits in different annual reports can mean nothing similar at all. I have demonstrated the point adequately elsewhere.

These defects which we have grouped under "terminological confusion" are serious insofar as they illustrate the undisciplined character of thought, and the consequential undisciplined character of practice. As financial statements are integral combinations of series of constituent statements, it is possible for them to have a meaning comprehensible to their users only if the constituent statements have consistent meanings; that is to say, if assets are things having common features; if liabilities are things having common features; if past costs, present prices and future valuations are recognized to be quite distinctive categories, and are not mixed together as if they were the same in kind. Would you obtain your present financial position by adding the $1000 you may have paid for some B.H.P. shares ten years ago, the $500 you may now have in the bank, and the discounted amount of your prospective salary for the remainder of your working life? Try doing the sums; you will find there is absolutely no use which you can now make of the result.

Contradictions — by footnote, by changes in methods between successive dates of reporting, and by other means.

When a newspaper bears on its face a given date, we expect that the news it contains is of events or states at or about that date. We expect the whole thing to be consistent with what it says is the date, and we expect to be able to read and understand it by reference to our own familiarity with other things at or about that date. Or, if an article or report relates to some other time, we expect to be told, and we are told, what part of it relates to some other time and what that time was. It seems to me that financial statements, as they are today, are the one kind of news report which violates this common and reasonable expectation. And it seems to me that all those literary allusions which paint accountants as painstaking and meticulously careful and precise people are thoroughly undeserved.

If one finds a financial statement dated 30 June, 1969, one is entitled to suppose that, unless any other dates are given, the details and the narrations should be understood to relate to 30 June, 1969. This commonsense expectation is engendered by newspapers, periodicals, the letters we write and receive. But if we rely on it in accounting we will be deceived. In the body of the above statement we will find, say "Fixed assets, cost, $1.5m.". Here "cost" does not mean "cost at 30 June, 1969". It means cost at some other time. What time? Who knows? Only the accountant, probably: and the statement was not drawn up for his benefit. Or we may find "Cost or valuation", again with no date. Now, as we might think a valuation (i.e. at a recent price) is better than a long out-of-date cost price, this narration would confirm our expectation that the figures were up-to-date costs or valuations. Again we would usually be wrong.

The use of such vague terms as "cost" and "valuation" without dates under a general dated caption is concealed contradiction. One of the reasons for publishing information is to prompt thinking or further inquiry. If instead of such blanket terms, financial statements were to set down the dates at which the costs were incurred, readers might be prompted to ask themselves: But what are those assets worth now? Perhaps they would also begin to realize how useless is the information they are given now. And perhaps the vague terms continue to be used to avoid just these consequences!

Footnote explanations have been with us for some years. Some modern reports are, indeed, getting to look like the work of footnote-crazy pedants. The function of a footnote or "note to the accounts" is to explain, not to contradict or to confuse. This likewise is the function of notes in parenthesis.

In particular, the requirement of some jurisdictions that the market value of quoted securities shall be shown, by way of note if not otherwise, results in a direct contradiction in most cases. The 1960 accounts of Shop Investments (a U.K. company) are reported to have shown "Investment at cost £6250", whereas the market value was £180,625 (*Accountancy*, December, 1960). The 1961 accounts of Globe Telegraph and Trust Company (a U.K. company) showed investments quoted on British stock exchanges "at cost less amounts applied from net surplus on realizations, £9.25m.", whereas the market value was £32.30m. The book value of all quoted investments was £12.22m., whereas the market value was £37.95m. Curiously, by contrast with this, in the same year the directors wrote up the book value of an *unquoted* investment from £1.34m. to £6m. The shareholders' equity was shown as $15.65m.; if the market values of quoted securities had been used it would have been £41.38m. The earnings rate was 5.4 per cent on the published equity; it would have been 2 per cent on the adjusted equity! Which is a reader to believe?

One wonders what to make of some notes in the 1968 Conzinc Riotinto accounts. The total assets of the group are shown to be $423m., the total assets of the company to be $122m. Among the investments of the company are shares in a subsidiary the cost of which, $27m., is included in the balance sheet figures. The notes to the accounts give to these shares a market value of $755m. Among the assets of the group are listed shares in associate companies, the cost of which, $4m., is included in the balance sheet figures. The notes give the market values of these shares as $69m. A footnote to one note gives the company's equity in the net tangible assets of three unlisted associate companies as $47m., whereas the book value used in the

balance sheet is $33m. Certainly the large mining companies pose knotty problems of analysis. But some of these differences make one wonder whether the assets other than shares are not shown at far less than their present prices. They raise doubts for which there are no answers.

Companies which have overseas operations or subsidiaries give notes on the basis of currency conversion. Whatever assets you or I might have abroad, we would convert to the domestic currency at the rate of exchange ruling at any time we wished to discover our states of affairs. Not so for some companies it seems. The following kind of note is not uncommon.

> "Investments in overseas companies have been converted at rates of exchange ruling when the investments were made. All other overseas balances have been converted at the rate of exchange on (say) 30 June 1969."

Without the note readers might suppose (even though wrongly) that the commonsense thing, using the one rate of exchange, would have been done. The note says in effect that contradictory things have been done: the rate at 30 June both is and is not the proper rate to use for overseas assets at that date.

In this sense contradictions abound. The propriety of using a cost basis for assets is contradicted whenever a company departs from a cost basis to a valuation. The propriety of using a given depreciation method is contradicted whenever a company changes its method. The propriety of using for inventories, cost or realizable value or replacement price, is contradicted every time a company uses "the lower of cost or realizable value or replacement price". Or if one prefers to call these inconsistencies rather than contradictions, they could be fitted into the next section.

We hold these to be contradictions, however, by reference to the provisions of the law. The law requires the publication of statements which give a true and fair view of the state of affairs. It seems, from the security investment cases cited, that cost is deemed to give a true and fair view, that the law contemplates that cost does not give a true and fair view, but both are given in case readers choose to believe one rather than the other. This makes things just incomprehensible.

Inconsistencies — equal status of factual and non-factual amounts: addition of past, present and future magnitudes.

A statement of position is necessarily a statement of position at a point in time. We have no need to be too exacting about the point. But one thing which can be guarded against is stating a position which is non-factual and regarding a point of time as almost infinitely elastic.

151

In the preceding section we illustrated the treatment of security investments. We will take in another element of the same matter. All will admit that a market price of quoted securities held at a given date is not a price fixed by any definite person, least of all by the directors of any company which happens to be holding some of those securities. It is therefore a very different kind of number than a directors' valuation of shares of non-listed companies. There may, of course, be transactions in securities which are not listed. If there are any such transactions the price at which the shares changed hands would at least be some price, and as a price it would have some characteristic of the market prices of quoted securities. But what is a valuation?

Consider a relatively simple example. The 1968 report of Australian Paper Manufacturers Ltd. includes among the notes to the balance sheet the following:

"Land at Directors' Valuation 1962 .... .. $6,125,000
During the 1962 financial year the Company's land holdings were independently valued by Sworn Valuers. As these assets were not written up to the full amount of the valuation, they are shown as "Land at Directors' Valuation 1962.""

There is a similar note on Shares in Subsidiary Companies.

The question is "to what extent is the sum of money shown a factual statement in 1968?" In the first place an external or independent valuation, however made, is independent of the choice of the directors; in that respect it is like the amount of money shown to be on hand in a balance sheet, or the market price of shares held as assets at a given date. But if a smaller amount is shown by the decision of the directors, that amount lacks the independently verifiable character of the cash and the market values of shares. The auditors cannot, independently of the management, determine that the amount shown is an amount properly to be shown as a component of the company's position. And in any case, it is difficult to see what a valuation in 1962 has to do with the position of the company in 1968. It might have been of some help if the amount of the "sworn valuation" of 1962 had been given. But it is impossible to know what the money amount of the assets referred to might be in 1968.

When this valuation is added to other land "at cost", it is impossible to know what the sum means. And when there is added further, Buildings "at cost less depreciation", and Plant and Equipment "at cost less depreciation", it is even more difficult. For depreciation, as it is commonly determined, is another matter of managerial judgment and is not independently verifiable. And we are inclined to think that more often than not the amount of depreciation is not even a matter of managerial judgment, but the result of routine application of a bookkeeping rule, having no testable or

tested relationship to the diminution in the monetary amount of the assets from year to year.

Or take the 1968 consolidated balance sheet of John Fairfax Ltd. and subsidiaries. There are shown under "Investments", shares in listed companies, some at par, some at cost, some at "1964 directors' valuation", loans and deposits which may be supposed to be factual amounts at the end of 1968, all less a "provision for fluctuation in value". The latter is not a factual description of anything that had occurred up to the end of the year. In this case there are five entirely differently derived numbers, only one of which is a factual indication of how the group stood financially at the end of the year.

And of course they relate to past, present and future, which is the second point to be noticed in this section. Perhaps the most conspicuous examples of adding magnitudes which have different significances are found in the accounts of U.K. companies subsequent to the 1967 amendment of the Act. One of the amendments required the dates of valuations of assets to be shown. Consider the fixed assets of Brooke Bond Liebig and subsidiaries. There are separate figures for freeholds, long leases, short leases, and plant, transport and equipment. The totals are:

Balance remaining of valuation in		£	105,000
	1947		128,000
	1955		1,015,000
	1960		174,000
	1961		459,000
	1962		348,000
	1964		3,928,000
	1966		20,000
	1968		10,967,000
			17,144,000
Cost			39,214,000
			56,358,000
Less Accumulated depreciation			18,894,000
Net book value at 30 June 1968			37,464,000

Here we have all kinds of past dates and a present date, and a sum of £39m. for which we have no dates at all. But look at the dates. Everyone knows only too well that £1 of 1945 is in no sense equivalent to £1 of 1968, (in fact the purchasing power of £1 in 1968 was less than half what it was in 1945). Yet all these different amounts in different £'s are added up as though they meant the same thing. Or, put the matter another way. Suppose these valuations were approximate prices at the several dates of some parts of the assets on hand at 30 June, 1968. Everyone knows that prices and the structure of prices change from time to time. The addition of prices of things at different times can give no sensible aggregate of anything. Yet there it is. None of us would add up the prices we paid or the prices that ruled at times long past, and deduct depreciation calculated by some formula to find what our assets are now, or how we

152

stand in relation to the rest of the world now. Why what we would not think of doing makes any sense for corporations is impossible for me to understand.

In case there is any doubt about the above remarks on the idiosyncratic nature of the depreciation provision, another class of inconsistency may be mentioned. It is impossible for any reader to know whether a depreciation charge is legitimate or understated or overstated. And if an auditor accepts the cost price or a valuation and the depreciation rule adopted by a company, he cannot be sure that the result gives anything like the present money equivalent of an asset. It is therefore possible for a company to choose any method of the "accepted methods", any expected life, and any residual value it pleases; and to change these from time to time for good or any reason. Such changes have often been reported. There has been a rash of them in the United States recently; but in most reported cases, all that is said is that the method has been changed and the effect of the method on earnings per share. Nothing at all about any real justification by reference to the decline in the money equivalent of the assets. Here is the note to the 1968 accounts of National Steel Corporation on the matter:

> "Effective January 1, 1968, the corporation adopted the straight line method of computing depreciation for financial reporting purposes, however, it will continue to use accelerated methods for tax purposes. Provision has been made for the deferred federal income taxes applicable to this change. The effect of this change was to reduce depreciation expense by $21,158,822 and to increase net income for 1968 by $10,000,780 or $0.61 per share."

Not only does this illustrate the point that the choice of a method is not based on the factual financial characteristic of assets; it introduces another illustration of mixing figures purporting to show the state of things at a given date with future things *expected* to happen. Clearly the company expects to earn taxable profits in the future, and on that expectation, and the expectation that tax rates will remain the same, it has reduced the $21m. by the tax payable on it, $11m. No one surely would say that, as he expects to be 200 miles away in five hours' time, he is 200 miles away already. To incorporate the effects of expectations of the future in a statement of present position is to provide a mixture which has no present meaning at all.

General.

There is a growing tendency to add to the number of expected future contingencies included in financial statements. I believe this practice to be utterly misleading in a statement which is taken to represent how a company stands at a given time. Assets which *might* be worth more in the future than they are now, and liabilities which *might* have to be met in the future but which are not amounts now owing, are the experi-

ence of all firms. But these maybes are not present facts. And the history of business, commerce, economics and politics is full of cases in which maybes just did not turn out to be so. Why auditors are prepared to append clean reports to financial statements which contain so much that is guesswork about the future, when present facts are both necessary to users and more reliable, I do not know.

Information to Excess

Many of the observations made so far relate to the quality of information. There has been a growing tendency to require more information to be disclosed in financial statements. I am of the opinion that a great deal of this additional information has been required because what is already disclosed is defective rather than insufficient, and that attempts to patch up what is defective is no proper answer to deficiency.

In a very real sense the more information we are given about anything the more difficult it is for us to grasp the sense of it. Classification and summarization is our response to complexity. But the classification and summarization must be pertinent to the uses which are to be made of the information. Managers may quite properly require more details than investors. They are able to make use of details because they know the features of operations in a way no outsider can know them. Outsiders are not competent to judge in matters of detail; they cannot know all the details of all the kinds of companies in which they might invest. They need to know the broad and general effects of things on companies. There seems to have been quite a deal of confusion about what is appropriate for each class, and the additional information given in published statements is almost certainly not interpretable.

Inventories.

The basis of valuing inventories has long been required to be disclosed. Consider some of the forms of disclosure.

> "The amounts included for stocks have been determined on bases and by methods of computation which have been applied consistently and which are considered appropriate in the circumstances of the business of each Group subsidiary" (Reed Paper, U.K., 1968).

Simple; no jargon; but it adds nothing to the meaning of a £60m. item.

> "Certain metal refining and fabricating subsidiaries value their base stocks permanently employed at fixed prices, reviewed periodically, which are below market prices of the metals concerned. Adjustments rising from variations in the quantities involved are dealt with through Retained Earnings" (B.I.C.C., U.K., 1968).

How much below market value is the £60m. inventory referred to? When last was the review made of the prices of base stocks?

"Raw materials are valued at cost or average cost of purchase, and mined or quarried rock at the direct cost of mining. Finished goods are mainly valued at manufactured cost which includes direct works expenses. In certain subsidiaries, works, administration and selling overheads are included where considered appropriate." (B.P.B. Industries, U.K., 1968).

There are five families of methods here — all having quite different effects on the aggregate. What can the aggregate (one figure only is given) mean?

"Finished goods have been stated at amounts (less than cost) based on selling prices less allowances for selling expenses, profits and possible losses from style changes. Substantially all of the raw materials and the raw material content of the work in process have been priced at cost (last-in, first-out method) not in excess of market. All other inventories and supplies were priced at the lower of cost (first-in, first-out method) or market" (a U.S. Company, 1966).

This is as fine a bit of uninformative jargon as one could hope to meet. Even if a reader did know the technical significance of all the valuation methods referred to he could form no impression of what these effects might be on the one figure shown for inventory. Yet this may well be said to be a very explicit form of disclosure, so prone are we to accept words instead of meaning.

Fixed Assets.

Certainly too little information can be given about what in many companies is a very large quantum of assets. But the amount of information now being given by some U.K. companies is likely to give the impression that the facts are so complex that they are beyond grasp. Some 1967 amendments to the Act seem to have been the cause of this.

The 1968 accounts of Norcros Limited take a full page for the footnote to "Fixed Assets". There are two six-column sets of figures, one for the group, one for the company. The columns are for freehold properties, long leaseholds, short leaseholds, plant and other equipment, motor vehicles and a total. The narrations down the page are cost at December 1967, cost of additions, cost of inter-group transfers, cost of disposals, cost eliminated on disposal of subsidiaries, adjustment on conversion of overseas currency assets, and an aggregate of all these; then, under depreciation, there is aggregate depreciation to December 1967, amount provided in 1968, inter-group transfers, eliminations in respect of disposals, eliminations on disposal of subsidiaries, adjustments on conversion of overseas currency provisions, surplus arising on property valuations, and a net balance at December 1967 and the balance for December 1968. There are also a dozen or so lines of explanation. This constitutes a grid having up to 240 separate figures. In this case 80 of them are blank. But surely 160 separate figures to describe a couple of aggregates is going a bit far.

On top of all this is the absence of any information indicating how old the "cost" figures are. A more elaborate and more useless mass of information would be difficult to invent. Yet, in terms of the woolly idea current on the disclosure of information on the position of a company, this would be regarded as superlative. If the company had revalued its assets, or some of them, any number of times, as some companies have done, the final figures may have been more informative, but the detail would have been even more bewildering.

It is emphasised that the example is by no means isolated. And, by contrast, the detail given in American and Australian reports is far more skimpy, especially those that continue to use out of date costs or valuations. But for all its detail it is a poor substitute for a more realistic statement of present position, which is what one supposes to have been behind the amendment of the Act.

The Multi Digit Syndrome.

Consider excessive information of a different kind. Accountants have long treasured the idea of accuracy; a trivial difference may be the net result of two non-trivial differences, it is said. But given that accounts are properly prepared, and especially given that they have been audited, there seems to be no good reason for preserving the trivialities in the final statements.

Here are some figures from the 1968 consolidated accounts of Ansett Transport Industries:

Freehold land and buildings at cost		$12,366,807
Freehold land and buildings at independent valuation —		
1956 less amount written off	771,199	
1958 less realisation	272,042	
		13,410,048
Leaseholds at cost	11,457,147	
Leaseholds at independent valuation (1955)	46,342	
Leaseholds at Directors' valuation (1965)	97,000	
		25,010,537
Less Provision for Amortisation		4,031,644
		20,978,893

Was the directors' valuation of leaseholds of 1965 exactly $97,000 in the same sense as we suppose the cost of freehold land and buildings might be exact? It is at least highly unlikely. The final three digits in the total is thus a spurious degree of accuracy. It is so for other reasons, since the earlier valuations of certain items are likely to be vastly different from similar valuations of the same items in 1968. In another place in the accounts an Investment Fluctuation Reserve of $500,000 is set off against investments of a book value of $4.8m. Exactly $500,000? This suggests that at least the last five digits of any total figure are of doubtful accuracy. And as the market values of certain listed shares are $268,623 against a book value of

$497,450, it seems that the last six digits of the eight-digit balance sheet total are of dubious accuracy as a representation of the monetary amount of the company's assets at the balance date.

It should be clear that all this pretended accuracy is mythical, or pretentious. It is conducive to the belief that all the figures are equally exact and equally proper. And even if they were exact they would be unnecessary. For the only way in which financial statements can be interpreted is by means of ratios and percentages, and for most such purposes only the first three or four digits are significant.

General.

The point of these examples is simply that, in most of today's accounting, exactness over trivialities has tended and tends to push aside concern for the very qualities which make reports useful: properly condensed, up-to-date information, able to be digested because it is in comprehensible form, and uncluttered by jargon.

Real Time Accounting

When I was asked to address this convention I was specifically asked not to limit my remarks to the problems of accounting for inflation. I think I have discharged that request. But the mere form in which the request was cast — accounting for inflation, or the price level problem — makes me feel obliged to clear up some confusions, and to express my own view.

Inflation is a condition in which the purchasing power of money has fallen, generally by some substantial proportion, by comparison with the purchasing power of money at some other time. It is not descriptive of a condition in which the prices rise of the things which any individual person or company buys or sells; for at the same time the prices of the things which other persons or companies buy or sell may have gone down. Inflation relates to a fall in the *general* purchasing power of money or to a rise in the level of prices *in general*. It relates to general purchasing power it affects all prices denominated or measures made in monetary units. If a man or a company holds money while the level of prices in general rises, he becomes less well-off, less able to buy things in general than he was before.

But as we have hinted, the prices of particular things may go up or down at different rates than the level of prices in general. Thus if the selling price of a block of land I own goes up from $2000 to $2500 while the level of prices in general remains the same I am $500 better off. But if the price goes up in the same way while the level of prices in general rises by 10 per cent,

I am only better off by $300 of the later purchasing power; for the $2000 I spent is equivalent to $2200 of the later purchasing power.

There are thus two different factors affecting the change in wealth, the rate at which the prices of particular goods held change and the rate at which the purchasing power of money changes. If our aim is to report what has happened to a company from time to time we must report the effects of both of these changes, as they may and commonly do affect companies differently. The possibilities are:

(i) account for neither as it occurs — this is what is done in conventional accounting;

(ii) account for changes only in the prices of particular goods held — this is done partially whenever revaluations are made;

(iii) account for changes only in the general purchasing power of money — this is substantially the view of *Accounting Research Study* No. 6 of the Research Division of the A.I.C.P.A. It assumes that the prices of the goods held by a firm move at the same rate and in the same direction as a general index of prices;

(iv) account for changes in the purchasing power of money to the particular company. This has been advocated by some, but it results in the absurd position that, as every company has a different combination of assets, every company will be reporting in terms of different purchasing power units. Comparison of the absolute amounts of assets and equities and the use of those amounts for comparison with any other possible investment opportunity would be impossible;

(v) account for both types of movements as they occur — this is my own view. It is the only view which takes full account of what has happened and the only view which results in balance sheets which are factual at any time and financial statements which are interpretable by reference to any prices ruling at that time.

I am averse to using "gimmicky" descriptions; shorthand becomes jargon all too soon. I have refrained from calling this latter type of system a "real-time" accounting system. But that is just what it is. It is not a price level accounting system, nor a specific index system, and should not be confused with either.

The object of the system is to give, in statements of financial position, the present monetary equivalents of present assets and the amounts of equities in those assets at any given time. In general the present monetary equivalent of anything is its market resale price. Whether or not a company is going to sell an asset is immaterial; and whether or not it does subsequently fetch that price is immaterial. What we are trying

155

to do is find how a company stands in relation to the rest of the community; for how it stands is of interest to every party connected with it managerially or financially. We must therefore find approximate resale prices of assets, for the sum of these is the total command the company has over resources in general and the total amount available to or being used on behalf of the equity holders. Notice we said command over *resources in general*. The mere fact that a company has certain assets means it has command over *resources in particular*. But when, by using resale prices of those resources, we get the total amount of *money* which is equivalent to the assets held, we have made the particular into something of very general use. And that is what companies need to know, for it can be used in all kinds of calculations about buying and selling — assets, services, things it does not have or things it has and does not want — paying debts, raising loans and so on. The same information when published is equally useful to all outsiders, for it is an expression in general terms which all can understand — the worth in presently circulating units of purchasing power of what the company has and owes. Given two such statements of financial position we can readily deduce the profit: it is the difference between the monetary equivalents of the net assets of a company at two dates, provided only that the monetary equivalents are expressed in units of equal general purchasing power.

The things we have said to be wrong with financial statements are not new. They have been the very things which have prompted the development of the ideas just described. Notice what defects are eliminated:

(a) Assets are saleable things presently in possession: the amounts of assets are present market prices — this eliminates all the argument about cost, or market, or valuation, or whatever, and the confusions and contradictions which flow from them.

(b) Changes in the prices of things are brought into account whenever they occur, — this eliminates the lag in reporting which give rise to great differences between book values and commercial values, lags which have been to the detriment of shareholders and creditors alike: and it conforms with the circumstances, which prompt businessmen to vary their actions, investments and business operations, when they arise.

(c) The unit of account used in the balance sheet, and used to denominate the net income figure for any period, is the common monetary unit whatever its purchasing power happens to be at that time — this eliminates the aggregation of prices at different times expressed in monetary units of greatly divergent purchasing

powers; and it enables readers to compare and contrast the figures with any other prices or monetary magnitudes or quantities at that time.

(d) The need for lengthy footnotes is reduced, because the contemporary figures are given and readers do not need a clutter of out-of-date figures to help them guess at contemporary figures themselves.

(e) The state of affairs represented is a present state of affairs at the date the balance sheet bears and, being determined independently of managerial opinion, it is factual and therefore "true and fair" to all interested parties.

Conclusion

Financial statements at present are very similar to the pronouncements of the Greek oracles. The deliverances of the oracles, you may remember, were couched in terms which could be interpreted in more ways than one. Whatever course was chosen by those who consulted the oracle, the outcome could be shown after the event to tally with what the oracle said. The modern counterparts of the oracles, of course, are the astrologers, whose horoscopes are similarly vague. In an age in which knowledge and deliberate calculations have so extensively supplanted divination, it is odd to find such vague, contradictory and inconsistent pronouncements in published financial statements, as one might find in the pronouncements of the oracles and astrologers. One can scarcely avoid the conclusion that we have advanced little in this respect in over 2000 years. and to judge by the mounting criticism, the business community seems to think that is not good enough.

The fabric of accounting — both its so-called theoretical justifications and its practices — are shot through with fundamental errors. Its ideal form is not, however, very different from some of the practices which have been grafted on to the traditional modes of practice. Great numbers of the operations presently part of the accounting process would be the same; all dealings, one part of which entails a cash movement, would be the same for example. The major change required to eliminate most of the defects is a change in the representation of the balances of non-cash assets. But as most assets of most firms are non-cash assets it is a major change indeed.

The use that is made, in financial statements now, of market prices, net realizable values, replacement prices and so on, is indicative of the feasibility of what we are suggesting by way of improvement. If we could see these uses as evidence of the invalidity of the long-standing and more common practices, we might the sooner eliminate what's wrong with financial statements.

Patchwork Principles or a New Code?*

Ten years ago it seemed possible that the dilemmas and difficulties
into which the discussion and practice of accounting had run might soon
become things of the past. Those difficulties had impressed themselves
on leaders of the profession in the 'fifties so much that a new and
thorough examination of the foundations and function of accounting seemed
necessary. The American Institute reconstituted the Research Division
and set up the Principles Board in the hope - explicit in statements of
the time - that a clearly stated and closely integrated set of ideas
would emerge.

Since that time many have devoted their energies to the work of the
Research Division and the Board. Of their goodwill and assiduity there
can be no question. But the products of their labors may be contrasted
with the objects which the originators of the new scheme had in mind. It
will be recalled that the Special Committee on Research Program set out
three classes of propositions - postulates, principles and rules - which
should, ideally, be a complete and systematic account of what accounting
is based on and what form it should take.[1] We may say "what form
accounting **should** take", for the Special Committee envisaged that the
postulates would provide the "foundations" for the rules, and the rules
would thus be **necessary** consequences of the postulates.

Accounting Research Studies (A.R.S.) 1 and 3 were of the kind which
should have provided a general framework of ideas about the context,
functions and characteristics of accounting.[2] They were general in style
and wide in ambit. They were steps in the direction suggested by the
Special Committee. They may have had defects. They may have needed
elaboration and clarification.[3] Studies of specific accounting problems
may have shown whether there were defects and obscurities, if those
studies were carried out subsequently with the clear intention of
checking the adequacy of the general framework and producing a coherent,
self-consistent set of ideas and rules.

157

---

* Presented in Georgia State University, Atlanta, March 1970.

It is unfortunate that the subsequent studies of specific problems were not regarded as attempts to work out the necessary consequences of A.R.S. 1 and 3, as tests of the propriety of A.R.S. 1 and 3, or as providing evidence in support or rebuttal of any of the propositions of A.R.S. 1 and 3. Only by working backwards and forwards, between particular cases and general statements, is it possible so to modify the basic ideas or the rules they entail that a coherent set of general propositions and particular rules emerges. With one obvious exception (A.R.S. 7)[4], the Research Studies which followed these earlier general studies have no ostensible connection whatever with the propositions of A.R.S. 1 and 3. Instead, the greater part of the work of the Division and the Board has been in the same direction - piecemeal work on particular topics - as the Research Bulletin series which was believed in the fifties to have been unsatisfactory. The work seems to have departed materially from the goals stated in 1958.

There is a dangerous possibility that the very volume of material produced, of this highly specific but theoretically unconnected variety, may merely reinforce habits and practices which are the offshoots of the inadequate and unsatisfactory ways of reaching conclusions prior to 1958. Why, a **dangerous** possibility? Because the felt necessity of knowing what the newer publications contain tends to draw attention away from the principal sources of new and better ideas, namely, the appearance of anomalies and the resolute attempt to eliminate them.

One of the oldest habits of men is to rely on the sayings of their fathers and other authorities. There is perhaps some wisdom in this, for our antecedents cannot have been altogether unobservant or altogether misguided. But the history of ideas is a history of the discovery that inherited and long-venerated wisdom is incomplete, overburdened with useless excrescences, or irrelevant, or all three. In some respects, accounting is more likely to suffer from adherence to the voice of authority than many other fields of knowledge and expert practice. For, first, it is not easy to put to the test of usefulness in the world of commerce the more complex products of accounting.[5] Second, accounting has no tradition of scholarship based on observations or experiments which can be repeated or replicated by others independently. Third, its practitioners and teachers have long relied on the authority of judicial dicta, on legislation in the proper sense, and, more recently, on professional legislation or rule-making. And fourth, its practitioners and teachers have long accepted as feasible and proper the right of management (just another authority) to determine some of the magnitudes which appear in financial summaries published for the benefit of outsiders. There are few fields in which so many forces may interfere with the independent determination, by knowledgeable and inquisitive experts, of the prime characteristics of their special field of expertise.

Four Basic Ideas

To put into perspective the selection of ideas which we will consider, it will be useful to sketch the circumstances which gave rise to them.

159

The accounting of feudal officials to their lords was a necessary element in the management of their properties by absentee owners. The idea of officials using the money and goods of others in prescribed ways, dates much further back than feudal times and persists to the present. But the uses made of the means available were largely "domestic" uses; it was sufficient to require of officials that they gave an account of what was put into their hands at the beginning of or during any period of accounting defined by the visits to his estates of the owner. It was a kind of trusteeship accounting. It contributed to accounting the idea of **stewardship** in its simplest sense.

The rise to prominence of trade gradually gave rise to the distinction between domestic and commercial matters. Commercial ventures became larger and the contractual arrangements between venturers of longer duration. Ventures overlapped, so that firms concurrently carried on many ventures of different temporal duration. The exigencies of partners, and of members of corporations, were met by the sale of their interests in continuing ventures. The risks were often great and the returns correspondingly high; no exacting calculations or financial reporting would have thrown much light on the value of an interest in such firms. But their deeds and charters did provide for periodical meetings at which an account would be given of what had occurred, and decisions would be made on the division of the surpluses that had arisen. Hence the idea of **periodical financial reporting**, as distinct from whatever accounting owner-managers may have required for their own guidance.

160

Trade increased; firms grew in size and number; manufacturing increased, a less risky business than much of the earlier venturing; competition reduced the rate of profit yielded. Durable assets were acquired; loans were raised. The linkages between managers, members and creditors became more tenuous. Concern with the protection of lenders' interests gave rise in some places to mercantile agencies for the collation of financial information on borrowers. Abuse of the rights and interests of lenders focussed attention on ways of protecting them, especially with the rise of the limited liability company, which restricted the extent of creditors' remedies. The nineteenth and twentieth century legislation relating to corporations was directed quite specifically to the protection of creditors' interests. By this time the market in company shares was extensive, and shareholders also needed more exact information on profits and the safety of their investments. Buyer and seller would, each in his own interest, wish to know what rights in what properties and prospects he was acquiring or relinquishing. All these factors reinforced the desirability of a form of **accrual** accounting. Only by such an accounting could the complex of assets and equities of a firm be adequately represented at periodical intervals.

Concurrently with these changes various forms of taxation were introduced by governments, income taxation becoming the most common. The object of a tax is simply to raise public revenues, and the taxing authorities are in a position to dictate the base on which taxes will be levied. They may adopt, wholly or partially, the existing modes of commercial practice in choosing the base. But they are not constrained by the accounting rules which might be adopted by business firms for their better management, nor by the rules which might be imposed for the better guidance of creditors or stockholders. In the course of time the manner of calculating the tax base under income taxation laws has diverged from the manner in which income is calculated for other purposes. And the concessions and allowances made by taxing authorities have influenced the timing and style of investments in business assets. That different forms of calculation were required for tax administration than for other purposes strengthened (if it did not actually spawn) the general idea that **different kinds** of financial information are required for different purposes or by different classes of users of financial statements.

Some Kinds of Confusion

The incidents and changes described range over a period of at least 800 years, though the ideas which have arisen from them have had concurrent impact on accounting over a much shorter time. But even 100 years has been sufficient to give rise to unsystematic and undisciplined applications of those ideas and to yield a confused body of doctrine.

The stewardship idea was, from the beginning, an idea of periodical acquittance. The feudal steward was acquitted of his responsibility on each occasion when his lord visited the estate to take account of its administration. Once acquitted, the matters under review were not reopened. In modern parlance, the estate was a going concern; but, as in all going concerns, there is a limit to the utility of looking backwards. If the account given by the steward is accepted, best let him get on with the business from that time forward. Substantially the same idea is served by the annual meeting or the annual report of a modern corporation. Indeed, in some European countries the auditors of today recommend that the managers be discharged of their responsibility for the work and results of the past year, and the annual meeting so resolves. However, by some strange alchemy, this idea has become fused with the notion of the continuity of the business firm. The present "conventional" view of the stewardship idea (though it is not universally held) seems to be that the balance sheet is a cumulative account of the net monetary inflows and outflows from all transactions, from the beginning of the corporation, sanctioned by all past and present managements. The belief in the propriety of accounting on an historical cost basis is the result.

But this belief is nowhere held in its pure form. The accrual idea, necessitated as we have said by the continuity of business firms and the enduring and overlapping lives of assets and liabilities, is allowed to override it; but not consistently. On a strict interpretation the accrual idea could mean that the accounts of a period will take notice of effects, on the financial position of a firm, of past events of which the cash consequences have not yet been experienced. An example of this strict interpretation is the accounting for receivables and payables. The balances of these are the accrued consequences of past events.

It is commonly believed that the traditional methods of accounting for inventories and depreciating assets are also applications of the accrual idea. But they are not applications of the strict interpretation we have just given. They require that the accountant (or the manager) of a firm estimate some future event or events, and work **backwards** from those estimates to obtain the amounts of inventory or durable asset values. (This is the import of the idea that asset balances shall only be carried forward if they will have some future value in use to the firm.) And, what is more, the basic figures to which the estimates of the future are to be applied are, in the case of durable assets, generally the prices paid for those assets in the more or less distant past. We may very well estimate some future magnitude from some past and present magnitudes. But it is impossible to derive a present magnitude by applying some guesses about the future to some magnitudes of the past. At this point, however, we only wish to establish two points. First, in practice we are not sure what the result is of using "accrual" in two senses, though inconsistency of meaning can only result in aggregates of undefinable significance. Second, the two ideas of stewardship and accrual, both proper and understandable notions, have become mixed in the traditional doctrine, instead of being adopted, each fully and in its own particular way, into the general corpus of accounting doctrine and practice.

Consider now the periodical reporting of financial information. As an aid to stockholders and creditors, periodical reporting is useless unless the information reported is up-to-date. Now, it may seem that accrual accounting is a means by which information is brought up to date. It does serve. But in present practice only partially. The accepted practice of writing off inventory and other losses and discovered discrepancies (when the market values of assets fall below book values) brings the information up to date. However, there are other senses in which information is more or less up-to-date. If the market price of any asset held and used by a firm goes up or down, the rise or fall has substantially the same effect on the financial position of the firm as a discovered surplus or loss in inventory. Yet in traditional doctrine and practice they are not treated in the same way. Changes in the prices of assets held are quite generally disregarded; historical costs are retained. To that extent the resulting financial statements are not up-to-date.

Some confusion seems to have arisen, indeed, between the up-to-dateness of the information contained in the statements and the speed with which financial reports follow balancing dates. Certainly speed of publication is important. But it is a mechanical matter, unrelated to the quality of the information reported. If the prices of assets shown in balance sheets are prices of long ago, no amount of speed in publishing the statements will compensate for the out-of-date character of what is reported. Here, again, there is confusion of two ideas, one a matter of principle the other a matter of mechanics, leading to the neglect of the matter of principle.

The fourth idea we mentioned in the preliminary sketch is the notion that different parties need different information. As an example of the point we wish to make we will consider corporate income calculation. One of the objects of income calculation is to indicate what is available for distribution as a dividend from the operations of any year. It has long been held that it is not prudent of a company to distribute so much cash that it leaves itself unable to pay its creditors as their claims fall due. The two ideas, what is legally available and what may prudently be distributed, seem to have become fused; or if not fused, confused. There emerged the idea that income is something which is "realized", for conversion of goods to cash makes available cash to pay creditors and stockholders. The idea is reinforced by taxation practices. A prime consideration of taxing authorities is the ease of collection of a tax. There is therefore a tendency to make taxes fall on incomes as closely as possible to the point at which revenues arise. Now certainly revenues arise from the realization of assets (the sale of goods). But revenue is not income. Income is a calculated magnitude, and there enters into its calculation other magnitudes than revenue which are not realized. In particular, the credit entry for closing inventory, which is made in accordance with the accrual principle, is not a realized magnitude. While, therefore, we may speak of realized revenue (though the adjective is superfluous), it is not equally proper to speak of realized income. The idea of realized income cuts right across the accrual principle. It interferes with the flow of information to stockholders and creditors, by tending to the suppression of increases and decreases in the prices or values of assets held. If such increases and decreases are regarded as changes in financial well-offness (income), the realized income idea

163

affects the reporting of income per share and rate of return. In any case it affects adversely the computed values of assets per share or per bond, and judgements on the rate of financial growth of companies. It thus interferes with judgements of efficiency and of other matters which periodical reporting is expected to promote.

The principal point here, though, is that in trying to provide different kinds of information for different kinds of "users" in the one set of statements, the additional notion of realized income is introduced which is inconsistent with the accrual principle.

The Direction of Reconstruction

In this brief survey we have tried to show that several ideas, each central to the doctrine and practice of accounting, have become abraded or warped in the course of time under the influence of other ideas. The demonstration could be extended. But we have chosen to concentrate on few ideas only, and those of the most general kind rather than more complex and specific ideas. We have chosen these because if the common or general ideas are defective, it is certain that the more complex ideas, being based on the more elementary and general, are also defective.

The question posed by our title may now be approached. Must we accept every new idea which arises from a variation of circumstance, retaining meanwhile an old idea across which it cuts? Can we tolerate such a profusion of ideas that they warp and wear down one another? Must we find a fit place for every idea which has crossed the consciousness of some inventive ancestor who sought to rationalize an anomaly by formulating a new precept? No. To do this is passive. It makes the shape of thoughts present and practices to come the mere consequence of the accidents of history, instead of the creation of intelligence applied to the novel and more complex settings in which we find ourselves.

There is no reason why we should continue to live with the plethora of ideas which have been thrown up on the strand by the waves of circumstance and undisciplined invention. Accountants profess technical knowledge of the modes of doing business, of the relationship of money and monetary calculation to the conduct of business. Given this, we can **decide** what particular ideas relate to what particular phenomena. We can **decide** what particular combination of ideas (elementary notions and inferences based on them) is necessary and sufficient to provide the kind

164

of accounting which any given set of environmental conditions, or any given kind of institution, seems to require. There are warrants of many kinds for believing in the propriety of deliberately constructing a new code.

There is a telling example, for instance, in the political history of the United States. Nevins and Commager, in **The History of the United States**, give the following account of the Constitutional Convention of 1787:

> At the outset the delegates tacitly agreed that they would not revise the Articles of Confederation, but write a wholly new Constitution. In this decision they exceeded their powers. The Continental Congress had called the Convention "for the sole and express purpose of revising the Articles of Confederation." But, as Madison later wrote, the delegates, "with a manly confidence in their country", simply threw aside the Articles and went ahead with a new form of government. It was, as Hamilton remarked, a revolutionary step, and an eminent authority, John W. Burgess, later declared that if Napoleon had done such a thing, it would have been pronounced a **coup d´etat**; yet we must remember that many of the states had specifically instructed their delegates to create a union adequate to all exigencies of the crisis.

It was no small achievement; Gladstone was to say of it, "the American Constitution is the most wonderful work ever struck off at a given time by the brain and purpose of man."

The history of scientific enterprise is full of examples of occasions when new circumstance, the accumulation of new empirical knowledge, gave rise to the rejection of clumsy systems of ideas, and their replacement by new systems which more satisfactorily embraced both the old and the new factual knowledge. Some of these were major revolutions. The switch in the manner of regarding the relationship between the sun and the planets, initiated by Copernicus, the establishment of the nature of the process of oxidation by Lavoisier, and the atomic theory of Dalton, are examples. In other cases the changes in the extant systems of ideas entailed major exercises in redefinition. In **The Structure of Scientific Revolutions**, Kuhn describes this as changing the meaning of established and familiar concepts. Of one of the variables of the laws of mechanics, mass, Kuhn observes: "Newtonian mass is conserved; Einsteinian is convertible with energy. Only at low relative velocities may the two be measured in the same way, and even then they must not be conceived to be the same."

It seems to be entirely feasible in accounting, therefore, to abandon the patchwork products of responses to increasingly complex commerce, and to reconstruct the main notions into a self-consistent and empirically significant system. We will illustrate the possibility by reference to the small group of common ideas already discussed.

Stewardship and the Accrual Principle

We will grant that owners or stockholders require a periodical account of managerial stewardship. In particular, we grant that the old idea of stewardship in the custodial sense persists; and that this entails an accounting for the legitimate use and disposition (according to a company's charter and the powers delegated to its executive) of the cash and other properties which pass under the control of managers. This task can properly be served by any form of reporting based on records which show all stocks of money and goods and all obligations at the beginning of a period, all movements in money and goods during the period, and the stocks of money and goods and the amounts of obligations remaining at the end of the period. It does not matter, for this kind of custodial accounting, what money values, or whether **any** money values, are assigned to the non-monetary assets of the company. It is necessary only that all movements, of money, claims to money, and goods, shall be described, so that explanations can be given of any movement when they are called for. And to give assurance of the correctness of the "account", there is, of course, the normal audit process.

There would be nothing misleading about this "account". Certainly no manager or accountant could be allowed to vary the money amounts set beside any goods, if what was required was an account of stewardship in the custodial sense. And **in** any form of custodial report it would be improper to say anything about any asset or liability based on what the custodian expects to happen in the future. He will have to report that if and when it does happen.

But this kind of report would not be informative of any financial characteristic of the company as a whole, or of the economic performance of management-cum-company. Ever since accountants began adding the

166

numbers appearing in inventories of assets and equities, it has been recognized that there is something to be learned of an enterprise as a whole from the sums and differences and ratios of groups of amounts represented in accounts. There is a kind of stewardship **additional** to the custodial kind. For not only do managers have the custody of assets, they also have the powers to use them: how well they **use** them is just as much a matter of interest to stockholders as how well managers **protect** company assets. Today stocks are freely transferable; the stocks of many companies are available to any investor; and the financial publicity laws and regulations are intended to enable stockholders to judge between the performances of different companies, on the basis of authenticated financial statements. These judgements of performance, on the basis of aggregate figures, cannot properly be made unless the numbers assigned to individual items in the statements are of the kind which can properly be added and presently understood. And, as in the case of custodial stewardship, periodical judgements of performance cannot properly be made unless the reported information embraces just the events and effects experienced by the company between the beginning and the end of each year.

The accrual principle serves just this purpose. But only if it is fully and strictly applied. It would be useless to bring into account the accrued effects of some things and to leave out the accrued effects of others. If the prices of some goods held during a year have risen or fallen during the year, the effect is an effect occurring in that year. It would be a distortion of the year's results and position not to show the effect. If the prices of some goods rose and the prices of other goods fell during the year, it would be a distortion of the year's events to include the effect of the fall and to exclude the effect of the rise. In both the cases cited, the financial statements would be a misrepresentation of performance. If we are concerned with managerial stewardship, it seems proper to give credit for buying in advance of rises in prices, and to mitigate credit to the extent of declines in the prices of goods held. Indeed, a manager may have had to put up with some falls to take advantage of some rises. Only a strict application of the accrual principle will give a fair indication of performance. Furthermore, only a strict application will have the effect of bringing all prices up to date, so that they can be added legitimately and interpreted by readers in the context of other current prices.

Again, if the prices of some goods are **expected** to rise or fall in the next or succeeding years, it would be a distortion of the year's events to bring into account the expected effects of those rises and falls. If an obligation is **expected** to arise in a future year but is not an actual obligation at the end of a given year, it would be a distortion of the year's events and of the closing position to bring it into account. These are not cases of the accrual principle, and they interfere with stewardship judgments. There are other devices for dealing with expected events - the retention of income, for example - without distorting the periodical reports of what has occurred.

168

The stewardship of management is not, of course, a relationship between abstractions. The managers of a firm may change from time to time, voluntarily or involuntarily. It should be clear that the performance of no particular manager may be properly judged if events occurring under the direction of a prior manager or which may occur under the direction of a future manager are permitted to cloud a contemporary report. Nor is there any value in attempting to discover the trend in the performance of a company and its management if the figures of successive years are made fuzzy by overlapping.

There is a way of judging the performance of a company and its management additional and superior to comparison of performance year by year. We have no "natural", instinctive or fixed notion of what the rate of return on the assets of a company or the dividend from an investment in its stock should be. Our only source of guidance in these matters is the reported returns on investment of other companies and the dividends their stocks yield. Valid comparisons may be made, however, only if all companies calculate their results and positions consistently in every year. If all companies accrue the effects of all events, completely, in each year, the **mode** of calculation will be uniform, the resulting figures will be comparable, and the relative differences in performance will be discernible.

It should be clear that none of this cuts across the custodial stewardship idea. In the course of accounting for and accruing the effects of events right up to the end of each year, all dealings will have to be brought into account. The intimacy of the connection between stewardship, in the broader interpretation we have given it, and the strict application of the accrual principle should be apparent.

Different Users of the Same Information

And both ideas entail some kind of periodical reporting. Periodical reporting is not a mere nuisance as some imply, an arbitrary cutting up of the life of a firm. It is necessary as a guide to the worthwhileness of courses of action and of investments. We mentioned earlier that the financial publicity laws were directed to protection of the interests of both stockholders and creditors; and we mentioned the popular idea that different kinds of information are required by different kinds of people (or for different kinds of decisions). We wish now to examine the relationship between these two notions.

There are some who regard financial statements as serving stockholders only. And stockholders, they say, are interested in the product of income calculations, not with the messy particulars of balance sheets. This lop-sided emphasis may be a convenient way of pushing aside the imperfections of today's balance sheets. But just as it is still necessary to entertain the idea of stewardship in the custodial sense, it is still necessary to consider the financial statements as aids in the protection of creditors' interests. The custodial obligations of managers run as much to creditors as to stockholders; the law and administration of bankruptcies and liquidations evidence the point. There is ample ground for asserting that the solvency of a firm and the safety of creditors' interests remain elements of the firm's position on which creditors need to be informed from time to time.

169

It may be true that bankers and other financiers are always willing to lend to borrowers, some borrowers. But it does not follow that any particular indigent borrower can borrow at any time. And if the firm does borrow it still has the task of repaying under the conditions and at the times stipulated in the contract. It is thus of consequence to managers that they know the relationships between obligations and the means of meeting them, continuously. And not only the immediate means, cash, but also the cash equivalents of all assets, any combination of which may, in an appropriate circumstance, serve to meet an obligation or assure a creditor that an overdue obligation can be met. All firms encounter situations from time to time in which solvency is strained. To be forewarned of a drift in that direction is the surest way of avoiding its severest consequences.

170

But we wish also to tackle the "different users, different information" question. Are stockholders and creditors interested in different information? It seems unlikely, at least. Both may be said to be interested in the rate of return on the firm's assets; for this is an indicator of financial or economic efficiency. Both may be said to be interested in the firm's rate of return on net assets, or stockholders' equity; the interest of stockholders is more direct, but creditors will be the safer if the rate of return on equity is relatively high than if it is relatively low, for stockholders have so much more to lose by insolvency in the former case. Both may be said to be interested in the firm's debt to equity ratio, for each class will want to consider whether its interest is likely to be strengthened or weakened by further issues of securities. New stock issues for example may strengthen the security of lenders; new bond issues may weaken the security of lenders, and of stockholders, while raising the rate of return by increasing its riskiness. Both classes may be said to be interested in short run liquidity; drifts in it may indicate to stockholders the likelihood of new security issues, and to creditors the necessity of closely watching their own share of the firm's payables. And for all these purposes, of course, only fully accrued figures, up-to-date asset prices, are serviceable.

We conclude that, certainly, different users may make different uses of the information given, each in his own interest, just the same as a buyer and a seller of stock may make use of the same information. But that is an entirely different thing from asserting that different kinds of information are necessary.

But what about taxable income? Is that not a case in which a different user requires different information from that which might be of use to stockholders? No. A statement made for taxation purposes is a highly specific document. It is generally considered to be a confidential document. Generally its confidential character is protected by law. Such a law has thus exactly the opposite intention to the financial publicity laws. It is therefore mistaken to treat a statement made for taxation purposes as falling within the same category as financial statements or reports proper. The taxation laws affect financial statements in one way only. They enable the amount of the liability to taxation to be calculated. In this respect they are no

different from the terms of a bond issue. Those terms enable accrued
interest to be calculated and the amount repayable in the near future to
be determined; but they introduce no novel accounting principle. If we
take this view we have no reason to modify the general course of
accounting simply because of the specific provisions of the tax laws for
asset valuation or any other matter. We are able to rely on the accrual
principle, strictly and fully applied, without any other stratagem.

Some are not content to do this; they regard our suggestion as
superficial. They say that the tax rules in force at any time have a
distinct effect on the decisions of firms; and, that being so, the
content of those tax rules must contain some element of reality. If, for
example, the tax laws permit the use of LIFO for inventories, there must
(they say) be some element of propriety in LIFO valuation for general
reporting purposes. And if there is such a law as the "investment
credit" law, it must (they say) affect the way in which assets are valued
for general reporting purposes. It is undeniable that tax rules affect
decisions. But it is entirely improper to expect financial statements to
disclose the separate effects of tax rules on decisions. Financial
statements describe the consequences of all decisions, actions and
unplanned events together; to untangle them is impossible. As for the
use of tax rules for financial reporting purposes, this may be challenged
directly. The LIFO rule was introduced as a way of reducing the tax
burden in a period of rising prices from the level imposed by the use
of historical cost accounting in taxation. The "investment credit" and
similar devices have had the same intention and effect. These tax rules
are thus to be understood in conjunction with other tax rules, as
attempts to mollify the harshness of other already existent tax rules.
They have no independent status as valuation principles. Their benefits
or burdens fall on specific years, just those years in which the actual
tax liability of a taxpayer is modified by the tax rules. And they fall
in the form of a variation in the tax payable in respect of those years,
and on nothing else in the accounts whatever. Tax rules in respect of
asset valuations have no place in general financial reporting: in respect
of the liability to taxation, tax rules provide the raw material for
accrual calculations, purely and simply.[6]

171

Review

When new situations confront us they **seem** to demand new solutions. In the excitement of the novel and the urgency of finding ways of meeting it, we are apt to invent new words, new devices, new doctrines. We scarcely pause to ask whether the old words, devices and doctrines are still serviceable. Instead of making external change an occasion for appraisal of the state of the art of accounting, we make a fetish of change. We **must** have new principles, no matter what the old ones are, and no matter how harshly the new and the old may work against one another. That the result may be a patchwork; that a superabundance of ideas and terms is a threat to disciplined discourse; that we may be tripped or trapped by the ornate and the superfluous; these things do not seem to bother us.

What's superfluous? We have long had the accrual idea. It means the assignment to successive periods severally of all the effects which had a bearing on a firm's financial position in each such period. Strictly the "matching" idea means the same kind of thing. And the "allocation" idea also means the same kind of thing. But the mere fact that we have three terms has encouraged the development of three quite different ideas. People as diverse as novelists and scientists have pointed out that words come to have careers of their own; instead of being their masters we become their slaves. Or perhaps their fools! For not only do we have synonyms for accrual which we do not regard as synonyms; we introduce and tolerate other words and ideas which are inconsistent with accrual. The notion of realization, applied to income, cuts right across the accrual idea. For "accrual" means bringing into account all effects falling within a specified period; "realization", in its conventional setting, means bringing into account only some kinds of effects. Similarly the common rules for valuing fixed and current assets differently cut across the accrual idea; for they permit changes in the prices of current assets - but not of fixed assets - to be brought into account. Indeed the practice of setting up ideas and propositions in such a way that they cut across one another has reached such a stage that a new "explanatory" idea has been introduced to the literature - the "trade-off".[7] We are told that accuracy may be traded off for increased relevance; that there may be trade-offs generally among relevance, quantifiability, verifiability and freedom from bias. The whole idea

172

is, of course, so confused and confusing that it is no wonder we are not given the rates of exchange!

No system of ideas or practices can advance while ambiguities and contradictories infest it. Its exponents and practitioners are inevitably forced into inconsistent positions, finding themselves obliged to accept contradictory conclusions because their premises are contradictory; and that is a condition which is neither professionally comfortable nor consonant with a service ethic. The basic ideas must be so stated and linked to one another that they are not contradictory, but complementary, reinforcing or mutually supporting. We need a few broad and sweeping ideas with sufficient auxiliary ideas to produce a useful network.

173

From the ideas we have discussed we may choose accrual as an example of a broad idea, ranging across the whole of the accounting for continuous enterprises. Realization on the other hand is an idea of limited use (which is to say, we should use it in a restricted fashion if we wish to avoid a head-on clash with accrual). Stewardship, once a narrow idea, may legitimately be extended to embrace its old meaning and a newer meaning; the extension does violence to nothing and adds substance to the idea. The "different users-different information" idea seems to be the product of some confusion of decision-inputs. It seems impossible to say that any factual information, as information, is not pertinent to any decision-maker. It is quite possible and proper to say that different users make use of given information in different ways, or with different ends in view. These are examples of the ways in which ideas may need to be sharpened, extended, cut down or rejected, if we are to have a new code.

It is difficult to escape an uneasy feeling that many today - practitioners and teachers - are adding to our difficulties. The tendency is widespread to view every new commercial device as an occasion for a new rule, instead of attempting first to find whether the existing rules are adequate. The divergence of the tax-base from accounting income has led to tax allocation proposals; sale and leaseback arrangements have created confusion through over-extension of the accrual idea; new types of securities are giving rise to difficulties over the meaning of income per share; mergers have saddled accounting with some highly suspect reporting devices. These and similar things confront us because we have been indiscriminate in applying or extending the basic general ideas of accounting.

The basic ideas are, I believe, embodied in the simple proposition that, to do thoughtfully anything at all, we need up-to-date knowledge of where we stand, complete knowledge of how we got there, and knowledge which is relatable to the knowledge we have of alternative possibilities of action. This applies as much to financial action and knowledge as to any other kind. I have attempted to build on the substance of this proposition.[8] I have found it necessary to extend, reject, select, and trim ideas which have grown freely in the permissive conditions of accounting discourse. No breeder of fine stock or flora concedes equal survival rights to everything that turns up in his field. Exercise of the same care in accounting is the only way in which we may supplant the present insecure patchwork with a new code of tight, interlocked and mutually supporting principles.

Ten years ago we might have expressed the same view, may have hoped it would prevail. But these ten years must have given additional weight to the belief that patchwork will not do.

174

FOOTNOTES

1. "Report to Council of the Special Committee on Research Program, **Journal of Accountancy**, December 1958.

2. Maurice Moonitz, **The Basic Postulates of Accounting**, Accounting Research Study No.1, 1961; Robert T. Sprouse and Maurice Moonitz, **A Tentative Statement of Broad Accounting Principles for Business Enterprises**, Accounting Research Study No.3, 1962.

3. For some comments of the present writer, see "The Moonitz and Sprouse Studies on Postulates and Principles", **Proceedings** of Conference of the Australasian Association of University Teachers of Accounting, Canberra, January 1964.

4. Paul Grady, **Inventory of Generally Accepted Accounting Principles for Business Enterprises**, Accounting Research Study No.7, 1965.

5. See "The Linked Logics of Practice and Pedagogy", **Proceedings** of Conference of the Australasian Association of University Teachers of Accounting, Newcastle, August 1968.

6. For other argument see R.J. Chambers, "Tax Allocation and Financial Reporting", **Abacus**, December 1968.

7. See **A Statement of Basic Accounting Theory**, American Accounting Association; and for some comment on trade-off, see Chambers "The Mathematics of Accounting and Estimating", **Abacus**, December 1967.

8. In **Accounting, Evaluation and Economic Behavior.** Many of the terms used in this work have different referents than the same words have in traditional accounting usage.

175

The Anguish of Accountants

IT would be an exaggeration to say that many accountants are bothered and anxious about the state of their art. Generally speaking, they have been firmly taught to do what they do, and they have been firmly taught that it is right to do what they do. Official pronouncements of their professional bodies generally continue to affirm what they were taught, with perhaps an occasional and slight modification. Articles and speeches by their leaders and colleagues encourage them to continue to do what they do. And they are reasonably well paid for doing what they do. There is not much cause for anguish.

Of course, what I have said about accountants can be said about the general body of specialists in any field. Most technical specialists have a very limited view of the impact of what they do. If their actions conform with the rules familiar to them, they are confident that they are right. Usually they will be backed up by the majority of their professional peers if anything goes wrong— because they were all taught the same rules. They can shelter behind their professional associations or behind the corporations they serve, or behind the insurers who are prepared to shoulder some of their risks. Or they can shelter behind moralistic notions like the merits of free competition or the virtue of integrity, or the plea of honest mistake. They do not know or do not remember that most of the great tragedies of history occurred under the banner of just such mottoes as these. But mottoes, catch-cries and shibboleths are no comfort to those on the receiving end.

When I speak of anguish I speak of the small number of people who are concerned with the effects of what they do, or what others do, in the name of professional practice. I speak of the small number of practitioners who are genuinely perturbed by the criticisms of accounting, by the faults they see in it themselves, and by the personal misery which these faults visit upon trusting and unsuspecting persons they know. I speak of the small number of scholars and teachers who are dismayed, both by what disturbs practitioners and by the excuses, fallacies, myths and rationalizations which masquerade as the theory of the subject. I speak of such practitioners as Kenneth MacNeal, Leonard Spacek and Howard Ross, and of such scholars as William Paton and Henry Rand Hatfield and Henry W. Sweeney. There have been and are perhaps a few hundred like them, though none as outspoken. But what is a few hundred in the hundreds of thousands of accountants in the English-speaking world in the last 50 years? A small number.

It has always been a small number of anxious people who have been critical of long-standing (generally accepted) practices. It was not the consensus of housewives which has stimulated the demand for fair packaging. Perhaps most of them grumbled when they found their "economy-size" or "super-pack" or "mammoth-size" only partly full. But grumbling does not change a generally accepted merchandizing practice. It was not the consensus of heavy industry magnates which stimulated the control of atmospheric, riparian and tidal water pollution. It was not the consensus of car-drivers or car-manufacturers which is forcing manufacturers to make cars safer. Nor have these rejections of what were generally accepted practices been due to a small number of theorists conferring on the definition of "pollution" or "safety", with the object of so defining those terms that wastes, fumes and other effluvia could not be described as pollutants, and that existing cars could not be said to be unsafe.

A paper presented at the convention of the Australasian Association of University Teachers of Accounting held at Christchurch, New Zealand in August, 1971. We are indebted to the President of the Association, Mr. W. P. Birkett, M.Ec., A.A.S.A., Senior Lecturer in Accounting, the University of Sydney, and the author for permission to publish this paper as an article in the journal.

Signs of Present Anguish

Anxiety about the present practices of the many is the burden of the few. In the late fifties such people as Marquis Eaton and Alvin Jennings, officers of the American Institute of CPAs, were perturbed by the loose, piece-meal way in which decisions on practices had been made for some twenty years by the Committee on Accounting Procedure.[1] The fruit of this concern was the new plan of research activity announced in 1958, and still running. Twelve years have passed, years in which there has been more litigation against accountants in the United States than ever before in a similar period. There has been much cause for anguish. In early January this year (1971), a conference was held of 35 prominent CPAs under the chairmanship of the President of the Institute to consider again ways in which the present quandaries of the profession may be resolved. Among the questions discussed were:

Is it desirable or necessary to undertake a broad review of how accounting principles should be established? and,

Which elements in society have a legitimate right to participate in the establishment of accounting principles and how can that involvement be best achieved?

The Journal of Accountancy of February 1971, reporting the conference, pointed out that "The conference also took note of the fact that the American Accounting Association had recently appointed a committee to explore the feasibility of creating a public commission to determine how accounting principles should be established".[2]

The American Institute has been in the business of making recommendations and pronouncements since about 1917, and the American Accounting Association has been publishing statements on accounting principles since 1935. It seems strange indeed that after all that time the question is still being asked: How should accounting principles be established? And strange that it should be asked by the two organizations which have already devoted more time and effort to the discussion of principles than perhaps any other professional accounting organization in the world. These motions seem to suggest that both organizations have grave doubts about the efficacy of all the "research" recommendations, statements, opinions and prohibitions they have sponsored or uttered at least in the last decade.

I have no wish to predict (in June 1971) the outcome of the latest proposals of these bodies. I hope it will be better than I fear it will. My fear is based on the method proposed for the resolution of the questions raised: the method of committee deliberation. I have elsewhere pointed out that seldom, if ever, has a material advance

in knowledge been the work of a committee. But as belief in the method of committee deliberation persists, it seems worthwhile to state quite plainly the drawbacks of proceeding to resolve fundamental questions in this way.

The Failure of Research by Committee

Professional organizations, of practitioners and teachers, are usually administered by committees. Committee-men usually have limited service-lives under the rules of their association. Committees are usually expected to "get something done" in each term; they expect it of themselves, even if members of their associations have no clear expectations. Getting something done in a limited term means getting something done in a hurry. If it is a matter of making some physical arrangements, or carrying on some work with established precedents, a committee may be a very effective device for using limited resources. But research, the attempt to resolve significant questions of principle, is not one of those things. If problems of principle could be resolved by vote of a majority of a committee, we should long since have been free of present uneasiness. Why are the products of research committees so unimpressive, unproductive, unenduring?

In the first place, too often the work assigned to a research committee is far more extensive than it is possible to carry out in a limited term. If a fruitful way of proceeding were known and a limited problem were posed, it should not be impossible for a committee to produce some worthwhile work in a limited time. But, as the questions recently raised by the A.I.C.P.A. and the A.A.A. indicate, there is no agreement on a fruitful way of proceeding. And generally, the sponsors of research committees and their members have wanted to resolve some complex issue, or to do some big job—like writing a statement of basic accounting theory, or clarifying the meaning of business income—in their limited time.

Second, those who are invited to undertake assigned research tasks are, in a sense, pressed men. Some prestige attaches to committee membership, especially to research committee membership. Few of us like to refuse such invitations. But few indeed of the members of committees have been expert in the matters they have been invited to resolve. An expert on a matter of practical or theoretical principle will have qualified himself as an expert by giving the matter considerable thought on his own initiative, by marshalling his ideas about it and by writing, with due care and deliberation, at least a few significant articles about it. Among the members of research committees there have been few who qualify in these terms. More commonly, members of committees will not have written a line, before or after their committee service, on the issues they were asked to assist in resolving. On this ground alone it should not be surprising that, as Professors Mautz and Gray have pointed out, "substantial expenditures on

---

1. See generally *The Journal of Accountancy* in the latter years of the fifties.
2. News Report, "Conference Recommends Study of Efforts to Establish Accounting Principles", *The Journal of Accountancy*, February 1971, pp. 11-14.

research have not produced the hoped-for results"; and "one has difficulty in citing specific instances of progress in accounting practice which resulted from these efforts".[3]

Third, there seems to be a kind of deference to their sponsors on the part of committees. There is little evidence in their products of willingness to challenge the conventional wisdom. Skirt the primary issues, yes; talk about other tangential things, yes; but confront directly the propriety of existing beliefs and practices, no. This may be due to the belief that there is a compelling, an entirely convincing, rationale for existing practices, even if any particular committee cannot find it. It may be due to the guidance given, or to the implicit expectation of sponsors that a committee's work will confirm the merit of present beliefs or practices. It may simply be evidence of the incapacity of a committee to think through any issue closely to the point of challenging prevailing beliefs. But these attitudes, expectations and incapacities are so inconsistent with research, in the proper sense of the word, that they cannot be expected to lead to significant advances in knowledge or practice. We will never find out whether a boat is seaworthy without rocking it quite a bit.

Fourth, a committee is unable, by its nature, freely to engage and disengage from its immediate attention particular clusters of ideas in the search for worthwhile conclusions. To solve any problem it is necessary to hold the elements of the problem in sharp focus, while drawing successively on particular sets of ideas or experiences which promise, even if only vaguely, to assist in the solution. To solve any generalized problem, any problem of principle, the same process is necessary; but it is more difficult, since one must consider the *general* import of sets of ideas or experiences rather than their incidental or contingent features. It is possible for one person to take up, in succession, a series of possible ways of resolving a matter, to reject each way which fails, to remember the respects in which it fails and the respects in which it partially succeeds, to use these recollections in devising previously untried methods of solving the problem, and at last to reach a conclusion. It is possible, I say, but it is not easy. It requires concentrated attention, and, as the history of ideas shows, it often requires long periods of reflection, disengagement, collection of evidence and further reflection—all with the benefit of the memory of previous reflections. It requires the concentrated attention of one mind. But a committee has not one mind. It has many minds. At any stage in the deliberations of a committee, each member will have different sets of ideas in the back of his mind, waiting to be drawn upon, and each will tend to value those ideas differently from other members. Debate follows. Sharp lines are drawn, lines which

prevent the free association of ideas and lead to premature commitment. Committees are impatient with involved argument. They tend to brush aside evidence; their members can be depended upon to meet any specific evidence with counter-evidence, since they are concerned more with the impact of their own experiences on themselves than with the *general* import of those experiences and the experiences of others. They tend to seek verbal consensus rather than understanding, and to value convergence of opinion rather than the convergence of evidence.

These characteristics of committees I know at first hand from my own participation in, and observation of, committee work. The ambiguous phraseology and the mutually inconsistent arguments and conclusions of many committees bear them out. I have the greatest respect for the diligence and devotion of committee-men to their work. But diligence is fruitless if applied to inadequate tools. The new programme undertaken by the A.I.C.P.A. in 1958 seems to me to have expressed a judgment on the effectiveness of the Committee on Accounting Procedure and the Study Group on Business Income. The recent announcements of the A.I.C.P.A. and the A.A.A. seem to me to imply unfavourable judgments on the work of all preceding committees—research committees, advisory committees and all committees which have steered or influenced work published as research work. How the proposals for new committees can lead to better results than their antecedents I do not understand.

The Business of Research

In most fields, research is regarded as a specialized business in its own right. The business of practitioners is considered to be the solving of specific problems of clients. The business of researchers is considered to be the solving of general problems so that a useful general framework is available to practitioners in their dealings with clients. Practitioners may quite properly respect principles which are generally accepted among themselves. It is the function of researchers to question the substance of those principles and practices. Consensus of practitioners is no guarantee that what they agree upon is valid or useful, in principle or practice. The constant iteration of the phrase "generally accepted accounting principles" has clearly not stilled the doubts and anxieties of professionals. Researchers may not properly consider consensus or general acceptance in practice as any evidence of the validity or fruitfulness of any principle. The two different problem contexts of practitioners and researchers entail that each class has or should have a "mental set" appropriate to its own function. One cannot be a "true believer" and a critic at the same time. Attitudes, knowledge and technique differentiate between the one and the other.

The objects of the curiosity or inquisitiveness of researchers and practitioners differ. A researcher seeks to know as much as it is possible to know about a

---

3. R. K. Mautz and Jack Gray, "Some Thoughts on Research Needs in Accounting", *The Journal of Accountancy*, September 1970, p. 55.

limited range of phenomena. He may use any of an extensive range of devices—observation, experimentation, argument, simplification—to discover how things work or how they are connected. He is not satisfied with the general knowledge that certain things are related; he seeks to know how they are related in detail, how one thing follows another and the general laws or principles which justify the belief that, in general, certain effects follow from certain causes. A practitioner, on the other hand, must have an extensive knowledge of techniques which will serve in the full range of circumstances he may meet. He is curious about the practices and opinions of his peers on all of the technical matters which may engage his attention as a professional. It does him no injustice to say that his knowledge is less intensive and more extensive than that of a researcher; for it is beyond most of us to have both intensive and extensive knowledge in any complex technical field.

The attitudes towards existing beliefs or practices of researchers and practitioners differ. Research begins with doubt about the validity or propriety or efficacy of some prevailing belief or practice. A researcher wants to make sure. His inquiries are prompted by observed events which, if prevailing beliefs were dependable, should not have occurred. He regards these events as anomalies. Even a single anomaly may be of interest, for an anomaly—something contrary to or inexplicable in terms of known rules or laws—demands explanation. A professional practitioner in his relations with clients cannot for long indulge doubts. As an expert he is expected to be confident about his specialism, to resolve doubts by seeking second opinions if necessary. Anomalies mean little to him; he must give primary attention to the problems of his client even if his solution must be anomalous. He can take some comfort from the generally held notion that many of the anomalies of today become the standard practices of tomorrow; the history of ideas and practices lends this notion support. But being preoccupied with the affairs of one or more particular clients, he seldom considers which newly tried idea *should* become standard practice in future. To do this is a proper function of researchers.

There are significant differences in the pressure upon researchers and practitioners to solve their different kinds of problem. Ideally a researcher should be free of external pressure to produce results in the short run. To identify an anomaly may not be difficult. To identify it as an instance of a class of anomalies may be more difficult. To identify the cluster of beliefs on which a class of anomalies throws doubt may be more difficult still; for usually both well-developed systems of belief and conventionally developed systems of belief comprise interrelated sets of ideas. To gather evidence, to interpret it, to evaluate its relevance to the matter under inquiry, may require sustained patience over a long time. Pressure to resolve any significant problem is likely to prevent all proper measures being taken to consider the propriety of a solution and its superiority over other possible conclusions. I mention superiority, for to discover what is best at any given time is the dominant objective of research. Competing or contradictory conclusions or proposals always represent unsolved problems. A professional has little freedom to reflect upon the wider or long-run consequences of his solutions of clients' problems. He must resolve them speedily. The on-going affairs of his clients cannot be impeded by extended deliberations on matters of general principle; and his attention is commanded by the different problems of many clients. The pressure to reach conclusions speedily is intense. He will proceed by precedents, rather than by the extended process of collecting and sifting a wide range of evidence. Research under pressure proceeds in exactly the same way. Arguments, precedents and authorities take the place of evidence and analysis. This is excusable in practice: it is inadequate and inexcusable in research.

Both practitioners and researchers make use of analytical and constructive skills, but to different effect. A researcher is concerned with the common properties of many problem situations. He must apprehend their similarities and differences, distinguish the invariant elements from the contingent elements of events or classes of experience, endeavour to establish the empirical connections between events and the logical connections between propositions explanatory of events. He is anxious about gaps in any system which is presented as a possible explanation of observed events. For he wishes to construct a system of propositions which will serve as a general guide for the solution, in practice, of many problems of a given class. A practitioner is concerned with analysis of the immediate problem context of a client. His object is to construct a solution which is workable in that context alone, at least in the first instance. He may resort to invention, to ad hoc devices which will meet the circumstances of a client—and to different ad hoc devices to meet the circumstances of other clients. He may strive for consistency in his own practice, but he cannot foresee the effects of his innovations on the general practice of his art—whether those innovations will be adopted by others as precedents, and with what consequences.

There are sufficient differences in attitude and circumstance between researchers and practitioners to suggest strongly that it is difficult to expect effective research work to be undertaken by practitioners. Even if they have the best of intentions, and this may be assumed, the cross currents of practice are too numerous and pressing to leave them free to doubt, to explore, to await the emergence of evidence, to suspend judgment, to reflect upon the more extensive and more remote consequences of specific conclusions.

But the uneasiness of the A.I.C.P.A. and the A.A.A. is not to be attributed solely to the lack of reliable results from professionally sponsored or supervised inquiry. There is little satisfaction, it seems, with the products of the academic arm of the profession.

The academic arm is usually considered to be the body of teachers. It seems to be supposed that all teachers are adequately equipped—have sufficient time and appropriate inclination or disposition—to be researchers. Some such expectation is entertained by large sections of the body academic itself. The supposition is unrealistic. Good teaching is itself a time-consuming and exhausting business. To teach a subject thoroughly requires much more than the following of some conventional textbook. If teaching is to prepare students for the future, and if the best products of research are to become the commonplace of the future, teachers have the task of introducing new ideas, of demonstrating their application and discussing their advantages, even though they are not originators themselves. To learn about what is new and to reduce it to assimilable teaching material is no small or simple task. Good exposition is no less important or necessary than good research. To expect that all academics shall do both well is to put a premium on mediocrity in both directions. But, in any case, there are some general flaws which tend seriously to qualify the value of research effort.

There is too great a tendency to rely on argument rather than evidence. Mautz and Gray have observed that "much accounting research has been . . . [in the nature of] a citation of authorities with argumentation to fill in any gaps".[4] It is true, but, for the advancement of knowledge, it is unfortunate. It is almost standard practice in the literature of disciplined and scientific inquiry to point out the defects of mere reliance on authorities, to show how it has impeded the advancement of knowledge. Many of the notions of traditional accounting have been, and I believe can be, supported by argument only. I have long been seeking one single piece of evidence to the effect that any kind of financial or commercial decision can be based on financial statements derived on the historical cost principle. I have sought in vain. I am inclined to believe that there should be a moratorium on argumentative defences (and the citation of authorities) until some firm evidence is produced which lends some support to the dependability, in practical problem-solving situations, of the products of traditional accounting.

There is too great a tendency to be superficial. There are some who urge that, as accounting is information-processing, all information-processing should be the province of accounting and accountants. Just a little care would show that the conclusion arises from a fallacious form of the syllogism. There are some who, sensing that accounting information is in the nature of financial measurement, blandly assert that all kinds of financial magnitudes are measures or measurements. Just a little analysis would show that some such mag-

nitudes are derived in ways that cannot conceivably be called measuring. In a recent article on research method by a professor who need not be named, it was said that "most accountants accept the use of historical cost as the primary basis of asset valuation". The view is widely held, but it is superficial and unsupported by any substantial evidence. Historical cost is not the basis used for cash. For receivables it is quite common to make some judgment about future collections. There are two elements, actual account balances and future estimates, both equally necessary to obtain the reported asset value; neither can be said to be primary. For inventories, the lower of cost or market rule makes market price of the same status as cost; neither is primary. For plant and similar assets, accountants use four separate elements —cost, an expected service life, an expected resale (scrap) price and some chosen pattern of amortization —to arrive at asset values. Cost cannot be said to be primary when three equally necessary and independent elements enter into valuation. If $2 + 3 = 5$, we cannot properly say that 2 is the primary basis of 5. All the elements 2, $+$ and 3 are equally necessary; none is primary. There will be no substantial progress while we are content to proceed from or to make such superficial statements as the one which prompted these comments.

There is too great a tendency to "explore" accounting from other directions—economics, psychology, statistics —of which the explorer has too little acquaintance. For example, there are many who hold that the accepted principle of economics entails the use of replacement costs in accounting. In the first place, this view disregards the function of accounting information as feedback on past performance. In the second place, it disregards the function of information on the actual financial state of a firm as a basis for immediate choices and actions. These two objections relate to accounting as such. In the third place, the view in question disregards the principle, accepted in economics, that *ex post* measures of wealth are made by reference to the market prices of assets and *ex post* measures of income are made by reference to changes in wealth. And, finally, it disregards the fact that the context of discussions of replacement costs in economics is the set of alternatives available to any firm but not yet acted upon. A little knowledge is a dangerous thing—particularly in what purports to be research.

There is too great a tendency, on the part of academics, to flee from reaching conclusions. It almost seems to be regarded as unacademic to stand firmly in favour of some proposal and against all others. You may have heard of the three-handed economist: on the one hand, this; on the other hand that; and on the other hand, something else. The many-handed accountant leaves him far behind. We badly need more one-handed academics—we would at least know what they stood for. I believe it is the function of research to demonstrate that a proposal is better than any competing proposal, the best of all at any time. If researchers felt compelled to demonstrate what is best they would be obliged to

---

4. *Ibid.*, p. 56.

grub for evidence. But there is so little willingness to stand firmly for any proposal, or to suppose it is sufficient just to accept all proposals, that the search for evidence is seldom even begun. From what some practitioners say, they would like to depend on the firm conclusions academic researchers reach. But weak-kneed ambivalence does not escape their notice. A prominent practitioner, commenting on a set of papers by academics at a conference last year remarked "We heard W, X and Y tell us about the pros and cons of several proposals, but the discussion did not reveal how strongly they supported the proposals. And then there was Z, who, contrary to the apparent rules of the game, said quite plainly that he believed in what he proposed"! One cannot expect one's conclusions to command respect if one does not respect them sufficiently oneself to stand for them.

Finally, even among workers who show some diligence, there is too little care given to the choice of a method of inquiry. There is an extensive range of research methods. But they are not all equally available or useful in all fields of inquiry. Experimentation is not available to astronomers or astro-physicists. Some forms of experimentation are not available to medical researchers. Experimentation is not available to political scientists, anthropologists, historians and economists. Nor to accounting researchers. Statistical methods are useful in fields where the subjects of inquiry are in some important sense uniform. They are not useful where the phenomena under observation are in important senses unique. Opinion surveys may be valuable when it may be supposed that the referenda are known to respondents. But they are useless when opinion is sought on matters unfamiliar to respondents. The range of methods is not a "grab bag" from which any method may be freely chosen. The belief that it is has produced a vast amount of output in accounting which is, in my opinion, nearly, if not completely, worthless. There are examples of violation of most of the canons of inquiry in the literature of the last decade.

What seems to me to be the most fruitful method, which would supply the hard, empirical evidence of which there is such a serious shortage in the literature, has been almost entirely overlooked. It is the method of sustained observation of the consequences of particular practices, the intertemporal and international comparison of practices and their consequences. This is the method used by all researchers in fields where experimentation is impossible. There is a mountainous quantity of evidence on the consequences of using different accounting devices in the matters reported in the commercial and financial press, in the annual reports and histories of companies, in the litigation and the professional wrangles which are among the proximate causes of professional anguish. This evidence is empirical in a sense in which much so-called empirical research of recent years is not—it is the stuff of financial and commercial experience. No doubt the

method has so few adherents because it is laborious and slow; perhaps also because it makes little or no use of sophisticated tools such as computers and statistics. But these are only drawbacks if we prefer instant prestige to enduring knowledge. I cannot agree with Mautz and Gray that "accounting suffers from lack of an established research methodology". What accountants have failed to do is to make the most fruitful choice from among many established methods of inquiry.

Where, from Here?

If the turmoil, the anxiety and the outright anguish of the past decade and longer are to be modified, it seems that some quite different modus operandi must be adopted. It does not seem to be fruitful to go on reorganizing old ideas in new papers, or organizing new committees when so many old committees have failed. The flood of new expositions of old ideas engorges the digestive apparatus of practitioners, students and teachers alike. We are forced to read it, especially if it is "official", in case there is anything important that we should know. But the very quantity of it and the diversity of it makes it almost certain that we are not informed by it. We have no time to reflect on it. We have no time to question or contest it. We may often have the feeling that it has all been said before, but before we can check that, there is a new batch before us. It is demoralizing. The February 1971 number of *The Journal of Accountancy* carried a filler in which appeared the following words attributed to "a Roman citizen", A.D. 60: "We tend to meet any new situation by reorganizing and a wonderful method it can be for creating the illusion of progress while producing confusion, inefficiency and demoralization." I doubt whether the editor had his tongue in his cheek; but it makes an interesting contrast with the proposals, cited above, announced in the same issue of the journal.

I believe there should be an entirely different mode of relating practice, teaching and research—a division of labour such that each branch of the profession respects the other for its specific skills and functions, and each makes greater efforts to benefit from the special skills and knowledge of the other.

Take first the academic arm.

There should be a clear understanding that teaching is a distinctive and demanding function, no less respected and valued than research. Teaching is in fact the process by which, in due course, the novel ideas of one generation become the accepted doctrines of the next. It is not just a vehicle for passing on old traditions. Teaching is well done if a teacher understands present professional practice and present dilemmas, the contribution of contemporary research to the resolution of those dilemmas, and the necessity for reducing both to a form in which they can be absorbed, as knowledge and as challenge, by each year's brood of hopeful and anxious novices. For those who like to teach, there are sufficient demands in these exercises to leave little time or effort for dabbling in research. There is no question that good teaching and research go hand in hand. But this does not mean that all teachers can or should engage in research themselves. In most well-developed fields there is a strong demand for good teaching, good exposition, apart from and even if there is no clear demand for research. Research has always been to the taste of few. It makes little sense to force it on the many.

As for researchers, there should be far greater respect for evidence and the accumulation of evidence than there has been. Debate is not altogether uninstructive. But it soon becomes sterile if there is no injection of new evidence. The unfolding of new commercial, financial and professional events, their similarities to and differences from past events of the same class, provide a continuous flow of live evidential material sufficient, I believe, to discipline the imagination and focus the attention on how well past practices have worked, how well present practices are working and how well proposed practices might work. How well things have worked cannot be resolved by argument without evidence. Unless we attempt to resolve the dilemmas of practice and the debates of theorists by reference to evidence other than the dicta of other accountants, the academic arm of the profession will continue to exhibit the fragmentation which confuses and attracts the scorn of practitioners.

There should be more direct confrontation of innovative suggestions by counter-argument and counter-evidence. At present almost any suggestion, however poorly supported by evidence, can become accepted into the corpus of what is taught and what may be cited as authoritative. Instead of a literature we have a "litterature". At present there are about four or five main systems of accounting which are contenders for general approbation. They have been expounded almost ad nauseam; but the amount of intensive, critical analysis and the amount of evidence for or against them are meagre indeed. There is also a continuous outpouring of arguments and suggestions on particular matters not directly connected with these main systems, and as little critical analysis and evidence for or against them. I have always believed that the object of research is the establishment of a better-organized body of knowledge, a body of knowledge with greater cohesion and consistency than any alternative system of ideas. Scattered effort, proposals unconnected to any main stream of ideas, unwillingness to probe intensely the foundations of conclusions and suggestions will not lead in that direction. They are parasitical, cancerous, at a time when we need all our energy to establish a well-organized body of knowledge.

And, what of the practising arm of the profession?

I believe it should vacate the field of research. There is no other technical specialism, to my knowledge, the practising arm of which involves itself in "research" activity as much as the accounting profession. There is no other profession, to my knowledge, the general members of which take part as freely in debate about the products of research activity without benefit of the evidence on which conclusions are based. There is no other profession, to my knowledge, which has spent so much time and money in a decade—only to be asking at the end how should its principles be established. There is no profession, to my knowledge, which has devoted so much effort to expounding what others have already expounded, and so little attention to the new suggestions of researchers working independently of it.

But to vacate the field of research does not mean to have no interest in it. Researchers and practitioners both entertain the expectation that research will lead to advances in practice. But there would be more disciplined research if practitioners refused to take notice of research work unless or until the products of inquiry had been thoroughly debated by researchers themselves, were substantially supported by evidence, and were in the form of tightly constructed and well defined proposals. At that point, but not before, it would be profitable to have a small committee of practitioners as appraisers or referees of research conclusions. The work should be ready for its severest examination, with evidence, argument and comparison well laid out. To my knowledge there has never been an intensive appraisal by a group of professional practitioners of any proposal of independent researchers.

It is not uncommon in other fields for expert practitioners to undertake experimental exercises based on research findings, to see how they work in practice. The task is undertaken by leaders in the profession, for their professional skills and reputations are safeguards against foolish experimentation. Researchers do not have the means of running forms of practical experimentation; they can only offer proof of feasibility in general terms. In any case, it is a proper check on research conclusions that expert practitioners should try them out. And the object of the exercise is not to convince proposers, but to convince other practitioners; a demonstration by leading practitioners is far more effective and convincing to the general run of practitioners than a demonstration by researchers themselves. In all this, of course, I presume that the leaders of the profession earnestly wish to advance its technique; as for the costs and the risks, they would be far less than those associated with present "research" exercises by the professional bodies and their members.

It is a common practice in other professions and technologies for professional organizations to support financially the work of independent university researchers, without expecting short-run pay-offs. More of this in the field of accounting would be less costly than attempting to duplicate or triplicate work done elsewhere. I know that the granting of financial aid is a hazardous business. But there are safeguards. If the profession is concernd that its practices shall be founded on a well-organized body of knowledge, it could properly expect that applicants for financial aid should demonstrate that their projects have some clear connection with the resolution of some significant dispute or with the better organization of some comprehensive system of ideas. It goes without saying that any applicant should be expected to demonstrate his capacity in the matter he proposes by the extent of his work preparatory to and directly bearing on the issues he intends to explore.

The division of labour suggested, the development of mutual respect by all three classes of people mentioned, and the development of mutual involvement and interdependence seem to me to offer some prospect of relief from the concern, anxiety and anguish which has plagued reflective members of the profession. To arrange things so that well-developed new ideas seep into the profession through its teachers and professional leaders is, in my view, far more promising than the introduction of a "second legislature", after the manner of some recent technical directives and prohibitions.[5]

My answers to the problems which worry the A.I.C.P.A. and the A.A.A. may be simply stated. Is it

5. Professor Paton has some pointed words on the matter in "Earmarks of a Profession—And the APB", *The Journal of Accountancy*, January 1971, pp. 42-3.

desirable or necessary to undertake a broad review of how accounting principles should be established? I think it is unnecessary. It is necessary only to follow the same well established and fruitful steps taken in all scientific inquiry. Those steps should be well known. Let those researchers who will follow those steps carefully and rigorously be encouraged; and let there be some serious effort, on the part of leading professionals, to evaluate and to test those conclusions or proposals which emerge from the evidence accumulated and analysed by researchers. Which elements in society have a legitimate right to participate in the establishment of accounting principles and how can that involvement be best achieved? Expert professionals, practitioners and researchers, only. Only those who know well the impact and the technicalities of professional work can have a legitimate right to determine its style. Medical, legal, engineering principles are not established by democratic vote or deliberation of the technically uninformed. Neither should accounting principles be so established. As for the involvement of practitioners and researchers, let there be respect, each of the other's function, skill and duty. Let each be auditor of the other in his special way.

Thus may we have fruitful concern instead of fruitless and persistent anxiety.

183

Prospect on Graduation*

Today is a beginning. You who have graduated, and most of your friends, will no doubt see it as an end - an end to some years of disciplined toil and dependence. But I and my colleagues hope you will leave here today with some sense of the excitement of a beginning, rather than with the anticlimactic feeling "well, that's over".

One of the main functions of the University, according to the Spanish educationist Ortega, is to give men and women the capacity to live "to the height of their times". This imposes on University people the endless task of exploration and invention, of discriminating between the trivial and the significant, of confronting the myths and folklore of each age with more reliable knowledge. You have benefitted from the fruits of these processes; some of the things you have learned as undergraduates took eminent scholars decades, indeed generations to learn. But, your sojourn here of three years or so is probably too short for you to have seen the emergence of knowledge that is genuinely new. Some of the ideas that scholars began tinkering with before you came here are still only in embryonic form. The ongoing inquiries of the University are thus already making out-of-date the things you learned in last year's lectures. Today could well mark the beginning of your intellectual obsolescence.

On the other hand, today marks the beginning of your intellectual self-propulsion. You go from here to forty years of commercial, professional and academic life - years in which the world's affairs and the best ways of analyzing them may change radically. It is not yet forty years since Keynes' **General Theory of Employment, Interest and Money** revolutionized the teaching and practice of economic analysis and policy making. And there have been many less spectacular changes in the interval. How well you succeed in living "to the height of your times" will depend on the survival of your intellectual curiosity and self discipline. That is in your own hands.

---

* An address on the occasion of an Economics Graduation ceremony in
the University of Sydney, 14 April 1973.

To speak of my own field, if I may, the last forty years have seen a major crisis emerge in the study and practice of accounting. Commercial failures and fancy footwork have marked the progress of traditional practice from one embarrassment to another. Misrepresentation of the profits and wealth of companies has occurred on an alarming scale. The Reid Murray group in Australia, the Atlantic Acceptance Corporation in Canada, the Penn Central Railroad in the United States, Investors Overseas Services of Geneva, the Pergamon and Handley Page companies of the United Kingdom, and the JBL group of New Zealand - to name just a few - have provided examples of serious misrepresentation. Against most of this misrepresentation the law provided neither protection nor remedy to investors and creditors who lost hundreds of million of dollars. In a far greater number of cases, companies - again around the world - have disclosed, suddenly, enormous increments in wealth and sometimes enormous losses, almost literally at the stroke of a director's or an accountant's pen. Closer to home and of a somewhat different class was the recent Weekly Statement of Central Banking Business of the Reserve Bank of Australia. There a loss of some $300 million on foreign assets, following revaluation of the dollar, was thrown into an item described as "loans, advances and all other assets" - as if in fact no loss had been made. The habit of accountants and their masters of showing things otherwise than as they are is no less objectionable because it is a habit. Indeed it is in direct opposition to the object of publishing financial information, namely that those who deal with companies shall be fairly informed. It is a case of massive pollution of the information streams on which many private and public judgements depend.

The consequences of misleading information are far-reaching in countries which make extensive use of the corporate form of business. Figures on company wealth and profits are used by economists in research and advisory work, by agencies or tribunals administering taxes, tariffs, bounties, prices and wages, by bankers, insurers, brokers, investors and creditors. In one way or another, these figures affect the growth of particular industries, the employment opportunities available, the wages we earn, the prices we pay, the taxes we pay - and of course the national income. For the optimal distribution of a country's resources is impossible unless we are continuously and reliably informed of the yields of investments in their present employments.

186

The alarming things about the distortive and manipulative practices to which I refer are that they are universal, that they are all permissible under the law in this and most other countries, and that they survive in spite of their proven capacity for misdirection. No doubt many people will find it hard to believe that lawyers, brokers, managers, professional accountants and legislators, many of whom have passed through these halls, can and do put up with such notoriously unreliable information sources. But the evidence is massive and unmistakable. It only goes to show how securely myths and folklore can shore up old habits of specialists who see only individual trees - never the forest.

Which brings me to a final point. We like to think that a University education will have given you a glimpse of the forest, so that you will see both individual things, events, ideas, and their systematic relations. But the neat subject boxes so dear to teachers often work against this expectation. In proper academic fashion I could give handfuls of footnotes on eminent practitioners and teachers of accounting who misinterpret economic doctrine, and on well established economists, statisticians, historians and so on who use accounting information quite unaware of or indifferent to its defects. I am reminded of a jibe of Mark Twain. The length of the Lower Mississippi River, he noted, had been reduced, by cutting off some of its many bends, by 242 miles in 176 years, "Therefore", he says, "any calm person who is not blind or idiotic, can see that in the Old Oolitic Silurian Period, just a million years ago next November, the Lower Mississippi was upward of 1,300,000 miles long and stuck out over the Gulf of Mexico like a fishing rod. And by the same token any person can see that 742 years from now the Lower Mississippi will be only a mile and three quarters long and that Cairo and New Orleans [now 1000 miles apart] will have joined their streets together and be plodding comfortably along under a single mayor and a mutual board of aldermen. There is something fascinating about science", he concludes. "One can get such wholesome returns of conjecture out of such a trifling investment of fact".

Building mountains of conjecture on one´s own few chosen facts and ignoring the rest is more common than we often suppose. It is the source of many of the chronic pathological conditions in administrative and professional affairs including those to which I have alluded.

It is given to few in any generation to enjoy the exhilaration which prompted Archimedes, fresh from his tub, to cry "Eureka", or which prompted Hillary, atop Mt Everest, to exclaim "We made the bitch". But the excitement of challenging the folklore, of weeding out the pretence, the pseudo-science, the sloppy thinking in your own fields, practical, professional or academic, lies before you all. That is living to the height of your times. Go to it with courage.

Accounting rules must be
consistent with
"the way things work"
and based on
fundamental necessity or
technological constraints.

accounting principles or accounting policies?

There was a time when people debated the character of "accounting principles." The debate was not particularly fruitful. It did not lead to a definite body of self-consistent rules. Grady's *Inventory of Generally Accepted Accounting Principles*[1] and exercises of a similar kind in other countries have all left open a variety of optional methods of accounting for the same kinds of assets, liabilities, revenues and expenses. The directors and managers of companies are free to choose, from the options, such particular rules as will serve their purposes. Companies have switched from Fifo to Lifo and back again, from straight-line to accelerated depreciation and back again. If there were a firm body of rules, switching of these and other kinds would long since have been outlawed.

The freedom of company officers to choose accounting rules has, particularly over the recent past, been tolerated on the ground that accounting methods are matters of company policy. There have been increasing numbers of references to the accounting policies of particular firms. Dale Gerboth, in an article directed to justifying the modus operandi of the Accounting Principles Board, speaks of policy-making by the APB.[2] There is a high-toned deceptiveness about the terms "policy" and "policy-making." On the one hand, they imply a superior source of direction (such as the board of directors), overriding all localized or merely technical considerations. On the other hand, they imply highly specific directives which, even given the same facts, may vary from policy-maker to policy-maker.

It is difficult to avoid the conclusion that people have switched from talk about "principles" to talk about "policy" to get around the awkward fact that diverse and contradictory forms of accounting co-exist. It seems to be thought that if we talk of policies rather than of principles we can tolerate the diversity. For, "of course," policies must have some definite justification, and diversity of policies must be expected because different people have different aims, and the same people have different aims at different times. Gerboth uses this argument in defense of the APB against critics of the Board's failure to lay down the "objectives" of accounting. He refers to the "shifting, contradictory and often unrecognized" objectives of even one person, and the "insuperable" difficulties of obtaining agreement about objectives among a group of people (p. 43).

We may admit the complexity of individual ob-

[1] Paul Grady, Accounting Research Study No. 7, *Inventory of Generally Accepted Accounting Principles for Business Enterprises* (New York, N.Y.: American Institute of CPAs, 1965).
[2] Dale Gerboth, " 'Muddling Through' With the APB," JofA, May72, pp.42-49.

jectives and the difficulties of securing agreement about objectives. But this is no cause for failing to state exactly what function accounting is expected to serve. Indeed every pronouncement of the APB must have arisen from some notion of the function of financial statements. The essence of the criticism of the pronouncements as a whole is that the function of financial statements and their contents is not clearly stated, and that, as between different statements or Opinions, quite different notions of function seem to be entertained. Progress toward better practice is unlikely while this state of affairs persists.

There are four aspects of the task of advancing accounting practice: (1) discerning what is wrong or defective in present practice; (2) knowing (or discovering) how things or actions are related to one another, and how symbols of things are related to thinking and acting; (3) devising rules which will lead to symbols which are useful or fruitful in the process of thinking about financial matters; and (4) convincing others that the rules are efficacious or imposing those rules on others. The order in which we have placed them is the order in which any attempt to advance practice should proceed. If there are no observed defects, no action is called for; no new rules need be contemplated. If there are defects, they will have become apparent through mistaken (because misinformed) action; new rules to remove the defects will be sought through reconsideration of the relation of symbols to thought processes. To enforce new rules, by persuasion or coercion, is the last step.

The greater part of the recommendations, opinions and proposals of official bodies (and of many individuals) is in the nature of the latter two of the four points. But unless proposals are firmly anchored in the former two points there can be no reasonable expectations that practice will be advanced.

What defects?
To a very large extent, the APB has concerned itself with problems of a novel or peripheral kind—leases, pension plans, the investment credit, oil and gas ventures, goodwill. Its exercises may therefore be said to have arisen from difficulties or defects. But have they been difficulties and defects which became apparent through the mistaken actions of those who relied on the products of existing forms of accounting? Generally no; at least no substantial evidence has been advanced to the effect that users of conven-

tional financial statements have been misled.

There have, of couse, been some pronouncements or Opinions on matters of a more general and fundamental kind, such as the statement on accounting for the effects of inflation. But even in this case the published material gives no evidence of financial statements users' having been misled and in what specific directions.

The difficulties to which attention has been directed are difficulties of accountants or difficulties said, by accountants, to exist. I do not deny that the difficulties experienced or feared by accountants deserve attention. But the difficulties of the users of the information produced are far more significant in terms of professional performance or competence.

Is it more important that leased assets should be accounted for in one way or another than that there shall be a relatively small margin (for difference of opinion) between the possible figures for reported profit? An issue which affects the reporting of a limited number of companies is surely less pressing than an issue which affects the reporting of all companies.

Is it more important that the costs of pension plans be accounted for in one way or another than that the financial positions and results of any two companies shall be directly and easily comparable? Again, no. Pension plans may be widespread and spreading; but they are far from being as general a problem as the comparability of companies through their financial statements.

We may appear to be attacking the priorities of the APB and other such bodies. But the matter is deeper than that. The calculations of net income and the representation of financial position are based on certain general rules. The solution of any less general problem is bound to be sought in those general rules. But if the rules are themselves defective, the solution of a less general problem by recourse to those rules will be defective also. In particular, if the general rules are self-contradictory in that they result in widely divergent figures on the basis of the same data, at the option of accountants or managers or directors, the solution of any specific problem is likely to be some rule which has (or alternative rules which have) the same effect—a solution which therefore multiplies the possibilities of divergence.

First things should come first. Consider the APB Opinion on reporting income per share. It is an exercise of great virtuosity, coping with all sorts of possibilities. But what is the point of all this while reported income can be such a variable figure?

Recall Greer's demonstration, as long ago as 1938, that the profits over eight years of a group of companies could have been as little as $125 million or as much as $275 million according to the accounting rules used.[3] And Spacek's demonstration

191

[3] Howard C. Greer, "What Are Accepted Principles of Accounting?" *Accounting Review*, March 1938.

of 1960 that, by the use of different rules, income per share could be as different as $.80 and $1.79.[4] And Savoie's 1963 demonstration that net income could be as much as $624,000 and as little as $28,000, given the same data.[5]

Recall that U.S. Steel increased its 1968 reported income by $94 million by a change in its accounting methods. And that in the same year TWA increased its net income by $18 million; National Steel upped its net income by $10 million; and B. F. Goodrich boosted its earnings per share from $2.76 to $3.25 —all by changing accounting methods. Recall the differences between reported income and subsequently revised income in the *Yale Express (Fischer v. Kletz)* case, the *BarChris (Escott v. BarChris Construction Corp.)* case and many other cases like them. These are only a handful of the large number of cases which show how unreliable a reported income figure may be as an indicator of what has actually happened to a company during a year.[6]

When there is so much latitude in the basic figure, it seems quite pointless to engage in highly refined exercises over the calculation of income per share. The latitude, in fact, points to a fundamental defect which should have received attention prior to any consideration of peripheral problems. Noncomparability of figures is as widely complained about as the desirability of comparable figures is asserted. Complaints from beyond the profession cannot be stilled by asserting that the defects do not exist (as is sometimes done in official responses) or by turning one's back on them (as is done when complaints pile up without any sharply directed attack on their specific causes).

General allusions to feedback have become quite common in discussions of changes in modes of accounting. But the examples cited above suggest that the feedback they represent is disregarded. Surely no company can really increase its income by a stroke of the pen! And surely, therefore, there is something very wrong with a code of rules that enables companies to switch rules when they think it necessary to give income a shot in the arm!

Knowing or discovering how things work

The appearance of complaints or anomalies is evidence that things are not working as they should, or as others expect them to work. But the causes of complaint will not be removed by a decision or policy which is promulgated without consideration of the way in which things do work or should work or may work better. No amount of consensus among accountants on a new rule or an old one will remove

[4] See T. A. Wise, *The Insiders* (Garden City, N.Y.: Doubleday & Company, 1962), pp.37-38, 203-236.
[5] Leonard M. Savoie, "Accounting Improvement: How Fast, How Far?" *Harvard Business Review*, July-August 1963.
[6] An extensive selection of examples of these and other defects and anomalies is given in the present author's *Securities and Obscurities* (Melbourne, Australia: Cheshire Publishing, 1973).

defects or anomalies unless the rule is consistent with the way things work.

To get down to brass tacks—a company is better off or worse off financially (richer or poorer), as a consequence of a year's business events, by a definite amount. Admittedly there are some difficulties in

---

Specific rules relating to particular classes of assets, equities, revenues and expenses are useless unless they improve the exactness of the general indicators. . . .

---

finding this definite amount. But it can be described. It is the increase or decrease in the net wealth of the company. Net wealth is a commonsense idea. It is total wealth less debt. It is an important idea. It has much to do with what a company can buy and what it can borrow. It is thus significant on its own account. But it is also significant because from two consecutive figures for net wealth the rise or fall in net wealth may be computed. Net wealth and changes in net wealth are not the products of accounting. But, because to know their amounts is important, the accounting must be designed so as to produce those amounts. If there are difficulties, necessitating approximations, at least we know the kind of figure that is the ideal to which we are approximating.

Here are a few relatively simple ideas—net wealth and the periodical change in net wealth. I have never seen it contested that these figures are of use and interest to investors, creditors, managers and others. By the use of them or their components, *and in no other way*, we may discover the relation of short-term assets to short-term equities (solvency), the relation of debt to equity (leverage) and the achieved rate of return. I have never seen it denied that these indicators are of use and interest to investors, creditors, managers and others. We know that a low current ratio is risky; and that a high current ratio may be less profitable (for a given class of trade), but it is also less risky. We know that high leverage (for a given class of trade) tends toward the maximum gains available from a given shareholders' equity, but that it is in some respects risky. We know that low leverage is less risky and that it indicates the possibility of raising the rate of return through borrowing. We know that, other things being equal, a high rate of return is preferred to a lower.

We know that solvency, leverage and rate of return are significant to the kinds of people who use financial statements, even though we do not know, and cannot know, how any person may "weight" the three in making a judgment. We know how these things "work" on the profits and the prospect of survival and growth of a company, and how knowledge of them severally may "work" on the judgments of users. With this knowledge, and with the intention that users shall have information which gives good indicators of solvency, leverage and rate of return, we can determine to construct a set of rules which will yield that information.

This set of ideas is a limited and relatively simple set. But it concerns itself with the way in which the financial statements and their contents may be put to use. Specific rules relating to particular classes of assets, equities, revenues and expenses are useless unless they improve the exactness of the general indicators mentioned. The indicators of solvency, leverage and rate of return are derived by using different combinations of parts of the same set of interlocked or interrelated financial statement figures. If the present indicators are misleading—and there is much evidence to this effect—there is good reason why their defects should be tackled together. Dealing separately with different classes of event or transaction or element of financial position may well lead, and has in fact led, to oversight of the connection between aggregative financial information and its use in financial analysis and decision-making.

Some will affirm that investors, creditors and managers may need, or may like to have, other and quite different information than has been specified. The point is conceded. But this in no way reduces the need for information of good and dependable quality on solvency, leverage and rate of return. It has been urged that cash flow statements should be produced, that price-level adjusted information should be produced supplementary to the financial accounts, that budgets for the next period should

---

Accountants have been singularly indifferent to the idea that a set of clearly defined specifications of the quality of the product of accounting is necessary.

---

be produced, and so on. But none of these things can make good the deficiencies in the financial statements on position and results. They have in fact diverted attention from the financial statements proper. Those statements, the only source of a particularly useful set of indicators, remain as defective in that respect as they were two decades ago.

To the best of my recollection the APB has never specified the particular acts or deliberations on which accounting information may be expected to shed light. I have not seen it argued that this or that rule, of the alternatives available, will result in a better indicator of solvency, a better indicator of leverage, a better indicator of rate of return or a better indicator of all three. Whenever a firm statement of a rule is made, it is stated or implied that that rule is better than others. But it is no better simply because of its choice. It is only better if in some way it improves the quality of the present indicators of significant financial features of companies.

Knowing how things work, how they are interlocked and related to one another, how one may lead to another—these are basic bits of knowledge necessary and indispensable to the removal of any defect or anomaly.

Devising rules

If a man intends to make a screwdriver, he must do to his raw material such things as will fashion a screwdriver. He has an objective, in the jargon of the literature. Stripped of jargon, this simply means that he must direct his actions to producing a thing which serves as a screwdriver serves. We would think him a poor craftsman if we asked him for a screwdriver and he produced a corkscrew. (Unless of course we wanted to drink the "screwdriver"—which digression only serves to emphasize the necessity of knowing what is wanted, what job "it" is expected to do).

Accountants have been singularly indifferent to the idea that a set of clearly defined specifications of the quality of the product of accounting is necessary. The very general words "objectives" and "goals" have been widely used. But general terms are notoriously open to varied interpretation. This, of course, is able to speak (as we have noted) of the "insuperable" difficulties of obtaining agreement among a group of people about objectives. To do any specific job, however, we must have limited and exacting specifications which are consistent with whatever general goals we espouse. If this were an "insuperable" difficulty, it would be impossible to go into any toolstore and ask confidently for a screwdriver; the different, shifting and contradictory "objectives" of all the makers of screwdrivers would have resulted in so many different products that the chance of getting "a thing to turn a screw" would be quite remote. Yet, you *can* buy screwdrivers anywhere.

As the example suggests, to look at the general objectives of the toolmakers or the general objectives of the tool users, rather than to the function of the tool, will not help in the making of the tool. There are in fact no different, shifting and contradictory objectives of makers of screwdrivers *when they are making screwdrivers*. Their attention is not distracted by the fact that some people want hammers and saws besides screwdrivers. They get on with the job of producing a piece of tool steel with a blade at one end, a shank in the middle and a firm handle at the other end. Because that is the kind of thing which men can use to turn screws. It would be a useless exercise for the "Screwdriver Standards Board" to sit in committee and formulate a "policy" that screwdrivers should have no blade—when the screwdriver-buying public wants a bladed tool.

The same sort of common sense applies to accounting. If we know that information of a certain kind is necessary for specified purposes, that knowledge dictates the shaping of the information. Tool-makers make tools for specified purposes. They do not make "screwdrivers" with a blade at one end, a serrated shank, and a hammer handle because some tool users may want a screwdriver, some a saw and some a hammer.

What rules shall be adopted is strictly a matter of technology, not of policy. If it is accepted that the kinds of information indicated in the previous section are necessary for the kinds of calculation and judgment there mentioned, the rules to be adopted in shaping the raw material may be speci-fied. The qualities desired in the end product (ac-counting statements) are not "desired" in any whim-sical sense, but desired because only if the product has those qualities can it be connected with or re-lated to other things by the user. We can work back-ward from the desired qualities to the rules for pro-

> The only policy which can properly be adopted by an accounting rule-making body is that it will devise rules leading demonstrably to figures which firms or clients and outsiders can confidently use in watching over their interests.

ducing a product which has them. This, of course, is how any well-designed product is made. It is otiose to point out that this is *not* the way in which officially promulgated rules have been devised.

Policy-making is "choosing which" when the choice is a matter of opinion or taste or some other personal or organizational criterion, and not simply a matter of technology. But neither rules nor poli-cies can have any prospect of attaining desired states or results unless their makers first have a clear no-tion of the ways in which things are related to one another. A debtor, *knowing* the consequences of not paying his debts as they fall due, may take steps to see that he always has the means of paying; or he may take the risk of inconvenience or bankruptcy. One or the other of these two steps is his policy, a course chosen in the knowledge of the relation be-tween two kinds of event. But he cannot choose not to pay and also choose at the same time to avoid inconvenience and bankruptcy.

Similarly, if we know that knowledge of a debtor's position or net wealth will assist him in avoiding inconvenience or bankruptcy, rules should be devised which provide that knowledge. Account-ants cannot tell whether those they serve may, in a given set of circumstances, choose to remain solvent or to risk bankruptcy. But they can indicate position or net wealth, regardless of a firm's or client's policy in this respect. And that knowledge will be useful whatever the firm's policy. But if these considera-tions are set aside in favor of compliance with such inventions as the original cost and matching doc-

trines (as they are often applied), the firm or client is deprived of the very knowledge which, surely, no one would deny is needed.

The only policy which can properly be adopted by an accounting rule-making body is that it will devise rules leading demonstrably to figures which firms or clients and outsiders can confidently use in watching over their interests.

Acceptance, persuasion or coercion

The final step is to have chosen rules adopted gen-erally. Let there be no delusion about the origins of rules or policies. Whether they are good or bad, they emanate from small groups of people. Rules are not made democratically; they are made by small groups. They are not enforced by democratic process; they are enforced by small groups to whom the power of enforcement has been entrusted. If persuasion is resorted to, instead of enforcement by specific sanctions, the persuasion is done by small groups.

A small group is more able to focus attention on the elements of a knotty problem than a large group —but only if its members agree in the first place that they will be bound by the laws and rules which it is beyond their power to change. If those laws and rules are specified, the superstructure which is built on them is the more likely to be accepted or en-dorsed generally. For those to whom they are ex-posed, or those who act upon them, can no more object to the fundamental laws and rules than they can object to the law of gravity. And if they object to any element of the superstructure, they can object only on the ground that the inferences drawn by the small group are demonstrably inconsistent with the fundamental laws and rules. They cannot object simply on the ground that they are of a dif-ferent opinion.

All of which suggests that chosen rules will have a better chance of acceptance and survival if they are shown to be based on fundamental necessity or technological constraints. Official pronouncements are notoriously short on such demonstrations. They may be accepted and survive a while notwithstand-ing this, due to the position of power of their promulgators. But King Canute, though king, could not stem the tide by a policy statement.

Consider some of the things which it is beyond the power of any rule-promulgating (or policy-making) body to change. It cannot change the real-world importance of solvency. It cannot change the amount of profit which a company makes in a year; for profits are made in marketplaces, not in counting houses. It cannot change the basic rules of addition and relation. It cannot change the ten-dency for prices to move, and in different directions and at different rates. It cannot change the signifi-cance, in all commercial and financial dealing, of the contemporary market prices of goods and services. Any theorist or policy-maker can choose to ignore any one or more of these things. But only at the risk, like Canute, of getting his feet wet and his face red. Any theorist or policy-maker who prefers to avoid these consequences must construct principles, rules or policies which respect the constraints mentioned above and others like them. And when he has done so, he will be able to justify those principles or rules against all comers; for they rest not on his opinion but on the unavoidable realities of interpersonal dealings in financial matters.

Needless to say, the present practice of accounting and the pronouncements of the "policy-making" bodies do not respect the abovementioned constraints. Yet apparently the profession and the public it serves must continue to accept the consequences. To quote Gerboth again, the mode of operation of the APB "admittedly violates the commonly accepted virtues of orderliness and completeness, but commonsense norms are not necessarily criteria for policy-making excellence. When those criteria are eventually derived from penetrating inquiry into the [business] policy-making process, excellence may well be found in the seeming irrationality of present practice" (p.47). But surely there are no good grounds for preferring the disorderly to the orderly, the incomplete to the complete, and the seemingly irrational to the rational! It should be no cause for wonder that disorderly, incomplete and seemingly irrational propositions should attract the attention of Charles Horngren's 1,000 dogs.[7] The only way in which rules, policies or problem-solutions of the disorderly, incomplete and seemingly irrational kind can come to be accepted is by the brute force of naked power. And that has never been the course of reasonable men.

Conclusion

"Muddling through" is the typical way in which scientific and technological work is advanced. But it is systematic muddling. If something is tried and found wanting, it is set aside. Something else is tried. But when people learn the corpus of modern knowledge in a given field, they do not have to go over all the old steps or learn all the outmoded curiosa by which that knowledge progressed to its present state. The hand-me-down dogmas of an earlier time are relegated to the history books. Only the stuff that has stood the test of usage over time remains as part of the present state of knowledge.

It is the misfortune of accounting and accountants that there is so little determination to set aside hand-me-down dogmas which have been found to be so defective in use. Will anyone deny that the cost prices of assets have nothing to do with the capacity of a company to pay its debts, borrow money or buy other goods? Will anyone deny that figures based on unamortized costs have nothing to do with the assessment of leverage? Will anyone deny that a rate of return based on income and asset values computed according to the original cost rule cannot properly be compared with the prospective rate of return on a feasible alternative? Will anyone deny that asset values based on price index adjusted historical costs have nothing to do with the tests of solvency, leverage and rate of return just mentioned? Will anyone deny that different kinds of costs and prices added together can have no real significance in financial calculation or dealing?

If these things can be denied, let them be openly denied; and let the denials be made so clear that no one will use accounting information for any of these purposes. If they cannot be denied, there can be no good reasons for retaining rules (or policies) which quite positively, though implicitly, deny them. If the clichés of the textbooks and the pronunciamentos of the past could be set aside, and if attention were focused on the representation of what actually happens to the financial affairs of companies as they go about their business, the "muddling" might be more fruitful. "Muddling" might in fact turn out to be "muddling *through*." ■

195

---

[7]The allusion is to Charles Horngren's quip, cited by Gerboth, that the APB often feels like "a lone tree in the midst of 1,000 dogs."

ACCOUNTING PRINCIPLES AND THE LAW

The Companies Acts of New South Wales and Victoria provide that the Corporate Affairs Commission (N.S.W.) or Registrar of Companies (Vic.) shall maintain a registry of certain documents on the affairs of companies. These documents include a copy of the audited accounts, which are part of the annual return of a company. The Commission may refuse to register or receive any document which (a) contains matter contrary to law; (b) by reason of any omission or misdescription has not been duly completed; (c) does not comply with the requirements of the Act; or (d) contains any error, alteration or erasure (s.12(5)).[1] The Commission may require the defects to be made good. Any person aggrieved by a refusal to register or receive a document or by any other act or decision of the Commission may appeal to the court.

The object of the section is to give the Commission some regulatory power over the contents of the accounts and required annexures thereto. If there were no such supervision and no sanction such as refusal to register, the Act would certainly fail to secure that the public ("any person" who wishes to inspect registered documents) would be adequately informed. There would be no way of ensuring that the provisions of the Act or the terms used in the Act or Schedules to it were uniformly and equitably interpreted by different companies.

Attention has—at last—been drawn to this object by the recent announcement of the New South Wales Commissioner for Corporate Affairs on qualified audit reports.[2] A qualified audit report signifies that there has been some unresolved difference of opinion, between the directors and the auditors of a company, on the amount which, when disclosed in the accounts, would give a true and fair view of its financial position and results. The accounts of some companies have, for several recent years in succession, attracted audit reports which were qualified in respect of the same matter. The Commissioner (Mr F. J. O. Ryan) stated: "I am of the view that a conflict of opinion between the directors and the auditors as to an accounting

---

[1] References to sections of a Companies Act, except where otherwise indicated, will be to sections of the N.S.W. Act.
[2] News release, "Qualified Audit Reports", 13th November, 1972.

principle which may affect the truth and fairness of accounts ought not to be allowed to go unresolved year by year". He foreshadowed the possibility that if other measures, independent of the Commission, were not successful in eliminating such conflicts of opinion, the Commission might well approach the Supreme Court, "in appropriate cases, for a declaration that accounts containing an auditor's qualification of the type under discussion failed to give the true and fair view required by the Act".

In that it mentions "the true and fair view required by the Act", the Commissioner's statement holds promise of breaking new ground. The phrase (or its antecedent "a true and correct view") has been in use for over 100 years. For example, the model (optional) articles of association appended as a schedule to the English Acts of 1856 and 1862[3] provided that the auditors should "state whether, in their opinion, the balance sheet is . . . properly drawn up so as to exhibit a true and correct view of the state of the company's affairs". But since that time there have been few circumstances in which the courts might have had to consider or elucidate the meaning of a true and correct, or a true and fair, view. I know of no dicta on the matters. Nor do I know of any standard legal text or treatise which attempts to attribute a meaning to the phrase.

This is strange, since these words are the only general specification in the statutes of the quality of the contents of the accounts. They are key words. In many litigated cases in which false, misleading or fraudulent accounts have come under notice, the line of the prosecution has been to establish fraud or deceit in respect of particular matters. The general principle has not been a central issue. But the sheer number and notoriety of the cases where particulars have been in dispute (whether before the courts or only in the public press) have been sufficient to call for some closer attention to the intention of the statute.

Some references by legal scholars to the phrase suggest that their authors considered that the words stated plainly—without the need for elucidation—what the Act required. Thus:

"It was at one time said that a balance sheet need not disclose the true position of the company, that it deals, as regards assets, not with existing facts but with past history. It shows what the particular assets cost, not what they are worth. But this cannot now be said since the Act [U.K., 1948] in ss.147 and 149 now requires the accounts, balance sheets, etc., to show a true and fair view of the state of the company's affairs".[4]

197

3 19 & 12 Vict. c.47, An Act for the Incorporation and Regulation of Joint Stock Companies and other Associations; 25 & 26 Vict. c.89, An Act for the Incorporation, Regulation and Winding-up of Trading Companies and other Associations.
4 R. Buchanan—Dunlop, *Palmer's Company Precedents*, 17th ed. (Stevens & Sons, London, 1956), vol. 1, p. 604.

Gower has expressed a similar view, though he goes on to point out that the words of the statute have not had the effect which might have been expected. The values at which fixed assets are reported "may bear little relation to value as at the end of the current financial year".[5]

Gower gives no examples. Here are a few from the U.K. in respect of land and buildings:[6]

	Year	Surplus on revaluation	Balance of asset at year end
Boots Pure Drug Co.	1958	£13.4m	£ 26.1m
F. W. Woolworth & Co.	1963	£35.9m	£105.0m
J. Lyons & Co.	1969	£25.8m	£ 45.6m

The amount of the surplus on revaluation shows by how great a margin the previously reported figure fell short of an up-to-date value: a 40-50 per cent undervaluation, or an undervaluation by tens of millions, implies that "true and fair" has an extraordinarily flexible meaning in respect of the state of affairs of a company.

The 1967 amendment to the U.K. Companies Act required directors to comment on the relationship between book values, as reported in balance sheets, and the current market values of interests in land. The requirement is interesting: for if the accounts did in fact give a true and fair view of the state of affairs of a company, they should, *ipso facto*, give a true and fair view of that part of the state of affairs which related to interests in land. Apparently they did not; hence the new provision. And apparently they still do not, if the current market value of an interest in land is an element of a true and fair view of the state of a company's affairs. The market value of the freehold and leasehold properties of Montague Burton was said, by the directors, to be £19m in excess of the £52m book (or balance sheet) value in 1968. Rolls Royce directors in 1969 said that the value of land and buildings was £18m in excess of the reported figure of £18.6m. Similar discrepancies have occurred in the accounts of Australian companies.

What then can a true and fair view of the state of affairs and of the results of a period mean?

RULES OF INTERPRETATION

It is reasonable to suppose that, if any company or its officers was seriously to believe that its accounts might give rise to litigation in which the meaning of a true and fair view was at issue, they or their advisers would be guided by the rules relating to the interpret-

---

[5] L. C. B. Gower, *The Principles of Modern Company Law*, 3rd ed. (Stevens & Sons, London, 1969), p. 120, footnote 2.
[6] Other examples are given in R. J. Chambers, *Securities and Obscurities* (Gower Press, Australia, Melbourne, 1973), Ch. 6.

ation of legislation. In any case, whether or not any such cause of litigation was contemplated, it is reasonable to take the rules of interpretation as a guide to the meaning of the statute. It will be sufficient for present purposes to notice two such rules.[7]

The first is: adopt the plain and natural meaning of the words used, unless that meaning is contrary to the intention of the legislature, is contrary to other parts of the statute, or leads to patent absurdity.

The intention of the legislature, in respect of company accounts, is nowhere plainly stated, except by use of the very words in question. But there are numerous indications.

First, every balance sheet is required to give a true and fair view of the state of affairs of the company as at the end of a definite period (s.162(3)). The term "financial position" is also used (s.161A(1)(a)). It seems reasonable to consider "state of affairs" and "financial position' as synonymous. But neither is defined in the statute. Further every profit and loss account is required to give a true and fair view of the profit or loss of the company in the period up to the date of the balance sheet (s.162(1)). But neither is "profit" (or "loss") defined in the statute. These several terms may be considered to be technical terms, and we will deal with them again under another rule of interpretation. In any case, if the accounts are to *give* a true fair view of anything, their contents should not be misleading or false in any particular at the date or for the period to which they relate. Nothing that relates to events or transactions of a prior or future period has any legitimate place in the accounts. Further, since any person may inspect documents in the appropriate companies registry, it is implied that the contents of the accounts shall not be misleading to any person (e.g., shareholder, prospective shareholder, creditor, prospective creditor, and so on). Further still, since the prescription "true and fair view" occurs outside of the clauses relating to reports by the principal accounting officer, the directors and the auditors, it must be construed not as a view (or opinion) held by any or all of them, but a view (or representation or indication) of specified features of the company.

Second, the legislature cannot have prescribed that a true and fair view be given without intending that the information disclosed would be used; and it cannot have prescribed that the quality of the accounts would be backed up by declarations of the principal accounting officer, the directors and the auditors, without intending that the information should be reliable and a firm basis of judgments by users. On the one hand, the accounts have long been held to be the basis of creditors' judgments. The principle of limited liability removed creditors' recourse to members, but the principle of financial disclosure was intended to give, in its place, knowledge of the

[7] See P. St. J. Langan, *Maxwell on the Interpretation of Statutes*, 12th ed. (Sweet & Maxwell, London, 1969), Ch. 2, 3.

wealth and financial obligations of debtor companies. Only up-to-date information on the extent of the wealth and financial obligations of companies is reliable and relevant, as far as creditors are concerned. On the other hand, disclosure has long been regarded as the "cornerstone" or the "fundamental principle" of investor protection. Shareholders and prospective investors cannot intelligently appraise the prospects and risks of companies, and hence the prospects and risks of their investments, without more or less exact and up-to-date information. It seems reasonable to suppose therefore that one aspect of "a true and fair view" is the exactness and up-to-dateness of the figures which represent it.

Third, if solvency, risk and the respective interests of members and creditors in a company's assets are to be known or judged (a corollary of the second point just mentioned), the figures must be of a certain kind. Asset figures should represent the contemporary money amount of the wealth of a company, and the profit or loss should represent the change in net wealth (assets less liabilities) other than changes due to new contributions or withdrawals (by way of dividends) by shareholders. The contemporary money amount of the wealth represented by any asset is its net selling price.

There are indications in the statute that such selling prices (or market values, or realizable amounts) are deemed by the legislature to be pertinent. Some may consider them to be vague indications. But taken together with all other points, they are at least supportive. Where any current asset is shown in the accounts at an amount greater than the directors expect it to realize, the directors are required to write down the asset to its expected realizable value or to make provision for the difference, presumably by a charge against the year's profits (s.162(7)). Whatever the basis adopted in obtaining the book value of listed security investments, their current market value must be shown somewhere (Ninth Schedule, cl.7(5)). And, as we have noted, the English Act requires directors to comment on the difference between book values and current market values of interests in land. It seems reasonable to suppose that an informed appraisal of the state of affairs of a company depends on there being available information on the current selling prices of assets—since these realizable values are the basis of a company's solvency, of the shareholders' and creditors' equities in the company's assets, and of the power of the company to borrow on the security of its assets.

Admittedly the task of constructing the intention of the legislature is not without hazard. But there are at least indications that a true and fair view of the state of affairs at a stated date and of the profit or loss of a period requires that the figures disclosed shall relate to a specified date or period and to no other; that the figures shall be up-to-date figures; and that they shall, in respect of assets, be approximations to realizable values.

200

Some might hold that this interpretation is contrary to other parts of the statute. In effect the Act provides that non-current assets shall be shown at an amount not exceeding the amount "which it would have been reasonable for the company to spend to acquire that asset as at the end of the financial year" (s.162(7)(c)). Such an amount is not, of course, the money equivalent to a company of the asset it then has, and would not, in ordinary usage, be considered to be a measure of the wealth of the owner of a like asset. Further, the Ninth Schedule requires to be shown in respect of fixed assets or investments the cost, or a valuation, thereof and the amount written off since purchase or valuation. But such provisions as these are over-ruled by s.162(9). Directors are required to provide such additional information and explanations as will give a true and fair view of the matters required to be disclosed, if the stipulations of the Ninth Schedule do not themselves lead to this end.

Finally, it cannot be said that the interpretation we suggest leads to patent absurdity. In ordinary usage, no person would calculate his wealth at a stipulated date otherwise than by taking the money equivalent or selling prices of his non-cash assets and subtracting from it the amount of his financial obligations at that date. His financial position would be represented by a statement of all his assets, at current selling prices, of his debts outstanding (whether immediately due or not) and the difference between these figures, which is his net wealth. He would use selling prices, not because he intends to sell any or all of his assets, but simply because the price at which others will buy is the only indication of the money equivalent of his assets at the time.

A further rule relates to the interpretation of words and phrases which may have both an ordinary and popular meaning and a technical meaning. Words are interpreted in their ordinary sense unless from the context it is clear that they should be interpreted in a way which is special or peculiar to a certain trade or profession.

Now the phrase "a true and fair view" (or its antecedent "a true and correct view") did not, at the time of their introduction to the statutes, have a special or peculiar connotation among accountants, or in the accounting profession. Nor, as far as I am aware, did it have any peculiar connotation in any other like profession. If it had come to be interpreted at the time of its introduction, the phrase could only have been given a popular or non-technical interpretation.

Since that time there have been attempts by the accounting profession to make clear its interpretation of the phrase. For example, Statement D1.1 of the Institute of Chartered Accountants in Australia reads, in part:

"A true and fair view implies appropriate classification and grouping of the items and therefore the balance sheet needs to show in summary form the amounts of the share capital, reserves and

201

liabilities as on the balance sheet date and the amounts of the assets representing them, together with sufficient information to indicate the general nature of the items.

A true and fair view also implies the consistent application of generally accepted principles. Assets are normally shown at cost less amounts charged against revenue to amortise expenditure over the effective lives of the assets or to provide for diminution in their value. A balance sheet is therefore mainly an historical document which does not purport to show the realizable value of assets such as goodwill, land, buildings, plant and machinery; nor does it normally purport to show the realizable value of assets such as stock-in-trade. Thus a balance sheet is not a statement of the net worth of the undertaking and this is normally so even where there has been a revaluation of assets and the balance sheet amounts are based on the revaluation instead of on cost."[8]

202

Notice that the phrase is said to "imply" appropriate classification and consistent application of generally accepted principles. No objection can be taken to this on the face of it. But there is no elucidation in the statements of the Institute (or of the English Institute) of the *kinds* of amounts which should or must be used for a true and fair view to be given. And there is, in fact, no body of generally accepted principles by reference to which this matter may become clear. Insofar as the magnitude of the items shown in accounts are what concerns investors and creditors, the statement deals with form and not with substance. Consequently companies can and do use intrinsically different valuation rules for different assets, Any given company, for example, could value some of its inventory at cost, some at selling price, and some at replacement price; some of its security investments at cost, some at a valuation selected by the directors, and some at selling price; some of its plant at cost less depreciation, and some at distant and some at recent valuations less subsequent depreciation; some of its buildings at cost, some at cost less depreciation, some at valuations less depreciation; some of its land at cost, and some at valuations. These different kinds of amounts would be added. But it should be apparent that the addition cannot possibly yield a total which has any sensible, commercial meaning. If it has no such meaning, the balance sheet cannot properly be said to give a true and fair view of anything.

Further, any company may change the way in which it values any asset, and companies do make such changes from time to time notwithstanding the Institute's allusion to consistency. This can only mean that "generally accepted principles" is too vague a phrase to specify the kind of information which will give a true and fair

---

[8] The Institute, *Statement D1.1 Presentation of Balance Sheet*, December 1963.

view. Further still, as between any two companies, quite different
rules may be used to value similar assets. Now many of our personal
judgments or opinions about companies arise from comparisons of
the figures of two or more companies. If the companies have used
different valuation rules, comparisons of their figures would be fruitless
or misleading. In effect, although the accounts will appear to be based
on the same test—a true and fair view—they will in fact represent
quite different views of the positions and results of the several
companies.

The conclusion seems unavoidable that there is no technical
meaning which can be ascribed to the phrase "true and fair view", no
technical meaning, that is, which is well-stated and well-understood
among accountants. It might be noted at the same time that there is
not, in the official technical literature of accounting, any clear description of what is understood by "state of affairs" or "financial
position" or "profit".

In these circumstances it seems that "true and fair view" and other
technically undefined words must be construed as having their "plain
and natural" meaning; especially since the figures derived by the
varied use of rules derived from or described as "generally accepted
principles" lead to manifest absurdities and a denial of the right of
investors and creditors and others to be informed.

There is just a possibility that if the court is called upon to
adjudicate on the matters raised by Mr Ryan, a more dependable
interpretation may be given than that now current among accountants. The Cohen Committee and the Jenkins Committee both cited
and endorsed the substance of a statement of the Institute of
Chartered Accountants in England and Wales which included the
sentence: "It has long been accepted in accounting practice that a
balance sheet prepared for this purpose ['to present information to
the proprietors, showing how their funds have been utilized and the
profits from such use'] is an historical record and not a statement
of current worth". To this Mr Justice Wallace was moved to say:
"I venture, with all deference to Lord Jenkins' Committee . . ., to
ask as regards the concluding phrase of this quotation relating to
'current worth'—why not?" He continued:

> "It is a little difficult for a lawyer to detect why either expediency
> or the practice of the accountancy profession can authorize
> departure from ordinary principles of construction applicable to
> a statute. When we observe the wealth of detail required by the
> Ninth Schedule and the overriding requirement in s.162(11) that
> the accounts must give a 'true and fair view' of the state of affairs
> of the company and of its profit or loss (with accompaying verify-
> ing statements and declarations by directors and secretaries and
> severe penalties for breaches), it seems legitimate to ask: where
> is there room for the 'historical record' doctrine as a fully satisfy-
> ing compliance with the statute?

203

... To me, the word 'true' (curiously enough) simply means what it says—it is for the legislature and not accountants and directors to alter the natural meaning of the statute. But how could the legislature possibly change the wording even if it wished so to do?"[9]

His Honour has not been alone in questioning the dubious sources of practice and the effects of practice on subsequent events. Commenting some thirty years ago on litigated disputes in the U.S.A. involving valuations for dividend purposes, Professor R. J. Baker observed:

"... whether we like it or not and whether we are wholly aware of it or not, the accountants may be making our law ... If the case is well-tried, with submission of accounting literature as evidence and accounting testimony and depositions, what accountants of standing do and say makes the decision."[10]

It is now notorious that "accountants of standing" do and say things which are vastly different. The Pergamon-Leasco affair and the Westec case provided examples (there have been many more cases) of extraordinarily diverse "views" of profits on the part of different accountants. There have been a number of hypothetical exercises by prominent accountants which have shown how diverse may be the products of "selective accounting"—choosing rules to bring about the *appearance* of higher or lower profits, as directors or managers wish.[11] There can be little that is true or fair while the possibility of such manipulation persists, and while the diversity of rules which are equally acceptable to accountants permits it to persist.

The present position has recently been summed up in a remark by Bayless A. Manning, then Dean of the Stanford School of Law:

"It is clear that what we call accounting and the standard methods of accounting are of remarkably limited usefulness for purposes of figuring out what is going on in the real world of economic activity."[12]

The observation is equally pertinent to Australia, the United Kingdom and the United States. So also are the following remarks from a 1969 report for the U.S. Federal Trade Commission:

[9] R. A. Woodman (ed.), *Record of the Third Commonwealth and Empire Law Conference* (Sydney, 1965, Law Book Company, 1966), pp. 333-336.
[10] Cited by William P. Hackney, "Accounting Principles in Corporation Law", *Law and Contemporary Problems*, Vol. xxx, No. 4, Autumn 1965 (Duke University), p. 822.
[11] See Chambers, *Securities and Obscurities*, Ch. 8, 13.
[12] Henry G. Manne (ed.), *Economic Policy and the Regulation of Corporate Securities* (American Enterprise Institute for Public Policy Research, Washington, 1969), p. 85.

"If accounting is a tool designed to facilitate a rational assessment of business success or failure, its techniques should give a timely and accurate representation of an enterprise's current operations, permit comparison with results in previous years, and allow comparison with other comparable enterprises.

As currently practised, accounting does not always meet these expectations. On a number of key issues, generally accepted accounting principles permit a range of reporting choices that can materially alter reported company operating results. There need be no consistency in the treatment of depreciation charges, inventory valuation, the expensing of research and development, and other factors. The specific method of reporting selected by management may be changed from one period to another. It may be said categorically that accounting statements often are neither consistent over time nor comparable between firms."[13]

It must be open to serious doubt at least, if not to absolute denial, that the legislature ever contemplated that published accounts could be or should be capable of manipulation—or that such manipulation could be considered to be perfectly "legal" because the "accepted" rules of accountants tolerate it and indeed make it possible.

The infrequency with which the purport of accounting figures has come before the courts may lead many to suppose that there are no dicta on the matter. There is, however, an excellent discussion of it in the judgment of Fletcher Moulton L.J. in the *Spanish Prospecting Co.* case—excellent, I judge, because it seems both to express the intention of the law and to indicate what users of accounts in commercial affairs need to know of the profits and states of affairs of companies. I quote sparingly from the judgment which should be read in full:

" 'Profits' implies a comparison between the state of a business at two specific dates usually separated by an interval of a year. The fundamental meaning is the amount of gain made by the business during the year. This can only be ascertained by a comparison of the assets of the business at the two dates. For practical purposes these assets in calculating profits must be valued and not merely enumerated. An enumeration might be of little value. Even if the assets were identical at the two periods [dates] it would by no means follow that there had been neither gain nor loss, because the market value—the value in exchange—of these assets may have altered greatly in the meanwhile . . . To render the ascertainment of the profits of a business of practical use it is

---

[13] Staff Report of the Federal Trade Commission, *Economic Report on Corporate Mergers* (U.S. Government Printing Office, Washington, 1969), p. 120.

205

evident that the assets, of whatever nature they may be, must be represented by their money value.

But though there is a wide field . . . for variation of practice in these estimations of profit in the domestic documents of a firm or a company, this liberty ceases at once when the rights of third persons intervene . . . In the absence of special stipulations to the contrary, 'profits' in cases where the interests of third parties come in mean actual profits, and they must be calculated as closely as possible in accordance with the fundamental conception or definition to which I have referred."[14]

Note especially that profits are said to imply comparison between the state of a business at two specific dates. It is therefore necessary first to find the state of the business. The basic steps are to find the amount of the assets (by reference to "market value—the value in exchange"), the amount of the liabilities (by reference to known obligations to creditors at the specified date) and the amount of the shareholders' equity (the difference between the amounts of assets and liabilities). The difference between the amounts of shareholders' equity at the two dates will then be the profit of the intervening period. The "well-defined legal meaning" of profits, as the learned judge expounds it, coincides (as he says) "with the fundamental conception of profits in general parlance". And it is the meaning ascribed to profits by economists.[15] Where the general level of prices (and the purchasing power of money) varies from one date to another, economists would take the difference between the amounts of the shareholders' equity at the two dates only after those amounts had been reduced, by use of a price-index, to common purchasing power terms.

Few works of legal scholars have come to my notice in which the authors have considered accounting practices analytically rather than

[14] In re The Spanish Prospecting Co. Ltd. [1911] 1 Ch. 92 at 100-101. Some are disposed to dismiss the passage as obiter dictum. But the definition of "profits" is quoted, with apparent approval, in C. M. Schmitthoff and J. H. Thompson, Palmer's Company Law, 21st ed. (Stevens & Sons, London, 1968), p. 662.

　　See also Baxt, "True and Fair View—a Legal Anachronism" (1970) 44 A.L.J. 541.

[15] "Income . . . equals the value of the individual's consumption plus the increment in the money value of his prospect which has accrued during the week; it equals Consumption plus Capital accumulation." J. R. Hicks, Value and Capital, 2nd ed. (Oxford University Press, 1946), p. 178. "Personal income may be defined as the algebraic sum of (1) the market value of rights exercized in consumption and (2) the change in the value of the store of property rights between the beginning and end of the period in question . . . without regard for anything which happened before the beginning of that interval or for what may happen in subsequent periods . . . The essential connotation of income, to repeat, is gain—gain to someone during a specified period and measured according to objective market standards". H. C. Simons, Personal Income Taxation (University of Chicago Press, 1938), p. 50. The appropriate definition of corporate income is obtained by replacing "consumption" in these passages with "dividend payments".

as they are. Comment is usually descriptive, or based to some considerable extent on the precedents of accountants' practices. However, a 1932 article by Berle and Fisher hints strongly at the use of current market values for inventories, marketable securities and fixed assets.[16] And the U.S. Securities and Exchange Commission, although it has ordinarily enforced the traditional rules of asset valuation (based on original cost), has on some occasions required disclosure of the market values of fixed assets.[17]

A complete form of accounting which proceeds to calculate financial position and results in the manner suggested by the preceding paragraphs has been developed. A substantial body of the evidence which supports it, a brief indication of its style, and a draft of the alterations and additions to the Act and the Ninth Schedule which would give effect to it, are given in my recently published book, *Securities and Obscurities*.

207

Some Present Problems

With the above observations in mind, even without requiring the adoption of the form of accounting I have proposed, it is of interest to give attention to the matters referred to specifically by the N.S.W. Commissioner of Corporate Affairs in his statement of 13th November, 1972. The matters in respect of which confused and disputed accounting have occurred are extraordinary items in profit and loss accounts, "deferred" taxes, and depreciation of buildings.

Extraordinary Items of Profit or Loss

Whatever scheme of asset valuation and revaluation is used, the whole of the difference between the amounts of the shareholders' equity at the beginning and end of a period (excluding new contribution and dividends) must be regarded as a gain or profit (or loss, as the case may be). Only if this is done will the profit and loss account and the balance sheet be consistent with one another; only thus will the change in shareholders' equity be fully and explicitly accounted for. As Fletcher Moulton L.J. pointed out, certain "arbitrary" practices have come to be followed—depreciation calculations based on cost, the exclusion of "gains and losses arising from causes not directly connected with the business of the company, such, for instance, as a rise in the market value of land occupied by the company". But these, as he said "rest on no settled principles". Some of these practices involve splitting total gains or losses of a

---

16 A. A. Berle Jr. and Frederick S. Fisher, "Elements of the Law of Business Accounting", *Columbia Law Review*, Vol. xxxii, No. 4, April 1932.
17 See, for example, Robert H. Scott, Jr., "Disclosing Current Values of Fixed Assets in Corporate Reorganizations", *Cornell Law Review*, Vol. 55, 1970, p. 285; Homer Kripke, "The S.E.C., The Accountants, Some Myths and Some Realities", *New York University Law Review*, Vol. 45 No. 6, December 1970, p. 1151.

particular kind so that some part appears in the profit and loss account above the line showing net profit of the year, while the remainder either appears "below the line" or is carried directly to a reserve account. Thus unusually large losses or writing down of debtors' accounts, inventories or other assets may be dealt with otherwise than as a charge made in arriving at the net profit of a year, only a "normal" charge being made in arriving at net profit. But this cannot be said to be conducive to the giving of a true and fair view of the profit or loss for a period, since it leaves the determination of the amount of the profit or loss in the hands of company officers.

The common argument for so splitting total amounts of gains or losses is that investors want to be able to form an opinion of the scale of profit which can be relied upon as recurrent. Investors may well wish to know this—though, because business is at numerous and varied risks, there can be no assurance that what is reported as profit from the "ordinary" or "normal" business of a company will recur. But it does not follow that investors do not want to know the *total* amounts of the gains or losses of a year, inclusive, that is, of all unusual profits or losses. Lopping off the "unusual" parts of such items, even if they are shown elsewhere, is unwarranted interference. If the whole of the amounts are shown, investors may average out the reported profits of past years, if they wish to form an opinion about the general scale of profits of a company. However, if the whole of the amounts are not shown in the profit and loss account proper, large unusual amounts (which in many cases should have been charged or credited over previous years) will not enter into the calculation of such averages. A possible exception is an adjustment made in respect of some item of an earlier year which has become necessary in the light of knowledge not available in that earlier year. But as the same reasoning applies to this as to the other cases mentioned already, it seems better to show it above the line with appropriate identifying detail or footnote.

Profits and losses of every sort, therefore, should appear above the line representing net profit of the year. There is nothing to stop companies from showing, separately but above the line, the amounts of unusual or non-recurring profits or losses. Shareholders and investors are, I believe, entitled to expect the whole of the net profit (or increment in shareholders' equity) to be shown clearly and in one place.

These suggestions are generally in line with Statement D1.2 of the Institute of Chartered Accountants in Australia,[18] but they go beyond that in two respects. Statement D1.2 recommends exclusion of "prior period adjustments" from calculations of the net profit of a given

---

[18] The Institute, *Statement D1.2 Profit and Loss Statements (Net Profit, Prior Period Adjustments, and Extraordinary Items)*, June 1970.

year. Certainly there is some merit in the point that what belonged to a prior year should not be included in the current year. But the possibility that prior period adjustments could be numerous or large, and that they could escape being reported in the profit and loss account of *any* year, seems good ground (in the absence of a better form of reporting) for reporting them above the line in the year in which they are discovered. The second respect in which my suggestion differs is in the inclusion of gains or losses on asset revaluations. Statment D1.2 says nothing on this. The present position is that assets may rise (or fall) in value for years without the knowledge of shareholders; and that, if and when the rise is brought into account, millions may pass to a reserve account without passing through the profit and loss account as a gain (or loss, as the case may be).

It may be said that these two items could give rise of quite misleading impressions, if treated in the way suggested. But it is better that directors shall be obliged to explain unusual items which appear in the profit and loss account, than it is, by showing them below the line or elsewhere, to create the possibility of them being overlooked when investors and their advisers turn to calculate averages or trends.

209

Deferred Tax Accounting

The calculation of net profit of a year by reference to the change in net assets entails knowledge of the amount of liabilities at the specified date. In any case, the statutory reference to the state of affairs of a company requires that the liabilities of the company at the end of the financial year be stated. The Chartered Institute Statement D4[19] recommends that provisions be created for deferred taxes, where the amounts of tax assessed or assessable due to special provisions of the tax laws are less than would be "normally" assessed or assessable; and that these provisions should be classified in balance sheets as non-current liabilities. The companies particularly affected by the recommendation arc mining companies, but there are other classes of business which are subject to similar tax rules.

The substance of Statement D4 has not had a happy history. Some auditors have found clients convinced, or have convinced them, of its merit. Some have failed to qualify reports on the accounts of clients who would not accept it; and some have qualified their reports. This mixture of responses can only tend to confusion of the securities market and of individual investors.

I set out briefly the main grounds on which the recommendation is assailable. Argument at greater length was given in my article "Tax Allocation and Financial Reporting", *Abacus*, December 1968.

[19] The Institute, *Statement D4 Treatment of Income Tax in the Accounts of Companies*, November 1970.

A deferred tax provision is in no sense a liability at the date of any balance sheet. It is not legally due or constructively due to the tax authority; for subsequent assessments to tax are contingent upon the earning of taxable profits. At the very best, such amounts are no more than contingent liabilities, and could perhaps be treated by footnote in the same way as other contingent liabilities.

If they are brought into the accounts proper as liabilities, the accounts will not represent the consequences of events and transactions up to the balancing date; the accounts will include hypothetical consequences of future events which may not in fact occur. There is no more reason for providing for deferred taxes than there is for including other items of cost or gain which may arise at some future time. The inclusion of such things would make the balance sheet and the stated profit a mixture of fact and speculation—a mixture which could not possibly be regarded as giving a true and fair view of the profit or loss of a period and of the state of affairs at a specified date. The whole exercise would be a violation of the long and strongly held view that accounts are necessarily and properly historical in character.

210

There seem to be eminently sound and practical reasons for objecting to deferred tax accounting. To show deferred tax as a liability increases the debt to equity ratio, and, on the strength of a liability which is not a liability, reduces a company's apparent borrowing power. Because it reduces reported profit and reported shareholders' equity, it distorts calculations of the rate of return on shareholders' equity. Furthermore, whatever may happen in the future, the function (and, it seems, the legislative intention) of the substantial relief from taxation in the early years of the life of depreciating assets is to create a surplus which a company is as free to use as any other surplus. To earmark this surplus as a liability defeats the function and nullifies the intention.

There are ways of coping with the differential time incidence of tax concessions and burdens which are open to fewer objections. One is the noting of a contingent liability, mentioned above. Another would be the creation of a named reserve to be included among the shareholders' equity accounts. Another would be the indication in the profit and loss account of the "benefit" in a given year (by comparison with "normal" charges) of the concessions available under the tax rules of the time. None of these is as objectionable as the reporting of a liability (often large in amount) which is not a liability.

In short, the treatment of "deferred" tax as a liability is wrong in principle and in description. It smoothes out the burden of taxes, in a manner inconsistent with their time-incidence. It does so by recourse to speculation about the future courses of profits and of taxes. It surely cannot be held to lead to a true and fair view of the state of affairs and the profits of a company year by year.

Depreciation of Buildings

It is undeniable that buildings are subject to wear and tear and technical obsolescence. But accounting is concerned with financial features, not physical features, of assets. It is also undeniable that the user-value of building space—and hence the market value of buildings—may go up or down. The market value of a great deal of building space, particularly in urban and industrial areas has gone steadily upwards. Whether or not the fall in value (depreciation) through wear, tear and obsolescence is offset by the rise in value (appreciation) through pressure of demand, is a matter for discovery in any particular case. But as accounting is concerned with the financial significance of assets, it certainly cannot be held as a general rule that buildings only fall in value, that they are subject only to depreciation.

Fletcher Moulton L.J., in the judgment already mentioned, observed: "The value assigned to trade buildings and plant is usually fixed according to an arbitrary rule by which they are originally taken at their actual costs, and are assumed to have depreciated by a certain percentage each year, though it cannot be pretended that any such calculation necessarily gives their true value either in use or in exchange". This is fair description of and fair comment on the common practice. If the balance sheet gives neither value in use nor value in exchange, there is serious doubt it giving a true and fair view in respect of buildings.

211

Statement D5 of the Institute of Chartered Accountants in Australia[20] describes depreciation as the net cost of a fixed asset during its effective working life, and "net cost" as the diminution in value from its cost to its residual sale price on disposal. The object of providing for depreciation is thus to write the value of the asset down to a resale price or value in exchange. If resale price on disposal is to be taken into account from the date of purchase or construction of a building, the depreciation calculation involves speculation about the life of the building and the movement of resale prices for as much as 30 or more years in the future. Whether a building will have a resale price 30 years hence equal to half its original cost, or twice or ten times its original cost, or zero, is anyone's guess.

Much of the discussion in Statement D5 evades reference to this speculation by the simple supposition that buildings will have nothing more than a scrap value 30 or so years hence. (The supposition entails an annual charge for depreciation). This is justified on the ground that the owner or purchaser will want to demolish the building, and that the resale price of the building and the land on which it stands will thus be the price of the land itself. But, first, what a

---

[20] The Institute, *Statement D5 Depreciation, Depletion and Amortisation of Fixed Assets*, November 1970.

future owner may intend to do has nothing to do with the value now of a property to its present owner. Second, it is certainly not the general case that land and buildings are sold with the object of demolishing the buildings. And, third, the allocation of a hypothetical future price as between the land (the whole price) and the building (zero) is an entirely gratuitous allocation.

Statement D5 notes that a number of Australian companies have revalued fixed assets, and recommends that in such circumstances depreciation should be based on the revalued amount. However this is inconsistent with the definition of depreciation given in the Statement and reproduced above, unless "net cost" can be a negative figure and depreciation is interpreted as including appreciation. If the Statement had endorsed revaluation as firmly as it endorses the provision for depreciation it might have been unobjectionable. But insistence on one without the other is biassed, lop-sided, and cannot be conducive to the giving of a true and fair view of profits or losses or of the state of affairs.

The problem is complicated by the fact that land and buildings are often acquired as one parcel of property. Statement D5 (para. 32) says that the book values of buildings should be distinguished from the book value of land. Where the two assets are acquired as one parcel, the splitting of the cost is at best arbitrary, as is the splitting of the resale price on disposal mentioned above. Arbitrary splitting is itself not conducive to the giving of a true and fair view of the consequences of transactions. The paragraph in question goes on to say that "an appreciation in the value of the land on which a building stands, whether or not recorded in the accounts, is not a valid reason for failing to charge for depreciation of the building itself". The point as issue really is whether anyone can work out the net cost of buildings (cost less resale price on disposal) when land and buildings are acquired in one parcel and are likely to be disposed of in one parcel (since one cannot sell a building of itself). It would be reasonable (if we were to grant the reasonableness of splitting the original cost between land and buildings) to insist that both appreciation of land and depreciation of buildings be shown; but it is biassed to insist on the charging of depreciation for buildings "whether or not [appreciation of land is] recorded in the accounts".

The Statement has not been readily endorsed in practice. Many companies have declined to provide for depreciation of buildings; some auditors have and some have not qualified their reports in consequence. The Institute has drawn attention, in Statement K1,[21] to the desirability of following the substance of its statements on principles and practices. It intends to seek explanations from members who as directors or auditors or otherwise are responsible for accounts which do not conform with its statements. Whether this will

---

[21] The Institute, *Statement K1 Conformity with Institute Technical Statements*, February 1972.

enforce compliance or lead to a spate of qualified reports remains to be seen. But the making of charges against revenue and of reductions in the net values of assets, where these are unwarranted by reason of rises in the current prices of assets, leads to distortion of debt to equity ratios, rates of return and assetbacking. This is good and practical enough reason for expecting objection to be taken to the practice recommended by the Institute.

Conclusion

The above analysis suggests that, in the absence of any clear specification of what is meant by a true and fair view of results and state of affairs, arguments for particular practices are bound to be fragmentary, inconsistent and strained. In the light of the years of struggling which have led to the present confusion of argument and practice, the only prospect of rationalizing accounting practices seems to lie in clarification, by law or through the Courts, of what shall be regarded as conforming with the present requirement of the law. A true and fair view cannot be given by financial statements which are made up of out-of-date, fictional and technically inconsistent pieces of information. Yet, a true and fair view must be given if informed judgments are to be made by the many parties who—sometimes in harmony and sometimes in conflict—have financial dealings with companies.

213

A Funny Thing Happened on the Way to the Counting House*

Jack Adderson, chartered accountant, came down to breakfast, shaved, showered and dressed in regular business suit. It was going to be a day of decision. He was an audit manager in a Perth professional firm, and he had been offered a salaried commercial position in Sydney which would almost double his annual income. He had a substantial equity in his Perth home, two small parcels of shares, a life insurance policy, a two-year old station wagon, and a small pleasure boat at the marina. If he took the Sydney job, he would face a higher average rate of tax on his income, and higher living costs — and he would want to buy a home in Sydney. There was the crunch; house property was much more expensive in Sydney than in Perth. He had been to Sydney, nosing about to find the prices of suburban houses, moderately better than his present home, in districts where he might choose to live. He found the price of the property he was disposed to buy to be about $80,000; legal fees, removal costs and additional furnishing costs would add to that another $10,000, he estimated.

"Well, Honey", he said to his wife, Jill, "today's the day. I have to give that Sydney firm an answer. Do we go or do we stay?"

"You've done all the figuring, haven't you?", said Jill.

"I've done some figuring, but I'm not sure that it helps", Jack replied. "We have a nice home here. We only paid $20,000 for it 8 years ago. Of course, we redesigned the kitchen; that cost $2,000. And last year we put in the pool — $3,000. To pay $80,000 plus extras for a home in Sydney when this one cost $25,000 sounds a bit steep".

"But, Jack, you said last night that the agent thought he could get us $50,000 for this house".

"Yes. But the inflation of the last few years has kicked up prices quite a lot. I don't know whether $50,000 is enough for a home on which we've spent $25,000".

"Never mind that. The agent knows his business, I suppose. $50,000

215

---

* The Institute of Chartered Accountants in Australia Student Society Luncheon **Address**, Perth, March 1975. The prices were prices of the time.

is what he thinks we can reasonably expect to get. Unless you really know better, that's the only idea we have of what it's worth. And, of course, we still owe $5,000 on it under the mortgage. That means we have $45,000 to start with".

"O.K., Honey. Then there are those shares. The 300 shares in Gold Diggers cost us $1800 four years ago, but today's price is $4. They must be worth more than that in the long run".

"No, no. You said we have to know today, not some day in the future".

"Oh, yes. So we have possibly $1200 from them. Then there's the 2000 shares in Steve Dawes, the chandlers. We paid $1 each and they've gone up to $2.50. So that makes another $5,000, eh? And I think I could get about $1000 for the boat".

"That leaves your insurance policy and the wagon. I think we should hang on to them, don't you?"

"Yes. I found that the surrender value of the policy is only $1000, and if I have to start all over again we'll face higher premiums. And we must have a car. Setting those things aside, what does the rest add up to? Ummm. $52,200. If it's going to cost us $10,000 in removal and other basic costs, that would leave us $42,000 towards the Sydney house. That should be sufficient, with a mortgage loan on the property. I'll check with the bank or the insurance company and call you back later".

Enter Jack Junior, aged 15. "G'morning, Dad".

"Morning, Son. How did you get on with last night's homework?"

"I couldn't manage the English language piece. We had to explain a remark said to have been made to C. Wren by King James on first inspecting St Paul's Cathedral. He said: `It's amusing; it's awful; it's artificial´. None of that sounds as though he was pleased with it. Yet it is thought to be one of Wren's finest buildings. Scrambling around in the dictionary didn't help".

"That's not surprising. Many words have long had the same form but they have had quite different meanings. For what was once described as amusing we would now use amazing. Awful once meant awesome or awe-inspiring. Artificial once meant artfully constructed, well made. You'd have to check that with seventeenth century usage. Try some old

216

dictionaries or other books on the changing use of words. If it turns out as I said, you'll see that King James's remark was highly complimentary. Out of date descriptions are puzzling and they may be deceptive. You wouldn't now say you were 120 centimeters tall, when that was your height eight years ago — unless you wanted to deceive someone who couldn't see you himself".

"Thanks for the lead, Dad. I'll go look it up".

"Goodness, look at the time; I must be off. See you later, Junior. Good bye, Honey". (Smooch, smooch. Exit Adderson, senior).

* * * * *

Thirty minutes later Adderson was at his office desk. He had to check the audit work done on the accounts of three clients of his firm and their draft financial statements. We pass over all other details of the financial features of the clients except the following.

Client file A53 related to a company conducting a retail business in two suburban shopping centres. It had freehold title to the property it occupied in one of those centres, for which it had paid $40,000 some 15 years earlier. The file showed that the latest official valuation of the property was $150,000. Plans were afoot to redevelop a block of stores including that of A53, and $180,000 had been named as an offer by the developer. A53 was to have the right to lease part of the redeveloped complex, and the proceeds of the sale could be used in the company's business. On the ground that the property was a fixed asset, Adderson accepted the balance sheet valuation, at cost, $40,000.

Client file B21 related to a private company which among other things had acquired a quarter-interest, 100,000 shares, in another private company in a related line of business for $100,000 five years previously. The latter company had made losses aggregating 40 cents per share up to the latest balance date, but it was expected to become profitable in the future. Adderson endorsed the $100,000 valuation of the shareholding on the ground that it represented the cost of a permanent investment.

Client file C9 related to a light engineering company. It had entered into a contract with a customer for a fixed sum to develop and manufacture 10,000 units of a sub-assembly. The contract, written three years previously, stipulated a delivery date which had passed during the latest financial year, but the customer had taken no steps to cancel the contract. The development of the product had not been completed, but the costs of development, $60,000, had been included in the asset balances, in the light of the existence of the contract. Adderson agreed with this, since the amount would be recoverable when the order was completed.

* * * * *

Now Adderson knew that up-to-date selling prices of assets were needed to make any estimate of the feasibility of any plan of action by any client, and to choose between the merits of any alternative plans. He had been doing just that, over breakfast, for his own affairs, and using that kind of information. He would not know what plans or intentions the managers of the client companies might entertain before or after discovery of their financial states. But making plans and forming intentions are recurrent incidents in the conduct of business.

Adderson knew that the past costs of assets have no bearing on what the client firms could do by virtue of their asset holdings at any time. He disregarded the costs of his own assets - reluctantly perhaps, but nevertheless certainly - as his breakfast-table calculations proceeded.

Adderson knew that out of date terms and magnitudes and descriptions can be puzzling, misleading and deceptive. He'd told Junior just that only hours before. Yet, there he was, endorsing out-of-date descriptions, anticipating future outcomes, and ignoring up-to-date evidence, in the balance sheets of clients that would purport to represent the states of their financial affairs at specified dates.

What he found useless in thinking about his own affairs, somehow he thought would be useful to others concerned with their affairs. What he rejected in his own calculations, somehow he thought others could properly use in theirs. It would have been just the same if Adderson had been the chief of the counting house of any of his firm's clients.

Whatever could have happened on the way to the counting house?

218

THE ACCOUNTING D.Ts.[*]

The President of the English Institute of Chartered Accountants in
responding recently to a toast to the Institute drew attention to the fact
that the Latin word "Liber" which means "book", is also the root of the word
liberal, and is also associated with the Greek god Bacchus, the god of wine
and conviviality. As accountants are concerned with "books", he went on to
say, they may also be supposed to be liberal at some times and convivial at
others.

The title I have chosen, however, has nothing to do with the D.Ts.
which afflict over-zealous devotees of Bacchus. It relates to an affliction
described as double-talk and double-think to which, it seems, many accountant
are subject, even in their most sober moments. I first drew attention to
this affliction in 1957 in a lecture in the University of Melbourne. But I
am prompted to mention it again because examples of it continue to crop up -
and in more terrifying forms than some of the forms I identified nearly
20 years ago.

George Orwell's <u>1984</u> is not an accounting textbook. But its description
of "doublethink", the underlying philosophy of the rulers of Orwell's Oceania,
cannot be surpassed as a description of the common philosophy of accountants.
"Double-think means the power of holding two contradictory beliefs in one's
mind simultaneously, and accepting both of them ... The process has to be
conscious, or it would not be carried out with sufficient precision, but it
also has to be unconscious, or it would bring with it a feeling of falsity and
hence of guilt ... To forget any fact that has become inconvenient, and then,
when it becomes necessary again, to draw it back from oblivion for just so
long as it is needed, to deny the existence of objective reality and all the
while to take account of the reality which one denies - all this is
indispensably necessary". The whole notion makes interesting fiction; and
<u>1984</u> has slipped into common language as hinting at the terrifying shadow of
twisted authoritarianism. But in accounting it is no fiction. It is with us
now and has been for a long time.

Everyone knows that it is only proper, logically and practically, to add
like things to like. Accountants, of course, are great adders. They add up
accounts; they add up balances of accounts in balance sheets. They, like
everyone else, learned that unlike things cannot be added. They learned it
in primary school very likely. They know it to be a fact that adding unlike
things only yields nonsensical aggregates. But when they enter the counting
house they promptly forget this fact, take up a contradictory belief, and
proceed to add up money sums which are as unlike as chalk and cheese. They
add present amounts of cash, prices paid years ago for security investments
and land, prices paid for depreciating assets less hypothetical deductions
based on guesswork about the future, prices expected to be received in the

---

[*] Address to the Annual Meeting of the Geelong Branch of Australian Society
of Accountants, 27 February 1975.

future for some types of inventory, ruling market prices for other types of inventory, and replacement prices (i.e., the purchase prices of goods not yet in possession) for other types of inventory. These past, present and future amounts have no common, or like, quality; they cannot properly be added. Yet accountants do it all the time - until they go home to their personal affairs, where it is quite inconvenient to stick to the counting house rules and they become commonsense people again.

"The process has to be conscious", said Orwell, "or it would not be carried out with sufficient precision". The counting house rules are followed quite consciously. There are special bits of reasoning which are said to justify all those different valuations; and those special bits of reasoning make the accountant unconscious of the folly of adding up unlike things - as Orwell said, relieving the doer of any "feeling of falsity and hence of guilt". It's quite easy when one has mastered "doublethink".

220 Every accountant knows about the accrual principle. It means that the effects of events in a year are brought into the year's accounts even though the ultimate effects of those events are yet to be experienced. It's a good principle. Everyone likes to know what progress he is making towards some ultimate situation; we can ascertain progress even if we don't know what the ultimate situation will be. But accounting is not so simple. There is another principle called the realisation principle which says, in effect, "don't take account of beneficial effects until those effects have been realized". This is a classic example of doublethink, "of holding two contradictory beliefs in one's mind simultaneously and accepting both of them". A provision for depreciation, for example, follows the accrual principle. But if there is appreciation short of the date of sale, no account is taken of it - which is a denial of the accrual principle. Or put it another way, assuming that realisation is the dominant principle. Account is taken of appreciation when an asset is sold, but account is taken of depreciation before an asset is sold. Depreciation is the opposite of appreciation, as loss is the opposite of profit. There can be no good reason for treating one effect differently from its opposite. But one can do it without any sense of logical or practical impropriety by recourse to double-think.

Now consider consolidation accounting and equity accounting. Accounts, we are told, are kept for specific entities. A company is a legal entity with power to buy and hold assets, to borrow and to issue securities. A balance sheet purports to describe some features of the entity, in particular what it possesses and what equities outsiders have in the things it possesses. But what is a consolidated balance sheet? It purports to describe some features of a group of companies. But a group is not a legal entity. It does not possess the assets listed; it has no legal title to them, either by way of ownership or possession. It does not owe the amounts shown as liabilities in the consolidated balance sheet and it did not issue the shares outstanding as reported in the consolidated balance sheet. The financial statement of the parent or investor company based on legally enforceable rights, stands cheek by jowl with a financial statement, the consolidated statement, which is not based on legally enforceable rights. It is a clear case of holding two contradictory beliefs simultaneously, disregarding one of them when it "has become inconvenient, and then, when it becomes necessary again, drawing it back from oblivion for just so long as it is needed". To draw up a consolidate balance sheet _as if_ it were a good and proper balance sheet conceals the separateness of the ownership of assets and the liability to creditors of the legally separate companies in the so-called group. And here again we have double-talk. For we stand four-square for the principle of disclosure, and proceed forthwith to endorse a form of concealment.

Orwell referred to the simultaneous recognition and denial of "objective reality". One aspect of objective reality is that accounts are used by, and are required by law to be provided for the beneficial use of, shareholders, creditors and others. No accountant would consciously deny this. Yet the fact is forgotten when it becomes inconvenient. Shareholders, creditors and others obviously want to know the wealth of a company, the money's worth of it net assets. They want to know the periodical increase in its wealth - not simply the increase in the nominal amount of its assets but the real increase, for only the real increase is indicative of growth. They want to know what is legally available for distribution as dividends. Some of those outside parties make use of financial statements in connection with price regulation, wage negotiation and taxation and with judgments upon these matters. And few people would deny that those statements are intended to assist shareholders in making investment decisions. Yet in a series of official statements of the English Institute, the relevance of financial statements to every one of these functions or uses is denied (See <u>Securities and Obscurities</u>, pp.44-5). The mere mention of all these potential uses of accounts is acknowledgment of "objective reality", and of the proper connection between accounts and objective reality. The simultaneous denial of the usefulness of accounts for these purposes puts objective reality behind one's back - out of sight, out of mind. It's a case of double talk, par excellence.

Let's now take two up-to-date examples. At the International Congress in Sydney in 1972 it was widely reported that there was almost universal rejection of the historical cost basis of accounting. One could almost say "the dogs were barking it". <u>Since</u> the Congress, national and international committees have been hard at work preparing statements of principle or practice. And on what basis, do you think? Right, the historical cost basis. I tendered a criticism about a year ago of the proposed statement on depreciation. In the reply I received there occurred the clause "As long as we are committed to historical cost ... etc." I was foolish enough to suppose we were no longer committed to historical cost. But I did not reckon with doublethink. One of the projects currently in the international pipeline is accounting for inventories. And do you know what the full title of the project is? Accounting for Inventories under Historical Cost! There we are - able to reject historical cost at an international congress and equally able to go on issuing official statements on the historical cost basis from international committees which had their origin in or about the same time as that congress.

And finally there is the English provisional standard on accounting for inflation, which has been given wide circulation in slightly amended form in Australia as a Preliminary Exposure Draft. We will note first that it "does not suggest the abandonment of the historical cost convention" (para 3). But several paragraphs later, it says that the advantage of historical cost - limitation of the number of matters which are subject to the exercise of judgment - is impaired where the purchasing power of the monetary unit changes

significantly over a period of years (para 7). Now if the stated advantage
of historical cost is impaired, surely historical cost should be rejected.
Surely? No, not so surely if you have learned the art of doublethink. Para 3,
as I have said, does not reject the historical cost convention.

The method proposed has been called current purchasing power (C.P.P.)
accounting. The name suggests that the financial statements will represent
assets in terms of their current purchasing power. Para 10 refers to the
provision of "suitable information to enable users of accounts to understand
the effects of inflation on the results and financial position" of a company.
Para 1 of an explanatory appendix says C.P.P. accounting "looks at the
undertaking from the point of view of the purchasing power invested in it by
its owners and of the maintenance of that purchasing power". It all sounds
as though C.P.P. accounting will tell us some of the things we have long wanted
to know. But again we must reckon with doublethink and doubletalk.

C.P.P. accounting does not represent assets in terms of their current
purchasing power. All non-monetary assets (inventories, plant, buildings,
land, shares) are assumed to have risen in value at the same rate as the
general level of prices. This assumption will not yield values indicative
of current purchasing power - almost anyone who has held shares over the
last few years will be aware of that. C.P.P. accounting does not provide
information on the effects of inflation on results and financial position.
In an inflationary period the general purchasing power of money falls, but
the prices of particular non-monetary assets may rise or fall or remain
constant. By assuming that all such prices rise at the same rate as the
general level of prices, C.P.P. accounting does not give effect to differential
changes in particular prices, and therefore falls short of showing the effects
of inflation on results and financial position. C.P.P. accounting does not
proceed on the basis of maintaining the purchasing power invested in a company.
To do this it would have to take account of the current purchasing power of
all assets from time to time - which, because of the assumption just mentioned,
it does not do.

The claims made for C.P.P. accounting just do not stand up. Its arguments
are contradictory - and that is doublethink. And the results it yields are
contradictory of the results of the principal (i.e. conventional) financial
statements published with them - and that is doubletalk.

I would continue in this strain. There are many examples of the same
kind of thing. But I have chosen my examples because they are so general
in their coverage of accounting. Accounting doctrine and practice are riddled
with doublethink and doubletalk. The accounts they yield are double-tongued.
They have long served to cover up double-dealing, until in the end they have
brought double-trouble - to investors, financiers, bankers, and indeed to
accountants and auditors. Double-entry deserves a better reputation than that.

When I first used the doublethink theme, there remained 27 years to 1984 -
a long enough spell to eradicate doublethink and doubletalk. But much of what
has happened to accounting since is reminiscent of the witches' brew of Macbeth:

> Double, double toil and trouble
> Fire burn, and cauldron bubble.

The ingredients of accounting are becoming as odd as "Adder's fork and blind-worm's sting, lizard's leg and howlet's wing". Indeed the ingredients of accounting are odder. In so-called deferred tax accounting, there are reported as liabilities things which are in no sense liabilities. In consolidation accounting, things are represented as assets and liabilities of a "group", which is a fiction without legal or practical substance. In C.P.P. accounting, C.P.P. rules do not represent current purchasing power at all. In the light of all this, it is not surprising that some would foist on the profession and its clients the crowning glory of doublethink - or "multiple-think" - namely, multicolumn or multibased accounting!

To reject these follies we still have 10 years to 1984. Perhaps it's still time enough to give up doublethink, to repel the twisted authoritarianism of those who, in the guise of providing new standards, would turn the fine art of accounting into unintelligible gibberish. As you enter a new year I wish you well. I wish you not the Accounting D.Ts.

223

A Critical Examination
of Australian Accounting Standards

I suspect that relatively few people are aware of the total number of 'projects' presently in the hands of the Australian Accounting Standards Committee. I am relieved that I am not expected to cover them all. My brief limits me to a discussion of the statements of principle (or 'standards') issued by the Institute of Chartered Accountants in Australia and the Australian Society of Accountants to date. I take this to mean the statements of recent date issued by the two bodies. These are:

DS1.2   Profit and Loss Statements (issued December 1973)

DS4   Accounting for Company Income Tax (October 1974)

DS5   Depreciation of Non-current Assets (May 1974)

DS7   Materiality in Financial Statements (October 1974)

DS11   Disclosure of Accounting Methods Used in Preparing Financial Statements (September 1973).

To give the setting of my comments I indicate at the outset what I consider to be the proper order in which a standard code should be developed. I take as an analogy the design of any moderately complex product. For the output of accounting is a series of moderately complex products, and a code of standards represents the design or pattern for each particular product.

A. The design of a machine begins with a specification of what the functions or uses of the product are intended to be, and a sketch of the whole product consistent with that specification. If there is no such specification and sketch, there is no basis for choosing or designing the subsidiary or contributory parts of the machine. If the machine is intended to be used with other machines, it must be so designed that it 'engages' well with the features of other machines.

Financial statements and their contents have a specifiable set of functions and uses—to inform whoever seeks to be informed of the periodical profits and financial positions of companies from time to time, and in particular to yield indicators of solvency, gearing (or the relation of debt to equity), rate of return, divisible surplus, assets per share and similar specific features. The general style (or form) of the statements can be sketched. It must be such that the components of the indicators just mentioned are available. Any particular set of financial statements is intended to be used in conjunction with other sets of the same form (previous statements of the same company, current statements of other companies) and with other statements and calculations of different form (budgets, share price information, contracts and agreements restraining borrowings and out-payments such as dividends). These latter statements and calculations all relate to money and money's worth. The financial statements should therefore be so designed that in aggregate and in parts, they 'engage' well with other statements and calculations which are used with them.

B. Every machine consists of an interlocked series of 'sub-assemblies'. Each sub-assembly has its own part to play, and it must be designed to play that part. But each is also connected with the others, directly or indirectly. Each must therefore be designed to 'engage' well with the others. And of course the design of each and its connections with the others must be consistent with the specified function of the whole machine.

In respect of financial statements the 'sub-assemblies' are asset classes, liability classes, ownership interest classes, including in the latter revenue (or gains) classes and expense (or loss) classes. Each class should be defined (specified), and the manner in which each engages, directly or indirectly, with the others must be specified. There are several types of engagement. The total amount of assets must match the total amount of liabilities and ownership interests. The net gain or loss must match one of the types of change in ownership interests. The reference to totals and net figures entails that the figures must be capable of proper addition and subtraction (which are forms of 'engagement'). And since combinations of class or individual figures are used in conjunction with the 'other' types of statement and calculation mentioned under A above, the figures must be capable of proper addition, subtraction and relation to components of those other statements and calculations.

C. Each sub-assembly consists of parts. Each of the parts must be so designed that all parts of an assembly are consistent with (or fit) one another. The raw materials from which they are made, the processes through which they must pass and the tests of their quality must be specified.

The analogous aspect of financial statements is specification of the features of the descriptions and amounts of particular items or classes of items. The general features will already have been specified under A and B; thus, the particulars must not be inconsistent with the specified functions of the whole statements, and the particulars must be relatable to other particulars within and beyond the statements. The specifications of stage C link these necessary features with the raw material, the data relating to events and transactions. They explain how isolated bits of raw material are to be made into parts of a whole, internally consistent, and usable end-product.

There is a logic about this sequence which makes it the sequence chosen by the designers of products and the processes by which they are made. One does not begin with a clutter of bits and pieces, stick them together, and hope that the result will be functional. One starts with known functions and uses, and fashions the raw materials into parts and assemblies which are consistent

225

137

with those uses. The functions and uses specified in A above are known in respect of financial statements and their potential contents. It seems as simple as ABC to specify the characteristics of the parts which will produce statements serving well those uses.

However a glance at the Standards listed in my opening paragraph will show that these logical steps are not being followed. There is none yet on the balance sheet and no specification of the general functions of financial statements (Category A). There is no Standard in which assets, liabilities, owners' equity and changes in owners' equity are defined and their relationships indicated (category B). There are statements on taxes and depreciation which fall into category C, but the treatment of which depends on what should be said, but is not yet said, in categories A and B. Even granting that there may be delays in polishing up the 'missing' specifications, it cannot be expected that readers will properly understand category C specifications unless and until they are aware of the framework set by category A and B specifications. In any case, as I shall presently show, the absence of proper A and B specifications leads to oddities which are quite unservicable and avoidable.

Proceeding in what can only be called a higgledy-piggledy manner is neither new, nor local, of course. In 1950 I was a member of one of the first research committees set up by the then Commonwealth Institute of Accountants—the terminology committee. I tried to get the Committee to deal first with such general notions as 'income' and 'financial position', for the general framework would make all the subsidiary detail so much the easier. But without success. In 1961, I was invited to have a critical look at the new statements of principle about to be issued by the Institute of Chartered Accountants. I pointed out that there was no clear specification of what a balance sheet and income statement purported to represent or what functions they were intended to perform. Lacking such a specification it was impossible to judge whether any particular statement of principle was good or bad, wise or foolish. That too was disregarded. The same defect has been characteristic of English and American attempts to codify principles or to establish standards before and since; and in all cases the product has turned out to be unsatisfactory. What I was suggesting, and what I have suggested above, was simply an application of what is now described as 'management by objectives'. But that phrase seems as easy to ignore as it is to parrot. You've heard of the committee that invented the camel. For want of a sense of direction, many statements of principle have turned out to have more heads, legs, arms and humps than any camel.

There are some who, in defence of the present mode of proceeding, have contended that the aim of the statements being issued has been simply to codify present practice, and that the *next* step is to improve on those statements and the practices they endorse. But this claim won't hold water. The published statements and the exposure drafts which foreshadow the publication of 'Standards' almost universally propose deviations from what is presently, and commonly, done.

It is time to see whether the published standards are good specifications for serviceable products. It will be impossible to engage in a full analysis of all sections of each Standard. I have therefore been selective, taking notice of what seem to be significant points.

Profit and loss statements (DS1.2)

The main proposal of DS1.2 approaches an all-inclusive notion of profit (or loss) and an all-inclusive profit and loss statement. The statement is to include, and the reported profit is to take into account, all items of revenue and expense, and all other gains or losses '(both of a revenue and a capital nature), arising in the period from ordinary operations or other events and transactions, and even items relating to prior periods (para. 18). Adoption of the all-inclusive idea is commendable. It removes the possibility of carrying certain kinds of gains or losses directly to reserve accounts, a practice which conceals some part of the effects of a period's events. It would provide a full reconciliation of the opening and closing amounts of owners' equity (except for new contributions and dividends). It would also enable periodic profit to be described as the increase in the net assets in a period, thus making a point of the interlocking nature of accounts mentioned in the B section of my remarks on design. The definition given is revenue and other gains less expenses and other losses (para. 5). The profit figure should be the same however derived; but the definition given avoids the suggestion of interlocking and has led to the belief that income calculation is independent of financial position.

But, though it moves in the right direction, para. 18 is still baffling. It goes on to say that profit does *not* include gains arising on revaluation *except* gains arising from applying the equity method to shares held as assets, and *except* when an accounting standard provides for their inclusion. All this turns para. 18 into a hydra-headed monster.

Notice, first, that profit calculation excludes revaluation gains; but revaluation losses are not mentioned, although throughout DS1.2 gains and losses are almost invariably mentioned together. Presumably revaluation losses are to be brought into profit calculation. If so, the treatment of revaluations is lop-sided or biased. The old-fashioned notion of conservatism is the only ground on which this bias can be justified; but no attempt is made to justify it on any ground whatever.

Second, why exclude revaluation gains at all? A revaluation gain must be either a capital gain or a revenue gain, and the paragraph says both are to be taken into account. No reason is given for the exclusion. Para. 18 is thus patently self-contradictory.

Third, having excluded revaluation gains, it switches back to provide for the inclusion of revaluation gains arising under the equity method (on which there is not yet a Standard). No reason is given for the differential treatment of the two kinds of revaluation gain. Yet there seems to be even less reason for bringing into account equity method gains than for bringing in other

227

139

revaluation gains. Other assets (than shares in other companies) are wholly and obviously under the control of a given company and increases in their value accrue to it directly. On the other hand, the condition precedent to application of the equity method to shareholdings is only that the investor company shall have 'significant influence' (loosely defined) in the affairs of the investee company; and the gains do not legally accrue to the investor company, in any case. (See *Exposure Draft,* 'The Use of the Equity Method in Accounting for Investments in Subsidiaries and Associated Companies', September 1973).

Fourth, on top of this, there is a proviso allowing revaluation gains to be included if an (unspecified) accounting standard (perhaps some future standard) so provides.

Would para. 18 please make up its mind?

As if contradictions were not enough, there are obscurities as well. DS1.2 does not say what is meant by a gain, or a loss, or 'arising'. To be clear about these terms is necessary if we are to understand para. 18, which speaks of gains and losses arising; for nowhere is there any reference to the 'accrual' principle. Does a gain *arise* when the cost (or selling price) of an asset rises, or only when the asset is sold? Does a loss *arise* when the price of an asset falls, whereas a gain arises only when the asset is sold at a price above its book value? Does a revaluation gain *arise* when it is written into the accounts, or gradually (periodically) as the cost or value of the asset rises? (Note that revaluation is condoned, but periodical accrual of increases in value is not acknowledged as a proper step in profit calculation). What is meant by the reference to 'other gains and losses . . . arising in that period . . . even though they may relate to prior periods'? Does 'arise in' mean 'relate to'? If not, what is the difference? If, by chance, occasional revaluation gains are excluded because part of them *arose* in periods prior to the period in which they are brought into the accounts, why should they be excluded when it is provided that gains and losses relating to prior periods shall be taken into account in calculating the profit of a period? There is no rule against accruing depreciation, which is an unrealized expense or loss; why should revaluations (even though they are unrealized) be excluded generally when many of them may be corrections of previously excessive depreciation charges?

Further, para. 18 refers to gains or losses of a capital or revenue nature. But DS1.2 does not say what these are. Para. 8 describes as 'extraordinary items' some things which are commonly regarded (though not described in that paragraph) as capital gains and losses. But para. 18 says that they all must be taken into account in determining profit for a period. Now, if they are all taken into account, the 'capital/revenue' distinction must have been abandoned. I am entirely in sympathy with this, for the distinction has long provided a way of escaping clear disclosure of the effects of adverse movements in the prices of some assets. But I don't understand why the distinction is mentioned and why its former significance has been abandoned without benefit of discussion or explanation.

228

But enough of para. 18. Other paragraphs provide that the income tax applicable to, and brought into account in arriving at, the operating profit shall be shown separately, and that material extraordinary items and the tax applicable to each shall be shown separately. I find this rather curious. Taxes are levied on taxable income as a whole, not on parts of it, and not on operating income and extraordinary items in particular. The prescription is, I suppose, tied up with the prescriptions of DS4 to which I will turn presently. But it seems to me that in being over-fussy about details on the incidence of taxes, the possibility is created that readers will be overloaded with information which (even if it were correct) they are unable to interpret.

I have not drawn attention to the lack of clarity, the absence of reasoning and the contradictions of this Standard, merely as an exercise in disparagement. I am concerned with the practical consequences of it, with the confusion it should remove but which in some respects it only compounds, with the quality of the information which practice under it will yield. The gain or loss of a period must have reference to some 'quantity' with which the period began. That quantity is the opening amount of shareholders' equity. Every item which increases or decreases shareholders' equity should therefore appear in the profit and loss account. This is simple and clear. It links the profit and loss account with the balance sheet, making the two consistent. And it takes less space than para. 18 and the discussion leading up to it. There is no reference in DS1.2 to the argument over 'realized profit', nor is the accrual principle endorsed. Some stand should have been taken between these two ideas if only for the purpose of clarifying the meaning of 'profit arising'. But here, as in the 'incidental' reference to capital and revenue gains, there seems to be a notable reluctance to take a position or to clarify a source of confusion.

Accounting for company income tax (DS4)

The principal feature of this Standard is its advocacy of 'tax effect accounting'. My observations in this case will relate mainly to the principle at issue. Tax effect accounting is said to be preferred to 'taxes payable' accounting on the ground that it results in a better matching of expense and revenue (para. 4). Three variants of tax effect accounting are described; para. 14 expresses a preference for the 'liability method', and that is the method to which I shall give attention.

Tax effect accounting is justified by reference to 'timing differences', differences in the periods in which particular costs or revenues are brought into the calculation of 'pre-tax accounting profit' and 'taxable income'. Where the tax rules allow deductions at a faster rate (or bring in revenues at a later date) than the company charges (or credits) these items in calculating pre-tax accounting profit, a liability for future tax is 'assumed' to arise (para. 9). In the opposite circumstance an asset in the nature of 'future tax benefit' is assumed to arise. These assumptions—and therefore the whole notion of tax effect accounting—seem to be open to many objections.

First, a liability arises in a year only by virtue of an obligation incurred

229

141

in or in respect of that year. If a company appoints an executive under a five-year service contract, the liability for his salary and allowances for the five years does not arise in the first year. Likewise the deferred tax liability does not arise in the year in which it is created. It is owed to no one and recoverable by no one at the end of the year. It has none of the features of a liability.

Second, it is not necessarily recoverable 'eventually' by the tax authority. At the simplest level, future taxes depend on future taxable income; the liability may not arise through failure to make profits or through changes in the tax laws. At a more complicated level, if expenditures which are 'rapidly' tax deductible continue to be made year after year, the total of the accounting charges may not catch up with the total tax allowances for many years, if it does at all. And over those years the fortunes of the business and the tax laws may change significantly. (See A. D. Barton, 'Company Income Tax and Interperiod Allocation', *Abacus*, September 1970.)

230   Third some of the laws which allow accelerated charges for tax purposes are intended to give companies the benefit of rapid recovery of working capital. If less tax is to be paid in the short run there will remain a greater sum for other uses. But if a deferred tax liability is reported the intended advantage will appear to be nullified, since working capital is the difference between current assets and current liabilities.

Fourth, to report a deferred tax liability increases the debt to equity ratio merely by virtue of the assumptions on which it is based. This may cause a companiy to violate the terms of its bond indentures or debenture trust deeds. In fact, in one U.S. case the SEC was obliged to disregard an apparent violation of a bond indenture, because it insisted on tax effect accounting. I wonder who was protecting whom by this sort of inconsistency.

Fifth, to report a deferred tax liability instead of a corresponding increment to the shareholders' equity accounts, reduces the apparent amount of shareholders' funds employed and thus boosts the rate of return, simply on the basis of an assumption. This cannot be regarded as good reporting of the results and state of affairs as they really are.

Sixth, income tax, though treated as an expense, is not an expense which 'accrues' (para. 9 says the liability method is sometimes referred to as the accrual method). A company may earn a substantial 'operating income' and yet pay little tax because of, say, high tax allowances on new equipment. The amount of tax payable is in such cases (and quite generally) the *combined* consequence of quite different things. If special allowances unrelated to 'operations' can offset the gains from operations, it seems to be quite improper, and in violation of ordinary usage, to speak of 'accrual' of the expense (and the liability). Income tax is not an expense incurred in and for the purposes of any part of any business; this should be obvious, since companies which have no taxable income pay no tax.

Seventh, as for the 'better matching of expense and revenue' (para. 4), income tax is not an expense incurred in the earning of any revenue, and cannot be matched with any particular revenue. It has nothing to do with particular revenues, but with taxable income. That the tax laws may allow or disallow some items, or speed up or retard their allowance for tax purposes, does not entail that income tax is a tax on particular transactions or revenues. Like annual rentals, annual interest, annual dividends, income tax is an annual outlay (if it is payable at all); and there is no way of associating it (or them) with particular transactions.

Eighth, if we are to take the matching idea seriously and carry forward tax charges as a liability, surely we should also accrue the future income to which the future tax charge relates, and match the future tax liability against a future increase in assets. Otherwise 'matching' is a mere pretence. I have not seen any suggestion that this should be done; but I live in fear of some such proposal because of the growing extent to which guesswork about the future is being smuggled into accounts.

These are enough counter-arguments. Any one of them is a stronger argument 'against' tax effect accounting than the matching notion is 'for' it. DS4 attempts to counter none of them.

Other aspects of DS4 illustrate points made elsewhere in this paper. There is, for example, the lopsidedness or bias illustrated by the treatment of revaluation gains in DS1.2. A provision for deferred tax should *always* be raised *unless* it can be shown that, when the effect is due to be reversed, the company will incur equal or greater tax losses (para. 21). By contrast, the so-called asset, future tax benefit, should *only* be carried forward *if* adequate future assessable income is reasonably expected, *if* the company will continue to be eligible for the benefit, and *if* the legislation is not expected to change so as to eliminate the benefit. Notice how much more stringent are the rules about the asset than about the liability provision; it is a clear case of bias. Then notice how much fore-knowledge (or guesswork) is required in either case.

In the absence of any general statements of the nature of specifications A and B of my introductory section, I suspect that income tax is treated in DS4 without reference to its effects on the representation of financial position. My third, fourth and fifth counter-arguments turn on the use of the figures for analytical purposes. There is an allied point. The creation of a liability by assumption amounts to distortion of the facts. Textbooks for decades have given overstatements of liabilities as one of the ways of creating secret reserves—and for decades the creation of secret reserves has been frowned upon. Here, then, we have an 'approved' way of creating secret reserves; indeed an obligatory way, if there are sanctions against failure to follow the Standard.

I have never yet seen argument against the old-fashioned device of footnotes on contingent liabilities and assets to deal with contingent possibilities. It is far more defensible than 'assuming' that actual liabilities and assets arise out of timing differences. I shall presently point out that timing differences are *ignored* in another standard. It is hard to escape the impression that financial statements are becoming increasingly cluttered with fictions which obscure financial reality.

231

Depreciation of non-current assets (DS5)

One of the surest facts of commercial life is that the financial significance of assets changes from time to time. Purchase prices and selling prices change, some upwards, some downwards. There is appreciation and depreciation. They are counterparts of the same idea, change in price. Depreciation, both etymologically and by common usage means a fall in price. To accountants it means the same; for the process of writing off depreciation is designed to *reduce* the book value of an asset to its *selling price* by the time it is put out of use (para. 4). It seems to be reasonable therefore to deal with depreciation and appreciation at the same time and in the same place, just as DS1.2 deals simultaneously with profits and losses. But DS5 deals only with depreciation, which makes it lop-sided or biased from the start. There is no reference to appreciation. There are references to revaluation, but this is not intended to be a process analogous to depreciation accounting; 'it is considered preferable that depreciation be dealt with as a process of allocation, and not a process of valuation' (para. 11).

232

DS5 is pretty much a statement of the conventional depreciation accounting process. A 'depreciable asset' is a non-current asset having a limited useful life. 'Useful life' is the expected period or the expected physical service for which the asset will be employed in the business of the entity (para. 4). Depreciation is described as a decline in 'service potential'; but, like most other expositions, DS5 does not say what the term means. Depreciation accounting is a process of allocating the 'depreciable amount' (generally cost less expected recovery on disposal) over the periods (paras. 10b, 14, 15) or over the outputs (para. 16) which consitute the useful life of the asset. No attempt is made to argue that this process of allocation coincides with the decline in service potential; or with the wear and tear, and technical and commercial obsolescence which are said to be contributory to that decline. And, of course, no attempt is made to argue that the net amount (cost less depreciation) of any asset at any time is equal to the financial significance, or money's worth, of the asset at that time.

Because useful lives and selling prices on disposal are estimates of future magnitudes (para. 18), depreciation rates should be reviewed annually in the light of the latest estimates of useful life and expected selling price (para. 28). But there is no mention of reviewing the third element in the calculation of the periodical charge, namely 'the depreciable amount'.

Suppose a firm bought a machine for $1100 expecting it to have a resale value of $100 after a five-year service life. The net amount of the asset at the end of the fourth year would be $300. Suppose that early in the fifth year the price of the product of the machine was double its price in the first year, and that the resale price of the machine was *then* expected to be $390 after a further three years' use. What will be the depreciation charge for the fifth, sixth and seventh years? I suppose there will be *credits* of $30 each year, so that the total charges (200, 200, 200, 200, —30, —30, —30) will be equal to the 'depreciable amount' (cost, $1100, less revised resale price, $390). But we run into 'service potential' difficulties. If service potential is a physical notion, then presumably

144

the new life estimate means an increased service potential estimate, and a lower charge (but not a credit) for each of the last three years than for the first four years. But if service potential means cash generating potential (a financial notion), the charges for the last three years should (on average) be greater than for the first four years (and again, certainly not a credit). These anomalies would not arise if the 'depreciable amount' were to be revised annually, taking account of appreciation where necessary. But DS5 is stuck with the anomalies, for the total charges cannot exceed the depreciable amount (para. 12) and the depreciable amount is based on cost (paras 4, 11). (The definition of depreciable amount allows that some other amount may be substituted for cost; but that is a license to do anything at all, not a rule. For that reason I ignore it). But there is more trouble ahead.

Para. 19 avers that 'it has become a common practice to depart from the historical cost basis of accounting by periodically revaluing some or all' depreciating assets. I suspect that 'periodically', which usually means regularly or in every period, is a mistake, for it is certainly not common to revalue regularly. That apart, if departure from cost is common, either the departure should be censured (since the cost basis is preferred), or it should be endorsed and systematized (dropping the cost basis and making the accrual of appreciation the preferred practice). DS5 does neither. Confronted with contradictories, it shows itself to be spineless, unprincipled.

Land is, by implication (para. 6), excluded from depreciating assets. But if depreciation is to be regarded as a process of allocation (para. 11), there is no good reason why the 'net cost' of land should not come under the same rule as other assets. Land has a limited useful life in the business of many companies. It often becomes just too expensive to hold urban or suburban land when rates and taxes rise, when the costs of financing 'operations' rise, and the rising resale price of land makes its disposal increasingly attractive. Its service potential 'whilst used in the business' declines to the point where it is lost. I suspect that an exception is made of land because commonly land appreciates and DS5 does not countenance appreciation. Or perhaps the exception is made because the notion of service potential is switched from a physical notion (expected life or output) to a financial notion (as potential generator of cash). Whatever the reason, the making of special cases for particular assets in any class represents the breakdown of a rule or the line of argument which supports it. There would be no breakdown if appreciation were regarded simply as the counterpart of depreciation.

A special point is made of depreciation of buildings. 'The limitations of the long-term service potential of buildings are well recognized and are demonstrated in a practical manner by the continual demolition of existing buildings . . .' (para. 21). 'Long-term service potential' joins the list of undefined terms. That apart, the line of argument is a gross exaggeration. Buildings are not being continually demolished. Very few of the buildings demolished in the building booms of the last twenty years would have been less than thirty years

233

145

old, and many were much older; that doesn't represent continual demolition. Many old buildings rose, and many existing buildings have risen, in value (irrespective of the land they occupy) for exactly the same reasons as those given for land—'limited supply and increasing demand' (para. 22). The same paragraph takes issue with those who 'argue against requiring the depreciation of buildings, on the ground that any decline in the service potential of a building is likely to be offset by an increase in the value of the land itself'. If appreciation and depreciation had been dealt with in parallel, this argument could have readily been answered—take in the appreciation of land *and* the depreciation of buildings. And this would take better care of the 'sufficient distribution' problem of private companies than does para. 23. But DS5 closes itself against this simple solution. 'Increases in the value of land and/or buildings are part of another problem which requires an accounting solution independent of the question of building depreciation.' What the other problem is and why it requires an independent solution we are not told.

234

No one could object to charging for depreciation of a building if and when it did fall in value, or even in service potential, whatever that is. But it seems entirely objectionable to charge depreciation from the first occupancy of the building (para. 31) on the ground that some day, in the unspecified future, its service potential will diminish. It will be recalled that a whole new style of accounting for taxes was built on 'timing differences' arising from the tax laws. Here is a case in which timing differences are *created* within the accounts— depreciation is to be charged periodically without regard for the periodical change in the value or price of the asset. The line of argument against depreciation of buildings quoted above from para. 22 is really directed against the undervaluation of assets. However, the blanket insistence of DS5 on depreciation of buildings is, just like DS4 on future tax liability, a 'legitimized' way of creating secret reserves.

Para. 35 requires that the purchase cost of freehold land and buildings should be apportioned between land and buildings. This is necessary, of course, only if separate provision for depreciation of buildings (based on cost) is insisted upon. But no help is given to anyone who wants to know how to do it. It has long been freely admitted that all apportionments of costs or prices or outputs to one or another of joint 'causes' is quite arbitrary. But arbitrariness (and its consequences, ambiguity or unreliability) does not seem to matter to the draftsmen of DS5. Indeed, though described as 'allocation', the process of accounting for depreciation which it describes is 'apportionment'. And it may lead to other arbitrariness. Para. 34 acknowledges that the process may write off more or less than the difference between cost and actual proceeds on disposal. The difference is to be brought into account as profit or loss, as the case may be. But if a company foresees the possibility of this and revalues the asset, DS1.2 (as we have seen) excludes the gain on revaluation from the profit calculation. The differential treatment of realized and unrealized increments is purely arbitrary.

In sum, DS5 has several deep-seated flaws. It does not treat appreciation and depreciation as similar, and to be treated similarly. It accrues one but not the other. It attributes appreciation to supply and demand, but fails to regard supply and demand as also affecting depreciation. Its notion of depreciation is essentially a physical notion applied to initial cost, whereas accounting is, or ought to be, concerned with financial notions. It fails to recognize that cost has nothing much to do with service potential or its orderly amortization. It would cost a forger no more to produce a die for printing $3 notes than for $2 notes. The physical service potential of both may be equal, but the financial characteristic of the $3 die would be zero, immediately. I wonder what the service potential of DS5 is. Certainly it is not designed smoothly to engage with other parts of accounting doctrine and with other types of financial calculation.

Materiality in financial statements (DS7)

'Material' and 'materiality' are words intended to distinguish the significant from the trivial. Synonyms of 'material' are 'substantial', 'important', 'significant'. They have reference to the setting in which some judgement or decision is to be made. Where the potentially pertinent information is complex or extensive, it is commonly condensed—at the cost of some detail. Specification of what is qualitatively material is a safeguard against excessive condensation. For example, to report one figure for 'cash and receivables' may be regarded as excessive condensation. Where the information is quantitative and different in relative size, some bits of it may be relatively insignificant, and may be merged with other bits which are qualitatively similar. Specification of what is quantitatively material is also a safeguard against excessive condensation. In either case, what is material should have reference to the problem setting of the user, not the producer, of information.

DS7 begins with an indication of matters on which 'decisions on materiality' must be made. By way of illustration it refers to disclosure of an item, an accounting method, a change in accounting method and its financial effect, a departure from an accounting standard and its financial effect, a correction of an error in the accounting records (para. 5). Then: 'an item should be considered material if its omission, non-disclosure or mis-statement would result in distortion of, or some other shortcoming in, the information being presented' which would influence (presumably mislead) users of the statements (paras 6, 12). But what is a 'mis-statement', a 'distortion', a 'shortcoming'? To understand the definition of material, we must have some idea of what is a 'proper statement', a 'fair representation' and a 'statement free of shortcomings'—in short, what is the *ideal* style of a set of financial statements. This should be known at the outset; it is part of the specifications of category A of my opening section. But, of course, there is no such specification among the published standards.

Paras 7 and 8 identify as the 'prime users' present and potential investors and creditors. Reference is made to the 'information needs' of users, but we are not told what those needs are. We are told 'it is rarely practicable to . . .

235

147

meet the requirements of all possible users'; but we are not told what requirements of what users cannot be met. This is crucial. For if we do not specify the requirements which *can* or *should* be met, we cannot stipulate what is and is not material, nor understand in what way any element of the accounts is or is not material. The *general* requirements of users—'prime users', wages and prices tribunals, workers and their unions, governmental officials and analysts and advisers to any of them—are given in my category A. That information is obtainable uniquely from financial statements. Its users are all interested in money amounts payable or receivable (as debts, interest, dividends, wages, prices). Clearly, then, all items should be shown at their money equivalents at the date of each set of financial statements. Given this singular and uniform basis for all items, it is simple to describe 'distortion' and 'mis-statement' as deviation from a fair approximation to the money equivalent of an item. The question of quantitative materiality would then arise only where there were divergent, but apparently equally reliable, bits of evidence about the money equivalent of an asset.

236

But DS7 has no such sheet-anchor. It says: 'When considering the amount of an item, it should be compared with an appropriate base amount'. In the case of income account items the appropriate base amount is the operating profit. In the case of a balance sheet item, it is the lower of its own balance sheet class total and the total amount of shareholders' equity (para. 16). If the amount of an item is ten per cent or more than its appropriate base amount, the item is presumed to be material; if five per cent or less, it is deemed to be immaterial; if between five and ten per cent, it depends on the 'circumstances' (para. 17). The whole of this seems to refer to the *separate* disclosure of the amounts of items—and that is only one of the five examples mentioned in para. 5 of 'questions which may have to be settled by reference to materiality'.

How shall the materiality be judged of the financial effect of a change in accounting method? or of the financial effect of a departure from an accounting standard? Or of a mis-statement? Or, since para. 5 also refers to the disclosure of an accounting method, how shall the materiality of this kind of disclosure be judged? Changes in accounting method, departures from an accounting standard and mis-statements may yield greater or less amounts than if they had not been made. If there were any quantitative guidelines for such things, they should take the form, 'plus or minus a stated percentage'. The quantitative guidelines of para. 17 obviously have nothing whatever to do with the materiality of these differences or deviations.

Instead of limiting itself to qualitative and quantitative materiality as I described them in the first paragraph of this section, DS7 seems to be over-ambitious. It sets up a series of possible problems but fails to offer solutions or assistance for 80 per cent of them. Which seems to be a material shortcoming. And even the general dicussion of what is meant by materiality suffers from a material lack of clarity.

Disclosure of accounting methods used (DS11)

The variety of methods of deriving the figures which can appear in financial statements has long been notorious. It has been widely recognized as a serious impediment to analysis of the financial features of particular companies and comparisons of two or more companies. It is forty years since George O. May proposed that companies should describe their accounting methods. There has in the interval been a great increase in the valuation notations and footnotes given in financial statements. But none of it has removed the impediment to interpretation and comparison. And I do not expect that DS11 will do so.

By way of preamble, DS11 points out that 'over recent years considerable progress has been made in reducing the choices available between acceptable accounting methods' (para. 2). It has escaped my notice. If there has been any reduction it has certainly not been considerable. And in a number of respects (such as equity accounting, deferred tax accounting and price level adjusted accounting—for each of which there are alternative methods) we are confronted with choices we never had before. Para. 2 continues: 'Nevertheless, there still exist, in relation to some business activities, choices between two or more acceptable accounting methods, although a particular one may be considered preferable having regard to the circumstances of a specific business entity'. 237

One may read all those words without having a clear idea of what they say. 'In relation to some business activities'; which? 'Having regard to the circumstances'; what kind of regard? and what circumstances? 'A particular method may be considered preferable'; why 'may', if the circumstances really do make one method preferable? The paragraph is so loose that, even though it hints at some restraint, it allows any firm to use any accounting method it considers preferable. It is not a very fitting preamble to a remedial proposal.

Para. 4 says that, because a particular method can have a substantial impact on reported results and position, users must be made aware of the methods used for a proper appreciation of the reported information. I would like to know how a user gains a proper appreciation of results and position by being told, for example, the bases on which its several assets are valued. If one is told that land is valued at cost, buildings at cost less straight-line depreciation, shares according to the equity method, inventories at the lower of cost and market—what proper appreciation does one get of the reported information? None whatever in my view. *If* there were a *standard* basis of valuation, I could see some merit in stating that a different method had been used and stating the quantitative difference arising from its use. But there is no such standard.

Diversity in accounting hits users who wish to make interperiod and interfirm comparisons; for comparisons of figures are useless unless the figures are derived by substantially the same rules. There is not a word about this in DS11. And there is no way on earth by which a mere statement of the (different) methods used in two sets of statements would enable a reader to adjust the figures so that they would be based on substantially the same rules. No one outside the firm, not even an expert accountant, could do it.

Para. 4 goes on to say: 'The basic concepts of "going concern", "consistency", "accrual accounting" and "matching of costs and revenues" are presumed to underlie all financial reporting unless it is stated otherwise'. Now if these are *basic* concepts, it seems improper to contemplate departure from them, even if the departure is 'stated'. There should, one would expect, be some compulsion, some sense of commitment, to follow what is described as 'basic'. But, as it seems, any firm can escape the compulsion or commitment simply by disclosing its departure. However, there is a more serious point.

Exactly what these concepts are is nowhere explained. It appears to be taken for granted that each of the terms connotes a specific idea which is held in common by accountants. But this is patently not the case. The traditional going concern notion (which is said by some to support accounting on a historical cost basis) has been under attack by almost everyone who proposes an alternative to historical cost accounting. The consistency notion is implicitly set aside by every rule of the 'either-or' variety, such, for example, as the inventory rule 'lower of cost and market'. The accrual notion is not evenly applied, as our earlier discussion of appreciation and revaluation shows. And 'matching of costs and revenues' (the original form of the phrase) has become converted to 'matching of expense and revenue' (with a rather different meaning) to support tax allocation; and just for that reason, I suspect, since I know of no other setting in which it occurs. Clearly the four terms do not stand for commonly shared concepts. If it must deal with them (and others like them) at all, DS11 should specify the particular connotation the terms are to have.

Para. 5 says: 'Where knowledge of an accounting method adopted would be significant in the interpretation of financial statements, the method should be disclosed'. However, where that knowledge is significant is not disclosed. It could be significant if some other company were to use a different method and some user wished to compare the two companies' financial futures. But how does the accountant of any company know which other company will be compared with it? and how does he know what method that other company will use in its reports of the same period? It does not seem too much to expect that some clue would be given to 'where knowledge of the method . . . would be significant'.

Para. 6 deals with disclosure of changes in accounting method. Its stipulations would improve interperiod comparability of financial statements. But it does nothing to improve interfirm comparability.

Superficially, DS11 *appears* to be desirable, since a 'proper appreciation' of reported figures is desirable. But its stipulations do not remove the impediment to comparison which is the consequence of diversity. There is grave danger that it may be supposed to do so and that the impact of any drive to reduce diversity will be lessened by it. It is vague, ambiguous and permissive—and easy to swallow. In medical parlance, it is a placebo—'a medicine given to humour or gratify a patient rather than to exercise any curative effect'.

238

Conclusion

I have chosen to examine what seemed to be important rather than trivial features of the published standards. It is important that any standard statement shall deal clearly with its topic so that accountants, for whose direction it is intended, shall understand clearly what they are expected to do, and why. It is important that the product of applying any standard (and all standards together) shall be serviceable, as information, to those who rely on financial statements for guidance in making judgements and choices or decisions. On both counts the statements exhibit, not isolated and different but, recurrent and similar defects.

At the simplest level there is lack of clarity about the meaning of pertinent terms. The style of the statements shows that definition is believed to be necessary; many of them have introductory 'definitions' sections like the opening sections of statutes. But many terms which are vital to the understanding of a prescription or its underlying argument are undefined. 'Arising' in 'profit arising' (DS1.2), 'service potential' (DS4), 'distortion', 'mis-statement' and 'information needs' (DS7) and terms like them are not defined; their meanings are certainly not obvious; and they are by no means trivial terms in the places where they occur.

There is bias, or lopsidedness, or differential emphasis, where opposite aspects of some general phenomenon should be treated as counterparts and logical equals. The differential treatment of revaluation gains (DS1.2) and of future tax liability and future tax benefits (DS4), the neglect of appreciation (DS5), the failure to deal with matters said to be pertinent (DS7)—these are examples. Some of these things may be due simply to oversight; some seem to be due to undisclosed predispositions (such as conservatism) of the draftsmen. In any case bias, by omission or emphasis, is a defect from which standard specifications should be free.

There are contradictions and incompatabilities. Periodic profit appears, at first glance to embrace all gains and losses—but there are exceptions, and exceptions to exceptions (DS1.2). There is implicit (and sometimes explicit) endorsement of the historical cost basis—but there is also explicit recognition, without censure, of other 'substitute' bases (DS5). Basic concepts turn out not to be basic, since they can be set aside (DS11).

Overriding all these specific flaws is the absence of any general indication of the functions of the information which financial statements alone can provide. The uses made of the information are known; specific uses have been mentioned, briefly but sufficiently, in five sections of this paper. But there is no reference in the standards so far published to the particular uses of the figures in analysis, diagnosis and judgement formation. It is as if accountants were being directed to construct a machine the capacity and function of which is not known, or is secret. It is reminiscent of the eighteenth-century prospectus for a project 'the nature of which is hereafter to be disclosed'. In the absence of such general specifications of the product and its uses, it should not be surprising that the

239

five statements do not stand up well to tests of the usefulness of the information they generate.

Three final observations.

The defects noticed (and others not mentioned) occur also in the exposure drafts issued on other topics. Whether they will be eradicated before those drafts turn into standards I do not know. I mention the point only to indicate that the defects are epidemic. It is said that mighty oaks from little acorns grow; so do mighty cancers from little deviant cells; and mighty errors from poorly designed arguments and instructions.

Second, many of the statements show unmistakable signs that they were not 'made in Australia'. No objection can be taken to importing good and clear statements of principle manufactured elsewhere. But, equally, there is no good ground for importing defective statements, especially when the defects have long attracted critical attention at home and abroad. We can do without Trojan horses.

240

Third, some may think that to follow my A, B, C, steps would be costly and lead to voluminous standard specifications. That need not be the case. To produce the present standards has been costly, and to eradicate what I see as their flaws (or even to debate their meanings in countless offices across the country) will be even more costly. The more we have of the same style the more costly it will be. As for volume, the five standards examined occupy some forty printed pages. The specifications of my categories A and B have been sketched in this paper in no more than a few pages. If some such statement of the functions and style of financial statements were adopted as a framework, I am confident that what now takes forty pages could be said in a fraction of the space with greater clarity, less hedging, less convoluted argument and greater overall consistency. To my mind Standards having these characteristics are what the profession (and its public) needs and deserves. And should demand, as a matter of professional idealism and integrity.

Fair Financial Reporting–In Law and Practice
October 28, 1976

It is a considerable honor to present this lecture, named for Dr. Emanuel Saxe. I have long known his name, his reputation, and his association with Baruch College. But I met him personally only a few weeks ago, to be charmed by his geniality and awed by his firm and detailed grasp of the past and the present of accounting. This lecture will span a period of the past up to the present, of which he will have far greater and more intimate knowledge than any of us.

The standard auditor's unqualified opinion avers that the financial statement presents fairly the financial position of the subject company at a stated date, and the results of its operations and the changes in its financial position during the year then ended. It goes on to refer to conformity with generally accepted accounting principles and consistency with their application in the previous year. The opinion is the end-product of the auditor's work. By virtue of it, the financial and commercial community relies on financial statements, takes them to be "fairly" indicative of what has transpired. But there are several reasons why that reliance or confidence is not, as yet, justified. Those reasons strike at the very heart of present accounting practice, for which cause they deserve close analysis.

AUDIT CERTIFICATE: REPORT OR OPINION?

The setting of the phrase "present fairly" may be approached by considering the nature of the document in which it now appears. No more than 50 years ago[1] that document was generally described as a "certificate." It began: "We certify that...etc." To certify, of course, is to give an assurance of propriety, or veracity, or authenticity. That, surely, is the basic function of auditing. Those who rely on accounts, even when "those" were primarily the directors and senior executive officers of companies, need some assurance that what the financial statements state is worth depending on. The document then described as a "certificate" contained other words which support this idea. The balance sheet was said "to correctly set forth the company's position", and the profit and loss account was said to be correct. Other phrases used were "correctly record," "exhibit a true and correct view," "properly drawn up so as to show," "represents the true financial position." Some of these words are traceable to English law and practice. As early as 1844 it was enacted that directors of registered companies should cause "a full and fair balance sheet" to be made up periodically. Much later "a true and correct view," and later still "a true and fair view," was required by law to be given by the financial statements. In a number of decisions, the English courts held that "the accounts must show the truth," that a balance must "convey a truthful statement as to the company's position," and that an auditor must see that the balance sheet "was a true and accurate representation of the company's affairs." The same ideas occur in the works of Hatfield and Paton of 40 years ago.[2] To assert the veracity or authenticity of the accounts was implicitly proper; there was no other reason than that for the engagement of an outsider to audit the accounts—in England or in the United States.

But "certify" did not seem to be the proper word to use in a report which also contained the words "in our opinion." As an editorial in the *Journal of Accountancy* of July 1931 opined: "It is absurd to speak of certifying an opinion." That is verbal quibbling, but it did have a point. From about 1931 "certify" was abandoned; the auditor's statement was described as a report; and it took the form: "We have examined the accounts...etc. In our opinion...etc." The change may have eased the minds of accountants. But it did not affect the function of the report. In a letter to the presidents of listed corporations in January 1933, the President of the New York Stock Exchange stated that the public response to an announcement of the intention to require audited statements with listing applications indicates clearly that "...independent audits are regarded by investors as a useful safeguard."[3] There could be no such safeguard if they were not believed to give assurance of the veracity or authenticity of audited financial statements.

More recently still, the auditor's statement has come to be described simply as an "opinion." This has removed the *appearance* of giving assurances of any kind to users of financial statements. But it has not removed the *function* of an audit or an auditor's opinion. It may have tended to cause auditors to relax their vigilance, especially under the cover of the phrase "in conformity with generally accepted accounting principles" introduced about 1939. However the number of legal suits involving auditors over the last 15 years should be warning enough that the use of the word "opinion" has provided no safe shelter.

The shift from "certificate" to "report" to "opinion" appears to signify a gradual attrition of responsibility for the veracity or authenticity of the contents of financial statements. The shift may now seem trivial or superficial. For decades, however, the profession has agonized over the forms of words it would adopt as descriptive of the audit report. And through that period of erosion, as we shall suggest, the substantive matters to which the report or opinion relates have gone unnoticed or suffered similar erosion.

"PRESENTS" WHAT?

The Balance Sheet. In the twenties, audit reports said of the balance sheet that it "correctly recorded the condition of the company's affairs," or that it "represented the true financial position of the company," or that it "showed the financial condition of the company," or simply that it "correctly set forth the company's position." For a time during the Thirties and Forties, reference was made to "condition" or "position" without the qualifying term "financial." For the last 25 years "financial position" has been in common use. In England and other countries taking their corporation laws from that source, the corresponding term for a very long period was "state of the company's affairs"; more recently "financial position" has come into use.

It is a striking curiosity, or oversight, or act of negligence, that nowhere in the vast professional output of statements on accounting and auditing practice, in the United States or abroad, has financial position been described or defined. There are countless and voluminous detailed descriptions or prescriptions on particular balance sheet items. But there is no general framework indicating what a balance sheet is intended to represent. The professionally endorsed view, in the United States and elsewhere, has long been, and still is, that a balance sheet is a list of account balances. But the rules for arriving at those balances never at any point make reference to the representation of a dated financial position.

Some of those rules are perfectly proper, even in the context of deriving a statement of financial position. If there are discrepancies between the book balances and the actually *discovered* amounts of cash and receivables and payables, those balances are adjusted to their discovered amounts. But for all other items, no attempt is made to assert that the *discovered* money amounts, at or near a balance date, shall be the basis of closing adjustments and of the balance sheet. And no effort is made to argue that, in respect of those other items, the balances are in any way related or relatable to financial position.

Notwithstanding this neglect or oversight on the part of the profession, it is tolerably certain that the rest of the financial community expects a balance sheet to represent the *wealth* at the command of a company and the respective legal-financial interests in that wealth at a stated date. Bankers, financiers, creditors and analysts are interested in aggregate wealth, its composition and its growth; in the relationship of money available (or shortly to become available) and money shortly to be payable—the current ratio: in the relationship of the money amount of total debt to the money amount of owners' equity in the net assets—the leverage ratio: and in the relationship of periodical net profit to the amount of net assets—the rate of return. None of these magnitudes or relationships is of any guidance or use unless the balance sheet *does* represent assets by their dated money amounts or dated money equivalents.

The characteristic features of wealth are well attested in the literature of economics. Everything which is exchangeable is a part of the wealth of its possessor (Smith, 1776; Cournot, 1837; Mill, 1848; Fawcett, 1863; Marshall, 1890; Hobson, 1911; etc.[4]) The magnitude of wealth is its "exchangeable value" (Smith), the amount which goods in possession "would sell for" (Mill), their "value in exchange" (Cournot), "marketable articles taken at their market value" (Hobson). From Smith to Keynes (1936),[5] wealth has signified the "power of purchasing" "unspecified goods at unspecified times"—in short, general purchasing power at a stated date. All of these usages of course conform with general usage and understanding. Further, when reference is made to persons or firms which borrow, net wealth or capital is the aggregate of wealth (calculated in the manner just described) minus the amount of outstanding debt (e.g., von Mises, 1949; Shackle, 1970).[6]

These references to the literature of economics should not be taken lightly, as mere "theoretical" constructions. Any examination of the publications of the stock exchange information services, any examination of the finance and accounting literature dealing with the interpretation and analysis of accounts, and any examination of the daily and periodical press comment on the states of business firms, will support the contention that current ratios, leverage and the composition of assets from time to time are of practical significance to a variety of persons or institutions concerned with

243

the financial affairs of business; a wide range of examples is given in Chambers, *Securities and Obscurities*. And given that these indicators are based on asset aggregates, it follows that all the component amounts of assets must be of the same kind; for otherwise the components would not be aggregable. It is futile to expect a "financial position" to be "fairly presented" if the asset components are represented variously by actual money amounts (e.g., for cash, receivables and payables), by historical costs (e.g., for investments in land and marketable securities), by depreciated historical costs (e.g., for plant and machinery, vehicles and buildings) and by such other odd amounts as LIFO, the lower of cost and market prices, and so on (e.g., for inventories). Aggregates of such amounts have no meaning whatever; they fairly present nothing in the nature of a dated financial position. Only if assets are represented by their "dated market values," "dated values in exchange" or "dated money equivalents" are their amounts aggregable, and in the aggregate indicative of a dated financial position.

The Income Account. Just as "financial position" has never been adequately described or specified, neither has "income." The usual unqualified opinion of an auditor refers to "the results of operations." This phrase, "the results of operations," is vague; for "operations" may be as extensive as all the events and transactions which affect a firm, or as restricted as whatever is meant by "normal trading operations." Attempts to limit its meaning have never been successful, as the persistence of the "all-inclusive" notion of income testifies.

In some jurisdictions, beyond the United States, the income (or profit and loss) account is expected by law to give a true and fair view of a company's "profit or loss" or "results" for the period specified. This may appear to be less confusing than "results of operations." But in any case, in those jurisdictions as in the United States, there has been no serious attempt to define income or results. It is still common to find the view expressed that "there is no single concept of income which is serviceable for all purposes," and then to find this taken as good reason for specifying no concept whatever.

In commonsense usage "income" is what comes in. In ordinary personal affairs what comes in is so much money per period. In commercial affairs what comes in is a consequence or resultant of revenues and outlays—both of money. That resultant is thus an *increment* in something which a company or firm had before (i.e., at the beginning of a period). For a purely cash business, the increment is a cash increment. But in all other types of business, what the firm has at the beginning of a period is its net wealth or net assets. The periodical increment is thus an increment in net assets.

Now, first, it is just as important for a firm to know the increment in its net assets as it is for a person to know his cash income. To know it enables the firm to compare increments of successive periods, to regulate its disbursements by way of dividends, to consider claims made against it for higher wages or lower prices, to plan accumulations of money or other assets to meet debts, to extend its business and so on. All of these matters entail getting money in or paying money out. It follows that if a calculated income amount is to be serviceable in these connections, income must be an increment in money or the equivalent of money.

Second, "increment" can only have a comprehensible meaning if the increment is the same in kind as the base from which it is calculated. An increment in a net asset total which includes assets at divergent valuations is meaningless.

From these two considerations and the perceding discussion of financial position, it should be clear that only a system of accounting which makes use of one valuation method will yield intelligible figures for assets and income, and figures which are consistent with one another; and that only if the valuation method is "dated value in exchange" or "dated money equivalent" will the balance sheet be serviceable as indicating "financial position" and the income account be serviceable as indicating a genuine increment in net wealth or general capacity to pay dividends, make new investments, repay debts and make other such financial arrangements. Further still, only if income and net wealth (i.e., capital employed) are thus calculated will the rate of return be a mathematically proper percentage and a percentage directly comparable with rates of interest or rates of return on straight money contracts.

This notion of income is supported by economists, just as is the notion of wealth already mentioned. The works of Simons (1938), Hicks (1946) and Lipsey and Steiner (1966)[7] are quite specific on the matter. The clearest judicial discussion of profits to my knowledge is that of Fletcher Moulton, L.J., in the *Spanish Prospecting Co.* case of 1911.

> Profit "is the amount of gain made by the business during the year. This can only be ascertained by a comparison of the assets of the business at the two dates [which define the year] ... Even if the assets were identical at the two dates it would by no means follow that there had been neither gain nor loss because the market value—the value in exchange—of these assets may have altered greatly in the meanwhile. ... To render the ascertainment of the profits of a business of practical use it is evident that the assets, of whatever nature they may be, must be represented by their money value."

245

Further, this is the notion widely entertained by those who rely on financial statements. The income account and the balance sheet are expected to be integrally related. They are expected to be "taken as a whole", even by those who have formulated the principles of present practice.[8] The statements cannot be significant "as a whole," however, unless there is a consistent set of rules governing the whole of their contents.

Needless to say, the present rules are varied, variable and inconsistent among themselves. Accounts based on them represent particular elements of company affairs in different fashions and cannot possibly convey any realistic impression of those affairs as a whole. And the availability of alternative rules makes it possible for companies to select sets of rules which "on the whole" grossly misrepresent income. There have been classic cases of this—in Australia, the Reid Murray Holdings affair and others in the early Sixties: in the United Kingdom, the Pergamon Press affair and others in the late Sixties; and in the United States, the Penn Central affair and others like it. In all these cases, the rules used were all tolerable under "generally accepted principles"; but taken together their effect was quite intolerable. The Chairman of the SEC, commenting on the Penn Central case, observed that "reported income was not of a character to make a contribution to the pressing debt maturities or liquidity needs of Penn Central, nor was it of the sort that might reasonably be expected to be evidence of continuing earning power."[9] Note the words "a contribution to the pressing debt maturities or liquidity needs." This clearly implies that " income" is expected to be indicative of a real money inflow, not just a conventionalized product of a conventional calculation.

"GENERALLY ACCEPTED ACCOUNTING PRINCIPLES"

The present audit report in some sense qualifies the words "present fairly" by use of the phrase "in conformity with generally accepted accounting principles." Reference in the report to "accepted principles of accounting" dates from about 1933, and the phrase "generally accepted accounting principles" from 1939. The abandonment of words suggesting "truth" or "correctness" is indicative of some apprehension that the figures being produced *could not* be described as true or correct; and the introduction of the reference to generally accepted accounting principles seems to have been intended to put users of financial statements on notice of what has been called the "limitations" of financial statements. But the notice is almost completely nugatory.

If there had been, or if there were now, an identifiable set of generally accepted accounting principles, or if "generally accepted" meant accepted by *most* accountants or reporting companies, the qualifying phrase would have been serviceable. But in fact there is scarcely a single practice or rule which is endorsed or followed by *most* companies or accountants; for almost every item in the accounts there are two or more possible rules. And there is no clear source of what are generally accepted principles. *Statement on Auditing Standards No 5* of the AICPA (July 1975) indicates the varied and diffuse sources of "accepted principles." They include (1) statements and interpretations issued by the Financial Accounting Standards Board, (2) APB statements and opinions, (3) AICPA accounting research bulletins, (4) AICPA accounting interpretations and statements of position, (5) AICPA industry audit guides and accounting guides, (6) industry accounting practices (7) pronouncements of other professional associations, (8) statements of regulatory agencies, such as the SEC, (9) accounting textbooks and articles and (10) common business usage. This whole array of sources is so open-ended that it is no exaggeration to say that *almost anything* can be a "generally accepted principle."

It is this undisciplined, unstructured character of the corpus of principles which has defeated the protective intentions of the legislation. Professor Sanders, a consultant to the SEC in its early years, was of the opinion that the Securities Act of 1933 was intended to require a balance sheet which was actually a statement of financial condition at a specified date.[10] Only such a balance sheet would "provide full and fair disclosure of the character of securities," as the title of the Act proposed. But the SEC itself, by adopting rules which have persisted ever since the Thirties, seems to have undermined that intention. For there is *no possibility* that a balance sheet, in which past prices of assets, present holdings of cash and estimates of future expectations, are aggregated, can represent the financial condition of a company at a specified date.

The present state of the art has been roundly denounced. Only a few years ago, Bayless A. Manning, then Dean of the Stanford School of Law observed: 'It is clear that what we call accounting and the standard methods of accounting are of remarkably limited usefulness for purposes of figuring out what is going on in the real world of economic activity."[11] A staff report of the Federal Trade Commission published in 1969 pointed out the desirability of accurate and consistent representations in financial statements but also pointed out that inconsistencies in practice made comparisons of the statements of successive years and of different firms impossible.[12] In a number of litigated cases, in the United States and elsewhere, defences based on practice in conformity with generally accepted accounting principles have been found insufficient, because those practices yielded unrealistic figures.

246

The list of sources of generally accepted principles mentioned previously should itself make plain the fact that the whole art is esoteric in the extreme. No one but an accountant is likely to have access to, or to be able to comprehend, the array of material specified. Which means that the whole intention of communication is circumvented. Accountants have been so concerned with their "mechanics" that they have disregarded the informative and instructive function of accounts. It is as if no one could expect to use a car or a watch unless he understood the principles of their construction. But as Professor Kripke has observed "...accounting cannot be a closed system based on rules that are meaningless and misleading to others."[13]

The recent proposal of the SEC (ASR 190, March 1976), that information based on replacement costs should be given in supplementary form, threatens to introduce even more variety and inconsistency into the accounting process. It is true that the figures are not yet required to be embodied in the accounts proper. But the open-ended nature of the proposal and the freedom of experimentation it permits, is almost certain, if past experience is any guide, to reinforce the present well established practice of idiosyncratic, non-interpretable, accounting.

In another place I have examined the notion of a "true and fair view" of position and results which is required in jurisdictions under the English pattern.[14] My examination was by way of the established law relating to the interpretation of statutes. Its conclusion is that "true and fair" must be interpreted in their ordinary and natural sense. I believe this to be well supported by the frequency with which references to "true financial position", full and fair portrayal of "the actual financial condition", "realistic reflection of the true situation" and similar words occur in the dicta of the courts and commissions in the United States and elsewhere.[15] There are no other words which could possibly describe the kind of information necessary for informed judgements of the wealth and progress of companies from time to time.

CONCLUSION

When the discussion of what financial statements purport to do gets fragmented, it is perhaps necessary to consider the fragments. What I have tried to do in this paper is to point out that hitherto the professional discussion has disregarded the major fragments—the meaning of "financial position" and the meaning of "results." These things have to do with real money's worth, not just with book balances. Book balances may be made up from imagination, expectation and wild guesses; but that was not the intention of the securities laws. They were and are good laws, in my view. It is only the practice under them which has gone astray.

A financial position cannot be expressed otherwise then by dated quantities of dated dollars, representing actual wealth at the stated date. And my wealth, your wealth and the wealth of any corporation cannot be stated otherwise than by reference to the values in exchange or market selling prices of assets. That is an idea common to and understandable by all people; it is therefore *fair* to all people who have dealings with companies. Results cannot be significant unless they represent an increment in wealth. And that too is an idea understandable by all kinds of people. Those are the basic ideas upheld in common criticisms of financial statements, in litigation where the propriety of financial statements has been in question, and by users of financial statements no matter what their financial interests have been. Never yet have I encountered any circumstances in which people anxious to know the financial positions and results of companies have wanted to know the historical costs, or the estimated future replacement prices, or the price level adjusted historical costs of assets. As representations of position and results those kinds of figures are meaningless, irrelevant. I have no time to expound here the style of accounting I have described as continuously contemporary accounting, CoCoA, for short. But because it is based on the periodical rediscovery of the money equivalents of assets, it alone gives up to date and realistic representations of financial positions and results. It alone is free of the subjective choices of accounting method and free of the subjective expectations of corporate officers. It alone would free auditors from the quicksands of the presently indefinable set of generally accepted accounting principles. Only of its products could it be boldly said that they *fairly present* the financial positions and results of companies.

NOTES

1. For the dating of the use of some of the ideas and terms to be mentioned I have drawn on the excellent survey of George Cochrane, "The Auditors' Report: Its Evolution in the U.S.A.," *The Accountant*, November 4, 1950.
2. For details see Chambers, *Securities and Obscurities*, 1973, Ch.3.
3. See Hunt (ed.), *Twenty Five Years of Accounting Responsibility*, Essays and Discussions of George Oliver May, Vol 1, p.127.
4. Adam Smith, *The Wealth of Nations*, 1776; Augustin Cournot, *Mathematical Principles of the Theory of Wealth*, 1837; J.S. Mill, *Principles of Political Economy*, 1848; H. Fawcett, *Manual of Political Economy*, 1863; A. Marshall, *Principles of Economics*, 1890: J.A. Hobson *The Science of Wealth*, 1911.
5. J.M. Keynes, *The General Theory of Employment, Interest and Money*, 1936.
6. "Capital is the sum of the money equivalent of all assets minus the sum of the money equivalent of all liabilities as dedicated at a definite date to the conduct of the operations of a definite business unit," L. von Mises, *Human Action*, 1949, p.262. Similarly G.L.S. Shackle, *Expectation, Enterprise and Profit*, 1970, p.28.
7. H.C. Simons, *Personal Income Taxation*, 1939; J.R. Hicks, *Value and Capital*, 1946; Richard G. Lipsey and Peter O. Steiner, *Economics*, 1966.
8. See A.I.C.P.A., *Statement on Auditing Standards No 5*, July 1975.
9. Staff Report of the Securities and Exchange Commission, *The Financial Collapse of the Pen Central Company*, 1972, p.x.
10. T.H. Sanders, "Accounting Aspects of the Securities Act", *Law and Contemporary Problems*, Vol 12, No 2, April 1937, p.195.
11. Henry G. Manne (ed.), *Economic Policy and the Regulation of Corporate Securities*, 1969, p.85.
12. *Economic Report on Corporate Mergers*, 1969, p.120
13. Homer Kripke, "The S.E.C., The Accountants, Some Myths and Some Realities", *New York University Law Review*, Vol 45, No 6, December 1970.
14. "Accounting Principles and the Law", *Australian Business Law Review*, Vol. 1, No. 2, June 1973.
15. For a recent interpretation of the U.S. law, consider the judicial opinion in *Herzfeld* v. *Laventhol, Krekstein, Horwath & Horwath* (1974): "The policy underlying the securities laws of providing investors with all the facts needed to make intelligent investment decisions can only be accomplished if financial statements fully and fairly portray the actual financial condition of the company."

ACCOUNTING PRINCIPLES AND PRACTICES — NEGOTIATED OR DICTATED?

One morning in 1966 I had breakfast in the Berkeley Faculty Club with an Italian epidemiologist. He had just been to an international conference at which the results of a carefully planned series of observations on a certain disease were reported. To the disappointment of those experts, the reported observations in a number of countries over five years showed no serviceable correlation between factors they had suspected to be causally related. To the surprise of my breakfast acquaintance, the conference decided to do the exercise all over again in the next five years. Said he: "They were experts in the design of tests and the making of observations. There was no hint of a flaw in their procedures. Left to themselves, experts in countries less wealthy than others would rather have tried something different than repeat a fruitless exercise. But the conference, in its unwisdom, decided to do it again".

The incident has parallels over and over again in the annals of accounting (as, indeed, it has in other fields of inquiry). We go no further back than 40 years. In 1936 the American Accounting Association sponsored *A Tentative Statement of Accounting Principles;* in 1939 it sponsored Paton and Littleton's *Introduction to Corporate Accounting Standards;* in 1966 it sponsored *A Statement of Basic Accounting Theory.* These were intended, as it seems, to be reasonably comprehensive statements of principle. The A.I.C.P.A. took a rather different route. Its Committee on Accounting Procedure (1939-1959) dealt with specific difficulties as they became troublesome. The Accounting Principles Board seems to have proceeded in the same fashion. The idea that there would emerge a comprehensive and consistent body of principles, rules and practices may have lurked beneath this work; but of itself it was piecemeal. The Financial Accounting Standards Board seems to be proceeding similarly. Corresponding committees in the United Kingdom, Canada, Australia and elsewhere have also adopted what is essentially an opportunistic, piecemeal program.

1

What makes all of these exercises parallel with that of the epidem-
iologists is that in essence they have all been the same in kind.
There have been repeated attempts to do the same thing; and that
has been to derive accounting principles by negotiation.

Principles by Negotiation

In this paper I shall give a rather wide meaning to negotiation.
It will embrace the deliberations of committees of accountants, and
of committees including accountants and other varieties of experts.
It will include negotiations and interchanges of a formal kind between accountants and other parties, such as the stock exchanges,
the legislature and its auxiliary apparatus and the regulatory bodies.
It will embrace the responses of the profession to the hints, demands or directions of regulatory bodies, the courts, the legislature
and the commercial and financial establishment. It will also include
the responses of individual practitioners to the express or imagined
hints, demands or directions of clients.

It may seem odd to use "negotiation" of such an array of different
processes. The common element in them all, however, is the adaptation of the services given or to be given, or the principles avowed
or to be avowed, to the differing demands of two or more parties.
The examples cited in an earlier paragraph of exercises within the
profession may not seem to be negotiation. But anyone who has
been involved in the work of professional committees will be aware
of the "political" nature of the process, of the fact that the members
of committees have differing understandings of the matters at issue,
and differing expectations of the personal and professional consequences of different possible "conclusions". The "trading" that goes
on in such committees is not usually as crude as primitive haggling
in the market place. But the effect is very similar. The majority of
the members reach some compromise with which, at least for the
moment and for the sake of the committee, they are satisfied. Professional responses to the hints, suggestions and directions of others
may not seem to be negotiated either. However, they are accom-
modations to the views of others exactly as are the conclusions or
recommendations of formal negotiating or deliberative bodies.

Responses to Hints and Suggestions. To consider first the responses of the profession to the hints and demands of others will
lay some foundation for the difficulties we shall contend to be the
Achilles heel of committees. Consider some examples.

2

(a) When, in England, the legislature was considering the incorporation of limited liability companies, it was strongly contended that financial publicity was a necessary protection of creditors, a *quid pro quo* for their loss of the protection of unlimited liability. An act of 1844 required that a "full and fair balance sheet" be prepared annually. Later acts required auditors to state "whether, in their opinion, the balance sheet (was) properly drawn up so as to exhibit a true and correct view of the state of the company's affairs." The phrase later became "a true and fair view." In a number of litigated cases, the courts affirmed that the accounts must show "the truth" or "the true financial position" of the company.[1] The response of the profession was to use the words prescribed by the statutes. But never yet has the profession officially stated what it considers to be a "true and fair view" of the state of a company's affairs or what it understands by "financial position" or "state of affairs."

(b) Both in the U.K. and in the U.S.A., in the early decades of the growth of corporate business, emphasis appears to have been given, outside of the profession, to the interests of creditors. The utility companies were the principal public borrowers, and their loan securities were the principal form of private investment until the early twentieth century. In the U.S., the work of the mercantile agencies and the publication in 1917 of the statement "Uniform Accounting," were expressions of the demand for financial information on borrowers. Liquidity and solvency were the focus of attention. Now, liquidity is represented by the quantum of readily available assets, and solvency by the quantum of any (and, in critical cases, of all) assets, in relation to outstanding debts. These quanta are pertinent only if the assets in question are represented by their value in exchange. The document "Uniform Accounting" (republished in 1918 as "Approved Methods for the Preparation of Balance Sheet Statements") was the product of a joint exercise which included the American Institute. It envisaged the possibility in some circumstances of an appraisal of property by "disinterested outside experts"; but its general tenor was that asset values were to be based on costs. The exercise gave a fillip to the engagement of auditors for financial statements on the occasion of issues of loan securities. But the substantive question of the appropriate mode of asset valuation was by-passed.

(c) When, by the twenties, there was much greater public investment in ordinary stocks, the amount of periodical income became of importance. There developed a tendency among accountants to

3

assert that the income statement had now become more important than the balance sheet. The assertion became, in due course, a part of the standard dogma, where it still persists. But the dependence of corporations on lenders has persisted also. And the amount of income cannot be properly judged to be adequate or inadequate without reference to a firm estimate of the funds invested, and in use year by year, to earn it. The switch in interest from the balance sheet to the income statement was thus an opportunistic response, prompted by a simplistic view of the whole security investment business, and possible only by neglect of the continuing importance of liquidity and solvency. There could have been a response which respected the needs of both creditors and investors, a response which saw the two statements as integral, having functions both singly and in combination. Instead of this the "shift in emphasis" laid the ground for continued denigration of the balance sheet, even to the extent of proposals that the aggregation of its elements could be dispensed with. To this I will return in the second part of this paper.

(d) "Truth in securities" was the catchphrase of the New Deal legislation which included the creation of the S.E.C. There were clear signals that financial statements were not what they were expected to be. The requirement of the Securities Exchange Act of 1934 that statements be filed annually was intended to secure that the information they contained was up-to-date. At least that was the expectation as it was seen by Professor Sanders who served as a consultant to the S.E.C. He said: ". . . Congress . . . doubtless was thinking of the balance sheet mainly as it is customarily described in its own heading, a statement of financial condition as of a specified date; in other words a statement of present condition."[2] But in practice it turned out that the statements brought up to date the accumulation of historical cost figures — that was all. What was meant by "truth in securities" was never adequately explored. The cost doctrine became embodied in the administration of the Act, and this hardened its grip on the allegiance of practitioners and teachers alike. Of course, there were some senses in which accounting became better through the force of regulation. But they were not substantive senses — as the range and severity of disputes, differences of opinion and academic debates of the last 40 years have testified.

Other such circumstances have indicated a need for substantive changes in principles and practices. But, in the cases cited and in others, (i) the response was generally a token response only, (ii) it

4

was related to the immediate source of irritation only, (iii) it was not conditioned by antecedent or concurrent events, constraints or requirements, as any attempt to resolve problems progressively might be expected to be. The corpus of principles or practices was built up under the successive influences of legislation, creditors and bankers, investors and analysts, litigation and disputes, regulatory bodies and stock exchanges, all subject to the reluctance of managers, and sometimes of accountants, to adopt new practices. There has always been the possibility that the impacts of these successive influences could have yielded a gradually improved and more generally serviceable style of accounting. That would have been the direction of "evolution", so widely preferred among accountants to "revolution" whenever proposals for reform are aired. Clearly there were occasions for the reconciliation of interests; but the causes of confrontation were side-stepped.

Committees on Principles. The multiperson committee has long been the butt of the humorist and the sage. We have heard recently of the "Abilene paradox," the purport of which is that any group of people will tend to do what none of them singly would think it reasonable to do. The idea is newly named, but it is certainly not new. Almost everyone knows that "the best committee is a committee of one;" and that "the committee to invent the horse, came up with a camel." I am indebted to Doug Thomas, of the Canadian Institute of Chartered Accountants, for a story of the same genre. The secretary breezed excitedly into the office of her boss. "Lindbergh has flown the Atlantic and has just landed in Paris," she said. He took no notice. Five minutes later she tried again. He still took no notice. Five minutes later she tried again. He looked up and said: "Miss Jones, any man with determination and his mind on his job can fly the Atlantic. But please tell me when a committee flies the Atlantic."

Assignment to committees of the task of devising or revising principles is doomed from the outset. I doubt whether I can put the reasons, as I see them, any better than I have done in another place.[3] A committee is unable, by its nature, freely to engage and disengage from its immediate attention particular clusters of ideas in the search for worthwhile conclusions. To solve any problem it is necessary to hold the elements of the problem in sharp focus, while drawing successively on particular sets of ideas or experiences which promise, even if only vaguely, to assist in the solution. To solve any generalized problem, any problem of principle, the same process is necessary. But it is more difficult, since one must

5

consider the general import of sets of ideas or experienecs rather than their incidental or contingent features. It is possible for one person to take up, in succession, a series of possible ways of resolving a matter, to reject each way which fails, to remember the respects in which it fails and the respects in which it partially succeeds, to use these recollections in devising previously untried methods of solving the problem, and at last to reach a conclusion. It is possible, as I said, but it is not easy. It requires concentrated attention, and, as the history of ideas shows, it often requires long periods of reflection, disengagement, collection of evidence and further reflection — all with the benefit of the memory of previous reflections. It requires the concentrated attention of one mind.

But a committee has not one mind. It has many minds. At any stage in the deliberations of a committee, each member will have his own set of ideas in the back of his mind, waiting to be drawn upon, and each will tend to value his own ideas differently from those of other members. Debate follows. Sharp lines are drawn which prevent the free association of ideas and lead to premature commitment; or fuzzy lines are drawn, and the members are not clear about the ideas which are being associated. Committees are impatient with involved argument. They tend to brush aside evidence; or, when evidence is adduced, each member can be depended upon to meet specific evidence with specific counter-evidence, since each member is concerned more with the impact of his own specific experience on himself than with the *general* import of his experience and the experience of others. They tend to seek verbal consensus rather than convergence of evidence.

What have we then, as the products of committees? The examples which follow are only indicative. Any wider range of committee products will provide further examples of the same features.

(a) We have statements (recommendations, or standards) on component elements of balance sheets and income accounts without prior statements on the functions of financial statements — attempts to build a superstructure without a foundation. American, Australian, English, and now international, standards have been published on a variety of components (inventories, depreciation, investments in other companies, and so on); yet there is no general statement which would provide the framework within which the "sub-problems" (of dealing with components) may be or should be solved.

It is quite odd that no serious attempt was made to elucidate the "objectives" of financial statements until the 1970s. In 1961 I drew

6

the attention of an Australian committee to the lack of a framework, a specification of the functions of accounting, which could discipline the statements it then proposed to issue on specifics. It was unconcerned. The fact that security analysts and others make use of financial statements to derive indicators of short-run solvency (the current ratio), of leverage (the debt to equity ratio), of profitability (the achieved rate of return) and other such financial features of firms, should have been apparent for decades. But I can recall no committee which has considered the provision of reliable indicators of these features to be a determinant of the objectives or functions of accounting and which has considered seriously the conditions necessary for the provision of reliable indicators. Certainly the Study Group on the Objectives of Financial Statements and the U.K. Sandilands Committee did not do so. It seems that committees are unable, or reluctant, to think problems through to fundamentals, or are simply content to deal with superficial aspects of their tasks.

(b) We have statements endorsing alternative rules on particular matters, the application of which depends "on the circumstances." The way in which and the reason why the circumstances should determine the particular rule to be followed are never indicated. The use of the phrase is indicative to me of dispute, or doubt, or disinclination to be rigorous, among members of a committee. The committee has no clear thought, or none that it wishes to put under the scrutiny of others. Its internal "negotiations" have broken down, and the only way to "progress" its business is to leave the matter unresolved. Of course, "depends on the circumstances" leaves the way open to abuse of the rules; for, sooner or later, companies which find themselves in some kind of distress will find reasons for choosing the rule which is most advantageous or least disadvantageous to *them,* regardless of the interest of outsiders in knowing what has actually occurred. If the matter is serious enough, why, there's good reason to have another committee to do the whole thing over again.

(c) We have statements, or recommendations, or standards, which are internally inconsistent or self-contradictory; or statements which in series are contradictory. Most of the committee products which have come under my notice contain examples. It is nearly 50 years since Canning pointed out that many of the component products of traditional accounting are incompatible and that the financial statements themselves are thus internally inconsistent. It is nearly 40 years since Gilman pointed out that certain of the accepted doctrines or conventions are incompatible. I and a few others have continued to point out the same and additional solecisms. Last year I undertook an appraisal of the five Australian "standards" then officially operative. At numerous places they can be shown to be inconsistent.[4] The U.K. Sandilands Report is also well-spiced with inconsistencies and incompatibilities.[5]

(d) In many cases we have representations of proposals made by others on the matter under consideration by a committee, and appraisals made by the committee, presumably in the course of reaching its conclusions. But, in some cases the representations are not exhaustive — in some cases they are misrepresentations; in some cases a committee's conclusions stand up no better than other proposals it has rejected on a given "test;" and in some cases a committee's own conclusions violate the very tests which it used to screen out other proposals.[6]

Group Interaction: Some have said that accounting is too important a matter to be left to accountants (as another has said 'war is too important a matter to be left to generals'). So, here have been committees which have included bankers, industrialists, economists, union leaders, lawyers, security analysts and so on; there have been forums, conventions and symposia which have enabled accountants to interact with others; and there have been committees of accountants which, "in the spirit of democracy," have included people in professional practice, in commerce and in academic positions.

(a) One of the earliest examples of group interaction was the Committee on Cooperation with the New York Stock Exchange in the early 1930s. I suspect that it laid the foundation for the later use of the phrase "generally accepted accounting principles;" but it resolved no matter of principle. The Study Group on Business Income, set up in the late forties, had a very diverse membership. But its Report included provisos, caveats, and dissents by almost every member of the Group. The U.K. Sandilands Committee also had a diverse composition. But, although its Report carries no minority reports or dissents, it has abundant evidence of what seem to be unsuccessful attempts to reconcile different viewpoints.

(b) There must have been numberless occasions in the last 40 years of confrontations between accountants and other types of specialists in conferences, seminars and conventions. The intentions of the organizers of these events may reasonably be supposed to have been to expose participants to the views and experiences of specialists having different functions, making different uses of financial information, or having different attitudes towards accounting — all in the interest, presumably, of finding ways of meeting more satisfactorily the expectations of users, or influencing the expectations of users, of financial statements. None of these exercises in which I have participated, and none that have otherwise come under my notice, has had either of these two effects.

(c) There have been "mixed" meetings and committees of accountants probably since accountants first organized themselves. The interests and attitudes of public, industrial and academic accountants have appeared, from their utterances, to be diverse and in some respects opposed. To temper the differences, to remove the appearance of differences and perhaps in the hope of removing some of the causes of difference, committees of public accountants have often had token representation of other classes of accountant, and advisory committees to university departments of accounting have had token representation of public and industrial accountants. The phenomena are widespread, international. But there is no evidence to the effect that any of these gestures of cooperation or collaboration have brought the different groups closer to the clarification, rationalization or integration of accounting principles. Indeed, it seems plausible that these associations have had the effect of turning aside some academic accountants from the pursuit of organized knowledge to the acceptance of opportunistic rules and practices, however disorganized they may be.

257

CPA — Client Interaction. There is relatively little public information on the extent of "negotiation" between CPAs and clients. The relationship between the two is confidential. But scuttlebutt is plentiful: and there is at least some firm evidence of interaction. Not all cases of the appointment of "new" auditors have arisen from disagreement over accounting principles and practices; but some have. Not all allegations that professional firms yield to the wishes of clients or managements are well-founded; but some are. Why, otherwise, should an auditor agree — as many have done — to a change in accounting or reporting practices, when one of the general principles, widely accepted, is consistency in accounting? Why, otherwise, should an auditor leave himself open to litigation — as many have done — by agreeing to the use of practices or principles which fail to present fairly the positions and results of companies?

There are, on the record, details of cases where the accounting has turned out to be far from realistic.[7] But even in less extreme cases, negotiations, discussions and agreements have, I am sure, led to innovations which have increased the variety of methods and rules available, when for years the profession's leaders have avowed the desirability of reducing the prevailing diversity. For every kind of asset and liability (with the possible exception of "cash") there are at least two possible, generally acceptable, treatments, and for many items there are more than two.[8] Given this battery of possibilities, it needs only a moderate amount of ingenuity to make a case for an unusual rule, or an unusual application of a rule, when the object is to *improve the appearance* of the position and results of a company in trouble, or to *tone down the appearance* of a company that has been unusually successful. I am strongly of the opinion that many of the rules which have become generally accepted got their start in life from auditor-client discussions or negotiations in anomalous circumstances. The rise of new practices and newer uses of old practices in anomalous circumstances should make them suspect from the start, as practices yielding information of general application and utility.

In some cases, auditors and clients have found justification for particular practices in the vagueness of laws and regulations, and in the specific dicta of the courts in litigated cases arising from that vagueness. But litigated cases also deal with anomalous circumstances. Judgments given in them may be taken as indicative. But a trial is in essence a form of negotiation directed to what is fair and just between the parties. It is not a means of deriving or elucidating general principles. Indeed, there have been cases where, for lack of clear principles, the courts have been more tolerant of aberrant practices than, in my opinion, they should have been.

The Fruits of Negotiations. The styles of action, reaction and inaction indicated have several things in common. First, they have been responses to irritants, not analyses of the causes or sources of irritation. Each such irritant has been treated as standing on its own, not as systematically related to others. Second, they have been largely cosmetic. By circumlocution and prevarication, they have made it appear that there's nothing wrong which cannot be put right by a little coloring or touching up here and there; or that the alleged fault is a fault of application and interpretation, not a fault of principle. Third, they have been evasive, seeking to attribute "problems" to circumstances external to accounting, rather than admitting that those problems have arisen from the fictions and simplifications endorsed within, and only within, the profession. Fourth, they have been "bargaining" exercises, implicitly or explicitly. The whole business of receiving submissions, holding hearings, issuing exposure drafts and tentative statements is a process of polling

10

opinions to see just how far it is possible to go, or just how little it is necessary to do, in any specific, critical setting. It is a means of getting the greatest satisfaction (the least disturbance of the accounting status quo — in technique or presige) for a given sacrifice. There is little risk of embarrassment, though there has been some; for, although proposals are exposed to the profession as a whole, few indeed respond, and fewer still critically; and although there may be external critics, their views can often be set aside on the ground that "they do not understand the nature of accounting."

None of these observations should be taken as critical of the integrity, the assiduity, or the sense of duty to the profession, of those who initiate and take part in the kinds of exercise described. I have worked with many of them and have long been acquainted with others. Their aims and intentions are all commendable in some sense, admirable in some ways. Yet, taking a general view of the whole of the products of negotiation over the past 40 years, it cannot be said that the time, money and energy laid out have been justified by the results. The same problems continue to crop up; obviously they were not mastered by those who, previously, had turned their hands to their solution. This is by no means the first time that has been said. But apparently, it has not been heard, or heeded. Like the colleagues of the epidemiologist at my breakfast table, accountants seem to have been bound, committed, to the same routines as were found to be fruitless before. What else, then, is possible?

Principles by Dictation

I gave a wide and general meaning to "negotiation." It includes what some would consider as "dictation." But I shall use "dictation" of something less open to debate than the prevailing opinions of dictators, legislators or regulators. The work of the engineer, the chemist, the surgeon, the agronomist and of all their sub-species rests on things more fundamental than negotiation, compromise, political considerations and the weight of "popular" opinion. None of these things produced the *technical* knowledge by which the earth's materials have been shaped to man's ends; by which the earth's scourges are being brought under control; by which heart, kidney and other transplants have become possible; and by which it was possible to put a man on the moon. Friction, corrosion, chemical interaction, disease, gravity cannot be legislated out of existence by democratic, autocratic or "othercratic" processes.

If Copernicus had taken a poll of his fellow astonomers, he would never have concluded that the immediate universe is centered on the sun. If Harvey had taken a poll of his fellow surgeons, he would never have concluded that the blood circulated. If Newton had taken a poll of his fellow philosophers, he would never have concluded that there was a physical law descriptive of the "mutual attraction" of massive bodies. If the conclusions these men reached had never been reached, many of the technical inventions of their successors would never have been made. Progress in knowledge and technology turns on man's understanding of the nature of things about him. It is *dictated* by "the nature of things". That is the sense in which I shall use the phrase "principles by dictation."

The Nature of Things. What, then, is meant by "the nature of things?" Creditors and potential creditors have long made, and still make, use of financial information as a guide to the reliability of debtors and the security of debts. Shareholders have long used, and still use, financial information as a guide to earnings and dividend prospects. These uses are "in the nature of things." It does not matter how many creditors and shareholders do actually make use of this information. The laws which make information about these matters publicly accessible are intended for those who wish to make use of it. These laws also are in the nature of things. These uses and laws require, they dictate, that information pertinent both to creditors and shareholders shall be produced by some class of persons in respect to all ventures having creditors and shareholders. And since, in fact, (i.e., in the nature of things) no person other than accountants, and no processes other than accounting, are engaged in producing systematic information on the assets, debts and incomes of companies, the accounting process *must* yield information pertinent to the observed uses and users.

The imperative form of the conclusion is to be distinguished from the imperative form of any negotiated dictum. It is a logical imperative, given the premises on which it is based. It is not simply a contractual or agreed rule governing the behaviors of those who consent to be bound by it. It is a rule, failure to follow which entails failure to perform the stipulated function — failure to supply pertinent information.

Accountants may agree to be bound by the rules which their professional associations promulgate, even if those rules disregard the logical imperative. But rules of the latter kind will always be open to attack because they are inconsistent with the nature of

12

things. The disturbances which arose from the attempted prohibition of "flowing through" the amounts of investment credits, and more recently, the stipulation of different treatments of foreign assets and foreign liabilities, are among the more obvious instances of the consequences of failure to take account of the nature of things. Unquestionably, the debate which follows the announcement of any such rule is political in its style and object. But the occasion for discussion, debate and the display of political muscle, arises only because of proposals which fail to take account of the nature of things.

The Relatedness of Things. It is in the nature of things that objects, events and classes of persons are related, and that the financial interests of different classes of persons in objects and the outcomes of events are related. It is quite possible to ignore these relationships, to treat all items in accounts as isolates, and to assert of them propositions which disregard or implicitly deny those relationships. This is the most notorious consequence of setting up a series of specific and separate committees to produce statements on specified balance sheet or income statement items. It violates the nature of things.

The so-called "income-statement viewpoint" which regards the income account as the more important of the two financial summaries disregards the facts (i) that users of accounts calculate rates of return, current ratios and debt to equity ratios, all of which depend on balance sheet figures (and all of which are relationships); (ii) that income statement components and balance sheet components are simultaneously determined, no matter what criteria are used; and (iii) that the residual balance of an income account is itself a balance sheet item. The whole body of rules which provides for different types of valuation for different types of asset disregards the facts (i) that financial statements are aggregative (otherwise the ratios mentioned above could not be calculated, or, if calculated, would be meaningless); (ii) that different types of "valuation" cannot properly be aggregated; and (iii) that different prices (or valuations) ruling at different dates cannot properly be aggregated. The Committee on Terminology of the American Institute many years ago rejected any suggestion to the effect that "depreciation for the year is a measurement, expressed in monetary terms, of the physical deterioration within the year, or of the decline in the monetary value within the year, or, indeed, of anything that actually occurs within the year." This view, still widely current, disregards the facts (i) that a depreciation charge is a (negative) component of income,

13

the amount of which purports to be something that did actually occur within the year; (ii) that the depreciation charge affects the reported balance of assets at the end of the year, and hence the understanding of readers of what did occur during the year; (iii) that all conventional methods of calculating depreciation do relate to a postulated decline in monetary value; and (iv) that all users of financial statements expect and presume that depreciation does mean a periodical decline in monetary value.

In all of these cases (and there are others like them) the originators and popularisers of the notions indicated have disregarded the relationships between different accounts or account balances, the relationships between components and aggregates, or the relationships between sources and uses of information. They have ignored logical and practical imperatives. In some cases, it appears that accountants have, by definition, created their own reality, when the proper function of definition is to represent reality. "The lower of cost and market," "sum-of-the years digits depreciation," "deferred debits" are inventions; they exist by definition only, having no real-world counterpart. They follow the rule of Humpty-Dumpty: "When I use a word it means just what I choose it to mean." But those who live by this rule seem to overlook the fate of Humpty-Dumpty. In any case, they derive no firm principles rooted in the nature of things.

The notion that there can be no firm principles is an outgrowth of Humpty-Dumpty-ism. There are two varieties of it. On the one hand, it is suggested that accounting is a matter of policy, not of principle.[9] On the other, it is suggested that to every user there is a specific kind of information, uniquely suited to his needs, which he can purchase at a price.[10] But promoters of these ideas do not live by it themselves. If they believed what they assert, their articles would have to be prefaced by a statement of "composition policy," or they would write in code and offer the "key" at a price. But they know better than that. They write (most of the time) in the vernacular, using all of the common rules of literary composition (which, for writers in any given language are part of the nature of things) presumably because they wish to be understood. All this, while denying that there are also syntactical and semantical rules which should govern the form and style of financial communications so that they will be understandable by others who know "the language" of money symbols and money statements.

Simple and Complex Devices. A simple device will serve a simple function. The amount of cash in my possession determines what I can spend immediately. Knowledge of that amount is instrumental in choosing; it is a "device." But knowledge of the cash I possess is not the only knowledge I may need for a variety of other "cash-connected" choices. For those I need a more complicated device, but still one which includes provision of knowledge of my cash holdings. The more complex or varied the function(s) of any device, the greater the number of conditions it must satisfy.

The products of accounting are expected, in fact, to serve a great variety of functions simultaneously. They provide information on particulars, on sub-aggregates, on aggregates; on relationships between particulars, sub-aggregates and aggregates; on changes from time to time in particulars, sub-aggregates and aggregates, and on changes in the relationships between them. The products of accounting provide these kinds of information to different classes of persons having different, and in some respects opposed, interests in the financial aspects of firms, and interests in the financial aspects of different firms. The products of accounting must therefore satisfy the conditions of aggregation, relation, intertemporal comparison, interfirm comparison and interpersonal communication — all simultaneously.

The products of present forms of accounting may or may not serve the stated function well. But we can say they are "expected to serve," since we can observe the uses made of the information provided even though it is (unknown to users) faulty. Further, we are entitled to say that the "products of accounting" are expected to serve well, because there is no other device by which the specified information may be acquired. On the other hand, it is not necessary to suppose that every user shall demand or use all the information or the same bits of information. Now, (i) since all users of information on a specific firm may advance or interfere with the interests of the firm or of others related to it, and (ii) since no information generator can know how specific information will be used by any specific user in any specific circumstance, the principles governing information generation can be no less than will provide information pertinent to all users and uses.

Some Principles by Dictation. All of the substantive matters mentioned in the preceding paragraphs are "in the nature of things." We may then sketch some of the principles they dictate. The kinds of information we will assert to be required are indicated by numbers; the principles entailed by these requirements are indicated by letters. "N/T" will be shorthand for "in the nature of things," and the word which follows it will signify the field of practice or study in which the stated proposition is accepted or established.

In respect of all firms, some person or persons or institutions can be shown to have use for knowledge of —

(1) the dated dollar amounts of classes of assets and of total wealth (gross assets) from time to time.

(2) the dated dollar amounts of debts or liabilities from time to time.

(3) the dated dollar amount of the owners' equity in the assets (or the amount of net assets) from time to time.

    A. Since financial interests in all assets run to creditors and, residually, to owners (N/T-law), (1) = (2) + (3). This, of course, is the standard balance sheet equation.

    B. Since (1), (2), and (3) are aggregates, their components must be aggregable (N/T — mathematics, logic).

    C. Since the components of (1) and (2) include money, money receivable and money payable, all other components must be expressed in dated money equivalent terms (inference from A and B).

(4) the nominal amount of the periodical increment in (3).

    D. Part of the increment (4) will be due to changes in the balances of monetary items (mentioned in C) due to transactions or exchanges of money for goods or debts (N/T — commerce). Call this part (d).

    E. Part of the increment (4) will be due to unrealized changes in the money equivalents of non-monetary assets. Call this part (e). Since there is no way of deducing dated money equivalents from previously dated money equivalents (N/T — economics), all added money equivalents must be ascertained by observation when required. This, of course, satisfies the objectivity, or independent verifiability, test.

(5) that part of (4), which represents a genuine increment in net assets in the period. This part is regarded as income or profit (N/T — economics).

    F. The increment, (d) + (e), is nominal. When, in the period under consideration, there has been a change in the general value in exchange of the money unit the nominal amount of the increment must be adjusted to take account of the effect of that change on the opening amount of net

16

assets (N/T — mathematics). The change in the general value in exchange of the money unit is ascertained by reference to the change in an index of the general level of prices (N/T — economics). Call the amount of the adjustment to the opening amount of net assets (f). Then the amount of income or profit is (d) + (e) — (f).

(6) information similar to (1), (2), (3), (4), and (5) on other firms.

G. Comparisons may not be made of the figures of any two or more firms unless those figures have been derived by substantially uniform methods (N/T — mathematics). All firms must, therefore, follow substantially the same rules.

(7) information of the kinds (1) — (6) for successive dates or periods.

H. Comparisons may not be made of the figures of successive periods unless those figures have been derived by substantially uniform rules (N/T — mathematics). Whatever rules are used must be used consistently.

I. Comparisons may not be made of dollar amounts when the circumstance mentioned in F above arises. But intertemporal comparisons of dated ratios of identically dated amounts may be made (N/T — mathematics).

There is indicated a set of principles (A to I), *dictated by the nature of things.* At no point is there any resort to mere convention. It has been taken for granted, for the present purpose, that the kinds of information (1) to (7) are in fact used; their uses have been indicated elsewhere.[11] But the conclusions follow from well-established and testable knowledge. No amount of argument, it is suggested, can upset them. It is a relatively simple matter to deduce from them a set of quite tight rules of practice. As in all applications of principle, there is an element of art; for the varied and contingent features of particular applications may give rise to difficulties. For the resolution of these, and to secure uniformity (see G above), committees may well serve and serve well. But they may not violate the general principles without violating the expectations of those whom accounting serves. Such a framework of principles constrains the imagination and inventiveness of individual practitioners, their clients, and rule-makng committees. It provides assurance against the invention of conflicting rules; and against the production of information which is inconsistent with the independently ascertainable financial characteristics of firms. Negotiable rules provide no such safeguards.

17

The Future

My conclusions, indicated in the previous section, are not dictates of mine. I have tried to make it clear that they are the dictates of existing, well-organized and well-respected knowledge. I have not tried to "re-invent the wheel." I have simply used the established principles of "wheel-making" for a specific task, as all wheel-makers do. And there is plenty of evidence to the effect that that wheel will roll.[12] The only real impediment to putting it to use seems to be the belief that devising a technical device is a political and not a technical matter. That belief won't stand up. It has not been fruitful.

There are, of course, political implications of advances in all fields of technical expertise. Perhaps the greatest in recent times have been the implications of splitting the atom, of the invention of non-biodegradable products, of the use of processes which produce noxious wastes, and of the invention of the contraceptive pill. All of these things have affected masses of people. In some respects they have been "good," in other respects "damaging." But we could not benefit from the good, or learn to control the damaging, without the technical knowledge which yielded those things in the first place. Accounting is no different. Its producers are necessary for the efficient conduct of commercial and financial affairs. If, as it appears, those products are defective, causing misdirection and "stock-market pollution," there may be political pressure to improve it, but the precise ways of removing its defects are technical, not political, matters.

There have already been indications that public authorities may take an increasing part in determining accounting principles. To some this is a horrendous prospect. But the precedents are plentiful. It is the business of government to carry on things in the public interest which the private sector is unable or unwilling to do. And after the initial trauma, most of those who feared the worst have found the consequences less disastrous than they expected. But that is a side issue. Governmental determination or regulation is, according to my definitions, an example of negotiation, unless its advisors and technical experts choose to be guided by the nature of things rather than by what is popularly palatable. And it could be forestalled, I believe, by determined efforts within the profession to establish principles and practices on more solid grounds than what is popularly palatable within the profession.

As I have said elsewhere,[13] there is the possibility of a more fruitful partnership between the professional and the academic

266

18

communities. It is the business of researchers to attempt to find *general* solutions to classes of problems. It is the business of practitioners to find solutions to *particular* problems within the framework of the best general solutions known. The two classes of task are different. The researcher is (or should be) prepared to regard apparently diverse events as members of classes of events. The accounts of any one company, for example, provide an instance only of the accounts of many companies; the researcher's inquiries and judgments relate not to what is "good" or "bad" about the accounts of a particular company, but what is "good" or "bad" accounting or reporting by companies in general. And ideally, his conclusions and judgments are derived from observation and inference, not from personal and political considerations. (Recall that there is not a single personal or political element in the illustration of the derivation of principles in the previous section of this paper.) The practitioner is, on the other hand, very much involved in the personal and political aspects of clients' affairs; that is the nature of professional service. And that is the very reason why he needs a firm body of established non-personal principles — to protect himself and his client from allowing particular exigencies to interfere with the proper practice of his art.

The division of labor, between researcher and practitioner is the mode of operation in all well-developed technologies. In agriculture, in engineering, in medicine and in the host of technical specialisms based on physics, chemistry and biology, this kind of partnership is taken as the "natural" way of advancing technique. The orientation of the researcher is scientific;[14] that of the practitioner is in part technical and in part quasi-political. Confusion of the two stultifies the advancement of both. There is no good reason why the professional and academic communities should not respect each other for the specific functions each performs — the professional relying on the academic to produce innovative and ameliorative suggestions, proposals, theories; and the academic relying on the professional to consider those suggestions and proposals in depth and to try them out (experimentally, in the first place) for their feasibility.

The situation at the moment is a complete "stand-off". The practicing profession, both individual firms and professional committees and boards, are doing *ab initio* things which have long been argued and developed by the academic community, instead of devoting attention to critical and pointed appraisal of those arguments and experimentation with their conclusions. The spate of publications by firms and professional committees around the world could perhaps be justified if it produced some new insights. But a very great part of it is straight repetition — with all the defects, and scarcely ever with acknowledgement, — of what some "academic scribbler" (to use Keynes' words) has done long before. And on the other hand, although the profession has the means of trying out the new ideas produced by academics, I for one have been told repeatedly that a new idea will not be accepted unless *I* can show it works; and I have, as repeatedly, been asked about the technical treatment of specifics when, as I see it, that is a more appropriate problem for professional practitioners who have access to so many specific instances which they could contrast and compare in the search for an answer. There is also a "stand-off" within the academic community, the holders of opposing views doggedly sticking to them when exposure to some practical wisdom and experience could well resolve impasses and free all for something more progressive than mere debate.

I am not at all sure of the immediate future. But of this I am confident — that unless a "private sector" or a "public sector" authority directs the processes of accounting in accordance with the nature of things, accounting will continue to be a questionable guide to the administration of business and the conduct of the securities market.[15] If the accounting job were well done, there could open up the prospect of a fairer and more efficient commerce. As in other fields, a more exacting instrumentation would make possible more exacting diagnosis of the course of business, with greater prospect than in the past of avoiding the association of accounting with the "seamy side" of more or less free enterprise capitalism.

I could hope that this would be brought about by the self-correcting processes of scientific observation and inquiry. But how soon it will occur depends on the wisdom of those who manage the affairs of the profession. Much has been said about "educating" the community at large to expect less than they do expect of financial statements. This is entirely the reverse of what the present situation requires. What seems to me to be necessary is a re-education of the professional community so that it *does* produce what the community at large expects. That's a task on which the budgets of all the committees and boards now in existence could more profitably be spent then on inventing square wheels. Perhaps it is a task which only the next generation of accountants will be prepared to undertake. And it will only be so prepared if it accepts that accounting principles and practices are directed by the nature of things.

If there were no better future for accounting than the determination of its principles, rules and style by the interplay of naked or thinly-veiled self-interests — that is, by the process of negotiation — then there would be no future for research in accounting. We would be wise to abandon accounting to the whims of the manipulators. Accounting would then be no better than flotsam and jetsam on the murky backwaters of commerce. Or, to change the metaphor, we would have reached the age of "manipulators' lib"; the bra-burning of the zealots of "women's lib" would have its parallel in the book-cooking of the zealots of cosmetic accounting.

However, accounting *is* functional. For informed private and public policy formation, systematic and reliable financial information is indispensable. The present period of debate and confusion will pass. It will pass the sooner if attention is concentrated on the technical means of making accounting more serviceable, consistent with its observable functions. It will pass the sooner if research is directed to a full, meticulous and systematic understanding of the fundamental shape and structure of financial and commercial affairs — that is, to an understanding of the technical nature of technical things.

269

FOOTNOTES

[1] See Chambers, *Securities and Obscurities*, 1973, Ch. 3.

[2] T. H. Sanders, "Accounting Aspects of the Securities Act", *Law and Contemporary Problems*, Vol. IV, No. 2, April 1937, p. 195.

[3] Chambers, "The Anguish of Accountants", *Journal of Accountancy*, March 1972.

[4] Chambers, "A Critical Examination of Australian Accounting Standards", *Abacus*, Vol. II, No. 2, December 1975.

[5] See Chambers, *Current Cost Accounting — A Critique of the Sandilands Report*, I.C.R.A. Occasional Paper No. II, July 1976.

[6] See Chambers, "Continuously Contemporary Accounting — Misunderstandings and Misrepresentations", mimeo, December 1975. Also note 5, above.

[7] See *Securities and Obscurities*, Chs. 11-13. Other cases have since been reported.

[8] "At least two" is supported by Davidson and others, *Financial Accounting*, 1976, Ch. 15. A much greater variety of possibilities is suggested in Chambers, "Financial Information and the Securities Market", *Abacus* Vol. 1, September 1965.

[9] See Chambers, "Accounting Principles or Accounting Policies?", *Journal of Accountancy*, May 1973.

[10] See Chambers, "The Possibility of a Normative Accounting Standard", *Accounting Review*, July 1976.

[11]See, e.g., Chambers, *Securities and Obscurities,* 1973, Chapters 4, 10.

[12]See *Securities and Obscurities,* passim. For pertinent analogies see the introductory section of "Evidence for a Market Selling Price Accounting System" in Sterling (ed.), *Asset Valuation and Income Determination,* 1971; and introductory section of "A Critical Examination of Australian Accounting Standards", note 4 above.

[13]See reference under note 3 above.

[14]See e.g., Robert R. Sterling, "Toward a Science of Accounting", *Financial Analysts Journal,* September/October 1975.

[15]See also Chambers, "The Missing Link in Supervision of the Securities Market", *Abacus,* September 1969.

270

Inflation and the Reform of Accounting Education*

From its title, this paper may seem to be quite limited in scope. Accountants are concerned with many other matters than inflation and its consequences; and only relatively recently has inflation been of sufficient concern to arouse widespread interest in new accounting proposals. But I shall attempt to show that some of the ideas which it now seems necessary to impart in the educational process, by reason of experiences of inflation, are quite contrary to many of the ideas which have long been accepted in traditional practice. My conclusions will, thus, relate to the general bases and products of accounting. I shall be concerned with fundamental ideas, not simply with the various solutions or makeshifts that have been advanced under the general description of "inflation accounting". For, if fundamental ideas are well-grounded in commercial and financial experience and well-attested by the work of other scholars, and if those ideas are taken seriously as the determinants of a mode of accounting, many makeshift solutions will be found to be fallacious in principle and misleading in practice, especially under inflationary conditions.

My theses will be as follows:

(a) That the role of opinion and judgement has been permitted to outweigh the role of knowledge in the teaching and practice of accounting.

(b) That the characteristics of money, prices and inflation are commonly misunderstood, and are not taken into consideration in the teaching of accounting and in the revision of accounting practices.

(c) That the fundamental conditions of aggregation and relation have been almost completely disregarded in traditional accounting education and practice, and that this oversight has seriously impeded the development of a method of dealing systematically with the consequences of changes in prices and in the general level of prices.

---

* Presented at the Fourth International Conference on Accounting Education, Berlin, October 1977.

(d) That these misunderstandings and omissions will be eradicated only by more comprehensive and more exact treatment, in the educational process, of the fundamentals mentioned.

Opinion and Knowledge

In all disciplined fields of technical expertise, there are found bodies of propositions which are regarded as basic knowledge. They relate principally to the subject—matters of their fields. In law, there are misdemeanours, torts and crimes. Among the phenomena of medicine, there are diseases, malfunctions and injuries. In physics there are solids, liquids and gases. I mention only some more or less commonplace elements of the subject—matters of these fields. The object of the educational process is to teach what is known about those elements, to teach how to discriminate between them, and to teach the relationships between the many propositions which express what is known, so that practitioners will understand the subject matter of their field of practice as a systematic corpus of well-established conclusions. A lawyer is not at liberty, then, to regard a crime as a misdemeanour; nor does a physician treat a disease as he would an injury. Both, in practice, may use their judgement in the application of their knowledge; indeed, both must use their judgement in taking or prescribing any course of action the outcome of which is not known with certainty. But both proceed from what they regard as known facts or conditions, which have known antecedents and which have consequences which are known in principle.

It should be the same in accounting. But it is not. It should be **known**, for example, that goods cannot be bought or debts paid without money or things convertible into money. But, in accounting teaching and practice, assets are not represented by the amounts of money to which they are convertible at the date of representation. It should be **known** that the wealth and the net wealth of a firm are of importance to its managers, its owners or shareholders, its creditors and other parties. But, in accounting teaching and practice, the methods of valuation of assets are inconsistent with the common practice of determining wealth and net wealth, and inconsistent with the doctrine of a long line of economists reaching back from the present day to Adam Smith and beyond[1]. It is acknowledged that financial statements are messages or signals to others; and it should be **known** that no financial message is interpretable

272

except in terms of dated amounts of money and dated prices. But, in accounting teaching and practice, a great variety of magnitudes is used, many of which do not correspond with dated amounts of money and dated prices. It should be **known** what functions are served by financial statements and exactly in what ways they serve. But, in accounting teaching and practice, those functions are not specified; and the whole of the recent debate over the "objectives" of accounting shows that there is no clear and agreed notion of what those objectives or functions are[2].

Now all of the things I have said should be known (and others I have not mentioned) would provide firm foundations for a set of practices. But all of them are swept aside by assertions to the effect that they are either matters of opinion themselves, or that any quantification based on them will be a matter of opinion. In particular, when prices and the general level of prices change or are liable to change, it is said by some that prices on a given date do not represent the "real" or "true" financial significance of assets to a firm. We are not told what amounts **do** represent "real" or "true" financial significance. However, the practice of using original costs implies that they are "more real" or "more true" than any other money amounts. But if prices at a given date do not represent real or true significance, then neither do original costs; for they themselves are prices at a given date or dates. This kind of self-contradiction almost inevitably follows from attempts to set aside what is known or knowable and to set up in its place some imagined, opinion-based, substitute.

The clearest possible illustration of the dominance of opinion over reliable knowledge is the great variety of methods of dealing in financial statements with non-cash items. In English and American practice, at least, there are potentially millions of different permissible ways of deriving balance sheets and net profit figures[3]. There are no rules by which choices must be made between these alternatives; commonly the choice is said to "depend upon the circumstances". This leaves the matter subject entirely to the opinion of accounting or other officials of firms. Users of financial statements might expect, and they should be entitled to expect, that similar assets of different firms at any stated date would be represented by similar amounts of money. But in practice this is not the case[4]. The variety threatens to become greater, and the result more chaotic, as attempts are made to deal with the effects of inflation. Under the current cost accounting (CCA) proposals of the Sandilands Committee, non-monetary assets could be valued at initial (historical) costs, at depreciated actual replacement costs, at depreciated index-adjusted costs, at net realizable values, at "economic" (discounted net cash flow) valuations, and at the lower of replacement costs and net realizable values[5]. The range of options is greater than under any previously endorsed system. The resulting statements would be an amalgam of opinions to a greater extent than ever before. It would be poor service, indeed, to the commercial and financial community which needs up-to-date facts to inform its judgements and discipline its hopes and expectations.

Once the status of opinion is established, it is almost inevitable that proposals for dealing with the effects of shifts in prices and in the general level of prices will be judged by reference to opinion rather than by reference to argument and evidence. A classic example relates to the rise to popularity of the current purchasing power (CPP) variety of accounting in the United Kingdom and elsewhere over the period 1973-75. Little in the way of reliable knowledge was advanced in support of it. No specific evidence was adduced to the effect that investors or creditors had demanded to know, or could make use of, index-adjusted costs of assets. Its upsurge could only have been sustained by sheer belief in the opinions or judgements of its proponents. There are numerous other examples of the same course of events in the history of accounting practices. Many practices owe their endorsement to the process, described by Keynes in another context, of "anticipating what average opinion expects the average opinion to be". Neither good teaching nor good practice can be based on such unstable foundations.

All business is risky. Inflationary conditions increase the hazards. In risky conditions it is imperative, if one seeks to avoid their direct consequences, to know the present facts of a firm's financial state and progress. The process is one of continual re-discovery of the facts. Certainly, dated statements of fact become out-of-date rapidly in inflation; but that only makes rapid re-discovery the more important. This conclusion is completely disregarded by the process of periodically calculating asset values and asset-usage charges by reference to initial costs and opinions on the rate and pattern of recovery or amortisation of costs. The only element in this process which is independently testable, and which can therefore be reliable is the initial cost; the rest is guesswork. If nothing else has done so, the experience of inflation has indicated strongly the necessity of basing accounting principles on firm knowledge, and the necessity in practice of basing reported information on discovered facts. The established doctrine, in a nutshell, is: Take some out-of-date facts; form an opinion of what has since occurred, calculate the present resultant of both, and **call** that the up-to-date facts. The new doctrine should be: Take some out-of-date facts; **discover** some up-to-date facts; **deduce** what has occurred in the interval. Only the latter process can yield reliable knowledge.

If, as I believe, it is the function of institutions of higher learning to inculcate respect for reliable knowledge, a necessary step is to counteract the emphasis that has hitherto been given to opinion. To rank opinion above reliable knowledge is anti-scientific. It lays the mind open to persuasion by demagoguery, shallow argument and specious panaceas, or to the swings of fickle fashion. There are better foundations than these for what should be taught and what should be done in practice.

Money, Prices and Inflation

The standard literature of accounting and finance has little to say about money as such. Writers and teachers seem to suppose that, as everyone engages in transactions at money prices, the behaviour of money and prices may be taken to be understood. But this is as dangerous an assumption as it would be to suppose that anyone who can use an electrical device is a competent electrician. Layman's knowledge is not sufficient for the training of experts in the money market or the accounting office.

Money and prices are treated at length only in the literature of economics. Money is commonly said to have three functions. It is the generally accepted medium of exchange, and the money unit is, thus, the common denominator of the prices of other goods. It is a store of value or general purchasing power; its possession represents the power of purchasing anything at all, up to the amount of money in one's possession. Thirdly, the money unit is the unit of account, in which all statements and records of transactions and their consequences are kept. These elementary notions would probably be granted assent by anyone. But the textbooks do not leave the matter there.

The prices of goods in terms of money are not invariant through time. Said Adam Smith, two hundred years ago: "At the same time and place, money is the exact measure of the real exchangeable value of all commodities. It is so, however, at the same time and place only" (**Wealth of Nations**, Book 1, Ch.5). There were at that time and later some who held that exchangeable value must be measured by reference to a standard, and that a standard of value should be invariant through time. Some held that labour provided such a standard. But, as the prices of goods and labour vary in terms of money and the value in exchange of money varies in terms of other commodities, there is no invariant standard of value. The values in exchange of goods are always subject to variation in response to relative changes in the supply of and the demand for goods. And the value in exchange of money for commodities likewise depends on the relative changes in the supply of and the demand for money and goods. In particular when the supply of money increases at a faster rate than the supply of commodities and services, the prices of the latter tend to rise; and that is what is described as inflation. Of course, all prices do not rise simultaneously and to the same extent, for the supply of and demand for commodities vary relatively to one another. It follows that, as changes in prices are staggered through time, the holders of different commodities will be affected differentially in any period. It follows, also, that holders of different net quantities of general purchasing power at the beginning of any accounting period during inflation will be affected differentially in proportion to those holdings. The two kinds of differential effect arise from different causes; generally speaking they are opposite in effect on the financial affairs of any person or firm, but not, except in the most unusual case, equal and opposite; and both effects fall on most persons and firms in any given period of inflation[6].

All of these things should be **known**; they are not matters of opinion. They are expounded in textbooks which deal with money, prices and inflation. They are, furthermore, matters of observable experience. They **can be known**, therefore, to those who use money units as units of account; and to teachers who teach them how to do it; and to others who are concerned with ways of dealing in accounts with the effects on firms of changes in prices and changes in the financial significance of the

276

unit of account. Further, they **should be known**; for if accounts do not represent shifts in the financial features of assets, debts and equities, there is no other way in which persons or firms can grasp the aggregate effect of those shifts. These things **can and should be known**. But they are **not** known; or if they are known they are disregarded. The evidence is extensive.

The current purchasing power (CPP) proposal advanced in the United Kingdom in 1973, and under discussion in other countries before and since then, disregards changes in the particular prices of particular assets from time to time. It entails the up-dating of the book values of assets by use of a **general** price index, as if the prices of all assets had changed in the same proportion; but it does not bring into the account of gains and losses the amounts of those increments in asset values. It takes account of the loss (or gain) in general purchasing power during inflation; but only in respect of net monetary items, not in respect of the net command of general purchasing power of a firm at the beginning of the year. These elements of the proposal are quite inconsistent with what occurs in inflation. In essence it disregards the effects of actual differential changes in commodity prices - one-half of the problem.

By contrast, the CCA proposal of the Sandilands Committee, and many other proposals, are based principally on replacement costs. Such systems take account, in some sense, of changes in the specific prices of assets, though they are not necessarily the assets in possession of the firm at balance date. Most of these systems disregard the loss in general purchasing power due to the depreciation (in terms of goods) in the money unit; they imply that the money unit is an invariant unit, when everyone knows it is not. Some proposals take account of the loss (or gain) in purchasing power in respect of net monetary items, as in CPP. But as we have said, that is only partial treatment of the effect of inflation on the net amount of the investment of the firm at the beginning of the year. In general, the CCA proposal deals with differential shifts in commodity prices but disregards the shift in the general purchasing power of money. It deals with one-half of the problem, that half which CPP disregards.

The Exposure Draft issued in 1976 by the International Accounting Standards Committee, "Accounting Treatment of Changing Prices", allows that account may be taken of the effects of changes in the purchasing

power of money (e.g. CPP) or of changes in the prices of commodity assets
(e.g. CCA), or of both. The debate surrounding all these proposals, and
the two proposals described briefly above, could scarcely have persisted
if the interlocked character of changes in specific prices and changes in
the general purchasing power of money were known and used in the course
of devising a solution to the inflation accounting problem. We shall
indicate presently that a comprehensive and systematic procedure for
taking both classes of effect into account is feasible.

Monetary Calculation

The literature of accounting has little to say about the
fundamentals of monetary calculation. There is much on interest
calculation, accumulation and discounting, project-evaluation and
budgeting, and ratio calculation. But almost all expositions of these
matters ignore the shift in the financial significance of the money unit
in the course of inflation. And there are few expositions indeed which
deal with the conditions of aggregation and relation.

Accounting is aggregative. Individual accounts are aggregative.
Balance sheets, income statements, budget statements and cost
calculations are aggregative. In the course of analyses or projections,
aggregates and sub-aggregates are related. So elementary is the
operation of aggregation, that apparently teachers and textbook-writers
take it for granted. The consequence is fallacious addition and relation
on an extensive scale, even in the absence of inflation and more so
because of it.

At its simplest, the rule is that only like quantities or magnitudes
may be added, subtracted and related. To cope with the variety of
circumstances in which the addition and relation of quantities and
magnitudes may be of importance, the rule may be amplified into three
general rules. **Rule 1**: Quantities to be added or related must relate to
like properties or characteristics of all items for which the aggregate
or relation is to be found. **Rule 2**: If the quantities are determined by
reference to some scale of quantities and some instrument calibrated in
that scale, the same scale must be used under the same conditions in
respect of all items or objects whose properties or characteristics are
quantified. **Rule 3**: Quantities ascertained by reference to different
scales or under different conditions may be converted to like quantities,
if there are logical or empirical rules connecting the scales (or the

278

units of the scales) and if there are empirical laws relating to the
quantities under specified different conditions. For present purposes
the "scale" is a scale of numbers of money units of dated general
purchasing power.

These rules are violated in every respect under traditional
accounting.

Rule 1. Consider a balance sheet containing two assets - Cash,
2,000; Land (at cost), 10,000. The amount of cash represents general
purchasing power available to the firm at the balance date. The amount
representing land is an amount of general purchasing power paid out at
some past date. It does not represent general purchasing power
accessible to the firm at the balance date. The amounts are unlike, not
only as indicators of accessible general purchasing power, but also in
all other respects. Their addition violates the rule. For greater
reason, any balance sheet which includes items at "depreciated cost",
"replacement cost" and "the lower of cost and market", together with cash
or liabilities payable in cash, violates the rule.

Rule 2. Consider the same example. The amount representing land is
an amount of general purchasing power at a date different from the
balance date. Since the value in exchange of the money unit and the
prices of commodities vary from time to time, the two amounts will have
been ascertained under different conditions and in units of different
financial significance. Their addition violates the rule. For greater
reason, every accumulation of prices paid at various past dates violates
the rule.

Rule 3. As no attempt is made, in traditional accounting, to
convert past amounts of money, ascertained by reference to one scale, to
balance date amounts in the "balance date scale", this rule is simply
disregarded. The more obvious violations of the rule occur in proposals
relating to inflation accounting. CPP accounting employs a general price
index for up-dating the cost prices of assets. But, as the prices of
assets do not change in accordance with changes in that index, the index
does not provide an empirical rule connecting differently dated prices.
There is, in fact, no such rule; if there were, the "uncertainties" of
the market place would not exist; no one would make mistakes; all would
have perfect foreknowledge. The same stricture applies to the use of
specific index numbers for the calculation of replacement costs, as

279

endorsed by the Sandilands Committee and others. Both types of proposal violate the rule.

As there are no empirical rules for calculating prices at one date from prices at another, the only way of discovering prices at different dates is by observation. Observations made at any given date yield magnitudes under the same conditions expressed in common units, units which are common both in name and in financial significance. Further, as all balance sheets contain cash, receivables and payables balances, the only common property or characteristic by which all items can be represented is their money equivalent (for commodity assets, their net resale prices). Further still, if the money equivalents of all items are ascertained, the amount of net assets (total assets less liabilities) is a genuine, dated money sum. Now, although there is no empirical law relating specific prices at different dates, there is an empirical law relating the general purchasing powers of money units at different dates. The law is: the general purchasing power of money varies inversely with the general level of prices. It is therefore possible to convert the money sum representing net assets at one date to a corresponding sum representing equivalent general purchasing power at another date, even though specific asset prices cannot be so converted. A system based on the processes here mentioned violates none of the rules of aggregation and relation.

There is a second aspect of monetary calculation which deserves notice. It is said, in defence of the traditional use of different valuations for different assets, that they are "surrogates" for some "central" or "ideal" value. The argument has been used in support of proposals, such as the CCA suggestion of the Sandilands Committee, which entail the aggregation of replacement costs (RC), net realizable values (NRV) and economic, or net present (discounted), values (PV). Now there is no way whatever in which these three may be treated as surrogates or substitutes for one another, or for anything else. Consider any investment situation, which is the customary situation on which the argument is based. Note, first, that a replacement cost is simply a purchase price. The replacement cost of an asset presently in possession plays the same part in evaluative calculations as the purchase prices of any other similar or dissimilar commodity; we shall therefore, use RC to represent any such purchase price. Now, the NRV of any one or any

280

several assets represents a sum which is or could be accessible for any
other projects. Suppose there are three such projects A, B, C, requiring
the immediate outlay of RC(A), RC(B), RC(C) respectively. Now, if, for
example, NRV is greater than RC(A), there will be a sum of money which is
usable otherwise than for the immediate outlay; the proceeds of this use
must be taken into account in calculating the present value PV(A) of
project A. Likewise, if NRV is less than RC(A), the additional cost of
borrowing the deficiency must be taken into account in calculating PV(A).
A project being thus defined as exhaustive of NRV, that project will be
chosen which has the greatest PV, other things being equal. Clearly, all
three kinds of amounts, NRV, RC and PV, are used in the process, each in
its specific way. If any one of them was a surrogate, or was
substitutable, for the other two, there would be no way of discriminating
between projects in the manner described, which, incidentally, is
standard doctrine. The surrogate doctrine in the setting of balance
sheet construction is fallacious. It can only have arisen and survived
through neglect of the basic rule (Rule 1) of aggregation.

A third aspect of monetary calculation about which there is
confusion is the relation between physical and financial magnitudes. It
has long been customary to calculate periodical depreciation on the basis
of expected calendar life or expected output; to allocate rental and
other occupancy charges on the basis of floor areas occupied, and to make
other allocations on physical bases. More generally, some have held, and
some still hold, that the maintenance of operating capacity or
capability, in terms of physical capacity, is the base mark from which
profit should be calculated. But there is no constant or necessary
relation between physical inputs (or other physical magnitudes) and
prices or profits. All forms of accounting based on replacement costs
are based, in principle, on physical capacities; for in finding a
replacement price, whether or not the capacities of available near-
substitutes have changed, a price is found of the commodity which
physically (in description or output) approximates the asset held. But,
of course, when a firm is initially established and whenever new
contributions to it are made by investors or financiers, its endowment is
money, not physical goods. In all such cases there is no physical
capacity which must be maintained before a profit is struck, for there
was no physical capacity at the outset with which a closing physical

capacity could be compared. The cardinal concern of accounting is with
financial characteristics of assets, equities and operations. If,
therefore, there is any legitimate quantum which must be taken as the
base point from which the profit of a period may be computed, it must be
the net **financial** capacity of a firm, its net command of goods in
general, at the beginning of the accounting period. Following points
made earlier, that financial capacity is the aggregate of the money
equivalents of the firm's assets less the amount of its liabilities; or
the money amount of its net assets.

The Educational Prospect

Experience of inflation and the extended debate over possible
methods of inflation accounting have shown that practitioners and the
educational establishments have not been well prepared to deal with the
problem. Numerous elements of the present and proposed practice of
accounting have been shown to depend on unrealistic and fallacious
presumptions. These presumptions persist, it seems, because the
educational process has paid inadequate attention to some of the
fundamental components of economic knowledge and to basic features of the
logic of financial calculation. Without appearing to do so, the teaching
of numerous ways of dealing with similar facts and events undermines the
rules of aggregation and relation which are learned in the course of
secondary education. The dominance of the teacher, in the teacher-
student relationship, is no more evident than in the manner in which
accounting students are induced to forsake their previous learning and to
proceed in ways inconsistent with their "commonsense" dealings with money
and goods. Of course the fault does not lie entirely with the
educational institutions; the fallacious presumptions are widely held in
the profession at large. But as scholars and critical observers of
practice, and as teachers of those who enter practice, the educational
establishment has unequalled opportunity for rectifying the confused
state of doctrine and practice.

Reconstruction is possible. By way of illustration there is the
system I have described as continuously contemporary accounting[7]. It is
consistent with, because it is based on, the characteristics of money and
prices and the rules for aggregation and relation outlined earlier. It
yields financial statements based on the dated money equivalents (or
values in exchange) of assets. Income or net profit is calculated by

reference to net revenues, price variation adjustments and a capital maintenance adjustment. Net revenues are the ascertained net inflows of money and direct claims to money. Price variation adjustments are the unrealized differences, positive or negative, between book values and discovered money equivalents of assets at balance date. The effects of all changes in prices in an interval are thus brought into account, in net revenues for goods sold, or price variation adjustments for goods unsold at balance date. The algebraic sum of net revenues and price variation adjustments is reduced by the capital maintenance adjustment, the counterpart of which is a transfer to a capital maintenance reserve. The amount of the adjustment is the product of the opening amount of net assets and the proportionate change in the general level of prices (given by an appropriate general price index). The effect of the adjustment is to secure that profit is calculated with reference to general purchasing power at the end of the period equivalent to the general purchasing power of the net assets at the beginning of the period. The adjustment thus takes account of the shift in the general purchasing power of money. And the system as a whole takes account of both shifts in specific prices and shifts in the general purchasing power of money, the two concurrent types of change experienced in inflationary conditions.

283

The system has been described and contrasted with other systems elsewhere[8]. Its practical propriety has been evidenced by a wide variety of commercial and financial events in the United States, the United Kingdom and Australia[9]. The relevance of its products to the choices of managers, investors and others has been demonstrated. Its feasibility is attested by its use in New Zealand, by a number of companies independently or under an experimental study by the University of Waikato on behalf of a government committee of inquiry into methods of inflation accounting[10]. It has been found to be readily teachable to undergraduate students for over ten years. It has been exposed to over a thousand accountants in Australia and New Zealand over the past four years, without serious objection to any part of it.

However, the important point for present purposes is the possibilities this system illustrates. It is possible from fundamental knowledge to construct a style of accounting which deals systematically with the differential effects on firms of changes in prices and in the general level of prices; and, in the case of firms having international operations, with the differential effects in different countries of changes in prices, the general level of prices and rates of exchange[11]. Many of the deficiencies of traditional practice have arisen from **ad hoc** remedies for transient problems; for **ad hoc** remedies have a habit of becoming part of the corpus of rules or principles. Those deficiencies are only likely to be eradicated by reconstructing the rules of practice in the light of firm knowledge of the ways in which money quantities, prices and statements expressed in money units bear upon the deliberations of managers, investors, creditors and others.

The literature of economics and the literature of calculation and measurement have not been developed with the problems of accountants in mind. It cannot be expected that a ready-made solution to accounting problems will be found in that literature. There is not, for example, any form of regular measurement or calculation which makes use of a unit of continually varying significance, such as the significance of the money unit during inflation. It cannot be supposed that students who have undertaken studies in other fields will adapt what they have learned to the setting of financial calculation and representation. To do that is the task of their teachers. The confusion over inflation accounting shows quite clearly that the task has not been done rigorously or systematically. What has been learned from those experiences is not simply a **method** of dealing with the effects of inflation - for the matter is still in debate. But there are indications of a **programme** for reform. Its elements include:

(a) greater recourse to the literatures or ideas of fields related to accounting; for, if accounting doctrines are inconsistent with those of economics, law, finance, metrology and administrative studies, no coherent understanding of the function of accounting in financial affairs will emerge;

(b) clearer and closer analysis of the roles of observable facts and speculative judgement (opinion) in human affairs; for, if the two roles are confused, no firm foundation can be laid for a style of accounting which will engage satisfactorily with exploratory, diagnostic and evaluative calculations;[12]

(c) closer attention to the functions and characteristics of money and the relationships between money, prices and price levels; for, if the features of money as a medium of exchange are notunderstood,

15

neither will be the functions of the money unit as a unit of account;

(d)   more discriminating attention to forms of monetary calculation; for, if the functions of singular and aggregative information are distinguished, and if the rules of aggregation and relation are understood, there is less likelihood of undisciplined and **ad hoc** responses to emergent problems.

The educational process has in recent times been viewed as a means of preparing people to "fit into" the community in which they will live and work. The transmission of present knowledge and beliefs is certainly **one** of the functions of education; the teaching of traditional accounting doctrines exemplifies it. But it is also one of the functions of the educational establishment to discriminate in what it teaches; not to endorse and generate respect for mere tradition or dogma, but to reshape what is poorly constructed; not to make students live comfortably with fallacious rules and practices, but to establish respect for superior rules and practices by recourse to basic knowledge, argument and evidence. Many elements of the debate on inflation accounting indicate that this task has yet to be done. It should be done in the interest of advancing the intellectual integrity and the practical relevance of the work of both the educational and the practising branches of the profession.

285

Notes

1. e.g. "The power which that possession (of wealth) immediately and directly conveys to him, is the power of purchasing". Adam Smith, **Wealth of Nations**, 1776, Bk. I, Ch. V. At the more recent end of the time span mentioned: "The firm's fortune at any moment comprises the market value at that moment of all the material objects and legal rights which it then possesses, plus the money it has, plus the debts owed to it less those it owes to others". G.L.S. Schackle, **Expectation, Enterprise and Profit**, 1970, p. 28.

2. The specification given in Chambers "The Functions of Published Financial Statements" (**Accounting and Business Research**, Spring 1976) is believed to correspond with the uses made of financial statements, but it cannot be said to be "accepted" in the profession.

3. See Chambers, "Financial Information and the Securities Market", **Abacus**, September 1965.

4. An investigation of James E. Parker ("Testing Comparability and Objectivity of Exit Value Accounting", **Accounting Review**, July 1975) showed that, for 26 firms holding a specified asset, the dispersion of book values was significantly in excess of the dispersion of market resale prices, and that the major cause of dispersion in book values was accounting estimates (i.e. opinions, judgements) - not accounting methods.

5. **Report of the Inflation Accounting Committee**, London, 1975, Ch. 13. For extended comment on this and other features of the Report, see Chambers, **Current Cost Accounting - A Critique of the Sandilands Report**, I.C.R.A., Lancaster, 1976.

6. L. von Mises, **Human Action**, gives one of the clearest and most economical sketches of these differential effects on pp. 409-10 of the 1949 edition.

7. The development of the system from elementary principles, greater in variety than those mentioned in this paper, is indicated in Chambers, **Accounting, Evaluation and Economic Behavior**, 1966. See also footnote 8.

8. Chambers, **Accounting for Inflation** and **Accounting for Inflation - Methods and Problems**, University of Sydney, 1976.

9. Chambers, **Securities and Obscurities**, 1973.

10. The inquiry was begun in 1976 and was still in its early stages at the time of writing this paper.

11. Chambers, "Accounting in an International Economic Community", **Journal U.E.C.**, January 1972.

12. See the article referred to in Note 2.

The Construction of Accounting Standards*

1.   It is a rather curious fact that there has never been, to my
knowledge, a formal statement, by any of the professional bodies which
have engaged in standard setting, of what statements of standard practice
are intended or designed or expected to do.

2.   A number of things are, of course, implied. It is implied that
accounting standards and the standardization of practices are "good
things" - but there is not a single standard that does not allow options
in specified or unspecified circumstances. It is implied that
promulgated standards represent the best practice, for, surely, it would
be pointless to require less than the best practice - but, seldom, if
ever, is there an explicit line of argument to the effect that a standard
is better than alternatives; and the permission of options leaves in
doubt what is best. It is implied that the application of standards will
yield serviceable information to users of accounts - but there is no
specific demonstration to the effect that the information yielded is
serviceable in any specific use. It is implied, generally, that non-
conformity with standards is a "bad thing", and a cause of disciplinary
action - but there is evidence of non-conformity on a significant scale,
and no evidence of disciplinary action on a similar scale. It is implied
that the standards as a whole are consistent among themselves and with
the requirements of the Companies Acts - but there is no general
framework which would secure consistency; no attempt to define "state of
affairs" or "financial position" or "profit" or a "true and fair view" of
those things; and no attempt to demonstrate consistency with the Act.

3.   It is not sufficient that all of these things be implied. An
implied constraint or condition can easily be overlooked, or set aside,
by any person or committee given the task of constructing a standard.
Especially is this the case when the development of standards on
particular topics is assigned to different persons or committees. None
can be sure of the constraints or conditions accepted by others,
explicitly or implicitly in respect of work done concurrently, or
implicitly in respect of work already done.

287

---

* Presented at the Western Australian Congress of the Australian Society
  of Accountants, Busselton, May 1978.

4. All this talk about what is implied, presupposed or assumed may seem to be pointless to some people. Practical men, anxious to get on with the job, may think that things will fall into place, that there is no reason to design standards with reference to any general blueprint. But the same practical men would never commission the building of a house without plans and specifications. They know very well that no manufacturer of trucks, or refrigerators or anything else, proceeds without specifications of the uses of those products and without designs and specifications of the parts and sub-assemblies which, when put together, will satisfactorily engage with one another in the way users expect, so that the whole product will do the jobs users expect them to do.

5. Accounts are no different. A set of accounts is a whole product, made up of sub-assemblies, and intended or expected to be serviceable for particular purposes. An accounting standard is a specification for a sub-assembly. A set of accounting standards is a specification for a whole product. But if there is no specification of the job to be done by the whole product, there can be no satisfactory design of the product or its sub-assemblies and parts. The result will be higgledy-piggledy accounting - and I am afraid that is what we have.

6. Some assets are valued at their current purchasing power (cash and receivables, for example). Some are valued at their original costs. Some are valued at depreciated original costs. Some are revalued at amounts higher or lower than original costs. Some are valued at market resale prices. Some are valued at the lower of cost and market prices, a fiction of illegitimate parentage. What the sum of all these values has to do with financial position at a stated date no one can tell; it has no practical meaning and no practical use. Yet all of those valuations are endorsed or made obligatory under accounting standards. In essence, the standards devised, in Australia and elsewhere, endorse hand-me-downs from an undesigned, unstandardized past; a past in which all kinds of rules of thumb have yielded values which it has suited some firm or company to use in its particular, and often fleeting, circumstances. Cosmetic has been piled on cosmetic to the point where the face of a company may have nothing to do with its appearance.

7. A substantial number of cases involving misrepresentations arising

288

under accepted standards or principles have come to public notice. The amounts have run to millions and tens of millions. That being the case, it seems that the construction of accounting standards should have begun in the market place with inquiries as to what functions accounts can serve, and should have proceeded at the drawing board to devise a blueprint for accounts which would serve those functions. Those steps have not been taken by standard-setting bodies. I propose to outline the process by first stating a principle and then outlining the consequences of it. For simplicity I shall speak of the accounts of companies; but that does not interfere with the generality of anything I shall say.

Relevance

8.   First, there are many persons or companies who are interested in the solvency and the profits and the rates of return of companies. Those persons and companies include investors, creditors, suppliers (who become creditors), workers (who become creditors), customers (who become debtors), other companies (either as competitors for custom or competitors for the supply of investable funds). We may include governmental agencies and regulatory bodies and tribunals. There is no need to assert that all members of these classes do or would use information on solvency and profits, or how they do or could use it. But as knowledge of solvency and profits is useful to some people, and may be useful to many, it is imperative that proper indicators of them shall be given in accounts. This cannot be ensured by any standard or standards without specifying the components of an indicator of solvency, and specifying the meaning to be given to "profit", and deducing from those specifications the kinds of amounts which will give the required indicators. Those kinds of amounts could be said to be **relevant** to users of accounts.

9.   There is no discussion of these matters in any standard that has come to my notice. Relevance is mentioned in one statement on standards, but that statement provides no discussion of what is relevant. The only kinds of amount usable in an indicator of solvency at any time are the dated money equivalents of assets and the dated money amounts of liabilities. It is pointless to say that liabilities will be met out of future cash flows, not out of assets accessible at balance date. For first, other liabilities arise after balance date which will be required to be met out of future cash flows. Second, information on future cash

flows is not given in accounts, and is therefore not accessible to interested parties; and, in any case, future cash flows are conjectural and therefore not reliable information. Third, no lender or trustee under a loan agreement or trust deed can discover whether the terms and intent of the agreement are in fact breached by a borrower unless the dated money equivalents of assets and the amount of liabilities is known from time to time. And fourth, although debts may be payable under contract at future dates, any such debt may become payable immediately on breach by the debtor of any provision of a loan contract or of any provision of the law relating to debts and debtors.

Aggregation

10. Financial position (of which solvency is one aspect) and profit are features of a company as a whole. They are aggregative in nature, and in fact. It follows that all amounts in accounts should be capable of proper aggregation. The aggregation of amounts which are quite different in origin and kind, such as the amounts mentioned in para 6, would be effectively outlawed if attention were given to the principle of aggregation. This is not a theoretical principle but a principle of practical action. No practical guidance could be obtained of the short-run solvency of a company by adding its cash and receivables to an inventory valued at the "lower of cost and market"; such an inventory value has nothing to do with capacity to pay or to provide cover for liabilities. Nor has the initial cost less a calculated provision for depreciation anything to do with the matter.

11. The amount of cash and the amount of receivables have an obvious relation to the capacity to pay debts and to do anything else necessary to carry on a business. So has any other amount which is equivalent to a cash amount at any date. The only money equivalent (para 9 above) which can properly be added to an amount of cash, and the only kind of amount which can be considered as having a direct relation to the payment of debts, is the net resale price in respect of non-money assets. It follows that the amounts at which assets should be shown in a balance sheet which is to give an indication of solvency to all the parties referred to in para 8 are their dated money amounts or dated money equivalents.

Objectivity or Independent Testability

12. Accounts are indicative of financial position and profit only if

their component amounts relate to the actual assets and liabilities of the company. What accountants or directors may "think" those amounts should be is beside the point. The object of auditing and the function of auditors is to give assurance that the accounts are realistic and not conjectural (the statement enunciating one standard makes reference to "financial realism"). The only way in which an amount may be independently checked by an auditor is by reference to evidence arising otherwise than from the stated opinions or estimates of company officers or directors. There is no way of independently checking what another "thinks". It follows that the dated money equivalents of non-money assets, their net resale prices, should be determined by reference to external evidence; for any amount so determined is capable of independent testing or verification, by other officers of a company or by its auditors.

13. This is a long-standing principle. It underlies the use of costs as evidence for original entries. It underlies the counting of cash, the taking of inventories and the independent verification of receivables and payables. But, at every point where independent evidence is not available, the principle is disregarded. It is disregarded in the usual form of the depreciation provision and in the determination of other amounts which are matters of conjecture, expectation or opinion. It is almost completely thrown to the winds in the current cost accounting standard. But without it there is no sheet-anchor on which third parties may rely for relevant information and on which auditors can depend as defence against allegations of lack of care.

Comparison and the Accrual Principle

14. If successive balance sheets have been derived in the manner described, the comparison of the net assets of one date with the net assets of another will indicate the increment which has arisen in the interval.

In the absence of inflation, this increment is the profit of the intervening period. There is no other way of verifying a profit than by verifying the amounts of the assets and liabilities of a company at successive dates. The increase in the amount of net assets will have arisen partly from buying and selling transactions, and partly from accrued gains or losses not evidenced by transaction documents. The amounts of all such accruals will be the differences between the prior

291

book values and the independently ascertained amounts of assets and liabilities at balance date, and the book values would be adjusted accordingly. All adjustments to the balances of asset accounts may be described as price variation adjustments. Those adjustments take account of specific changes in the amounts of the net resale prices of assets.

15. The accrual principle is well established. It is intended to make accounts comparable, notwithstanding that cash received or paid in settlement of accounts may not occur at the same rate in successive years. It serves the more general idea of incorporating in the accounts of specific periods the effects of transactions or events occurring specifically in those periods. But it is a principle which, like all good principles, should be applied **consistently**, not simply when prices fall (as in the case of "depreciation", which strictly means a fall in price) but whether they rise or fall. And it should be applied to all assets.

Comparison and the Aggregation Principle

16. When inflation occurs, the significance of the dollar as a medium of exchange and as a unit of account changes. At the end of a year there are no longer any dollars of the same general purchasing power as at the end of the previous year. The net assets at the two dates will be in differently dated dollars (dollars of the same name but of different general purchasing power). The increment referred to in para 14 above will then be a nominal increment. So that a proper difference may be taken between the two amounts of net assets, the amount at the close of the previous year must be converted to a number of dollars of the end of the year of account which is equivalent in general purchasing power to the general purchasing power of the net assets at the end of the previous year. This is done by adding to the amount of net assets as of the end of the previous year the product of that amount and the proportionate change during the year in an index of the general level of prices.

The amount of that adjustment will be deducted from the increment referred to in para 14, and a corresponding amount will be added to the balance, at the end of the previous year, of the shareholders´ equity accounts. The net amount of the increment will be a genuine increment in the general purchasing power accessible to a company — a genuine amount of **profit**. Although the amounts of price variation adjustments are

292

nominal and the amount of net revenues is nominal (both being differences between amounts of differently dated dollars), the amount of profit is made homogeneous with the closing balance sheet by reason of the fact that its calculation entails the comparison of (adjusted) opening and closing amounts of net assets expressed in dollars of equal purchasing power.

Interfirm Comparison and Uniformity

17. The users of accounts referred to in para 8 judge the positions and performances of companies comparatively. It is impossible to compare the features of two or more companies by reference to accounts unless those accounts have been compiled in a uniform manner. The use of quite specific rules, without alternatives for "special circumstances", is the only way of ensuring that accounts are kept in a uniform manner. If any company or its directors wish to explain why the position and results are as they turn out to be, they have the opportunity. It is contrary to the basic principle of the company law that accounts should be kept in such a way that legitimate inquiries are frustrated or avoided by the manner in which accounts portray the consequences of transactions and events. The rules indicated above are quite specific, and are therefore conducive to proper comparison.

Intertemporal Comparison

18. Users of accounts may make judgements of the positions and states of companies by reference to previously reported figures, for one company or for two or more companies. The necessity of consistency of accounting from year to year has been mentioned. But comparisons of absolute amounts of money in successive years are impossible if the purchasing power of the money unit and the relative prices of different assets have changed.

It is nevertheless proper to compare ratios derived from the accounts of successive years, if those ratios are themselves based on amounts which are properly aggregable and relatable. All significant judgments are in fact based on ratios (the current ratio, the debt to equity ratio, the rate of profit on net assets, and so on). A uniform method of accounting will ensure that these ratios are properly indicative of the state and of shifts in the state of a company or companies from time to time.

The Construction of Standards Generally

19. The preceding paragraphs have dealt with the main principles which should govern the setting of accounting standards. They have indicated some of the consequences those principles entail. Whether any one agrees with those consequences or not is not relevant to the present discussion. The point is that the principles themselves are not contestable. It cannot be denied that knowledge of solvency and profit is pertinent to all who have direct or indirect financial interests in companies. It cannot be denied that these are aggregative aspects of companies. It cannot be denied that the aggregation of unlike amounts is useless for any aggregative purpose. It cannot be denied that prices change and that the general purchasing power of money changes, and that these changes affect the positions and results of companies. It cannot be denied that comparisons between companies and across successive intervals are made. It cannot be denied that serviceable comparisons depend on consistency of accounting and uniformity of accounting. None of these is a matter of opinion. Collectively they provide a firm foundation for standard practices, for they entail no wilful or questionable assumptions and require no questionable conjectures.

20. It seems that standards promulgated in the past have taken far too seriously the kinds of information which the managers of companies may wish to use, for internal purposes or to convey to outsiders the impression that companies are making steady progress. But the company law on accounts is written for the benefit of outsiders. Managers may make whatever calculations, conjectures, allocations and apportionments they think fit for their purposes. But if any of these conflict with the fair representation of the financial relationships of a company with the world about it, they serve neither managers nor outsiders in the manner in which accounting standards and accounts based on them are expected to serve.

21. A financial executive's tool-kit has a number of tools, balance sheet, profit and loss accounts, budgets, present value calculations and so on. None of these serves the same function as another, and none should be designed to serve any purpose alien to it. A dated balance sheet indicates a dated financial position; for that, dated money equivalents of assets are serviceable. A dated profit and loss account represents the profit or loss; for that, costs and selling prices and

dated money equivalents are serviceable. A budget represents a prospect
based on dated money equivalents at the outset and expected (conjectural)
receipts and payments (purchase or replacement prices) during an
interval. A present value calculation is a conjectured indication of the
discounted net prospect of the use of several assets or services in
combination; for that, expected purchase prices and expected selling
prices are serviceable. A calculation of an expected minimum product
price may entail the use of actual or conjectural costs, including
replacement costs. Observe that to each of the kinds of statement or
calculation there is a limited and specific class or limited classes of
basic data. In principle, it would be as foolish to use a past cost in
calculating a prospect, as it would be to use a prospective amount in
representing a past amount.

295

22. This principle of design seems to have been completely overlooked by
the proposers of accounting standards. It has been said, in respect of
some standards, that one basis of valuation could not be serviceable for
all purposes, and that therefore a mixture of valuation bases is
permissible. The premise is true, as the previous paragraph indicates.
But the conclusion, in respect of balance sheets, is false. It is as
absurd, and in practice as useless, to put in balance sheets the kinds of
conjectural amounts which must be used in budgets, as to put a hammer-
head on a saw-handle (the result of which might be described as a "hee-
haw").

23. Many of the standards, in Australia, the United Kingdom and the
United States do little more than codify rules and options that have
survived from the past. Some people have asserted that they have
survived because they are "the fittest". That is a comfortable way of
escaping any judgement about what is the fittest. If only the fittest
had survived, there would be much less debate about rules and standards
today; and nothing like the present scale of operations of the standard-
setting bodies in the countries mentioned and elsewhere. If only the
fittest had survived, there would have been no cause for the extensive
litigation against company officers and auditors over the last twenty
years, running in particular cases to millions of dollars. If only the
fittest had survived, there would have been no occasion for the inquiries
and investigations into accounting practices and principles which
governments and governmental agencies have found to be necessary,

especially those of the Metcalf Committee in the United States over the past two years.

24. The standard-setting bodies seem to have been completely oblivious of these things. None of the standards in any of the countries mentioned recites the specific difficulty, problem or obnoxious consequence of existing practices, which made necessary the statement of a standard practice. With no such problem in view, and under specific notice, it is no wonder that difficulties, problems and obnoxious consequences have not been resolved or eliminated by the standards.

25. The higgledy-piggledy order in which topics have come up for consideration is evidence of the unsystematic work of the standard-setting bodies. Surely it would have been wise **at the outset** to specify what was meant, or was understood to be meant, by "financial position", "profit" and a "true and fair view" of these. These are terms used in the statute, terms which require definition or clarification, since they determine the whole setting and style of the consequential accounting operations. But not only have these things not been specified at the outset; they have not been specified at all. It is as careless as if a builder were to proceed to construct the third level of a building without a care about its foundations.

26. Many people seem to have thought that a reorganization of the formal arrangements for setting standards would overcome the deficiencies of past efforts. It may help. But what is far more important than that is a new attitude towards the task; a determination to apply the intellect to discrimination between what is useless and what is useful, rather than the supine and undiscriminating acceptance, as useful, of any practice or rule which someone in the past has been able to get away with. Some people are of the view that a governmental body could do a better job than the "private" efforts of professional bodies have done. Such a body could hardly have done a worse job. Others believe that the task should be left to the private, professional sector; it surely should be able to do better. I take no side in that argument except this: that the legislation should specify the general quality expected of accounts in the public interest, for there is no other body in a democratic community that is charged with the preservation and protection of the public interest. But, given that specification, neither a public exercise nor a

rigorously to consider the steps by which the quality standard may be converted to a corresponding set of specific practices consistent with it.

27. The credibility of the profession and its products has long been and continues to be under fire. It will remain that way while notoriously unsatisfactory and permissive practices persist. If the profession is to make its standards respected and respectable, it must root out the permissiveness which enables non-standard practices to masquerade as standard practices. As a basis of professional disciplinary action, in the only sense relevant to the public it serves, the profession's standards are useless unless they are unequivocal. Standards which allow alternatives, or multiple choices none of which is "wrong", are in effect misrepresentations themselves; for they purport to constrain but provide ample opportunities for escape from constraint. That deludes both the profession and its public.

Conclusion

28. The deficiencies of the present process of constructing standards are not localized. They are virtually world-wide. There is no other field, to my knowledge, in which practices, that have been shown to give rise to damaging consequences, have been allowed so liberally to survive. A profession stands or falls by the quality of its products. The principles I have outlined earlier in this paper are principles which are directed to the quality of accounts. Some of them are entirely consistent with other statements of accounting principle. Some go further, to quite fundamental aspects of accounting. Yet none of them is contestable, in my opinion. If, in anyone else's opinion, they are contestable, I should like to know. What I should like more to know, in that case, is the ground on which any such principle is contested, for I know of none. If those principles are incontestable, the only reasonable process of standard construction is to work out the necessary consequences of those principles in the form of a set of prescriptions. An attempt to sketch the process is given in the body of the paper. No other process has yet been found to be fruitful. The process I have sketched and the result of it could extricate the profession from the morass in which it has floundered for so long. The only question is whether the profession has the will to extricate itself, or is content to muddle along as it has done, so fruitlessly, in the past.

297

4. The Functions of Accounting Standards

Summary

4.01   *The general function of accounting standards is to ensure that company accounts are of generally serviceable quality. Quality standards protect the users of accounts from misdirection; they provide the basis of disciplinary actions taken in the interest of maintaining the quality of company accounts, and of defences by those charged; and they provide the basis of defences against influence directed to the production of misleading accounts. Product quality standards determine the standards governing inputs and processes. The Companies Act provides a product quality standard for company accounts. Input and processing standards may not properly permit or require departure from that quality standard. Given a clear specification of the quality standard expected of company accounts, the professional bodies may properly be expected to develop appropriate input and processing standards.*

The Quality of Financial Information

4.02   All goods and services deliberately designed and produced have an identifiable function. What they are designed or intended to do determines how and with what materials they are made. A screwdriver is designed to drive screws. Its blade, shaft and grip must be designed with that in mind. A manufacturer must take account of the uses for which a product is designed in the choice of the materials and processes by which it is constructed. The fitness of a product to perform its function is the principal and primary object of design. The choice of materials and processes is subordinate to considerations of fitness to function or quality of performance. To secure that all screwdrivers of a given kind are of uniform quality, the manufacturer may lay down standards of performance of the product, and standards for the materials of which it is made and for the processes by which it is made.

4.03   Where there are many producers of a class of goods and many different users or uses of any such goods, there may be general standards relating to the quality of the end product. Especially is this the case where some goods must engage with, or be compatible with, others if they are to be serviceable. The manufacturers of electrical appliances, plugs, and flexes or cables, must so design these products that they will engage with one another and be compatible with a specified supply of electrical power. Any manufacturer may (within limits) choose the materials and processes which enter into his products; but they must be such as to yield a technically serviceable product. The financial statements of companies fall into the category of things which are produced by technical processes (the processes of accounting), by a wide range of producers (companies and the accountants and auditors who serve them), for technical use by a wide range of consumers (investors, creditors, managers and others). The varied uses of information yielded by the kind of accounting described in Chapter 3 were there indicated. Information on one company is expected to be compatible with information on another; otherwise comparison is futile. It is expected to be compatible with contracts, undertakings and understandings between many different parties; if it is not, there could be no consensus between these parties. To secure fitness to function in respect of all accounts, the inputs and processes of accounting may also be the subject of standards.

4.04 Product quality standards and input and processing standards are necessarily complementary. But input and processing standards will not of themselves ensure that a product is of serviceable quality. For that reason, among the standards developed by national standards associations there are examples of both. Since both are complementary, it may reasonably be expected that accounting standards should include examples of both. And since product quality standards determine the inputs and processes which are appropriate, it may reasonably be expected that the development of input and processing standards should be preceded by the specification of quality standards for financial statements. It will be shown hereafter that the accounting standards hitherto published by professional bodies are substantially input and processing standards, and that they have been devised without reference to the features which would ensure that the end product is of serviceable quality.

4.05 For many years the accountancy profession has been concerned with establishing some degree of similarity between the accounts of companies, and some degree of consistency in the accounts of each company. This concern has been prompted by the known diversity of practices and by the disputes which have arisen from diverse or questionable practices. The response of the Institute of Chartered Accountants in England and Wales ("the English Institute" hereafter) was to publish "recommendations"; the Institute of Chartered Accountants in Australia ("the Australian Institute" hereafter) followed the same course. In these cases, as in the United States for some twenty years, the subjects of professional pronouncements were determined by what appeared from time to time to be particular matters causing some confusion in practice. Recommendations or statements on these problem topics may have tended to improve the general degree of uniformity of practice. But there was no statement of the general function of the accounts of a company as a whole which would have served as a product quality standard governing all recommendations on particular matters. The publication of recommendations, so described, was almost tacit admission that no quality standard for company accounts could be specified.

4.06 Not only was there no statement which would serve as a product quality standard; there were quite specific indications that accounts could *not* be expected to be useful for many purposes:

"A balance sheet is therefore mainly an historical document which does not purport to show the realisable value of assets such as goodwill, land, buildings, plant and machinery; nor does it normally purport to show the realisable value of assets such as stock-in-trade. Thus a balance sheet is not a statement of the net worth of the undertaking and this is normally so even where there has been a revaluation of assets and the balance sheet amounts are based on the revaluation instead of on cost." (*Recommendation* N18, "Presentation of balance sheet and profit and loss account", English Institute 1958. Substantially the same words occur in *Recommendation* D1.1 of the Australian Institute, 1963, 1970.)

". . . the results shown by accounts prepared on the basis of historical cost are not a measure of increase or decrease in wealth in terms of purchasing power; nor do the results necessarily represent the amount which can prudently be regarded as available for distribution, having regard to the financial requirements of the business. Similarly the results shown by such accounts are not necessarily suitable for purposes such as price fixing, wage negotiation and taxation, unless in using them for these purposes due regard is paid to the amount of profit which has been retained in the business for its maintenance." (*Recommendation* N15, "Accounting in relation to changes in the purchasing power of money", English Institute, 1952.)

300

It appears, thus, that a balance sheet prepared according to professionally endorsed principles could *not* be taken as giving an indication of up-to-date realisable values of assets, *nor* an indication of net worth; and that the results (profits) are *not* a measure of increase or decrease in wealth in terms of purchasing power, and are *not* necessarily serviceable in price-fixing, wage negotiations or taxation. Subsequent to the 1963 case, *Hedley Byrne & Co. Ltd* v. *Heller and Partners Ltd,* the English Institute sought Counsel's advice on the accountant's liability to third parties. The opinion, published in 1965 for the guidance of members, stated that "the purpose for which annual accounts are normally prepared is not to enable individual shareholders to take investment decisions". It appears that the accounts to which the above observations relate were considered to be useless for most of the purposes for which accounts are, in fact, used. On the basis of such a full catalogue of uses which could *not* be made of accounts, it would have been impossible to construct a product quality standard.

Product Quality Standards

4.07   The object of a product quality standard is primarily to protect the user against the inadvertent use of a good or service the technical qualities, or fitness to function, of which he cannot judge himself. Users of company accounts are not in a position to assure themselves of the propriety of the information given in accounts. The user may be well able to understand the meaning of solvency and to deduce from a balance sheet whether a company appears to be solvent or not; and he may have a commonsense notion of profit. But he will not ordinarily know the accounting processes by which the reported figures are derived. He will not know whether the accounts were prepared consistently for a given period, or were prepared consistently from year to year, or were prepared in a manner consistent with the accounting of other companies. He will not know whether the accounts of different companies have been audited consistently, or whether any of the reported amounts are realistic in any sense. He must rely implicitly on the information provided. If that reliance is not to be misplaced, the information provided must be of serviceable standard, serviceable for any of the purposes for which it may be used.

4.08   A second object of a product quality standard is to protect the producer from improper allegations of misrepresentation. Allegations of misrepresentation in accounts may arise from many directions. Aggrieved investors and creditors may bring suit against companies and their officers and auditors in some circumstances. Criminal actions may be brought in others. Disciplinary actions may be brought against accountants by professional bodies. A variety of other parties may dispute the reported figures though they have no recourse to legal or other formal remedies. The Continental Vending Machine Corporation case (*United States* v. *Simon et al*, 425 F. 2d 796 (2d Cir. 1969)), has shown that, at least in some jurisdictions, it is not a sufficient defence on the part of auditors to claim that a mode of accounting conforms with, or is not in violation of, generally accepted accounting principles. Only if the information is of serviceable quality can an allegation of misrepresentation be rebutted. And only if serviceable quality is specified can the accountancy profession exercise any disciplinary authority over the performance of its members, of a kind that can be seen to be fair as between different members.

4.09.   A third object of a product quality standard is to protect the quality of financial information against self-serving or misguided manipulation of accounts. The amounts of reported profits of companies are the most readily available index of their success. To *appear* to be successful in this sense is in the self-interest of company officers who are aware that to be *actually* successful in this sense is in the interest of investors, creditors and other parties associated with companies. In the light of the beliefs and expectations of managers and directors and in the absence of a firm quality standard, the accounts may be made to indicate success or differing degrees of success. A firm quality standard would protect employed accountants and auditors against pressure to publish information of an optimistic but unrealistic kind. A firm quality standard would, indeed, protect managers and directors themselves against the often unforeseen and unforeseeable consequences of reporting what they would like to report "in particular circumstances", when the facts are otherwise.

301

The Quality Standard of the Companies Act

4.10   The Companies Act does in fact provide a product quality standard for accounts. It stipulates that the accounts to be made out and laid before a company at each annual general meeting shall include a profit and loss account "giving a true and fair view of the profit or loss of the company" for the preceding financial year and a balance sheet "giving a true and fair view of the state of affairs of the company as at the end of the financial year" (s. 162). The Act does not amplify or indicate the meaning assigned to "true and fair". But the phrase is recurrent and may, for that reason, be considered as a dominant element of the safeguards the Act seeks to provide. The phrase is used with reference to the keeping of accounts (s. 161A (1)), the statement by the directors to be attached to the accounts (s. 162 (10)), the statement of the principal accounting officer to be attached to the accounts (s. 162 (12)), additional information to be given in certain circumstances by the directors (s. 162 (9)), and the report of the auditor on the accounts (s. 167 (2)). However, the Act is ambiguous in certain respects which deserve notice before considering the general quality standard which the Act prescribes.

4.11   The Act requires that the directors shall state whether in their opinion the accounts are drawn up so as to give a true and fair view of the profits and state of affairs of the company. The auditor is required to make a statement which is described in identical terms. *It seems to the Committee that the required statement of opinion relates not to the quantitative contents of the accounts, but to the manner in which the accounts are drawn up.* The verbal form of the provisions does not require the directors and the auditor to report whether the accounts give a true and fair view in their respective opinions. Had this been intended the sections would have been constructed differently. Instead of providing that the directors shall state "whether in their opinion the profit and loss account is drawn up so as to give a true and fair view of the profit or loss for the financial year", the section would have had to provide that the directors shall state "that the profit and loss account is drawn up so as to give a true and fair view, in their opinion, of the profit or loss for the financial year". This would have made "a true and fair view of the profit or loss" and "a true and fair view of the state of affairs" simply matters of opinion. But that does not seem to have been the object of the sections. Section 161A requires that a company shall keep such accounting records as "correctly record and explain the transactions and financial position of the company", and shall "keep its accounting records in such a manner as will enable true and fair accounts of the company to be prepared from time to time". The Act implies that, such records having been kept, there is a true and fair view of the profit or loss and the state of affairs, which will be given if the accounts are properly drawn up, but will not be given otherwise. The Committee believes that the construction of the relevant sections does not permit the inference, drawn by some, that "there are as many true and fair views as there are viewers". This latter inference can only be drawn if the sections relating to the required statements by directors and auditors are taken in isolation, instead of in the context of the accounts provisions as a whole.

4.12 Perhaps it is due to the common but questionable interpretation just mentioned that the accounts of companies are commonly considered to be subject to certain discretions on the part of directors as to amounts to be shown in the accounts. The Act requires the directors "to cause" accounts to be made up (s. 162); and it requires directors to give additional information to that required by the Ninth Schedule if such information is necessary to give a true and fair view (s. 162 (9)). It also allows certain options in respect of the layout of the information, as between the formal statements and the notes accompanying them. But none of these provisions may be taken as giving directors the right or duty to determine themselves the amounts which appear in accounts. The directors of companies are responsible for the general oversight of many matters not within their personal competences or under their personal direction. In those matters with which they are not familiar, they may and do rely on skilled service and advice *(Re Brazilian Rubber Plantations and Estates Ltd* [1911] 1 Ch. 425; *Re City Equitable Fire Insurance Co. Ltd* [1925] Ch. 407). The same applies to the accounting and accounts of companies; they are technical matters with the details of which directors would not ordinarily be familiar. In any event, it would be manifestly improper deliberately to give to directors, no matter how honest and well-intentioned they may be, the power to determine the amounts shown in the accounts, when the accounts are intended to be indicative of the financial performance of companies under *their* direction, performance for which *they* are accountable.

4.13 The intention of the legislature may have become confused by certain judicial dicta which seem to be echoed in the provisions of the Companies Act. In *Newton* v. *Birmingham Small Arms Co. Ltd* [1906] 2 Ch. 378, Buckley J. observed: "The purpose of the balance sheet is primarily to show that the financial position of the company is at least as good as there stated, not to show that it is not or may not be better." In *Young* v. *Brownlee & Co. Ltd* [1911] S.C. 677, Lord Dundas said: "I am not at all prepared to lay down as a general proposition that

302

it is illegal for directors to make a low valuation of stock or other assets, in order to create a reserve in view of future or contingent liabilities. I think such action is *prima facie* within the range of their discretion". Earlier judgments seem to have been less permissive. Stirling J., in *Leeds Estate Building and Investment Society Ltd* v. *Shepherd* (1887) 36 Ch. D. 787, considered that a balance sheet was to be "a true and accurate representation of the company's affairs". Rigby L.J., in *Re London and General Bank Ltd, ex parte Theobald (No. 2)* [1895–9] All E.R. 953, considered that "A full and fair balance-sheet must be such a balance-sheet as to convey a truthful statement as to the company's position". It is difficult, if not impossible, to reconcile "true and accurate representation" and "truthful statement" with any understatement of the amount or value of assets.

4.14   To come to present circumstances, the Companies Act which specifies that a true and fair view of the state of affairs and profit shall be given, at the same time provides that the amounts shown for current assets shall be no greater than they are likely to realize in the ordinary course of business, and that amounts shown for non-current assets shall be no greater than their reasonable replacement costs (s. 162).   These provisions place a ceiling on what may be shown, but no floor. It is impossible to be assured in that case whether assets are shown at amounts which are significantly or trivially less than the prescribed ceiling, especially in the absence of statutory interpretation of "true and fair view".

303

4.15 A further element of the case law seems to have left its mark on the statute. In certain cases relating to the amount of divisible profit, a distinction between "fixed" capital and "circulating" capital was made or relied upon. For example, in *Verner* v. *General and Commercial Investment Trust* [1894] 2 Ch. 239, Lindley L.J. said that "fixed capital may be sunk and lost, and yet . . . the excess of current receipts over current payments may be divided, but . . . floating or circulating capital must be kept up". It has been deduced from this that amounts invested in fixed assets may, but need not, be written down by charges against current revenues, but amounts invested from time to time in current assets must be so charged to maintain the "floating or circulating capital". By further inference, it is supposed that so-called fixed assets may properly be valued at cost or depreciated cost, which may be long since out-of-date, whereas current assets such as inventories must be valued at some approximation to their recent prices, and will be so valued since they are charged off sequentially against the revenues arising from their sale. There is no merit in such differential modes of valuation. In the ordinary conduct of business it is quite proper and not uncommon to liquidate investments in "fixed" assets for the purpose of financing trading operations, and to acquire fixed assets out of funds which previously were used in trading operations. Only a single and common basis of valuation will indicate the funds available or accessible to a company for any of its purposes. The Mineral Securities case is an example of the confusion that may arise from alternative modes of valuation, for the discrepancy mentioned in para. 2.09 above arose from the different possible classifications of security investments.

4.16 On an appropriate occasion, in the interest of more disciplined practice under the Act, such sources of ambiguity should be removed from the statute. However, we are of the opinion that the over-riding quality standard of the Act is a proper standard, and proceed to consider it in some detail.

True, not False

4.17 At its simplest, the requirement that a true and fair view shall be given of certain matters means that a false view shall not be given. If all statements which may give a false view of a company's profit or loss and state of affairs were to be eliminated, it should be possible to identify what will give a true and fair view. Some statements which will give a false view may readily be indicated. A statement of the amount of an asset as it was at some date other than the date of a balance sheet will not aid the giving of a true and fair view of the state of affairs of a company as at the balance date. Thus, the amount of any valuation made at a date distant from any balance date will, in principle, give a false view. A statement of the cost of any asset, whether the cost was incurred at a date remote from or close to the date of any balance sheet, will not aid the giving of the required true and fair view. For if the state of affairs or financial position of a company embraces its capacity at a balance date to pay its debts and to meet its other obligations, and to provide security for any debt or obligation, and to carry on or vary its operations and investments, the cost of an asset provides no indication of that capacity.

4.18 The accounts provisions of the Act refer to the profit or loss and the state of affairs of the company. These are aggregative features of a company "as a whole". The treatment of particular components of them is subordinate to the giving of a true and fair view of those aggregative features. But the addition, as in a balance sheet, of the amount of money on hand, the cost price of some assets, the revalued amounts of some other assets, and the market selling prices of some other assets, cannot aid the giving of a true and fair view; for the aggregate of such heterogeneous amounts is meaningless, and false in the context of the requirements of the Act. No such aggregate can properly be related to the amounts of the money obligations of a company by any creditor desirous of knowing the extent to which his debt is covered, or by any trustee for debentureholders charged with ensuring that a borrowing company is not in default of the terms of a trust deed. No shareholder can rely on such an aggregate for an indication of the solvency of a company, or of the assets employed per share, or of the fairness of any takeover offer or bid.

4.19   The references of the Act to the profit or loss and the state of affairs of a company can only be taken as referring to some real features of the company. They cannot have reference merely to some features of the accounting records, such as the balances remaining in the accounts at the end of a year. If there are differences between the actual discovered amounts of assets and liabilities and their book values, the book values must be adjusted. The results of the company, its future and the interests in it of all users of accounts, turn on the actual or real amounts of assets and liabilities from time to time. Anything which differs from a fair representation of the actual or real amounts of assets at a given date or the actual or real profits for a given period is false. Any amount which expresses what is prospective, or what is expected or hoped by the managers or directors of a company, would not constitute a proper part of the representation of what is actual or real at the end of any financial year. Accounts which include any amounts that are not representative of the real amounts of assets, liabilities or profits, at the date or for the period stipulated, are false as indications of the profit or loss and state of affairs of a company.

4.20   The use of outdated and variously dated amounts in accounts, the use of the costs of assets in balance sheets, the aggregation of significantly different kinds of amounts, and the use of unrealistic or expected or conjectural amounts in accounts are all permitted under "generally accepted principles" and the standards to be considered in Chapter 5. Yet each of these practices is contributory to the giving of a false view. When they are used in conjunction, there is no way of telling how false the view is. The falsity is "corrected" in part by the realization of assets from time to time; for, on realization, the financial significance of an asset is determined. For that reason, the accounts of many companies may, in fact, be less false than the combination of the four sources of distortion mentioned may suggest. But as some assets are held over many years, and as, under present accounting standards, some book balances are conjectural and remain so for long periods, there are long intervals over which accounts may be false to a material extent. No accounting standard may properly endorse any of the practices mentioned. It may be noted, in passing, that the style of accounting referred to in Chapter 3 has none of these features.

Fair, not Unfair

4.21   Whether the phrase "true and fair" is to be taken as specifying a single characteristic of the view given by accounts, or as two different characteristics, is not determinate. It is difficult to imagine that a true statement can be unfair. It may be uncomfortable or unpalatable. But that does not make it unfair. However, the possible uses of accounts, or information drawn from accounts, may be considered in an effort to elucidate what is fair. As before, it may be stipulated that fair means "not unfair". Fair and unfair can only be interpreted, in the context of accounts, as instructive or misleading to a user of accounts.

4.22 The management of a company consists, to a considerable extent, in arranging and negotiating the terms under which investors, financiers, suppliers, employees, customers and others will join in and continue to support the conduct of its operations. All have financial interests in the outcome of those operations, and those interests are potentially in conflict. For example, the higher the prices of a company's products, the greater is the amount of money available to purchase supplies or to pay wages or to pay dividends (provided, of course, that higher prices do not result in loss of trade). In this case, the customer is placed at a disadvantage, to the advantage of the recipients of money from the company. Whether a company will charge higher prices may depend on a unilateral decision of the company's management, taking account of the possible side-effects of doing so; or higher prices may emerge from direct negotiation with customers. In any case, the matter at issue is whether a larger or smaller amount of money shall flow from or to parties of one class and a relative advantage or disadvantage shall accrue to parties of other classes. That is the focal point of negotiations or decisions, insofar as their outcome turns on financial considerations.

4.23 There are many such potential conflicts of interest. The reinvestment of profits for growth, diversification or research and development (a managerial interest) is at odds with the payment of dividends out of profits (a shareholders' interest). The relevant financial indicator is the relationship between profits and dividends. A fair assessment of the facts cannot be made unless profits and dividends are money amounts similar in kind. The payment of debts (a creditors' interest) may be at odds with the payment of dividends (a shareholders' interest) if the funds readily accessible to a company are limited. The relevant indicator is the relationship between the funds readily accessible and the amounts of debts outstanding and dividends proposed. An assessment of the fairness to parties of each class, of the actions or proposals of the management, cannot properly be made unless the representation of funds accessible is substantially similar in kind to the amounts of debts and dividends. Claims for increases in wages (an employees' interest) may be at odds with claims for increases in dividends (a shareholders' interest). The relevant indicator is the relationship of wages (or the level of wages generally of a company) to dividends (or to profits, since reinvested profits are expected to yield benefits to shareholders). The level of taxes payable (a governmental or public interest) is at odds with the interests of parties which might otherwise benefit directly (customers, employees or share-holders). The relevant indicator is the relationship between taxes payable and profits.

4.24 Such potential conflicts of interest as these may become actual at any time. The immediate parties in any given case attempt to assess the fairness (in the interest of each party, as it is seen by that party) of the present arrangement or any proposed rearrangement. What is judged to be fair or equitable by one party must be capable of being seen to be fair or equitable to others. In financial matters, that rests on the accounts. Yet, attention has been drawn on occasions, in trades union publications, to the irrelevance, obscurity and unreliability of some of the elements of company accounts. Governmental bodies, especially those concerned with price regulation and governmental purchase contracts, have complained of the diversity of accounting methods and the unreliability of their results. Associations of companies and directors have themselves found cause to be concerned about the quality of the profits computed by established processes, particularly with reference to the levels of taxation and prices. When so many parties of different interests and skills may have recourse to company accounts in negotiations with companies, it seems clear that "a fair view" can only be given if present and potential interests in a company's assets or gross revenues are represented in factual money amounts, and otherwise in terms that are up to date, readily comprehensible, and uniformly interpretable by all parties. Anything else would be unfair to some party, and may turn out to be inimical to all parties and the company itself.

4.25 For example, a company may have in contemplation the raising of additional funds by an issue of shares or other securities. Favourable profits and correspondingly favourable amounts of assets make the task the easier, and the servicing costs more favourable to the company. The raising of the money at favourable interest or dividend rates may be represented as advantageous to the company. But if the reported amounts of profit and assets are the greater by reason of the inclusion in them of conjectural or otherwise unrealistic amounts, prospective investors in the issue are to that extent misled. Workers and suppliers may be induced in the light of the reported figures, and in the light of the success which those figures and the new issue imply, to seek higher wages and other factor prices, when in fact the company is not able to meet them. To explain that, notwithstanding the reported figures, the company cannot meet increased charges would entail damage to the trust in the management and in the company of those who seek renegotiation. On the other hand, if no explanation is given and higher wages or prices are negotiated, the future of the company and those dependent on it may be prejudiced. The interlocking nature of the accounts entails that errors in some amounts may influence a variety of the indicators used by different parties. Errors in the amounts of accounts receivable and inventories, for example, affect the amount of profit, the current ratio, the debt to equity ratio, the asset backing of shares and the rate of return. Judgements made of the company may therefore be materially astray; and in ways which differentially affect parties who are concerned with only some of the indicators mentioned. No source of such misdirection can yield accounts which are generally fair to all parties dependent financially, in any way, on the success of a company.

307

The Interpretation of Statutes

4.26 It has been contended that the phrase "a true and fair view" has come to have a meaning other than the ordinary meaning which lay persons may ascribe to it. But, in the first place, it is required to occur in statements by directors and auditors which are intended to be informative to all persons, lay or professionally qualified, who use accounts. If the phrase were to have an unusual meaning, unknown to lay persons, the statements of directors and auditors could be of no generally understandable significance. It is not imaginable that the legislature could have intended that consequence. In the second place, although the professional recommendations assert that a true and fair view *implies* the consistent application of generally accepted principles, nowhere do they say what a true and fair view *is*.

4.27 As the phrase occurs in an act of the legislature, some guidance is obtainable from the canons of interpretation of statutes. There are two general rules. The first is: the plain and natural meaning of the words used is to be adopted unless that meaning is contrary to the intention of the legislature, is contrary to other parts of the statute, or leads to patent absurdity. The second is: where words and phrases may have both an ordinary and popular meaning and a technical meaning, they are to be interpreted in their ordinary sense, unless from the context it is clear that they should be interpreted in a way that is special or peculiar to a certain trade or profession. Neither before nor since the enactment of the statute have the professional bodies stated any special or peculiar meaning which should be assigned to the phrase in question. The statement mentioned in the previous paragraph to the effect that a true and fair view implies consistent application of generally accepted principles is of no assistance, since it has been shown in numerous litigated cases and other circumstances that the application of generally accepted principles may lead to patently untrue and unfair accounts. It seems therefore that the plain and natural meaning of the phrase must be adopted, in accordance with the rules of interpretation.

4.28   The quality standard represented by "true and fair" does not, of course, stand by itself. The statute refers to "profit or loss" and "state of affairs" as the matters on which a true and fair view shall be given. It may be suggested therefore that statutory definitions of profit or loss and state of affairs are necessary to make clear the intention of the statute.

4.29   Profit or loss in relation to a corporation is defined as "the profit or loss resulting from operations of that corporation" (s. 161). The Ninth Schedule refers to a number of specific items that would be part of the calculation of a profit or loss; but no general statement other than the above definition is given. The definition does not exclude any particular gain or loss, nor the outcome of any operation or class of operations; it is completely inclusive. Whether gains or losses arise from the ordinary trade in inventories, or from the holding of goods the prices of which rise or fall, is immaterial. The consequences of all transactions and of events occurring between transactions are embraced by "the profit or loss resulting from operations".

4.30   The Companies Act provides no definition or interpretation of "state of affairs" or "financial position". It has been suggested (para. 3.13) that these terms are synonymous. "State of affairs" is used in the Act with reference to a balance sheet; it can have reference therefore to no other state of affairs than the state of the financial affairs of a company. Now, it would be strange indeed if the legislature intended that the members of companies should have a balance sheet which does not represent the financial relationships of a company with the rest of the world. Such a balance sheet would not be indicative of the solvency of a company or of any other of the matters shown in Chapter 3 to be of interest to the parties associated with companies. Without such functions in view, it is impossible to imagine what use would be served by the publication of balance sheets. In any case, no specific or technical meaning has been ascribed to "state of affairs" by professional accounting or other organizations. The term should therefore be given its ordinary and natural meaning, which, the Committee believes, is the meaning assigned to it in para. 3.13 above.

4.31   It has been established that the accounts shall give a true and fair view of the dated profits and states of affairs from time to time; that true and fair should be interpreted in accordance with their ordinary and natural meanings; that variously dated cost prices or valuations, conjectural amounts, and practically improper aggregations, are not conducive to the giving of a true and fair view. It has been shown, on the other hand, that up-to-date money amounts, and a uniform method of valuation of non-money assets at their money equivalents, are serviceable and comprehensible to users of accounts. Accounts satisfying these conditions would be of serviceable quality. We turn to input and processing standards.

Input and Processing Standards

4.32 In the ordinary processes of accounting considerable attention is paid to some of the inputs. Amounts received and amounts paid are expected to be supported by documentary evidence, often checked by company officers other than those engaged in its accounting. It might be expected that there would be standards for the documentary evidence which is admissible as support for the recording of the financial consequences of all such transactions. There are such standards; the internal arrangements described as "internal control" are concerned, among other things, with performance according to those standards.

4.33 But when non-money assets are purchased, a company has so much less money and so many more other assets. The dated financial significance of the possession of money is its capacity at that date to buy goods in general, or any goods in particular, or to pay debts. But the dated financial significance of the possession of goods is not equal to the dated financial significance of the money spent to acquire them. It rises or falls as the resale prices of goods rise and fall. This is well known to all who buy and sell; it is an ineluctable fact of business life. A balance sheet which is to be serviceable in the manner described in Chapter 3 must therefore take account of this fact. The effect of such a rise or fall is an input which does not arise directly from a transaction, but its inclusion is nevertheless crucial. To ignore it and to continue to show non-money assets at their costs is to represent that a company's financial position is the same as before the money was laid out. To publish successive balance sheets in which assets continue to be represented by their costs is analogous to publishing a newspaper which contains the same "news" in successively dated issues.

4.34 A strong line has always been taken in accounting on the inclusion in accounting calculations of charges for depreciation. This is, in fact, an example of the recognition of the change from time to time in the dated financial significance of some non-money assets. The object of depreciation charges is to reduce the book value of depreciating assets to their expected resale prices by the date at which they are expected to be put out of use. Although the basic and common meaning of depreciation is a reduction in price, the usual way of making annual charges for depreciation is by a calculation, which only by chance will reduce the book value at the end of a year to its financial significance at that date. There are no standards for determining the annual charge or the money equivalent of the asset at balance date by reference to independent information. Accounting standards designed to secure the serviceable quality of accounts should include standards for ascertaining the appropriate amounts.

4.35 The money equivalent or financial significance of an asset may, of course, rise above the amount paid for it or above a previously ascertained and reported amount. That is appreciation. But not only is appreciation disregarded by the usual application of depreciation formulae; accounting for appreciation is actively discouraged, in respect of depreciating and other assets. In applying the accrual principle, a selective rule is commonly used: take account of all accruals which reduce the reported amounts of profit and assets, but not of accruals which increase these amounts. This practice is described as conservatism. But it is clearly contrary to the giving of a true and fair view both to overstate and to understate the amounts of profits and assets. An input or processing standard designed to produce accounts of serviceable quality cannot properly require or enjoin any such discriminatory practice.

309

47

Diverse Calculations and their Purposes

4.36 Several quite distinctive types of financial calculation are made for various purposes in the ordinary conduct of business. The purpose of some budgetary calculations, is to yield indications of the expected future money amounts of profit and assets. Except for the amounts of assets at the base date from which such calculations are made, the inputs to these calculations are all conjectures; and the estimated future money amounts of profits and assets are also conjectural. The purpose of other such calculations, net present value or discounted cash flow calculations, is to enable managers to discriminate between the prospective outcomes of different possible future projects. With minor exceptions, the inputs to these calculations are conjectural. The purpose of other such calculations, actual and prospective cost accounts, is to provide guidance on quite specific facets of a company's operations, such as the processing costs of products or the costs of carrying out specific policies or the prices at which products might be offered for sale. These three kinds of calculations are made for internal managerial purposes; they may quite reasonably include such conjectural or hypothetical amounts as are considered necessary. Lastly, there are the periodical accounts, the purpose of which is to represent the aggregative consequences of past operations and the financial positions of companies at stated past dates. As this information is entirely historical, and in principle verifiable, there is no occasion for the inclusion in it of conjectural amounts.

4.37 The different purposes of these calculations entail that the inputs to and outputs of each of them shall be different in kind. The prospective purchase (or replacement) price of an asset is serviceable in budgetary calculations; as an indication of prospective commitments, not as indicating resources available. It has nothing to do with reporting the consequences of past transactions and events. The net present values of possible future projects are serviceable in choosing between them; but they are not serviceable in the construction of budgets, and they have nothing to do with reporting the consequence of past transactions and events. The actual costs of assets and operations are indicative of the actual cash outlays made; but they are only one-half of the inputs to profit calculations, and they have nothing to do with the subsequent representation of a company's financial position. That some actual or proposed accounting standards endorse the use in accounts of original costs, replacement prices and net present values ("capitalized values"), is evidence of the failure to identify these magnitudes with the particular purposes of the calculations in which they occur. If there were input and processing standards for each of the several kinds of calculation mentioned in para. 4.36, clearly related to the function served by each kind of calculation, there would be no confusion about the relevance of particular inputs to their appropriate calculations. There would be no confusion of what is apposite for internal calculations with what is necessary for company accounts on which parties external to the management of a company will rely.

4.38 It is possible that external parties make use of company accounts for guidance about the future prospects of companies. Trends in profits and liquidities and other features of companies may be used for this purpose. It may be supposed, by some, that this possible use of accounts entails that reported profits should be indicative of what is "normal" or "sustainable" or "prospective" profit, and that the balance sheet should be consistent with this. However, the Companies Act provides no support for any such belief. It requires specifically that the accounts shall relate to matters which (at the date of any annual general meeting, for example) are past. Any input or process which has the effect mentioned is not in accordance with the express intention of the Act. To "capitalize" interest paid on projects in the course of development, and thus to exclude them from the profit calculation of the year in which interest is paid (except in the circumstances of s. 69 of the Act) is one such process. To defer the recognition of losses occurring in a given period and to "amortize" them over a series of future periods is another. Such practices as these confuse the facts relating to the past with intentions or expectations of the future. Their persistence indicates the necessity of input and processing standards which are consistent with the required quality standard of accounts.

The Setting of Standards

4.39   The task of the Committee does not extend to the construction of particular standards. The observations of this Chapter have therefore been suggestive only. It has been necessary to refer to particular practices by way of illustration. But the necessity of a general standard relating to the quality of the accounts as a whole is not thereby overshadowed. Insofar as the quality standard specified in the Companies Act may, for lack of interpretation in the past, be misunderstood, it seems necessary that its interpretation be elucidated. This may be done by an amendment to the Act, giving an interpretation; or by a more elaborate and clear description, in the Ninth Schedule, of what is required to be shown in the accounts; or by separate legislation or regulation. A suggestion in the latter direction is made in Chapter 8. Given that the quality standard is sufficiently clear, the development of input and processing standards in respect of the many and varied items which may appear in accounts may properly be the principal concern of the standard-setting apparatus of the professional bodies.

311

The Future of Accounting:
An Accountant's Manifesto[*]

Accounting has a brighter future than its past. Of that I have no doubt, for its past has been murky and muddled in the extreme. Its future is bright, for the utility of accounting information in the formation of business and governmental policy is increasingly being recognised. That information can inform investors and creditors in a far better way than in the past. It can inform price and wage negotiations, regulatory processes, taxation and industry assistance policies, the supervision of national and international enterprise in general, and so on. Never have so many uses been made of accounting information as are now made.

313

But it will serve in all those directions only if it is well designed to serve. And that is still a task before us. It is a task that demands some dedication, some grit and some determination. If my remarks do nothing else, I hope they might clear the air of some of the things that confuse or threaten to confuse our vision. The things I speak of are the clichés, the bits of homespun philosophy, and the catchwords which we adopt in place of thought.

First, I hold the view that the accounting profession should, as far as its techniques are concerned adopt nothing but the best. I've no doubt many suppose that we are doing what is best. If that were the case why does there persist so much criticism, litigation, uneasiness — all round the world? Far too often we are virtually coerced into doing **"something"** which is poorly thought out, devised in haste. Indeed, in discussions I have heard in the main English-speaking countries it has been said repeatedly that we cannot expect to get ideal solutions to problems. Why not? We may not **get** ideal solutions – but we certainly won't unless we keep the pursuit of ideals before us. I deplore the attitude which presumes that we must put up with patchy makeshifts – that is a denial of the responsibilities of professionalism.

Second, I hold the view that accountants alone are able to resolve their technical problems; and I deplore the view that accounting is too important a matter to be left in the hands of accountants. If we renounce the right to do our own thing as well as possible, we make the

[*]   Australian Society of Accountants, New South Wales Division, **Address**, Sydney, May 1978.

business we profess the creature of every power group which would seek to coerce us. It is foolish and a denial of the expertise we claim, to suggest that we do not know what the financial and commercial community needs of the profession; for to know that is our proper business, and we need only to look carefully about us to see what those needs are. If there are any who do not know what is expected of us, let them abandon the right to direct and influence the profession until they know better – and let them leave the guidance of the profession to those who do know.

Third, I hold the view that accounting principles and practices and the products of them can be matters of firm knowledge, and I deplore the opposite view that accounting is and cannot be otherwise than a matter of opinion. If any man asserts – and many have done so – that the greater part of the contents of financial statements are matters of opinion – he sells his profession short. If we have no hard and solid core of principles we will continue to be the butt of those who know even less than ourselves, to the greater shame of and diminishing respect for the profession. There is no surer way of white-anting the profession or allowing others to subvert it than admitting that it rests on opinion rather than solid and firm principle.

Fourth, I hold the view that the public esteem of the profession rests on its standard of technical competence – and I deplore the view that public esteem depends on deliberate exercises in so-called "public relations" development. Good wine needs no bush, they say. A good profession likewise needs no bull-dust. No amount of self promotion will secure anything of lasting value. As long as technical solecisms, misdemeanours, fallacious practices persist, protestations of probity will be laughable. And if all those things are swept away, puffing is unnecessary. I reject the idea that we need to resort to the same propagandist exercises as makers of products which depend on puffing. As I said earlier, there is no denying the demand for financial information of quality. The only justification for p.r. then is that it is a counter to criticism when we can't, haven't the wit to, introduce technical solutions which will remove the cause of criticism. And that is the course of an intellectually bankrupt – not of an intellectually vigorous – profession.

Fifth, I believe that the profession has nothing to fear from government, or business, or any other sector or the fourth estate provided it attends scrupulously to doing its job well. I deplore the

314

view that governmental supervision in one fashion or another is to be feared, or is retrograde. Government and governmental authorities are the only kinds of authorities which can properly give weight to the public interest. Every private business firm, professional association or other organization has significant private or sectional interests to promote. Private sector organizations would be foolish to disregard the public interest in what they do; but their actions must, by the very nature of their constitutions, be geared to private interests. In this the profession should be realistic. But if its practices are of the highest possible quality no external scrutiny can do it harm. Its strength will be the strength of ten, because its heart is pure.

Sixth, I believe that the profession should be intensely self-critical. I deplore the view that we all must stand behind any pronouncement, judgement or standard advanced by officers or committees or councils. If you watch closely you will see that exhortations to stand behind one proposal, scheme or authority are parts of the processes of demagoguery – they are the recourse of persons, committees or councils who have no adequate grounds for confidence in the propriety of their proposals. A professional association can have more spirit, liveliness, vigour if it is actively self-critical than if its members are adjured to support and supinely support the status quo. I get tired too of being invited to be constructively critical. Why shouldn't you or I or anyone else be destructively critical. In the construction trades, wreckers get paid handsomely for destruction. If the profession wishes to rebuild any part of itself, it is good prophylaxis to tear down whatever stands in its way. Don't worry – there are enough conservatives among us to see that the profession survives – but without self-criticism we remain open to the sharper and more destructive attacks of the rest of the world.

That is my manifesto.

I have stuck to matters of a general nature – but they all affect the mode and manner and efficacy of practice. The profession has wider and greater opportunities for service than ever before in its history. But those very opportunities bring the profession and its practices under wider and closer scrutiny. Old excuses and apologetics will not protect it from criticism.

Usefulness — The Vanishing Premise in Accounting Standard Setting

In the interval of some forty years over which attempts have been made to set up general bodies of accounting rules or standards, the idea of putting a man on the moon was conceived. The idea was turned into history — ten years ago. Of course it was costly; and to devote a large sum to the project was certainly a political or quasi-political choice. But whether it was feasible was not a political question. It was a question — or rather a whole host of questions — of technical knowledge and expertise. In the course of answering those questions (for they were all answered), it is certain that a vast number of specifics were tried and found to be wanting in some respect, under increasingly severe or increasingly numerous tests of adequacy. It seems hardly likely that the task of devising a set of serviceable accounting standards is a more demanding task. Yet it remains unfinished. I suggest that the reason lies, at least in part, in the phenomenon of the vanishing premise.

Trial and Error

In all scientific, or otherwise disciplined pursuits, we proceed by what is loosely called 'trial and error'. If anything 'tried' turns out to be in 'error', because it does not procure what it is expected to procure, it is regarded as 'on trial' until something else is found that is 'less in error'. The object of all research and development is to replace what is less effectual by something more effectual in bringing about what is desired or intended. The process has been described as a process of finding successively better approximations to an ideal — whether an ideal tool, an ideal programme or an ideal theory. It entails the search for flaws in a device or practice, the search for means of reducing those flaws and the rejection of devices or practices (or parts of them) which are the 'more-flawed' in favour of others that are 'less-flawed'. The method may be described, more exactly than 'trial and error', as *trial and error-elimination* (Popper [9]).

This has not been the method characteristic of accounting. The accounting method has been rather a method of *trial and error-accretion*. By no other method could there have been developed such a diverse and numerous set of rules or practices as those now available and permissible. If that diversity had given rise to no problems, there would be no concern about it. There would have been no cause for the professional bodies to devote so much time and effort to devising standards, and no reason for public officials and members of legislative bodies to express concern for the lack of standards. But quite evidently there is something 'wrong', something 'more in error' or 'more-flawed' than is tolerable by leaders of the profession and influential outsiders.

What is 'right' and what is 'wrong' — or, to put it less sharply, what is tolerable and what is not — can be interpreted in two ways. There is an old-fashioned dictum: 'the king can do no wrong'. A similar dictum has guided, or sheltered, other autocracies, of which, in our generation, the professions are examples. It can be made to appear that the practices of a profession are not wrong if it is maintained that what the profession agrees to do, or what is 'generally accepted', is right. However, to maintain that a practice is generally accepted requires some test (or 'trial') of general acceptance; for example, an expression in favour of it by the professional constituency. There has not, as far as I can recall, been any attempt thus to put on trial any of the practices or rules that have come to be described as generally accepted. It may therefore be an error to maintain that any practice said to be generally accepted *is* generally accepted. In any case a vote by the professional constituency in favour of any rule or practice could only be said to decide what the constituency *deems,* or will thereafter deem, to be *generally accepted by it.* It could not decide what is accepted by or acceptable to any other constituencies such as the users of its products. One precautionary or remedial step against the possibility of bias on the part of a limited constituency is to widen the constituency. In accounting this has taken the form of seeking to involve some groups beyond the professional group. Opinions have been sought from 'selected' outsiders. There have been occasional surveys of the opinions of outsiders, such as brokers and analysts, on their general attitudes towards specific accounting systems or towards particular bits of information. There have been invitations to outsiders to join in ventures intended to lead to specific prescriptions, often outsiders 'friendly' to the proponents of those prescriptions. But neither for limited nor wider constituencies has the polling process been used seriously (by extensive and randomized inquiry) to determine what is accepted or acceptable.

The second, and more fundamental, interpretation of what is right or wrong does not turn on what is accepted or acceptable, but what is demonstrably serviceable. No king, by edict, and no profession, by general agreement, can make the ratio of the circumference of a circle to its diameter equal to 3. No generally accepted accounting practice can make a company more profitable or more creditworthy than it is. Some practices may create illusions of profitability or creditworthiness. Illusions may be serviceable to their creators, for they may stave off confrontation with others. But illusions are of no service to those who want indications.

If tests of serviceability were obvious, we would make no errors. They are not obvious, however; for several reasons. *First,* skills are learned from teachers or superiors. In that setting the learner is at a disadvantage. He is junior in status, knowledge and experience to his mentor. He is seldom disposed to question what he is taught. Even if he has some doubts about particulars they are likely to be suppressed, since he has no means of appraising the grand design of which the particulars are presumed to be a part. The educational adventure, often depicted as a process of learning how to think, turns out to be a process of learning to think as the mentor thinks. Once that indoctrination is complete, whatever errors may have been absorbed come to be accepted as 'special features' of the field under study. Needless to say, that description of learning is not limited to accounting education and training; all kinds of skills are the product of indoctrination in the prevalent doctrines.

Second, what is learned is reinforced by the conventions of practice, the standards of practice of one's peers, whether or not they are embodied in formal statements of standards. As long as those standards are the products of the same indoctrination process, or of those who have gone through it, their flaws (if any) are not likely to be obvious, and the circumstantial pressure to conform with the practices of one's peers and to respect the wisdom of one's professional leaders tends to the suppression of doubts about the adequacy of one's learned skills.

Third, the products of most skills serve a variety of functions, and are commonly expected to be ready to serve one function or another as the circumstances of the user dictate. The principal products of accounting — periodical financial statements — are multi-functional products. It is possible, and it has been the case, that concentration on serviceability in one respect or another gives rise to oversight of other respects in which financial statements should be equally serviceable. Debate over the priority of functions thus stands in the way of testing rules or systems by reference to multi-functional considerations.

Finally, it does not seem to have been clear what constitutes a test. A trial run, with the object of finding whether the operations necessary to obtain a specified result can be carried out, is not a test of the serviceability of the result. A sampling of opinions — are you in favour of this or that? — is not a test; for each respondent is disposed to respond in the light of his prior indoctrination or his immediate circumstances, rather than on the general merits of the subject of the inquiry. Especially is this likely to be the case when respondents are asked whether this or that is useful. I once heard an eminent U.S. accountant assert that no business could properly be conducted if accounts were permitted to take account of upwards revaluations of assets — in patent disregard for the fact that the practice was widespread beyond the United States.

The Vanishing Cheshire Cat

It is almost impossible to imagine how a complete style of accounting may be tested for usefulness. Users are many and varied. Their circumstances, and their specific interests in the corpus of information in a given set of financial statements, are varied. And if they 'find useful' the information they are given, it may well be because there is no other information by which they can judge its usefulness. These may be reasons why accountants have not been explicit about usefulness; why the word itself or the idea crops up and vanishes intermittently in accounting expositions, like Lewis Carroll's Cheshire cat.

But it is possible to be explicit about the usefulness of particular bits of information, and the usefulness of the particular terms and ideas with which argument or advocacy are clothed. A term is useful — in analysis, or advocacy, or practice — if its meaning is clear. A bit of information is useful if it can be shown to be clearly related to a process of thought, a choice or an action. If an accounting system or a specification for an accounting system is made up of components which themselves are useful, the system

319

73

may be expected to be useful. These will be the grounds on which, in the following analysis, certain ideas and the bits of information they entail will be said to be useful or not useful.

I have described usefulness as a vanishing *premise* on the ground that every advocate of a rule or practice would contend that the product of it is (or would be) useful. That it is a premise, a proposition taken as one of the grounds of a conclusion, may not always be clear. There is very little by way of explicit argument from premises to conclusions in expositions of accounting. But whether described as a premise or not, that in fact is what its function is.

The material to which attention is directed is a cluster of official or quasi-official expositions of U.S. authorities published during the 'seventies. They are Statement No. 4 of the Accounting Principles Board, *Basic Concepts and Accounting Principles Underlying Financial Statements of Business Enterprises* (1970), *'APBS4'* for short; the Report of the AICPA Study Group, *Objectives of Financial Statements* (1973), *'Study Group Report'* for short; FASB Exposure Draft, *Objectives of Financial Reporting and Elements of Financial Statements of Business Enterprises* (1977), *'FASB Objectives'* for short; FASB Statement of Financial Accounting Concepts No. 1, *Objectives of Financial Reporting for Business Enterprises* (1978), *'FASB Concepts'* for short; and FASB Exposure Draft, *Qualitative Characteristics: Criteria for Selecting and Evaluating Financial Accounting and Reporting Policies* (1979), *'FASB Criteria'* for short.

The choice of U.S. material is dictated by the general breadth of the items listed. In no other country has there been such a cluster of wide-ranging expositions. The material is relatively recent; it may therefore be taken as the fruit of attempts to establish standards dating back much earlier than the 'seventies; and it may be taken as in some sense indicating the present state of thought and practice in an influential country. There are some differences between the documents beside their authorship. *APBS4* is more comprehensive and detailed than the others; and, though it is the oldest, it is intended to serve until superseded (*FASB Concepts,* para. 3). *FASB Objectives* and *FASB Concepts* carry distinct traces of the influence of the *Study Group Report,* but certain of the matters dealt with in *FASB Objectives* were deferred for later examination in setting up *FASB Concepts* and *FASB Criteria.*

Functions of Financial Statements

For decades there have been brief indications of the functions of financial statements in the textbook and general literature. It might have been expected that when, at last, in the 'seventies, those functions came under closer attention, they would have been examined in depth, given ample analysis, and crystallized to the stage of being pointed guides to the contents of financial statements. However, the specifications remain vague and partial. Generally, it is contended that the function of financial statements is to provide information that is useful in making economic decisions (*APBS4*, para. 9; *Study Group Report,* p. 13; *FASB Objectives,* para. 8; *FASB Concepts,* para. 9). The decision-makers in contemplation are numerous, and the decisions they make range from decisions in their own interests to the efficient allocation of resources in the community at large (*APBS4,* paras 43-47; *Study Group Report,* paras 14, 17-30; *FASB Objectives,* paras 4-9; *FASB Concepts,* paras 9-16).

320

Now it is unquestionable that much information is used, beside that contained in financial statements, in the kinds of decision-making referred to — technical, financial and economic information, some of the factual and some of the conjectural kind. If the information provided of *one* kind is claimed to be useful, the claim must be specific, sufficiently specific to indicate that it is a necessary kind of information, and (if to produce it is costly) that it is not otherwise available. To indicate that it is necessary entails demonstrating the particular points in the decision-making process at which some or all of the information may influence choice. I shall presently show that scarcely any attempt is made to do this. But there is a prior question: what is meant by 'financial statements'?

Business decisions, by insiders or outsiders, depend in part on factual knowledge of the financial performance of a firm in the past, in part on knowledge of the means available or accessible to it at the time of decision-making, and in part on estimates of the expected financial outcomes of the courses of action then under consideration. We may pick on any singular aspect of the financial affairs of a firm — say, its cash holdings. Any significant decision of the firm will be influenced in part by the drift of its cash holdings in the past, in part by the amount of its cash holdings at the time of making a decision, and in part by the expected future drift of its cash holdings consequent upon the alternative decisions it may make. These three kinds of information on cash holdings are distinctively different; but they are used in conjunction. For example, if the past drift has been downwards and the present holdings are small, *one* pertinent aspect of the decision will be the prospective capacities of alternatives to reverse the drift. If the three kinds of information are embodied in 'statements', as they well may be, all three statements could be called 'financial statements'. If they are so called, their distinctive differences are not identified, and no clue is provided to the design of any one of them. Their distinctive functions may be confused, so that one kind of statement may be treated, in exposition or practice, as if it were expected to serve in a way that only another kind of statement can serve.

The reference to information that is useful in making *economic* decisions casts a very wide net. All three kinds of statement would be caught in it. The vagueness and generality of the documents cited provide an escape from the disciplined discussion of details. It would have been more pointed, and more correct to speak of 'information useful in appraising the financial aspects of decision-situations'. If that had been said, the authors of the documents may have been obliged to say what the financial aspects of a situation are. But even a specification of function in those terms would have embraced the three kinds of statement mentioned. I shall turn to budgetary and other conjectural or exploratory statements later. In the sections that immediately follow I shall deal principally with periodical balance sheets and income statements, for those statements are the principal subjects of the documents considered.

The first point, then, is that at the very outset — the identification of the functions or objectives of financial statements — no interpretation is given to 'useful'. Unless some interpretation is subsequently developed, it is almost inevitable that the conclusions or rules put forward will be based on other premises than usefulness; or, where no distinction is drawn between statements that report on the past, statements that represent the present and statements that estimate the future, it is likely that the

321

specifications in respect of any of them will be confused.

Financial Position

For a couple of generations at least, a balance sheet has been held to be a statement of financial position. But very little attention has been paid to the meaning of financial position, or the usefulness in decision-making of knowledge of financial position.

APBS4 described financial position as the relationship between assets, liabilities and owners' equity at a particular time; financial position, it said, is represented in the balance sheet (paras 11, 138). But the information given is to be that 'required to be disclosed under generally accepted accounting principles' (para. 133). By way of elucidation the Statement gives 'seven qualitative objectives'; it will suffice to refer to four. *Relevant* information is said to be information that 'bears on the economic decisions for which it is used' (para. 88). This is simply 'usefulness' by another name. *Verifiable* information is information that is corroborable by independent measurers (para. 90). *Neutral* information is information that is 'independent of presumptions about particular needs and desires of specific users of the information' (para. 91). *Comparable* information is information that is free of differences arising 'merely from differences in financial accounting treatments' (para. 93). These specifications (and others) occur also in *FASB Criteria*. It might be expected, on this footing, that a statement of financial position would be factual (otherwise its contents would not be verifiable); that it would be free of the influence of the needs and desires even of the managers of firms, for they too are users of the information; and that 'differences in accounting treatments' would be proscribed — all in the interest of relevance or usefulness. The propriety of verifiability, neutrality and comparability may be established by a line of argument, one premise of which is usefulness. But the repeated reference in *APBS4* to 'generally accepted accounting principles' cuts across any such line of argument; those principles are said to rest on consensus (paras 27, 137). But consensus may have nothing to do with a line of argument, and clearly in the present case it has not. For, despite the catalogue of qualitative objectives, the Statement condones the then generally accepted principles which are inconsistent with the 'objectives'.

Further, to assert simply that financial position *is* the relationship between assets, liabilities and owners' equity provides no constraint on what shall be *represented* as financial position. There may (or may not) be an implicit presumption that the representation shall correspond, descriptively and quantitatively, with what is. But implicit terms or presumptions are no substitute for an explicit prescription. Only if it is said quite explicitly that a statement of financial position shall correspond with a financial position at a stated date is a constraint provided; and only then does it become necessary to justify the constraint in terms of the usefulness of the result.

The reference to 'statement of financial position' in the *Study Group Report* (pp. 35-6) is brief, vague and confused. The statement is expected to be 'useful for predicting, comparing and evaluating enterprise earning power'. But there is no indication of the components or aggregates that are useful in those settings (predicting, comparing and evaluating are different settings), or in what ways they may be useful. The discussion shifts uneasily between advocacy of historical cost and current value measures, making the choice dependent on unspecified 'circumstances'. That the choice is so dependent makes it evident that no clear and specific idea of the usefulness of the information was entertained by the authors of the document. In any case, the allusion to relevance (p. 57) should surely have ruled out historical costs; for values determined at a prior date cannot be said to be relevant at a balance date, either for the representation of a dated financial position, or for any decision to be made on the basis of a dated financial position.

The references to financial position in *FASB Objectives* are equally meagre. Statements 'that reflect the recorded state or condition of an enterprise at a particular time [are] described generally as statements of financial position' (para. 36). But there is no indication of what is understood by financial state or condition or position. It is said that 'an analogy is sometimes drawn between cartography and accounting and between maps and financial statements' (para. 41). A map whose features do not correspond in specified details with the terrain mapped is useless; but *FASB Objectives* does not draw the obvious inference that the elements of a balance sheet should correspond with the factual financial features of an enterprise at the date it bears. Indeed, the reference to 'recorded financial state' tends to make the record 'superior' to the facts. Yet no one would contend that a recorded cash balance that differed from the factual balance could be a legitimate element of a financial position.

To judge from the text of *FASB Concepts,* it has become possible to do without the term 'financial position' altogether. There are references to an enterprise's economic resources, obligations and owners' equity, but none to financial position as such.

The relevance to judgement and action of a dated financial position, representing the consequences of the past and the means of proceeding into the future, is scarcely deniable. Nor is it deniable that from time to time the components of financial position may appear in books of account at amounts that do not correspond with the facts; they must be discovered. But which facts are to be discovered if there is no adequate description of what is meant by a dated financial position? The 'all-encompassing' function of accounting as contributing to decision-making (*FASB Criteria*, para. 24) makes fine rhetoric; but it does not advance the elucidation of the substantive content of serviceable financial statements.

Financial Position — Aggregative

All allusions to financial position, and the general practice of drawing up balance sheets, entail that what is represented is aggregative. The aggregate amounts of assets, liabilities and owners' equity are determined; and there are sub-aggregates in each case. In the context of a double-entry system, balance sheet aggregations may be thought simply to be a check on the mechanical completeness of the record. But aggregation has a more substantial justification.

The very use of class names, 'assets', 'liabilities' and 'owners' equity', implies that the amounts by which the items in each class are represented are homogeneous amounts, properly aggregable amounts. Further, the way in which aggregates are linked in official expositions implies that the amounts of all three classes are properly aggregable (or subtractable). *APBS4* describes owners' equity as the excess of assets over liabilities (para. 132), and net income as 'the net increase in owners' equity . . . from profit-directed activities' (para. 134). If the amounts of the three classes (and of net income) were not homogeneous, the differences would not be valid differences. All the documents, whether explicit about the matter or not, contemplate that users of financial statements are concerned with aggregates, and, in particular, with the financial positions of whole enterprises.

An aggregative position cannot be represented by improper aggregations. Yet *APBS4* and all practice under generally accepted accounting principles tolerate improper aggregation. *First,* take a brief list of assets. Cash and receivables are balance-sheet-dated amounts; inventory at LIFO or the lower of cost and market is not a balance-sheet-dated amount; plant at cost less depreciation is not an amount similar to either of the two previous amounts; nor is land or listed securities at cost. Here are four distinctively different amounts that are added as if they were substantially similar in financial significance. But the financial significance of their aggregate is inconceivable. *Second,* since all prices are determined in the unique matrix of the price structure of the points of time when they are received or paid, no series of purchase prices incurred at different times can have any subsequently dated aggregative significance. Yet cost prices (or their unamortized residuals) are added as if they had a balance-sheet-dated significance. *Third,* if prices were paid for assets when the dollar denominators of those prices were themselves of different commercial significance (or general purchasing power), no aggregation of cost prices (or their unamortized residuals) can be a valid indicator of a position in balance-sheet-dated dollars.

There are thus three types of violation of the rules of aggregation or aggregative measurement in the type of balance sheet implicit in the principles of *APBS4.* There is a brief suggestion in the *Study Group Report* that the principal financial statements are, or may be, articulated (p. 38), but not in such a way that net income emerges as the increment in net assets of a period. On the other hand, there is an explicit suggestion that 'financial statements might contain data based on a combination of valuation bases' (p. 41). A reader might well ask, and the authors of the document should themselves have asked, what the significance might be of articulated statements containing heterogeneous bits of information. Further, although notice is taken of the claim of some critics of present practice that changes in the general purchasing power of the money unit should be recognized formally in financial statements (p. 16), no objective is stated which explicitly entails that financial position should be expressed in prices determined in a uniform setting and in balance-sheet-dated dollars. The matter is set aside in *FASB Concepts* as the subject of a further statement. There is brief reference in *FASB Criteria* to levels of aggregation (para. 8); but there is no discussion of the conditions under which any aggregation is valid. Since aggregation is such a pervasive aspect of accounting, and since users of accounts are concerned with aggregative positions and results, the conditions of valid aggregation surely are among the criteria for selecting component amounts.

If there is some sense in which in accounting, unlike other pursuits, the addition of heterogeneous amounts provides useful information, that usefulness must be demonstrated. Lay persons are not likely to be aware of the existence of improper aggregations. Seeing aggregates, they would expect, and consider that they were entitled to expect, that they represent genuine and realistic totals. But professionals should know the consequences of improper aggregation and the virtues of proper aggregation. That analysts derive indicators of position and progress from balance sheets, and that lenders expect the further borrowings of borrowers to be controlled by reference to balance sheet figures, are well known. But the products of analysis and the prospects of control are delusive if the data supplied are fictions — for that is exactly what invalid aggregates are.

Other fictions, of course, contribute to the fictional character of aggregates under generally accepted accounting principles. Allocations give rise to fictions; a lower of cost and market valuation is a fiction: a valuation based on straight-line depreciation or any other calculation by formula is a fiction. The burden of demonstrating that they are serviceable fictions, for balance sheet purposes, rests on their supporters. But that burden is not assumed if no distinction is drawn between fact and fiction, and if it is believed (without demonstration) that a mixture of fact and fiction can fairly present a financial position.

The 'historical principle' is widely invoked (*APBS4*, para. 35; *Study Group Report*, p. 45; *FASB Objectives*, para. 68; *FASB Concepts*, e.g. paras 42, 50). Dated original costs are certainly factual. But the 'accrual principle' is also endorsed (*APBS4*, para. 121; *Study Group Report*, Ch. 5; *FASB Objectives*, para. 34; *FASB Concepts*, para. 44). Now if the accrual principle is applied by recourse to internal conjectures or formulae, the factual character of an original cost is lost. And if the accrual principle is applied only partially (e.g. by disregarding upwards shifts in asset prices), the record is incomplete, and the upshot is non-factual. If the accrual principle were followed completely and consistently, by periodical accrual of the effects on an enterprise of *discovered* changes in prices and changes in the purchasing power of the dollar, the historical principle would also be satisfied; and the financial position at a balance date would automatically be represented in prices and dollars of that date. Failure to apply the principle completely and consistently leads inevitably to the arithmetical solecisms mentioned and the consequential misrepresentation of dated aggregative financial positions.

It is certain that the practice of aggregation and the accrual principle are intended to make a balance sheet more useful. It is equally certain that the documents and the arguments which underlie them disregard the relationship between usefulness and valid aggregation, and between usefulness and complete and consistent accrual. As a premise, 'usefulness' seems again to have vanished.

Financial Position and Risk

Examination in some detail of the particular uses made of information on financial position would have reinforced the propriety of valid aggregation. But the documents give only cursory attention to details.

The risks to which investments in and by an enterprise are subject are indicated generally in *APBS4*, Ch. 3. The assessment of risk is a 'critical element' in the decision-making process, says the *Study Group Report* (p. 18). The differential risks of alternative opportunities are noticed in *FASB Objectives* (para. 7). Risk is referred to in *FASB Concepts* (paras 33, 35, 38). But in no case is mention made of possible indicators of risk. The risk associated with the investments of an enterprise is a function of the risk associated with each asset class and the proportion of the total investment in each class. This entails a knowledge of asset composition in real up-to-date terms. The amount 'at risk', for any asset, is the money equivalent, not the book value, of the asset. The risk associated with an investment in the shares or debt of an enterprise is a function both of

325

asset composition and gearing (e.g., the debt to equity ratio). And since the numerator of that ratio is a dated debt, the ratio will only be valid if the denominator (equity or net assets) is a genuine dated money sum.

Consider three companies A, B and C with the following features:

	A	B	C
Asset composition	%	%	%
Cash and receivables	10	20	20
Inventories	30	20	20
Marketable securities	20	40	40
Land and buildings	40	20	20
	100	100	100
Debt to Equity Ratio	0.8	0.4	0.8

326

Each of the asset classes is subject to different risks. Therefore, on asset composition, A and B are differentially risky. They are also subject to different risks on account of their debt to equity ratios, for clearly B has greater reserve borrowing power than A and a lower interest burden than A. B and C are similar in asset composition but have different debt to equity ratios. How companies and investors in them would appraise the companies, no one knows; some people are risk-takers, some are risk-averse, and some are risk-mixers. But none of the percentage or ratio calculations provide serviceable indicators — of the state of any company, of the drift of that state over time, or of the relative differences between companies — unless the components are expressive of the dated money equivalents of asset classes.

This conclusion could have been reached, by some attention to detail, from the 'uses' specified in the four documents. *APBS4* refers to 'orderly adaptation to changed conditions' (para. 62). Changed conditions may refer to changes in asset composition or debt-dependence, or to changes in external circumstances that make a different asset composition or degree of debt-dependence preferable. And the means of adaptation is accessible funds. Simply to spell out these implications of orderly adaptation to changed conditions would give a more exacting indication of what is useful than is given in *APBS4*. The other documents allude to risk, but in no case to the possibility of assessing the risks to which an enterprise is subject by virtue of its asset holdings and debt at any time. If the potential usefulness of balance sheets for this purpose is ignored, less than full cover is given to the principles which should shape accounting.

Solvency is perhaps a more obviously pertinent feature of the financial affairs of enterprises; the risk of insolvency is of concern to all who may have financial interests in an enterprise. Neither solvency nor the current ratio (the usual indicator of short-run solvency) is mentioned in *APBS4*. Under 'creditors and suppliers', as users of financial statements, there is reference to taking action to 'enter suit or force bankruptcy or receivership' (para. 44). But there is no mention of the specific financial information which may prompt that action. Dealing with investors and lenders, the *Study Group Report* alludes to the capacity of a borrower to pay dividends and to repay borrowings (pp. 19-20). But there is no reference to specific indicators of the dated capacity of an enterprise to do these things. Although *FASB Objectives* alludes to the necessity of paying debts when due and paying for other services as required (para. 10), solvency is not mentioned. *FASB Concepts* refers to balance sheet information as helping to 'identify the enterprise's strengths and weaknesses and assess its liquidity and solvency' (para. 41). And *FASB Criteria* has some comments on the comparability of current ratios. But in neither case is any indication given of the information that is pertinent to valid assessment. It almost seems that insolvency is a rarity, beneath notice. Yet insolvency is not uncommon; and drifts in the measure of solvency are of interest to creditors and investors as indicating the prospect of growth or the prospect of new security issues.

Perhaps the current ratio, the debt to equity ratio and asset composition were regarded by the authors of the documents as 'part of financial analysis and . . . beyond the scope of financial accounting' (a comment made on 'earning power' in *FASB Concepts,* para. 48). But since usefulness is a desideratum, the usefulness of balance sheet particulars cannot be lightly dismissed. If the current ratio is used as an indicator of short-run solvency (it is given in all publications of security analysis services), the numerator must be indicative of capacity to pay short-run debt. But if inventory is valued at cost (on any basis) or the lower of cost and market, or if marketable securities are valued at cost, the numerator will not indicate ability to meet short-run debt. Only the current selling prices of those assets will serve. This conclusion could have been drawn by the authors of any of the documents cited. But, for lack of attention to the detailed information used by analysts and their clients, the conclusion was not drawn.

327

Turning to solvency in general — the relation of total assets to total debt — the same principle applies. For, if users wish to know *now* whether an enterprise will be able to meet its total debts as they fall due in the *future,* there is no better indication than its ability to *cover* that debt *now.* Knowledge of the future is not available now. But there is no point in compounding the uncertainty of the future, which confronts all users, with information that is not even relevant to the present.

It seems not unlikely that drawing the logical conclusion has been subverted by the notion that the asset valuation rules of generally accepted accounting principles yield 'going concern values'. But that notion is not analysed in the documents. In any case it is false. To maintain a going concern, steps must be taken to ensure its solvency. If it is veering towards insolvency, it must be steered back towards solvency. If there is no valid indicator of the approach of insolvency, no early warning signal, remedial steps are not likely to be taken. What was a going concern then turns out to be going no longer. The consequences of a decision made in the past may be materially different from the expected consequences. If they were not, there would be no occasion for 'orderly adaptation'. Since only the money equivalents of assets are pertinent to assessments of solvency or debt-cover, it is useless to represent any asset by any different amount. But this clear inference is a far cry from the inconclusiveness of the documents.

Financial Position — Point of Departure

By describing a dated financial position as a point of departure, I mean (1) a position on the basis of which managers may make choices and build plans of action (budgets), and

(2) a position in the knowledge of which outsiders may judge the prospects of financial association with an enterprise.

There is no suggestion in any of the documents that financial statements may *reveal* problem-situations. There is a reference in *APBS4,* under 'management', to evaluating the results of past decisions, assessing the nature and extent of financing needs, and projecting future financial position and income (para. 44); but there is no reference to the particulars by which those evaluations, assessments and projections may be guided or made. The emphasis on cash *flows* in the *Study Group Report* and *FASB Objectives* effectively sets aside the significance of knowledge of *stocks* of cash and the money equivalents of things convertible to cash from time to time. As mentioned already, *FASB Concepts* does not discuss the quantification of items appearing in financial statements; but it does allude to information that is serviceable in assessing prospective net cash inflows to the enterprise and to investors and creditors (para. 38). Nowhere is there reference to the *diagnostic* value of specific bits of information. A high and rising current ratio, a low current ratio, a high debt to equity ratio, a drift in asset composition, are all phenomena that may require action of a quite specific kind to be taken. Knowledge of those phenomena, and of any existent combination of them, may determine which, of any set of feasible alternatives, is more appropriate than, or is preferable to, another. This kind of usefulness is ignored.

The importance of getting and spending cash, borrowing and lending, and using non-cash means to generate cash (*FASB Objectives,* para. 32) is unquestionable. But an enterprise cannot choose between available opportunities for generating cash without knowledge of the cash available or accessible to it at the time of choice, for what is accessible determines which opportunities are *financially feasible.* Nor can outside users of accounts make any judgement about the ability of an enterprise to carry on as a going concern (whatever choices may be made by the enterprise) without knowledge of the cash available or accessible to it from time to time.

In the simplest case, it is sufficient to concentrate on the cash *on hand* when contemplating alternative outlays. In a slightly less simple case, knowledge of the cash on hand and shortly expected net inflows may be necessary. More generally, cash holdings are minimized (since they produce no income), and assets are held in other forms. In that case the amount of cash *accessible* is of consequence. The amount *directly* accessible is given by the sum of the cash on hand and receivable and the money equivalents (net resale prices) of non-monetary assets; that is the sum that could become available for any purpose, from the payment of short-run costs to the replacement of any asset and the making of any new investment. The amount of cash *indirectly* accessible, through borrowing, depends on what can be pledged as security. Loan applications may well be supported by cash budgets indicating the expected cash flows by means of which the debt will be discharged. But it is well known, and the *Study Group Report* (for example) points out (p. 19), that loan indentures or trust deeds generally specify restrictions on additional borrowing. The constraint is expressed by reference to the relationship between debt and equity. The loans obtainable depend (at least in part) on the current resale prices of assets at the borrowing date and the constraint on future borrowing is pointless unless the debt to equity ratio at subsequent dates is based on the then money equivalents of assets.

328

In any aggregative budgetary calculation, the expected amounts of transactions (themselves money amounts) are accumulated upon the opening balances of the budget period, which are the closing balances of the previous period. If those balances are not money amounts or money equivalents, that accumulation will be a further exercise in improper aggregation. The expected position at the end of the budget period thus calculated will not have been validly derived. It will provide no realistic indication of the subsequent position and no ground for judging whether the budgeted operations will yield a preferred combination of solvency, gearing and net income.

The authors of the documents cannot have been unaware of these uses of information on asset values. They cannot have been unaware of the fact that, even though lenders may have access to information not contained in balance sheets, other parties interested in the financial viability of an enterprise ordinarily have access to no other information than is contained in balance sheets. They cannot have been unaware that original costs (or unamortized balances) of assets give no indication of potential cash flows at any date; even at purchase date, since a purchase is made in expectation of the recovery of a greater sum through use or sale than the purchase price. Their failure to deduce the relevance of money equivalents can only be attributable to setting aside 'usefulness' and allowing some other undisclosed consideration to override it.

329

Cash Flows

No one can doubt the importance in a general way of cash flows, to enterprises themselves or to others having financial interests in them. But the treatment of cash flows in the *Study Group Report, FASB Objectives* and *FASB Concepts* specifies no time horizon over which interested outside parties are presumed to wish to predict cash flows. The use of 'prediction' in that setting is pretentious, empty to the point of being meaningless. Since no evidence is cited in support of the presumption, it remains doubtful whether many of those parties even try to make the specified predictions. It is at least as plausible to suppose that outsiders, informed of the total quantum of assets (however calculated), will take it for granted that in a market economy cash can be made available to meet obligatory or customary payments whenever the need arises. But one thing is certain. If cash flows in the short run are insufficient to meet debts and running costs, there will be no cash inflows in the long run. Short-run cash flows are crucial. Since the proximate indicators of short-run cash flows are the net resale prices of assets, it is an inevitable corollary of the position taken in the *Study Group Report* and *FASB Objectives* that assets should be so valued. But that natural and inevitable inference was not drawn.

Further, the emphasis on cash flow in the *Study Group Report, FASB Objectives* and *FASB Concepts* effectively sets aside the differential financial significance of cash amounts (stocks or flows) at different points of time at which the dollar denominator represents different purchasing powers. The changing financial significance of the dollar is an eminently observable feature of the environment and context of accounting. For that reason it should have been noticed and accommodated in any set of 'pervasive principles' of the kind given in *APBS4,* Ch. 6. But there it is said that the dollar is the unit of measure, and that changes in its general purchasing power are not recognized in the basic financial statements (para. 166).

Now no one supposes that an income of $20,000 per annum ten years ago is the same thing as an income of $20,000 today, or the same thing as an income of $20,000 will be ten years hence. The kinds of enterprise and investor implicit in the argument of the *Study Group Report* and *FASB Objectives* evidently take no notice of those differences. They are concerned with 'predicting, comparing and evaluating cash flows to them in amount, timing and related uncertainty' (*Study Group Report*, p. 20) — but *not*, apparently, in terms of their general purchasing power from time to time. The *Study Group Report* says that 'accounting measurements of earnings should recognize the notion of economic better-offness' (p. 22). But then it says: 'the earnings of an enterprise over its lifetime are measured by the difference between the net cash resources at the end and at the beginning of its life, adjusted for distributions to owners, or contributions by them' (p. 31). That difference will certainly not represent *economic* better-offness if the dollar has depreciated in general purchasing power over the life of the enterprise. No person with a modest experience of financial affairs would say that it would; and certainly no economist would make such a claim. It sits very uneasily with the contention that financial statements are useful in making *economic* decisions, as the Accounting Principles Board, the Study Group and the FASB have claimed.

330

Whether the past, the present or the future is in mind, cash flows are 'dated cash flows', flows of dollars of specific but different general purchasing power. If that is overlooked in the derivation of periodical financial statements or in estimates or judgements of future cash flows, the resulting information will be a jumble of mixed dollars, of no common use for predicting or evaluating prospects.

If cash flow considerations are to be accommodated in any framework of accounting, that accommodation should not be at the cost of losing sight of other significant features. Cash flows have to do with the maintenance of liquidity, with the dating of funding operations and investments, and with policies which influence the dating or timing of cash inflows and outflows associated with trading operations. Cash flow management is one aspect of performance; it is not a substitute for other aspects. Cash flow is no substitute for net income, whether the reference is to the past or the future. There are plausible reasons for separating realized net revenues (net cash inflows) from accrued measurements or decrements in an income account. But the heavy drift in the documents towards emphasizing cash flows threatens to push aside the usefulness of knowledge of net income to all decision-makers.

Net Income

A number of textbooks could be cited which associate accounting with the determination of wealth and changes in wealth. The official documents, however, tend to avoid the use of 'wealth'; though *FASB Concepts* notes that financial reporting 'focuses on the creation of, use of and rights to wealth' (para. 19). On that footing, 'net income' would represent the wealth created in a period. But what do the documents generally say?

Net income is defined in *APBS4* as the difference between revenues and expenses 'which is the net increase in owners' equity [in a period] from profit-directed activities that is recognised and measured in conformity with generally accepted accounting principles' (para. 134). I have already pointed out that the aggregations tolerated under *APBS4* and other statements are invalid aggregations. If the total amount of assets is derived by invalid aggregation, the difference between that amount and the amount of liabilities cannot be a valid amount of owners' equity at any date. The difference between two dated amounts of owners' equity so derived is, therefore, also an invalid difference. Net income does not represent a genuine increment in owners' equity both for this reason and to the extent that it is not based on a complete and consistent application of the accrual principle.

The *Study Group Report* describes net income or earnings as a measure of 'enterprise progress towards its goal . . . of producing the most cash for its owners' (p. 22). *FASB Objectives* says measures of earnings are information about an enterprise's performance (para. 34). But whether any given owner will remain interested in a given enterprise does not depend on earnings of itself; and earnings of itself is not a measure of performance. What is relevant to both is 'earning power'. But not the earning power of the *Study Group Report* which is said to be equivalent to cash generating ability; according to that notion an income of $100,000 would have the same significance whether $100,000 or $1,000,000 were invested to earn it.

Earning power is given by the rate of return on an invested sum. Curiously, rate of return is mentioned in *APBS4* only as a matter of interest to regulatory and registration authorities (para. 45). Return on investment is mentioned in *FASB Objectives* (para. 28) and *FASB Concepts* (paras 38, 39), in the latter case embedded in a discussion of cash flow prospects! But in no case is there a discussion of the components of the rate of return calculation, or a discussion of the conditions under which a rate of return is a serviceable indicator of performance.

The rate of return of a period is the ratio of the net income or earnings to the amount invested in the processes of earning it. Its simplest form is the rate of interest on a bond. But even those who deal with rates of return on security investments, such as bonds, include in income the accrued change in the period in the market price of the investment. Complete and consistent application of the accrual principle would yield a corresponding net income amount for a business enterprise. But what of the amount invested? In the case of a bond or a share in possession, the amount deemed to be invested at the beginning of any period is the market resale price of the security; for, if an investor has the opportunity of investing otherwise, that is the amount he could invest, and that is the common amount on which he would assess the prospective incomes from his alternatives in the course of choosing between them. The nominal amount of the security and what he originally paid for it have nothing to do with the choice. The corresponding amount of the investment in a business enterprise is the amount of net assets, where assets are valued at their money equivalents. Unless it is established that there is no good reason why the rate of return on bonds and on investments in business enterprises should have corresponding modes of calculation, the general nature of the components of the calculation are obvious; they are a genuine money-quantified increment and a genuine opening money-quantified stock or net investment. None of the documents attempts to show that rates of return on security and other investments should not have corresponding meanings and analogous modes of calculation.

The usefulness of an achieved rate of return lies in its aid to diagnosis on the part of managers or outsiders. Since one of the tests of performance is the rate of return on a risk-free investment, the rate of return *should* correspond with the bond rate. Apart from that, achieved rates of return for different enterprises should be computed by uniform processes if, on the basis of the achieved result, comparisons are to be made with the performance of other enterprises. *APBS4* deals at some length with comparability within an enterprise and between enterprises (paras 95-105). But the 'principles' and 'modifying conventions' it endorses cut across the conditions of comparability. The same can be said of the reference to comparability in the *Study Group Report* (p. 59).

The usefulness of an achieved rate of return is impaired if no account is taken of the change in the financial significance of the money unit during a period. It has been observed by many, and over decades, that the conventional accounting rate of return is misleading during inflationary periods, by reason both of the method of net income calculation and of the determination of the investment base. But, as in other respects, the documents offer no analysis of the components, such as might justify or challenge the usefulness of any specific rate of return calculation.

332

Let it be noted that the omissions under comment relate to a use of financial statement information which is acknowledged in the documents. The omissions represent failure to draw out the implications of what the documents assert. *FASB Criteria* refers to 'information that is *most useful* in decision making' (para. 25, emphasis added). It is not conceivable that what is most useful can be determined without some detailed analysis of the requisite properties of the information. If what is most useful cannot be shown to be most useful, by reference to the number of settings in which the information is used or to the number of different parties who make use of it, 'most useful' is empty verbiage. From the analysis given in the preceding paragraphs, a rate of return based on dated money amounts and money equivalents is pertinent in a wider range of settings than a rate of return based on other money-quantifications. But, whatever the reasons, the documents fail to reach that conclusion, or even to point in its direction.

Measurement

Measurement is a disciplined process. One of its objects is to remove from communications the vagueness of mere qualitative description. It enables one person to assign a *quantity* (say, a number of dollars) to a *feature* of some object or objects (say, a buying or a selling price) in a *scale in common use* by that person and others, so that others can make use of it in their judgements, decisions or actions. Measurements enable users of them to discriminate between larger and smaller objects (or classes of objects) in an exacting fashion. A systematic and consistent set of measurements enables users to relate one measurement in the set to another, as in the analysis of asset composition and the other forms of ratio analysis already mentioned.

It is implicit in discussions of the rules and processes of measurement that the object of which some feature is to be directly measured shall be present and observable to the measurer. If it were not present and observable, there could be no assurance that the quantity assigned to the feature or attribute of the object corresponds with the actual or factual quantity (no assurance of 'representational faithfulness', as *FASB Criteria* describes it); and there could be no possiblity of independent verification (as *FASB Criteria*, para. 54, for example, requires). If measurements of an aggregate or a difference (derived measurements) are to be found, (i) the feature of the objects to be measured must be the same feature, and (ii) the feature of the components must be measured in the same scale and under the same conditions, or the measurements made must be convertible to a common scale under common conditions. These rules of measurement are widely known and generally followed — except in the practice of accounting, as I have noted in respect of financial position and income.

The documents under examination all refer to measurements (*APBS4,* e.g. paras 144-168; *Study Group Report,* e.g. paras 22, 42; *FASB Objectives,* e.g. paras 13, 34; *FASB Concepts,* e.g. paras 43-45; *FASB Criteria,* e.g. paras 54-61). But nowhere is there a discussion of the disciplined steps by which measurements are obtained of the dated features of singular objects or of the dated features of an enterprise as a whole. It is not surprising, therefore, that neither prescriptions nor practices conform with measurement rules. Nor is it surprising that the documents tolerate the use of measures of heterogeneous properties in aggregative representations — explicitly in the *Study Group Report* (p. 41) and implicitly in other documents.

333

It seems never to have been noticed by the authors of the documents that adoption of 'measurement', as a description of what accountants do or should do, would have or should have cut down the options or alternatives which otherwise might be thought to be available. 'Measures' and 'measurement' have long been used, though sporadically, in the accounting literature. Indeed Canning ([4], pp. 199-200) specified the rules of aggregative measurement some forty years ago. However, not till the early 'sixties was more than superficial attention given to measurement. The use of the term 'measurement' has mushroomed since then But rather than a disciplinary use, a deliberate attempt to *make* accounting a measurement system, it has been a cosmetic use, creating an impression of disciplined observation and aggregation that is quite undeserved. Two options are available. The first is to abandon the use of 'measure' and 'measurement'. But since users need the results of disciplined observation as indications of progress and performance, that course is inconsistent with the notion of usefulness. The second is to *make* prescriptions and practices conform with measurement rules, so that neither references to measurement nor the products of measuring will delude users.

By contrast with what is now 'accepted', and with much that the documents tolerate, some of the alternative suggestions already made conform strictly with the rules of measurement. The money equivalents of assets are measures of a *single specified feature*. In principle they are *observable;* they can be measured. If observations are made at or near balance date, the measurements are made under *substantially similar conditions;* and in dated money units at that time, the *same units*. If income is to be equal to a change in owners' equity, and the measures of owners' equity at successive dates are expressed in different purchasing power units, the opening measure may be converted to an equivalent in balance date units by recourse to an index of changes in the general level of prices. At all points, the rules of aggregative measurement are satisfied.

Admittedly, the task of the FASB is as yet uncompleted. *FASB Criteria* 'contains no conclusions . . . about the unit of measure to be used or attributes to be measured' (para. 2). But references to measurement are so numerous in the documents that the usefulness of dated measurements and the conditions of valid measurement should by this stage have been made plain.

Different Information and Different Purposes

It is a truism that different kinds of information have different functions. If accountants were unaware of it, there would be no occasion to analyse what it entails. But they are aware of it. *APBS4* observes that 'information prepared for a particular purpose cannot be expected to serve other needs well' (para. 47). The authors of the *Study Group Report* believed that 'the objectives of financial statements cannot be best served by the exclusive use of a single valuation rule' (p. 41). This seems to be a variation on the different information/different purposes theme, for it led the Study Group to the conclusion that 'financial statements might contain data based on a combination of valuation bases' (p. 41). The Study Group, however, made no attempt to show that the simultaneous use of different values in financial statements would serve *any* purpose. The functional differentiation of different kinds of information deserves analysis.

First, aggregative information, sub-aggregative information and particular component information serve different functions. Aggregative information relates to whole enterprises, the whole of their assets, their liabilities and their net incomes. It yields dated indications of gross and net wealth, gearing and rate of return. No information less than the whole will provide such indications. Sub-aggregative information relates to facets of whole enterprises. It yields indicators of short-run solvency, asset composition, debt composition and income composition. Very little information on particular components is given in published financial statements; information on components (particular debts owed or owing, particular assets, particular sources of revenue) may, however, have a bearing on the decisions and actions of managers and other officers. If, for any reason, parts or sub-aggregates are to be related to wholes, then the information on the parts must be of the same kind as the information on the whole.

Second, information relating to the past, the present and the future serves different functions. These kinds of information are also derived by different processes. No purpose is served by treating all financial information as if it were the same in kind. Information on the *past* is *accumulated* as the events to which it relates occur; it is, in principle, *factual,* and any summary of it up to any date is reliable to the extent that the original observations and the subsequent processing are free of distortion. Information on the *present* is *discoverable;* it is, in principle, *factual,* and it is reliable to the extent that the observations faithfully represent the present. Information on the *future* is *calculable;* it is, in principle, conjectural or *hypothetical.* Though use may be made of it in deciding upon future actions, being hypothetical it cannot be said to be reliable in the sense that factual information is reliable. To *discover* the consequences of the *past* up to a stated *present,* the facts of the *past* and the *present* are relevant; the *future* has nothing to do with that. To estimate the possible consequences of *future* actions, both facts of the *past* and the *present* and *estimates* of the *future* are necessary.

These ideas may be brought together in a decision-making context. If the past has resulted in a financial position or a net income which is 'less than satisfactory' in some respect, the decision will be directed towards a more satisfactory outcome in the future. Given the funds accessible directly or indirectly to the enterprise (indicated by a statement of its financial position), and given the present purchase (or replacement) costs of goods necessary for a more promising result, it will be apparent what new investments are *financially feasible.* Notice that present purchase on replacement costs

334

are not funds accessible, but potential (hypothetical) charges against those funds; if such costs appeared amongst the balance sheet valuations, the statement of financial position would not be serviceable as an indicator of funds accessible. Next, if several competing projects are financially feasible, present value (DCF) calculations would indicate which is *preferable in terms of net inflows.* These calculations cannot be made without knowing the funds directly or indirectly accessible (from the sale of assets or from borrowing on the security of assets). Further, as DCF values do not represent funds accessible, their use in a balance sheet would make it unserviceable in this setting. Finally, to ensure that the project preferred on the basis of present value calculations will not have undesirable side-effects on financial position, budgetary calculations will be made, using the factual financial position at the date of choice and the same expected inflows and outflows as were used in the present value calculations.

This analysis identifies specific functions for each of the several different kinds of information: historical costs and selling prices for past income calculation; dated money equivalents for any dated statement of financial position; purchase or replacement costs for any prospective purchase; present (or DCF) values for evaluating competing prospective alternatives. A statement of financial position that contains historical costs, or replacement prices or DCF values, or that 'contains data based on a combination of valuation bases' as the *Study Group Report* (p. 41) suggests, is useless for any of the above steps in decision-making. Further, since the three 'time-classes' of information are used together in any significant problem-setting, similar bits of information of each class must be capable of being linked or associated if the potential consequences of any possible course of action are to be discoverable.

What, then, of external users of financial statements? Historical costs, when given, are given without purchase dates; no outsider could assess the present price or money equivalent of any asset so valued. Replacement prices and DCF values are founded on specific sets of assumed conditions and assumed intentions, of the significance or validity of which outsiders can form no idea. They would, in any case, tend to suppose that amounts appearing in a balance sheet represented funds accessible to an enterprise. On that assumption they would proceed to 'predict' future cash flows if they act as the *Study Group Report* (p. 20) suggests, or to 'assess the prospects' of future cash flows as *FASB Objectives* (para. 26) suggests. But their efforts will be vain. Historical costs are not indicative of future inflows or outflows. Replacement costs are potential outflows, not funds accessible or indications of future inflows. DCF values already represent future expected inflows. If outside users attempt to predict future cash flows on the basis of aggregates which include unamortized historical costs, replacement costs and DCF values, they mount one conjecture on a cluster of others; the meaning and usefulness of the outcome are unimaginable.

Despite all the attention focused on decision-making and prediction in the documents, none gives a clear indication of the points at which particular kinds of information enter into the process. The preceding analysis shows that quite specific kinds of information should be given in different kinds of financial statement (periodical accounts, budgets and DCF calculations), that no such kind of information is a substitute for another, and that all such kinds of information are used in conjunction in choosing or decision-making. Indeed, it turns out that the dated money equivalents of assets, though not

335

sufficient, are necessary at all stages of the process — finding a past result, stating a present position, discriminating between feasible and non-feasible prospects, and choosing between competing prospects on the basis of expected income and expected effects on financial position. If any kind of information is *more* useful, useful in more contexts, than another, it is that kind. Notwithstanding the observation of *APBS4* that 'information prepared for a particular purpose cannot be expected to serve other needs well' (para. 47), that kind of information serves a wide variety of 'needs' — and 'well'.

At no point has it been necessary to consider the idiosyncratic features of decision-makers, the users of the information. It should be apparent that *any* party interested in the financial affairs of an enterprise is interested in its solvency, its debt-dependence, its asset composition and its rate of return. All four are expressive of aspects of its performance, and any one or more of them may be suggestive of its trading and financing prospects. Accountants cannot know how the assessments of users will take account of the specific features of a given enterprise. They can have no idea of 'degrees of relevance' of information to particular users, or of the rate of exchange at which some relevance may be 'traded off' for some reliability (or any other characteristic) by any user — notions which *FASB Criteria* endorses (paras 35-36). In the light of that ineluctable ignorance, the only course to adopt is to ensure the 'representational faithfulness' of the indicators of solvency, debt-dependence, asset composition and rate of return — for between them, those indicators embrace every element of periodical financial statements.

To represent the periodical financial position and results of enterprises is one quite specific function, a function which is served by components of a quite specific kind. The failure to distinguish diagnosis from prognosis, to acknowledge that *both* are parts of the decision process, and to see the relevance to *both* of a faithful representation of financial position and results — this failure seems to be at the root of the slow and hesitant progress towards a more rigorous and serviceable accounting.

Conclusion

It is perhaps premature to judge what the outcome of the FASB documents still forthcoming will be. But there are no signs yet that the Board will come closer to grips with the detailed uses of financial information than it has done hitherto. The Board and its predecessors have shown a marked reluctance to deduce, from the perfectly proper premises they have stated or implied, the style of accounting they entail. There seem to be several reasons for this.

First, a great deal of the discussion is in terms of stereotypes and jargon, limited by the words and ideas it has become customary to use, however vague they may be. 'Objectives' is used of financial statements and financial reporting, as if those statements could, like people, have intentions or goals. Pens and paper and typewriters and computers and all other devices have *functions;* only those who invent them and make use of them can have *objectives.* The *function* of financial statements may properly be said to be to inform, whereas the *objectives* of those who publish them may be (and have often been) to inform partially, and indeed to misinform. Only if the distinction is drawn between the functions of devices (accounting rules, principles, and statements) and the

336

objectives of the makers or users of them, is there likely to emerge a body of ideas contributory to usefulness, or performance of function. As I have indicated, 'financial position', 'earning power', 'measurement', 'prediction', and other terms are used with little care for precision, and the discipline which arises from exacting definition is consequently lacking. To some it may seem merely pedantic to expect that words shall have definite significances. But Gresham's Law applies to verbal usage as much as to currency usage — 'bad usage drives out good'. Words are the stock in trade of devisers of statements of principle or standards. A poor, diluted or roughly handled stock can scarcely be turned to good use.

Second, there underlies much of what the documents say a prevailing belief that alternatives are inevitable, and that the choice between alternatives is a matter of policy. 'Policy issues arise whenever alternative accounting or disclosure treatments are possible' (*FASB Criteria,* para. 5). The belief provides a way of escaping choice, for anything is 'possible'. A tool maker may make a chisel out of soft steel; that is possible; but no matter how sharp its edge, it will be a useless chisel. If accounting information is to be relevant *and* reliable *and* understandable *and* verifiable *and* comparable *and* so on, the specification narrows down what is useful. The specification cuts out all 'possibilities' that do not meet it. But the idea of 'trade-offs' of elements of the specification (which probably dates from *A Statement of Basic Accounting Theory,* 1966, and which runs — in the form of caveats — like a scarlet thread through the latest of the documents, *FASB Criteria*) robs the specification of any incisive or discriminating character.

337

Third — and this is a corollary of the former two points — there is scarcely any evidence of a belief, on the part of the authors of the documents, that firm conclusions are to be derived by tight argument from specified premises. If tight argument had been the mode of proceeding, usefulness could not have been overridden as readily as it has been. Terms could not have been left unspecified. Trade-offs would not have been tolerable. Each idea or proposition would have had a determinate place in the line of argument, and each would have had to be consistent with the others. Vague terms and trade-offs can not be put to use, since both lead to ambiguity in premises and/or conclusions. Of course, where ambiguity prevails, it is impossible to reach any conclusion about what information is 'more useful' than other information of a like kind or 'most useful for decision-making' (*FASB Criteria,* paras 11, 25).

The FASB has indicated that in successive stages of its work on a conceptual framework, the generality of its earlier publications 'will give way to increasing concreteness' (*FASB Criteria,* para. 15). But it is not the generality of the expositions that is at fault; it is their vagueness, diffuseness and lack of a clear drive towards discrimination between 'possibilities' by reference to usefulness. While these things persist, there can be no dependable expectation that an orderly conceptual framework will emerge.

As I have already said, I have not chosen the American experience with any other consideration in mind than the extent of the official (or quasi-official) publications. In general, the same verbal habits, the same mode of proceeding, the same vaguenesses, have stood in the way of progress elsewhere. In a vague way, usefulness has been an implicit commitment of accountants, and accounting, for decades at least. But the fine and laudable things accounting *can* do — make possible increased industrial efficiency, make managers accountable, make companies accountable to the community at large, advance fair and informed negotiation, secure optimal allocation of resources, and so on — have been advanced, it seems, with an ideal in mind; with an eye on the stars, but with feet off the ground. Faith in generally accepted principles seems to have outweighted considerations of usefulness.

Usefulness, as I have said, seems to have been rather like the Cheshire cat — now you see it, now you don't. The ambivalence of the profession is captured in graphic fashion by some words of George Orwell:

> Doublethink means the power of holding two contradictory beliefs in one's mind simultaneously, and accepting both of them ... The process has to be conscious, or it would not be carried out with sufficient precision, but it also has to be unconscious, or it would bring with it a feeling of falsity and hence of guilt . . . To forget any fact that has become inconvenient, and then, when it becomes necessary again, to draw it back from oblivion for just so long as it is needed, to deny the existence of objective reality and all the while to take account of the reality which one denies — all this is indispensably necessary. *(Nineteen Eighty-Four)*

338

I used this passage with reference to what seemed to me to be the prevailing tone of accounting exposition in 1957 (Chambers [5]). It still applies — to 'usefulness', and the present style of accounting standards development. I fancy that in 1957 I expected that what was then at fault would soon be seen to be in error, and that some more down-to-earth way of devising accounting prescriptions would be tried. But nearly a quarter-century later the commitment to trial and error-accretion seems as strong as ever.

REFERENCES

1. American Accounting Association, *A Statement of Basic Accounting Theory*, 1966.
2. AICPA, Accounting Principles Board, Statement No. 4, *Basic Concepts and Accounting Principles Underlying Financial Statements of Business Enterprises*, October 1970.
3. AICPA Study Group on the Objectives of Financial Statements, *Objectives of Financial Statements*, October 1973.
4. Canning, John B., *The Economics of Accountancy*, Ronald Press, 1929.
5. Chambers, R. J. 'The Implications of Asset Revaluations and Bonus Share Issues', *Australian Accountant*, November 1957; *Journal of Accountancy*, August 1958.
6. Financial Accounting Standards Board, Exposure Draft, *Objectives of Financial Reporting and Elements of Financial Statements of Business Enterprises*, December 1977.
7. ———, Statement of Financial Accounting Concepts No. 1, *Objectives of Financial Reporting by Business Enterprises*, 1978.
8. ———, Exposure Draft, *Qualitative Characteristics: Criteria for Selecting and Evaluating Financial Accounting and Reporting Policies*, August 1979.
9. Popper, Karl R., *Objective Knowledge*, Oxford University Press, 1974.

Governmental Regulation of the Accountancy Profession*

Freedom under the Law

There is no such thing as a society in which everyone is free of constraints. A rabble only becomes a society when its members agree to submit, to a considerable extent, to what is deemed to be in the mutual interest of the members. Freedom from molestation, freedom to use the roads and other public places, freedom of speech — none of these is absolutely free. The freedom we enjoy in these and other respects is a regulated freedom. Notwithstanding that, we still think of ourselves as substantially and significantly free. We speak of "freedom under the law", not because the law and those who must enforce it impose constraints on us, but because they protect us from the wilful imposition by others of constraints on us. Freedom is bought with a price; the price is respect for the like freedoms of others.

It is a common complaint of this century that freedoms are being eroded. As commonly, the blame is laid on "the bureaucracy" or "the government". The complaint and the charge deserve inspection. Much of the erosion of freedoms, if it can be so called, has arisen from the increasing complexity of technology and social organization. Under the private initiative of inventors, innovators and promoters, there has come to the market labour-saving machines, and foodstuffs and drugs and textiles and other goods in great variety. The law had nothing to do with the production, initially, of these things, except to preserve the freedom of initiative of those who sought to exploit them. The law and the legislature came to have interests when the product of that initiative threatened the freedoms of others. Potentially injurious machines, foodstuffs, drugs, textiles and basic materials are brought under statutory and regulatory restraint when their use has been shown to be hazardous, to the users themselves or to innocent third parties. "No man is an Island", said John Donne, Any man who thinks he is a law unto himself must reckon with the law as it concerns itself with others.

The legislature is not the only source of regulation or constraint. The craft gilds of the twelfth and thirteenth centuries were the

* Presented at a State Congress of Australian Society of Accountants, Coff's Harbour, March 1980.

339

precursors of modern forms of **private** regulation. "The corporate form [in municipal corporations and craft gilds] was applied to a public purpose in which the widest considerations of social welfare and the social good were put before the interests of the corporation . . . The gild's fundamental precept was sound workmanship and fair dealing; its fundamental policy was economic security for all its members" (Cooke, **Corporation, Trust and Company**). These words sound very much like what might be endorsed today as ideals by trade and professional associations. But as early as the fifteenth century, the Parliament found it necessary to interfere with the "presumption on the part of the corporate gilds to regard their power of legislating within the gild as an absolute power"; for, as the Acts recited, many gilds and like bodies had made among themselves "many unlawful and unreasonable ordinances . . . for their own singular profit and to the common hurt and damage of the people". The acts of gilds, fraternities and other bodies corporate were made subordinate to national legislative policy and subject to review by the legislature. The erosion of what some have presumed to be freedoms thus has a long history.

The codes of conduct of the social organizations we know as professional associations are no less constraints or restrictions on their members than the laws and regulations of the society at large. The term "self-regulation" has been adopted to distinguish them from governmental or public regulation. The mythology has it that self-regulation is in some senses superior to public regulation. It is said to be more adaptive or more readily adaptable; it is said to be better informed, more finely attuned to the needs of the membership of a professional group and the needs of the public it serves; as a disciplinary device, it is said to be more prompt than the processes of the law, and fairer to members and the public than the often long-delayed findings of the courts. Some of these claims are altogether questionable, and I shall turn presently to question them. But the first and principal distinction between private and public rule-making (legislation or regulation) is that private laws are subordinate to the public law. Private legislation is not an alternative to public legislation. We cannot have self-regulation as a substitute for public regulation - unless, of course, self-regulation is as effective in serving the interest of the public ("we, the people") as any public law

340

can be.

In essence, the law is the general code regulating interpersonal behaviour. It makes explicit the rights and duties of persons filling one role in their relations with others filling other roles (buyer and seller, borrower and lender, employer and employee, and so on). Laws are designed to facilitate fair and reasonable relationships and dealings, and until it is demonstrated to the contrary, they are presumed to do so. What is deemed to be fair and reasonable may change from time to time; but if laws were not drafted on such a footing, they would command little or no respect, law-enforcement would be impossible or chaotic or arbitrary, and the courts would be jammed with litigants. Where the subjects of a law are the relationships between buyers and sellers of goods and services, the rule **caveat emptor** was long thought to be sufficient warning or protection to buyers. Even then the law provided the means by which buyers could inform themselves of the qualities of what they bought. There has since developed an extensive body of law regulating sellers. Much of it has arisen from the increasing complexity of goods and services sold, the consequential difficulty (on the part of buyers) of deciding on the quality of what was offered, and the increasing use of advertising. **Caveat vendor** is perhaps now as significant as **caveat emptor**. Indeed it seems to have been the "fundamental precept" of the gilds, for it entails "sound workmanship and fair dealing". And that, in turn, entails that the goods and services sold shall be serviceable, and that their quality shall not be misrepresented. That is what the constituents of a community may expect; and that, in essence, is what I think the law intends.

341

Sound Workmanship

What, then, is the relationship of all that to accounting? I shall not be concerned with the day-to-day internal uses of accounting information. The point at which accounting and its products become of legal interest is the point at which the interest of the public and the public interest in fair dealing are affected – financial dealings of a firm or dealings of a firm that affect the financial interests of other parties.

At the time when the formation of companies by registration was introduced in the United Kingdom, periodical accounts were regarded as a means of enabling creditors to protect their interests. The rise of mercantile agencies in the United States is traceable to the same source, creditors who needed to know the financial strength of their debtors. The first formal statement of "accounting principles" of an official nature in the United States (in the second decade of this century) arose from the same source, the use by bankers of the financial statements of customers. Yet almost all of the scores of cases in the last 30 years that have attracted public notice by reason of actual or incipient failure have shown that, as a means of helping to protect creditors (or of helping them to protect themselves) published financial statements have been far from serviceable. And the reported net profits of companies, which have been held to be the primary interest of investors in shares, have, at least as often, been equally delusive.

The UK Companies Act has been the subject of official inquiries about every 20-30 years. Some changes in the accounts provisions have resulted. The Australian State Acts have likewise been revised from time to time. The professional bodies have had opportunities of making financial community as they are claimed to be, it might have been expected that by now the Ninth Schedule and the accounts provisions of the Act would have been geared to the production of genuinely serviceable information. In the US, the SEC has had the responsibility for determining the style of accounting that would be serviceable "in the public interest and for the protection of creditors" since the mid-thirties. And since the SEC has maintained a working relationship with the professional body, the AICPA, the profession has had the means of making increasingly serviceable the output of accounting. On their own initiative, the professional bodies have, for up to sixty years, engaged in codifying technical rules. Research committees, boards and foundations have spent countless hours and millions of dollars on the exercise. But, from the persistence of litigation relating to the quality of accounts, and the express concern of some legislators with the rules and standards that have been developed, it is clear that **neither governmental nor private initiative, nor the combination of both, has yet been fruitful.**

Private Law and Public Law

In my view, the reason for this failure is that the private-sector committees, boards and professional bodies have never seriously sought a comprehensive answer to the question: "What is a serviceable accounting?" The expectation of the legislature is that accounts shall give a true and fair view of results and position from time to time. Yet, never since those words were introduced to the statute has there been a serious attempt, by the professional bodies or their offshoots, to state categorically what "true and fair" means as far as users of accounts are concerned, nor what "profit" and "financial position" (or "state of affairs") mean. If there is no disciplined use of those terms, there is no criterion for "sound workmanship" on the part of accountants, and no criterion for "fair dealing" between accountants and those who buy their products or services. And there can be no basis for "fair dealing" between those who buy and sell securities on the strength of what they are told about the issuers of securities.

343

The object of public legislation, as I have said, is to set the tone of interpersonal relations. Of necessity, words used in a statute are general terms, designed to embrace a wide range of particular instances. But in all those instances, the intent of the law is to serve, equally fairly, the parties whose relationships are in contemplation. Sound workmanship, or actually giving a true and fair view of financial results and affairs, is equally serviceable to accountants and their clients. It means reputation for skill and economic security to the one class and reliable information to the other.

If the general terms used in a statute are inadequately defined, a profession working under the statute would demonstrate how well it is informed and how well it is attuned to the needs of its members and the public it serves by giving increased specificity to those terms. At least, it would do so if it saw its "private law-making" or standard-setting as subordinate and auxiliary to the public law. The accountancy profession has not done that in respect of the key terms I have mentioned. Rather, its leaders have repeatedly stated that the meanings of those terms are matters of opinion, and one standard after another has provided options which accommodate different opinions. How the aggregate product of the profession – the financial statements of all companies – can serve financiers and investors (who must make comparisons even though the particular "products" are non-comparable), seems not to have concerned the profession. That being the case, the legislature (the government) is bound to intervene sooner or later; for it will find intolerable forms of private action which are actually or potentially

injurious to the interests of innocent parties. It will intervene to
stem "stock market pollution" in the same way as it has intervened to
control other forms of pollution.

The Alternatives

Which raises the question: "is government better equipped to do
this than the private sector?" The answer is by no means clear. I
expect that government and the profession alike would seek to do the job
by recourse to a committee. I see no special reason why governmental and
professional committees would necessarily differ in general competence;
both can draw men of professional skill and goodwill from the private and
the public sectors. I see no reason why governmental and professional
committees would be differentially "conservative" or "progressive". I
see no reason why both kinds of committee would not be equally served –
for better or worse – by their back-room staffs. Notice that I have not
considered a governmentally-appointed committee as a committee solely of
professional practitioners. So much for the similarities.

There are some potential differences. Professional committees of
the past have not been notably successful. They have, as it seems, been
bound strongly to the rules of conventional practice, permissive and
variant as those rules have been. Lacking the force of law, their
conclusions have had to have some assurance of support, even if the price
of support was toleration of variety and multiplicity of options. It has
been said that the conclusions of committees have often been influenced
by the exigencies of the clients of committee-members, rather than by
considerations of the general or public interest. Were it not for
reasons such as these, a greater degree of consistency or convergence may
have been characteristic of the conclusions on similar matters by
committees at different times and places. A governmental committee may
be free of some of these constraints. A governmental committee may be
reasonably expected to consider the rules or standards it devises as an
integral, if auxiliary, part of the general law. It may be more willing
than professional committees have been to consider the possibility of
altering the existing generalities of the law, or its specifics, if on
close analysis the law is found to be inconsistent with the prevailing
organization of commercial and financial affairs. In these last two
respects, a governmental committee may seem to have the advantage of
professional self-regulation; but even that advantage would be eliminated

344

if professional standard-setting were seen as, and made, an integral outgrowth of the intent of the general law.

We are so accustomed to think of government and public officials as "the bureaucracy" that we overlook the existence of private bureaucracies. The rule-making and administrative and disciplinary apparatus of a professional body is a bureaucracy. I am, of course, using the word descriptively, not disparagingly. Officials, public and private, must pay close attention to the minutiae of the rules which they administer. Otherwise they will be charged with biassed, capricious or arbitrary behaviour. For their own protection they give attention to refinements of the rules, to make easier the task of discriminating between cases and the task of giving effect to the disciplinary codes that govern the relationships between themselves and other parties and the relationships between other parties. All this is perfectly proper. But without a clear sense of what is serviceable and necessary, rule-making and rule-enforcement may become an end in itself, mere officiousness.

That is the direction, I fear, in which accounting standard-setting is running. If basic terms are undefined, if what is serviceable is not specified, alternatives in abundance will find their way, as they have done, into the rules developed. Professional performance will then be an expression, not of an ideal of professional service, but of the lowest common denominator of the rules. Self-regulation or self-discipline will then be farcical, for a sufficiently abundant set of rules will provide the excuse or justification for the crudest of practices. I do not despair of the profession's capacity for governing itself in the public interest. The concern of the law with the public interest, and the history of government intervention when the public interest is thwarted, are there for all to see. But if the profession does not look and does not see, it cannot blame others for trying to do what it has declined or failed to do.

The Prospect

As I have said, neither governmental nor professional instrumentalities have so far succeeded in producing a code yielding a serviceable accounting. What is the prospect of doing so?

Any reasonably regular reader of the financial press on company affairs will know that solvency, debt-dependence, risk and profitability are matters of common interest, at least to investors, financiers and creditors. Up-to-date indicators of these things are necessary if any company is to take prompt steps to counter a potentially harmful drift in any of them or to take prompt advantage of any external shift in its prospect of gain. Those indicators are equally necessary to outsiders, if they are to judge whether a company is able to avert difficulties or benefit from new opportunities. The common indicators of the features mentioned are: of solvency, the current ratio; of debt-dependence, the debt to equity ratio; of risk, the asset-composition; of profitability, the rate of return. Between them these ratios embrace every item in periodical financial statements. Now if up-to-date indicators are to be provided, every amount in a balance sheet must be an up-to-date amount; of debts, actual amounts owing; of assets, actual amounts accessible for the payment of debts, or of running costs, or for conversion to other assets if that is necessary or desirable. On that footing can be built a style of accounting that is serviceable, to all parties and in all circumstances. It would dispense with the need for many subsidiary standards, of the verbose, circumlocutory and often contradictory kind that we now have. Its valuation rules are minimal; so are its options. Henry Kissinger once said: "It is amazing what progress can be made when we have no options". Like progress could be made in accounting.

I am neither for nor against government intervention. But laws we must have for good order and fair dealing. It is perhaps not too late, even now, for the profession to make a fresh start, to reconsider its standards in the light of the general law and the demonstrable needs of users of its products. Failing that there will be government intervention. However, of one thing I am convinced. The only way of laying the ground for sound workmanship is by starting from what can be shown to be serviceable - in the manner suggested in the previous paragraph. Neither private nor public rule-making will succeed if it follows the tired and fruitless formulae of the past. If we persist in that direction, we shall perpetuate "unlawful and unreasonable ordinances with me greater expectations of the profession we serve.

346

The Institute of Chartered Accountants in Australia
26th Annual Victorian Congress

28th March, 1980

SHOULD ACCOUNTING AND AUDIT STANDARDS BE RELAXED FOR SMALL BUSINESS?

I suspect this question has engaged attention as a consequence of the elaborate rules that have been promulgated or proposed by the standard-setting authorities in Australia and elsewhere. You will no doubt be aware that the AICPA in 1976 resolved to distinguish between accounting firms which operate nationally and those which operate locally or regionally. The object of the demarcation seems to have been to require a different style or rigour in accounting for companies listed on the larger securities exchanges than for smaller companies. The US profession was at the time under critical notice of certain members of Congress and of committees under their chairmanship (the Moss and Metcalf Committees); and one of the considerations was the extent to which large professional firms were said to be dominant in the setting of accounting standards and the general regulation of practice. In mid 1977, as you may also recall, there was objection in the U.K. to the mandatory introduction of inflation accounting after the style of ED.18, arising, it seems, from apprehension of the complexities it would impose on small firms and their accountants and auditors. Since then, both in the U.K. and Australia (and in the US), inflation accounting proposals have been restricted in intended application to large companies whose securities are traded on the stock exchanges. I have over those years heard a number of criticisms of the usefulness to small firms of the information required by elaborate exposure drafts and standards, voiced by practising accountants whose clientele consisted principally of small firms.

I propose to tackle the matter on two fronts. First, I shall argue that an accounting standard should apply equally to all business, large and small. Second, I shall argue that accounting standards that are thought to be objectionable for small business are equally objectionable for large business. I shall conclude that what the profession, and the business community, requires is a more rigorous specification of accounting in general terms and less specific attention to details.

The Common Uses of Financial Information

It is widely held, and it is pointed out in most of the professional documents dealing with accounting, that accounting produces (or should produce) information of wide and general use. Managers, investors, creditors and other parties are all interested in the solvency, the debt-dependence, the asset composition and the rate of return of business firms, large and small. Owner-managers of small firms ought, perhaps, to be more concerned with these matters than those who have financial interests in large firms. Large firms tend to have larger purses, access to more varied sources of funds, and greater opportunities for risk-diversification, than small firms. The comparative disadvantage of small firms in these respects makes it highly desirable that their owners or managers shall be quite discriminating in the management of their financial affairs, that they shall have the means of being promptly and acurately aware of drifts in their solvency, debt-dependence, asset composition and profitability. Of course, the occasional liquidity strains and collapses of large firms indicate that prompt and acute awareness of the same things is a condition of survival, even of large firms. My conclusions will thus be quite general.

I have chosen to concentrate on solvency, debt-dependence, asset composition and rate of return since the measures of these features embrace all items that appear in balance sheets, profit and loss accounts, budgets and other financial calculations. The usual measures of those three features are the current ratio (current assets to current liabilities), the debt to equity ratio (total debt to net assets or owners' equity), the percentage of asset classes to total assets, and the rate of return (net profit to net assets).

It should be clear that a firm's ability to meet current debts out of current assets is only indicated if all current assets are represented by their money equivalents at a given date. This condition is not satisfied if inventories and marketable securities are shown at cost, or at any value other than their net resale prices at a given date. It should also be clear that a firm's ability to meet all its debts (or to "cover" its debts) is only indicated if all assets are represented by their money equivalents at a given date. Debts are potential money outflows debt-cover is not indicated by the cost prices (or unamortized costs) of any assets, or by any asset values other than their money equivalents. Even if assets are not intended to be sold, their net resale prices are the only up-to-date indications of potential cash inflows, exclusive of profit from their continued use. It should be clear that the risks consequent upon holding a given collection of assets can only be assessed by reference to the money equivalents of assets of different risk-

347

1

categories; and that those money equivalents represent what could be shifted, if necessary, to other risk-categories. It should also be clear that a rate of return that indicates the money-increment in wealth between two dates can only be calculated if assets are valued at the two dates of their money equivalents. Such a rate of return is comparable with other rates of return such as a bond rate, a bank interest rate, or a rate of return from other firms, companies or ventures.

The analysis may be taken further. If, by reason of an unfavourable drift in solvency, debt-dependence, asset composition, or rate of return, some variation in operations or policy is necessary in the following period, a budget (or a series of budgets) of an exploratory kind will be made up. The budget will proceed from a certain financial position at the opening date (the closing date of the past period); the expected effects of cash inflows, cash outflows and accruals will be accumulated; and the expected result at the end of the period will be calculated. Unless the opening position expresses assets in their money equivalents, the accumulation of cash inflows, outflows and accruals will not yield a valid and useful indication of the expected closing position — and useful values of the indicators mentioned above.

Finally, if we wish to introduce an adjustment for the effects of inflation in a period, it is a simple matter. The amount of net assets at the beginning of a period is expressed in "opening dollars"; at the end of the period all dollar amounts are "closing dollars". If the income of a period is taken as the difference between opening and closing net assets (excluding capital changes and income distributions), that difference is nothing but a **nominal** difference, if the general purchasing power of the dollar has changed. To reduce the difference to a genuine increment in general purchasing power, there must be deducted from it the product of the opening amount of net assets and the proportionate rise in the general price index in the period and the amount of that adjustment must be added to the opening amount of net assets. To put the matter in numerical form:

If opening net assets were	$(79)20,000
and closing net assets were	$(80)27,000
and the rate of inflation (the rise in the general level of prices) during the year was	10%,

the net income of the year would be
$27,000 − $20,000 − 10% of $20,000 = $(80)5,000

The opening net assets $(79)20,000 would be equivalent to $(80)22,000. The adjustment of $2,000 is described as a capital maintenance adjustment. The rate of return would be $(80)5,000 divided by $(80)22,000 or 22.7 per cent. It would be a proper or valid calculation since both the numerator and the denominator are both expressed in $(80). Notice also, that unless the amounts of assets were genuine discovered amounts at the opening and closing dates (not just calculated balances), none of the previously mentioned ratios would be proper indicators, and the application of the inflation rate to the opening (mixed balance of) assets would not yield a proper adjustment to income.

Common Uses Entail Common Standards

All of this is, I think, readily understandable — by small businessmen, and large businessmen and accountants. I don't think any would suppose that amounts other than the dated money equivalents of assets could give a dated indication of solvency or debt-cover or asset composition. And I think all would agree that dated indications of solvency, debt-cover and asset composition are necessary as guides to action when drifts occur (as they inevitably do) in the financial affairs of firms.

Not only that; the business of auditing is intended to secure that financial statements give a true and fair view of financial position and results from time to time. Ideally, the process of doing that is by checking that the asset balances are realistic balances.

Particular steps are taken, generally independently of client records and officers, to see that cash, receivables and payables are correctly stated, and that other assets reported to exist, do in fact exist. If the prices at which those other assets were shown were balance-sheet-dated prices, the accounting (and the auditing) would be consistent throughout; and the balance sheet could reasonably be said to give a true and fair view of the position of the firm at balance sheet date. But instead of that, traditional practice departs from consistency, allowing a whole variety of differently dated prices and calculations to take the place of discovered up-to-date prices. And the audit, which is thought to be independent verification of dated money balances, is independent verification only in respect of cash, receivables and payables. Now solvency, debt-cover, asset composition and rate of return must each mean the same kind of thing whether a business is large or small. It would be fatuous to think that a banker, or a financier, or an investor has a different notion of any of them according to the size of the business he is considering. Bankers, financiers and investors have the option of putting their money into a selection of business firms, varied in

2

operations and varied in size. None of them could validly choose between customers or clients, who are in effect competing for available funds, if solvency or profitability were different in kind (by definition of by mode of calculation) for different customers or clients. It follows that all firms large and small, shall prepare accounts in a substantially uniform manner, so that all users of those accounts shall be informed in like terms because all ratio calculations based on the accounts are uniform in origin and financial significance. It follows, as a corollary, that **all accounting standards shall apply equally to all business firms, whatever their size**).

Generally Serviceable Standards

I do not know of any extended and explicit argument, earlier than about four years ago, to the effect that the standards officially promulgated are "all right for large firms, but not for small". Even more recently, the signs of such a view are differently interpretable. They seem to stem more from the complexity of the inflation accounting proposals sponsored by the profession than from any other source. Large firms with "big" auditors, it is said, may be able to afford the costs of complex accounting; but why, it is asked, should small firms have to go to the same trouble? The force of the objection has been deflected by stated intentions to make newer forms of accounting or supplementary accounting mandatory only for large companies whose shares are publicly traded. But that is a deflection, not a remedy for complex standards.

If you examine the list of standards (or exposure drafts of proposed standards) in any major country, you will find that most of them relate to items other than monetary items — the "other assets" referred to in an earlier paragraph. Those standards (quite apart from inflation accounting proposals) are unnecessarily complex, simply because they have to cope with the varied prices, costs and calculation formulae which it has become habitual to use, and with the numerous alternatives it has become habitual to tolerate. But nowhere in all those standards will you find it contended that any enunciated standard contributes to reliable and up-to-date indicators of solvency, debt-cover, asset composition or rate of return. Of course neither in all those standards will you find it **denied** that a reliable and up-to-date indicator of those financial features of a firm is relevant to parties having financial interests in firms. The usefulness of those indicators is simply neglected.

According to the argument of the previous section only asset valuations based on money equivalents (net resale prices of non-monetary assets) will give reliable and up-to-date indicators. Unless that contention can be demolished, all standards which expound some other form of valuation are unserviceable, no matter how much or how little they have cost to develop, nor how much or how little they cost to implement. In particular (and since it seems to have been the proximate cause of disaffection with complex standards) CCA is unserviceable; for the financial information it yields, of itself or together with traditional accounts, does not make possible the derivation of reliable and up-to-date indicators of the kinds mentioned.

It cannot be argued that the thought processes or the environmental settings of the managers of large businesses differ from those of small firms. Managers and others having interests in large firms also have financial affairs on a small scale — their domestic affairs, for example. The managing of one's personal affairs — one's assets, income, savings and investments — are in principle no different from the managing of business affairs. I have never met a person who in his private capacity believed there is any merit in the varied methods of valuing and calculating found in traditional business accounting. Those methods can only be an aberration from commonsense, sanctified only by tradition and the indoctrination of textbook writers and standards setters. In sum, **the same grounds for finding standards objectionable or unserviceable for small business, make them objectionable or unserviceable for large business.**

A Rigorous General Standard

Perhaps that is all I may properly say, given the question posed in the title. This is no place to defend the financial statements, based on money equivalents, that have been said to constitute a serviceable accounting, or to answer technical questions on the details of such an accounting. But it is worth saying that there are at present substantial conflicts between what have been issued as standards or prospective standards. The most obvious example is given by the Australian publications. It has become necessary to specify that certain standards are to be understood "in the context of historical cost accounting", others "in the context of CCA". There are similar, but not so obvious, conflicts in the standards, or what for the time being serve as standards, of the UK and the USA. The concurrent publication of standards based on such diverse notions is deplorable. It is evidence of failure to resolve at the outset what kinds of information are serviceable to users — internal and external, large and small — of financial statements.

To resolve that question we must go, not to the **verbal context** of expositions of accounting systems, but to the **real-world context** of business and financial affairs. In that context, the only financial quantities that have significance are quantities of money held, owing and owed; buying prices of things bought or to

3

to be bought; and selling prices of things sold or available to be sold. No book values other than these have any function. We may allocate, apportion and calculate in any way we please — for exploratory purposes. But when the chips are down, when we want to know what we can do or must do financially, or what financial progress we have made, only actual money quantities and actual money prices count. That is quite a general principle.

In that context, it is a simple matter to say what "financial position" is. Financial position is the dated financial relationship of a firm with the rest of the world. As the assets of a firm at a stated date are the things available to it, to be sold or put to other use at its option or necessity, only their dated money amounts or money equivalents will indicate what is available or accessible to the firm. Only an income calculated by reference to the periodical change in net assets so determined will indicate the substantive product of a period's business. And only an accounting so devised will yield the pertinent and sensitive indications of position and progress which I have said to be relevant to the choices or decisions of all users of the financial statements of small and large firms alike.

You may or may not know that no accounting standard, domestic or foreign, has yet attempted to say what financial position is and what income is. Yet it should be apparent that worthwhile standards on specific assets, liabilities or equities cannot be devised unless they conform with what is understood by financial position and income. In the absence of such a disciplinary framework, it is inevitable that account-ing standards will be loose and vague, ambiguous and inconsistent, preoccupied with differential book-keeping detail, and unconcerned with the intelligibility or usefulness of the result. It can be shown that these are characteristics of the standards hitherto developed. I believe they arise from the lack of a gen-eral standard specifying the kind of information that is serviceable as representing financial position and income or profit.

A style of accounting based on the money equivalents of assets is, by contrast with traditional or "standard" practice, more rigorous, more serviceable and more intelligible; for everyone can understand what money quantities and money equivalents are, and what, in practical settings, they mean. A standard for that kind of accounting can be written in a page; with justification and explanation, in a booklet of a dozen or so pages. It might perhaps dispel the spectre of increasingly complex and numerous standards which seems to haunt small firms and their accountants and auditors — and do a demonstrable service for the rest of the financial and business community at the same time.

350

Company Accounting Standards*

1. Retrospect

My title is the title of the Report of the Accounting Standards Review Committee appointed by the NSW Attorney General in November of 1977. I expect that you would like to know something about the origin of the Committee, what it did and why, the outcome of its work and the prospective fruit of it.

The state of New South Wales has been the locus of the greatest amount of litigation relating to corporate affairs in the last decade. I will not canvass the reason for that. But it has also been the locus of the greatest amount of what seemed to be fruitless litigation. At least since 1967, the New South Wales Corporate Affairs Commissioner has expressed concern with the diversity of accounting. His 1967 paper on "A True and Fair View" presented at a New South Wales Convention of the Society was the first of a number of expressions of disquiet. Quite a number of cases of dubious corporate behaviour came under critical notice of the Commission in the early seventies, some issuing in investigations and some in litigation. But variant notions of profit and variant asset-valuation rules stood in the way of the prospect of establishing, by the processes of the Courts, a firm basis for distinguishing between misguided and fraudulent misrepresentation.

Meanwhile, from about 1971, the professional bodies of accountants had set their hands to the production of accounting standards. Between 1971 and the end of 1976, seven standards had been published on a variety of matters. The rate of output may have been impeded by the amount of attention given from 1974 onwards to the development of a standard on "inflation accounting". Several things about this standard-setting enterprise seem to have been of concern to the Corporate Affairs Commission or the responsible minister, the Attorney-General. The standards showed no sign of reducing diversity of practices, and the frequency of qualified audit reports. That the professional bodies should decide on rules or standards without adequate consultation with others affected by the decisions, or without independent review, left open the possibility that the standards proposed may not be in the

---

* Presented at the Australian Society of Accountants Regional Convention, Rockhampton, May 1980.

interest of all parties or in the public interest. The Attorney-General, addressing an Australian Legal Convention in July 1977, is reported to have said: "the question of accounting standards and the role of auditors is vital to a satisfactory resolution of the mess our (corporation) laws are in". He had come to the view that an Accounting Standards Review Board should be established to lay down accounting standards "supported by a legislative framework to ensure the responsible selection of standards and their effective enforcement". The matter had apparently been under study by the Corporate Affairs Commission; some information on its suggestions was published about the same time. They envisaged that the Review Board would include people "experienced in industry, commerce, economics, law and public administration". Its job would not be the formulation of standards but the appraisal of standards devised by others.

Following these reports in the Press, the then President of the Institute of Chartered Accountants proposed to me (I was then President of the Society) that we should seek an interview with the Attorney General, both to obtain clarification of his intentions and perhaps to inform him of some views of the professional bodies. I disqualified myself on two grounds. I had been openly critical of the standards that had been published, and critical, in-house, of much that was in the pipeline; I could not therefore hold myself out to be an impartial representative. Second, I was about to go abroad (among other things, to the Tenth International Congress in Munich), and if the discussion was to lead to some continuing dialogue it would be better to provide for some continuity of those engaged in it. I nominated in my place another general councillor of the Society. The interview took place, and by all accounts it was amicable. The Attorney General made it clear about that time that he did not intend to proceed in haste with the Review Board proposal and would be glad to have the proferred participation of the professional bodies on any committee he might set up on the matter.

A few weeks prior to this, on an informal occasion, I had discussed the press releases of early July with the Corporate Affairs Commissioner. He informed me that the Attorney General would welcome my comments on the proposals as they then stood. One of the last things I did before going abroad was to write to the Attorney General, briefly and generally. I took no objection to the idea of a Standards Review Board, but suggested that its task would be "enormously involved and protracted" unless the provisions of the legislation relating to accounts were made more exact and specific.

2. The Accounting Standards Review Committee

Four weeks later I arrived in Cincinnati, to find a telegram from the Attorney General's office inviting me to chair a committee which would include Mr T.S. Ramanathan and Mr H. H. Rappaport. This was an altogether unexpected development. I have sketched above all I knew of the background of the proposal. By telephone I obtained some clarification of the intention. The committee would include a nominee of the Institute and of the Society. Whether it was to be in the nature of a committee of inquiry or a Review Board of the kind that had been foreshadowed was not clear. A report was to be produced as soon as was reasonably possible. The invitation was personal (i.e., not in my capacity as President of the Society) and I considered at length whether its acceptance would entail any conflict of interest. I formed the view that, if any other person (whatever his associations) had received the invitation, he would have accepted it. There was a possibility that the Society's General Council or Executive Committee might consider the Presidency of the Society and the chairmanship of the committee to be incompatible; I decided to face that if objections were raised. I accepted the invitation.

On my return to Sydney in the latter half of October, the terms of reference of the Committee were hammered out. For some time there had been regular conferences of Australian and State Attorneys General designed to procure uniformity in the administration of companies and securities legislation. In discussions with the representatives of the professional bodies, the NSW Attorney General had agreed that the Review Board and its functions should be national in scope. But while there was no national organization for the purpose, each State would continue to deal with its own affairs in the light of its own exigencies. There was no reason why any State should not conduct an inquiry pertinent to accounting standards, or any other matter. (The Attorney General of South Australia, in fact, had already, in July 1977, announced the appointment of a committee to inquire into some other aspects of the profession). There were reasons, however, why a Review Board with the full powers outlined by the NSW Attorney General in July 1977 would be

353

premature. For example, if a State, on the advice of its Review Board, were to seek to enforce a particular set of standards in respect of companies under its jurisdiction, there could well be diverse standards across the country, contrary to the interests of all persons who might wish to make comparisons of the financial affairs of different companies. With these considerations in mind the NSW Attorney General resolved to describe the committee as the "Accounting Standards Review Committee", and that was how it was described in his press release announcing its establishment on 16 November 1977. He described it to me as a "steering committee on accounting standards". He expected its work to make "a useful contribution to the acceptance of the concept of a Review Board".

354

The immediate task of the Committee was "to examine the accounting standards which have been promulgated either in their final form or at the exposure draft stage by the accountancy profession and to consider any other standards coming to the attention of the Committee which should be considered in the interest of parties who use published accounting information". The Committee ("ASRC" hereafter) was to report to the Attorney General whether the adoption of standards promulgated by the Australian professional bodies "should be recommended to the Review Board when established".

The nominee of the Australian Society of Accountants to the ASRC resigned shortly after appointment; the Institute of Chartered Accountants in Australia offered no nominations. The Attorney General decided that the Committee consisting of the three previously named persons should proceed. Announcements in the press gave notice of the brief of the Committee and invited submissions to it. Some 15 submissions were received but neither of the professional bodies made submissions. And, for the record, there has to April 1980 been no official comment on the Report of the Committee (completed in May 1978 and published in December 1978) in the professional journals, and this is the first occasion when the Report has been the subject of a congress paper.

3. The ASRC Report – Company Accounting Standards

The Committee's Report (of some 170 printed pages) was completed in six months of strenuous effort. It consists of 10 chapters. The first was a summary of the whole. Chapters 2-4 dealt with the private and public interest in company accounts, the functions of company accounts

and the functions of accounting standards. Chapter 5 and an appendix of
22 pages gave a critical examination of 10 Australian standards or
statements in the nature of standards. The Committee concluded that none
of them could be recommended for legislative endorsement in their then
present forms. Chapter 6 dealt with price variation accounting, in
particular with CCA which in 1976 had been made the subject of a
"provisional standard". Chapter 7 dealt with accounting standards
abroad, with particular reference to the UK, the USA and the EEC. The
Report pointed out that in no case had the published standards or the
established practices been based on specifications of what was intended
by "balance sheet", "financial position", "profit" (or "income") and "a
true and fair view" of positions and results. Without such a framework
of the main ideas and the main products of accounting, there could be no
firm notion of the "quality" of accounting information and no foundation
for a systematic and consistent set of accounting standards. By recourse
to judicial dicta and practical considerations, the Committee sought to
make specific the meanings of those terms.

355

The Committee suggested that a statement of financial position (a
balance sheet) was expected to represent the financial relationships of a
company with the rest of the world - the assets it owned, the debts it
owed and the residual interest in its assets. A dated balance sheet in
which assets were represented by their dated money equivalents would be
serviceable and intelligible alike to creditors and shareholders and
other parties. The Report was to be a practical document; so, although
the Committee was aware of dicta of economists relating to wealth and
financial position that tallied with its specification, no reference was
made to that support. As for income, the Report described it as the
periodical increment in net wealth; this was consistent with descriptions
in the accounting literature and with dicta of the Court in the **Spanish
Prospecting** case. "True and fair" was broken down into (i) true - i.e.
not false with reference to dated position or periodical increment; and
(ii) fair - i.e. not unfair as a basis for negotiation or action by any
person having a financial interest in a company.

From these specifications, the Report proceeded to set out a general
accounting standard (Chapter 8). As the Report was an exploratory
document, authorised by the Attorney General of one state, it seemed
proper to set up the general standard with reference to the relevant

provisions of the NSW Companies Act and its Ninth Schedule which dealt
with the contents of published annual financial statements. In the
absence of interpretation in the Act, it seemed necessary to augment the
Act with the following sections:

> No balance sheet shall be deemed to give a true and fair
> view of the state of affairs of a company unless the
> amounts shown for the assets are the money amounts or
> the best available approximations to the net selling
> prices in the ordinary course of business of those assets
> in their state and condition as at the date of the
> balance sheet.

356

> No profit and loss account shall be deemed to give a
> true and fair view of the profit or loss of a company
> unless that profit or loss is so calculated as to include
> the effects during the year of changes in the net
> selling prices of assets and of changes in the general
> purchasing power of the unit of account.

Before proceeding to details, the Report set out a series of
qualitative specifications, of the kind that are commonly found in
expositions of accounting and of the kind that would secure the practical
utility of accounts. They included relevance to users, independent
verifiability, aggregability of component items, comparability,
completeness, consistency and interpretability. The general standard, it
was held, satisfies all of these specifications. The Report then set up
specific rules for all assets and liabilities referred to in the Ninth
Schedule, and for the calculation of income in accordance with the
proposed additional provisions quoted at the end of the previous
paragraph above. An appendix to the Chapter summarized the rules in a
form in which they might become the substance of an act amending, or
auxiliary to, the existing Act.

The treatment of group accounts was given a separate chapter
(Chapter 9). The prevalent method of consolidation accounting was held
to be misleading, on the ground that a "group" does not own assets, or
owe liabilities, or make profits. Although the professional view on
equity accounting was rejected, the Report proposed a more comprehensive
form of equity accounting for interests in non-listed companies
(including subsidiaries) and joint ventures. It also proposed

aggregative statements of the assets, liabilities, equities and profits of such companies and joint ventures. As in Chapter 8, there was provided an appendix that could be used, subject to deletion from the Act of references to consolidated accounts, as the basis of an act amending or auxiliary to the existing Act.

The Report was the first "official" document proposing a general accounting standard. It was the first to propose a single valuation rule (the money equivalent of an asset), and the first designed specifically to reduce inconsistency in principle and diversity in practice. It was the first such proposal based on explicit definitions of financial position, income and a true and fair view. It was the first to propose a method of dealing with joint ventures in a manner consistent with the treatment of other financial interests. This array of "firsts" may suggest one reason why the profession has found it difficult to take notice of the Report. But the "principles" on which the proposals were based are all principles of long standing; and the method of accounting from day to day would be unaltered. Only the periodical adjustments to take account of accruals would differ; and they would differ only because the accrual principle would be applied rigorously and consistently, instead of partially and inconsistently as is the present mode of practice. Because the proposals of the Report were specific and the asset valuations were to be based on recently discovered prices, the tasks of the auditing profession would be consistent with long-standing methods of verifying monetary items, and auditors would be free of the risks and uncertainties that otherwise have surrounded their work.

357

4. Old and New Evidence

Those familiar with my work over the last 20 years will know that the proposals of the Report have an extensive background. Takeover bids, asset revaluations (up and down), misleading features of accounts, official investigations, litigation and company collapses have yielded a rich harvest of facts indicative of the shortcomings of traditional practices and of the standards which have codified and reinforced them. In 1973 I put together a collection of this "evidence" for the reform of accounting in **Securities and Obscurities.** It pointed in the direction of real time accounting or continuously contemporary accounting (CoCoA), and in no other direction. No such collection of evidence has ever been put together in support of any other style of accounting.

Some new "evidence" is now in the process of being analyzed. Over the last two decades a great deal of work has been done by means of surveys intended to discover what financial information is deemed to be important by those having interests in the affairs of companies. The conclusions may generally be described as "soft" conclusions. The surveys have generally related to "kinds" of information (information about "what" should be disclosed) not to the "quality" of information; and frequently the test-material has been so voluminous that it has interfered with the drawing of clear and firm inferences. Last year I undertook a survey that would be more specific and more penetrating, though less technical. There is no fundamental difference between the ways in which people **think** about personal financial affairs and corporate financial affairs. Persons and corporations buy and sell, borrow and lend, save and invest, under the same laws and in the same institutional settings. They are equally interested in stocks and flows of cash and other forms of wealth and equally concerned to avoid bankruptcy or liquidation. It seemed plausible that, if individual persons were confronted with problem-situations of the kind and scale they might ordinarily encounter, their responses would indicate the kinds of information they found serviceable and the style of accounting that would provide that information.

The test-material consisted of 15 questions, most of them quantified, relating to such problem-situations. Every-day expressions ("your wealth", "your financial position", "what you could spend") were used generally instead of accounting terms. This was done to make the questions readily answerable by accountants and non-accountants alike, and to avoid the effect, on respondents, of questions that might evoke professionally or vocationally conditioned responses. A number of questions were designed to provide cross-checks on the responses to other questions. Some 1900 questionnaires were mailed; some 1100 responses were received, 67 per cent of them from accountants or accounting-oriented people, 33 per cent from others.

I shall mention only the results which bear clearly on a serviceable style of accounting. Asked what kind of valuation of non-cash assets would give the best indicator of their financial positions, the percentage responses were as follows:

	Accountants	Others	Total
What assets would fetch if sold	83	85	83
Prices paid for assets	2	1	2
Present purchase prices of assets	14	12	14
No response	1	2	1
Total	100	100	100

Asked what kind of valuation of non-cash assets would represent their wealth, the percentage responses were as follows:

	Accountants	Others	Total
Prices paid	1	1	1
Mixed valuations	5	5	5
Resale prices	92	93	93
No response	2	1	1
Total	100	100	100

359

In reply to three separate questions on "what asset valuation would be indicative of what could be spent" in a given context, the percentage results were as follows:

	Accountants	Others	Total
Averse to cost	98	95	97
Averse to cost less depreciation	96	93	95
Averse to replacement price	62	60	62

Some remarkably clear inferences may be drawn from these results. The "others" referred to included persons in banking and finance, legal practice and other trades and professions. So –

First, there is substantial similarity between accountants and others in the way they think of money quantities in relation to financial matters.

Second, 83 per cent of respondents associate market resale prices of non-money assets with financial position, and 83 per cent of accountants do likewise.

Third, 93 per cent of respondents associate market resale prices with assessments of wealth, and 92 per cent of accountants do likewise.

Fourth, at least 95 per cent of respondents find valuations based on cost to be irrelevant as indications of what can be spent; and a clear majority was averse to the use of replacement prices for the same purpose.

In the light of these results and the large proportion of accountants in the responding sample, it seems strange indeed that accountants, in the practice of accounting, should have adhered so long and so firmly to traditional accounting yielding balance sheets that are largely based on original cost prices; and strange that so much attention has been given to the promotion of a form of accounting (CCA) which to a large extent is based on replacement prices.

5. **The Functions of Financial Information**

The reason for these anomalies in practice and in the standards that have been promulgated seems to lie in the failure of the authors of textbooks and standards to discriminate between the differential functions of particular kinds of information in the course of using financial information in decision-making. Those kinds of information and their functions are as follows:

Historical costs and historical selling prices are inputs to the calculation of periodical profits; and profits are indicative of the success of past operations and guides to whether more promising opportunities should be sought in the future.

Dated balances of monetary items and market resale prices (money equivalents) of non-monetary assets are elements of dated statements of financial position; a dated financial position is indicative of the general financial consequences of past operations (on solvency, asset composition, and the relationship of debt to equity), and guides to what steps **may** be taken if all of those features are satisfactory, and to what steps **must** be taken if any one of those features threatens the continual and profitable existence of a company.

Replacement prices or current costs are elements of forward calculations (from any date, or from balance date), either for the purpose of determining selling prices of products or in respect of the general continued conduct of a company's business. They appear in such calculations not as indicating means available (that is indicated by financial position), but as prospective commitments of means.

DCF values or net present values are elements of forward calculations, made with the object of finding which, of alternative proposals, is the more or most promising of future net inflows. In making forward calculations, it is permissible to use extrapolations of the kind that apply price-indexes to costs or other ascertained prices; for no firm knowledge of the course of future prices is accessible. But no such indexed figures are necessary or useful in discovering past results or past-dated financial positions.

Since the latter two kinds of information (replacement or current costs and net present values) relate to forward calculations, neither has anything to do with the representation of past results and financial positions. In other words, they have nothing to do with the company accounting that is required by law. Certainly they have parts to play in the internal decision-making of companies. But without knowledge of past results and dated financial positions, no decision can be made as to what is financially feasible in the future, nor as to what projects or policies are in the best interests of a company, its shareholders and its creditors.

361

6. Conclusion

It is notable that none of the standard-setting bodies has made use of any such analysis as that given in the previous section, or has made any inquiry by survey or otherwise to determine what the users of accounts understand by financial position or profit. The consequence is that there are, now simultaneously current, standards based on historical cost styles of accounting and standards based on index-adjusted and replacement prices - a very messy state of affairs. Indeed, the latest US standard on "inflation accounting" (SFAS33) requires companies to calculate income and net assets on **three** bases at the same time, traditional, index-adjusted (CPP accounting) and replacement cost (CCA accounting). And the latest UK standard on the same matter (SSAP16) requires companies to publish historical cost accounts **or** current cost accounts, in each case with supplementary information of the other variety. It is inconceivable that the publication of such mixtures of information will resolve the question "what is serviceable information?" It must be obvious, too, that these "standards" cannot be claimed to be standards in any worthwhile sense; for they permit a greater diversity of practice than was the case before they were introduced.

On the other hand, it will be noted that the results of the survey alluded to in an earlier section are consistent with the proposals of the Accounting Standards Review Committee. The analytical and practical grounds for representing financial positions and calculating periodical incomes by the use of market resale prices were established some fifteen years ago. Yet none of the standard-setting bodies has given serious attention to such a system. Our recent survey suggests that users of accounts do, and will continue to, suppose that a statement of financial position is based on asset resale prices. It follows that they will continue to be misled if accounts are based on other rules.

I wonder how much longer accounting standards will be promulgated that fly in the face of analysis and evidence; and how much longer the statutes will continue to be so vague that such standards will be tolerated.

362

Regulation - The Future of the Accounting Profession*

Summary

1.   The professions - the accountancy profession among them - are
perhaps the most highly regulated pursuits. They are constrained in a
large degree by the nature of things. They are constrained further by
technical, ethical and social rules and considerations. That the
professions should be so constrained is consistent with the functional
importance of their arts and the inability of laymen to appraise
professional skill and performance. Regulation is inevitable for law and
good order. But where the rules that regulate conduct are varied and
optional, there is no order; following Gresham's Law, "bad rules drive
out good". That has occurred in accounting; hence the persistence of
criticism and the intermittent threat of further regulation. Regulation
on the basis of broad principle is generally more tolerable - and safe -
than regulation of details. And it is possible to have greater order
with fewer rules. But whatever the quantity of future regulation, and
whoever does the regulating, its benefits will be proportionate to its
respect for the common and well-known features of orderly thought and
conduct.

Regulation - For Whose Benefit?

2.   It seems to be the fate of accountants to be "pushed around". A lot
of what you do is governed by acts of parliament - the companies acts,
the taxation assessment acts, the bankruptcy act, and so on. How you do
it is regulated by those and other acts - acts relating to public
accountants and auditors - and by the rules and regulations of
professional associations and public regulatory bodies. You bind
yourselves under contracts with clients and employers who seem to be able
to demand that you do this or that, no matter how you feel about it.
Your professional associations appoint committees who tell you you should
undergo some intellectual recycling from time to time - it's called
continuing professional education. And now you submit to being pushed
around by a speaker on the future of being pushed around.

---

* Presented at a State Congress of the Australian Society of
  Accountants, Sydney, February 1981.

364

3.   To be regulated is to be pushed around according to rules. We do not object to being regulated if the rules which govern our conduct have an understood object. The common function of rules is to establish and sustain law and order. I, and you, and you, are the better off for law and order. We stand a better chance under law and order, than under chaos and disorder, of accommodating ourselves satisfactorily to the rest of the world. So law and order are not simply ends in themselves; they are conditions under which we can pursue our own ends with greater expectations of satisfactory outcomes than we could entertain otherwise. The rules relating to rights in property, to the rights and duties of parties to specific contractual relationships, to the rights of individuals to act or to require others to act in certain ways – such rules enable us to rely on, and to be relied on by, others. In a world in which so many things may occur at unpredictable times and in unpredictable contexts and combinations, it is a great help to know that, whenever a certain event occurs, an action of a specific kind on the part of one of a specific class of persons must follow. That knowledge reduces the extent to which we are at the mercy of chance, or of the power, wilfulness and individuality of others. To be pushed around – regulated – with that kind of end in view is generally tolerable; for if others benefit from the predictability of many of our actions, we in turn benefit from the predictability of many of theirs. We may call that the mutual benefit principle.

4.   The mutual benefit principle, however, seems never completely to override what may be called the individual benefit principle. To allow one's behaviour to be predictable is to forgo the possible tactical advantage of surprise. And if my behaviour is predictable there is always the possibility that what others gain from that fact may exceed what I gain from the predictability of their behaviours. This individual bias entails that rules relating to conduct and codes of conduct are universal in intent, but never universal in effect. Hence the law – enforcement agencies and the proclaimed penalties for infringement of the provisions of laws, regulations and other kinds of rule.

5.   The object of these disciplinary devices is to bring the greatest number of persons or instances of prescribed behaviour under the pertinent laws or rules. But again, not merely for the sake of uniformity, but for the sake of greater interpersonal reliance and

3

reliability. And if uniformity (lawlikeness) is not obtainable under a
given set of laws or rules, the laws or rules are changed so that as
large as possible a segment of the population of persons or instances are
made to fall "within the law".

6.   These considerations apply to all rule-making. Whether rules and
regulations are devised or implemented by private or public
instrumentalities, their objects include the creation and maintenance of
order, predictability and reliability. That object was of obvious
importance in the case of the accountancy profession. The rise to
prominence of the profession in England was associated with the Companies
Act, 1862, and the Bankruptcy Act, 1869. The increase in work under
these statutes "encouraged anyone with a slight knowledge of bookkeeping
to set up as an accountant, to prey on developing and dying companies".
The aim of the regional associations of accountants which promoted the
formation of the English Chartered Institute "was to combat public
indignation and horror at the large number of incompetent, unscrupulous,
untrained money-grubbers, who openly practised as accountants" (Geoffrey
Millerson, **The Qualifying Associations**, London 1964, pp 51-2, 68-70).
That professional bodies should assume the right to determine requisite
skills and other conditions of admission, syllabuses of examinations,
conditions of advancement and continuing membership and of cessation of
membership - subject always to general laws against arbitrary and
oppressive exercise of those powers - has been accepted since
professional associations emerged. Such rights of self-regulation,
indeed, date back to the craft gilds of the twelfth and thirteenth
centuries (Cooke, **Corporation, Trust and Company**, Manchester, 1950).
Their justification was that they encouraged good and discouraged bad
workmanship, making the work of qualified persons more generally
dependable.

A Professional Ethic?

7.   The wish to be considered by laymen as dependable experts contains
the germ of a professional ethic. The hallmarks of professions generally
have been said to be: "a high degree of generalized and systematic
knowledge; primary orientation to the community interest rather than to
the individual self-interest; a high degree of self-control of behaviour
through codes of ethics . . . and through voluntary associations . . .;
and a system of rewards (monetary and honorary) that is primarily a set

365

of symbols of work achievement, and thus ends in themselves . . ." (Bernard Barber, "Some Problems in the Sociology of the Professions", **Daedalus**, Fall 1963, p. 672). Of the four distinctive types of constraint or discipline implied in this description, three have some ethical feature – community interest, self-control, and accomplishment as one of its own rewards. The ethical elements are often supposed to be something distinct from the technical elements of performance; but they are also supposed to give some assurance of quality of performance. Are those suppositions warranted by the evidence?

8.   The Greek word that gave us "ethics" and "ethical" has reference to character and manners. It is understandable that many associations expect to have evidence of the good fame and character of those seeking membership, and that members shall respect the courtesies of interpersonal relations and the specific rules of conduct between a member and other members, and between a member and his clients. But both in character and manners there is a wide gap between the gross and the trivial. It is difficult to discriminate, within that gap, between what is tolerable and what is not; and difficult to establish the determination of a disciplinary body to uphold a standard of behaviour that is not specifiable. It is even more difficult for any such body to insinuate the impression that it might deal seriously with any evidence of technical incompetence, which is the very thing the public might need protection against.

9.   Millerson provides some information on disciplinary action taken by the English Institute over the period 1949-62. The following digests a more detailed table:

		Disciplinary Action	
		Expulsion	Other Penalties
I	Dereliction of statutory duties, crimes, misdemeanours	80	32
II	Ethical offences	12	51
III	Other failures and omissions	10	24

The offences of Class I are of the kind determined by courts and tribunals beyond the profession; the penalties were thus largely consequential. Of offences within the sole jurisdiction of the Institute, the cases are few and the penalties light (suspensions 5, reprimands and admonishments, 70). They may seem insignificant for an Institute whose practising membership rose from 5,600 to 10,500 over the interval. But we have no indication of the number of "complaints" considered over the period, so the general scale of disciplinary proceedings is not known. It is clear, however, that none of the 19 classes of offence given in the original tabulation alludes to technical incompetence as such, or to the exploitation of technical rules to the disadvantage of those who relied on their objectivity.

10. Now, we expect the general law and the legal and social sanctions against dishonesty and other misbehaviour to deal with the general morals and manners of men, professionals and laymen alike. We expect the disciplinary machinery of a professional body to concern itself more clearly with "professional ethics". And what is that? The same Greek word that gave us "ethics" gave us "ethos", the characteristic style of an institution or system, or the ideal of excellence upheld by a profession. Professional ethics relates not to the general morality of a particular class of men, but to a particular kind of morality or duty of that class. It is the duty of one, who professes to be expert, towards another who is in need of his expertise but who cannot understand it.

11. It is the burden of the professions to deal with matters not readily comprehensible to others. Where some men need skills that are beyond their understanding, the charlatan, the hack and the technical genius may all have a slice of the action. The protection of the non-skilled from exploitation by the unskilled and the unscrupulous subsists in the determination of the skilled to excel in what he professes and in the determination of professional associations of the skilled to weed out and expose incompetence. To think of professional conduct as "skill plus duty", the sum of two separate behaviours, is almost to treat it with contempt. Skill and duty must rather be seen to be welded, merged, all of a piece. The exercise of skill with respect for that skill, with a sense of duty to one's clients, and with an overall aspiration to excellence is of the essence of a professional ethic.

12. It is impossible to entertain a worthwhile notion of a professional ethic without regard for technical skill. That is the point at which the accounting profession has come under critical notice, the point at which there have been repeated threats to interfere with the self-regulation of the profession. Recall Barber's identification of "a high degree of generalized and systematic knowledge" as one of the marks of a profession and its members. It is generalized and systematic knowledge that enables the expert to deal with superficially different instances or situations in an orderly and consistent manner. It is that kind of knowledge that preserves him from self-contradiction, from charges of bias, and from attempts to undermine his skill and judgement. It is that kind of knowledge that enables him to claim that his art is disciplined, that in its practice he is self-disciplined. It is that kind of knowledge that assures him that the products of his skill are serviceable, in demonstrable ways, to the publics he serves; and that, where others than his clients are affected by what he does, their interests are not prejudiced. It is that kind of knowledge that gives him confidence in his fellow-experts, and the readiness to forgo individual benefit for the mutual benefit of members of his profession.

From Craft to Profession

13. There was a time when the skills and services of accountants were of private interest only. There was no firm body of technical rules based on the utility of the information yielded by accounting. Accounting was a craft, "an avocation based upon customary activities and modified by the trial and error of individual practice" (A.N. Whitehead, **Adventures of Ideas**, 1933, Ch. 4). But with the rise of public investment in private corporations in the mid-nineteenth century, the products of accounting came to influence the interests of others beyond the immediate masters and clients of accountants. The English legislature was concerned, quite properly, with the protection of the interests of those who would make corporate business possible – investors and creditors. Its expectations were indicated by references to "a full and fair balance sheet" and "a true and correct view of the state of the Company's affairs" in the model articles appended to the 1862 Companies Act. There were then no threats of governmental prescription of accounting rules, an ideal situation for the newly emerging profession to devise rules which would give expression to the qualifiers "full and fair" and "true and

correct".

14. But for the first half century of the profession's existence the professional bodies played no significant role in the development or endorsement of accounting principles. There was occasional litigation on asset valuation and profits. The cases were decided, as are all litigated cases, on their particular merits; no general principles were enunciated by the courts. In the absence of general principles the practice of accounting came to be shaped by the individual exigencies of business firms and the inventiveness of accountants. The textbooks used for coaching, or as authorities on practice, were written by practitioners; they recorded the state of practice with all its blemishes. Recruits to the profession absorbed its traditions from their professional mentors under apprenticeship. No attempt was made to weed out rules that would interfere with the ideal style of information alluded to in the legislation, or to consider what rules would yield the most serviceable kind of periodical information to the owners and managers of firms that did not fall under the provisions of the companies acts.

15. Meanwhile there began the process of reviewing the state of the companies legislation through parliamentary committees. In the U.K. there have been the Loreburn (1906), Wrenbury (1918), Greene (1926), Cohen (1945) and Jenkins (1962) Committees; there have been other such reviews in other jurisdictions and no doubt there has been a great deal of related work in ministerial offices over decades. Professional bodies have had the opportunity to make submissions on desirable and prospective changes in the accounts provisions of the acts, and some have done so. However, in the upshot, though the quantum of information required to be disclosed in company accounts has increased substantially, the rules governing the quality of that information have remained substantially the same. A true and fair view of results and financial position are required to be given; but neither by amplification of what that means, nor by the proscription of rules deemed to have a contrary effect, has practice been made more disciplined through the initiative of parliament or government.

16. As for the profession, about 50 years ago attempts began to be made to re-examine the prevalent corpus of rules. Cases like the Royal Mail case and the McKesson and Robbins case made it clear that there were

laxities and loopholes in practice; and litigated cases and official investigations since then have provided mounting evidence of the prevalence of loose and misleading practices. Professional associations have shown no lack of will to formulate recommendations and more recently to issue statements of standard practice. How is it then that, in spite of increased specificity of the statutes, over the 20 years in which professionally sponsored standard-setting bodies have been most active, criticism of the profession's practices has been more frequent and trenchant than before?

17. One class of reasons may be described generally as evasive. It has been held that since the legislature has not made clear what was intended by the true and fair view stipulation, the profession should not make the meaning of the phrase more precise on its own initiative. Perhaps so; but there was no reason why the profession should not seek to have the legislature make good the deficiency. It has been acknowledged that prevalent practices are deficient – have "limitations", to use a common euphemism – and that the public should be educated to understand the limitations of accounting. But no serious attempt has been made to find whether the limitations are unavoidable; and no scheme for educating the public has been advanced. It has been held that accounts should not be expected to be understood except by those who have taken the trouble to understand the principles underlying them. But that cuts right across the idea of a professional expertise needed, as we have said, by laymen but not open to informed appraisal by them. It has been held that if all business firms (and their accountants) were free to exercise their initiative in accounting, "market forces" would eliminate misleading and defective practices. But by what mechanism no one has yet explained.

18. A second class of reasons relates to oversights and omissions made in the course of attempts to improve the corpus of practices. The most common products of accounting are statements of profit and statements of financial position. But there has been no common definition or shared understanding of "profits" and "financial position" to guide or constrain usage or rule-making. The context of the use of the financial statements of firms is the making of analytical and exploratory calculations for the better conduct of negotiations, arrangements and relationships in a

market-structured setting. But many of the widely tolerated valuation
and quantification rules – the-lower-of-cost-and-market, straight-line
amortized cost, anticipation and deferral of revenues and charges – are
fictions, having no counterparts in market places. The most common
feature of accounting is aggregation, a process so widely spread through
human affairs that its rules might be expected to be well-understood and
respected. But, in the regular practice of accounting, kinds of
aggregation are made that we would not dream of making in respect of
personal affairs. It is well known that **different** information is
serviceable for **different** purposes. But universally in accounting,
different information is put together with the intention that a cluster
of different bits will serve a **single** purpose, i.e. will represent
financial position. The most common use of accounting information is in
conjunction or by comparison with other accounting and financial
information. But the reluctance to endorse uniformity as a principle
cuts right across the interest of information users in information that
is comparable at points of time, across intervals of time and across
arrays of firms.

19. These are fundamental solecisms, technical absurdities. They could
not have survived attempts to base accounting on "generalized and
systematic knowledge". They should not have survived the inquiries of
governmental committees, professional committees, and the submissions to
both by professionals and other users of accounts. They have survived
because of the firm allegiance of the profession to the presumptions of
traditional practice, and because of the inability or unwillingness of
others to challenge those presumptions. Long ago Whitehead observed that
"each profession makes progress, but it is progress in its own groove"
(**Science and the Modern World**, Cambridge, 1925, Ch. XIII). He saw great
dangers in this, for the upshot is that "the specialised functions of the
community are performed better and more progressively, but the
generalized direction lacks vision". There are antidotes to grooved and
visionless progress. But the profession's long-standing practice when
matters are in doubt is not one of them. That practice has been to rely
on part-time deliberative committees of professionals without any
obligation on their part to accumulate evidence and to base their
conclusions on argument from the evidence. Any given problem may be put
through that process repeatedly without resolving it. To change the

371

metaphor, let's call it the "revolving door addiction". It was noticed by the eleventh century poet - philosopher, Omar Khayyam:

> Myself when young did eagerly frequent
>
> Doctor and Saint, and heard great argument
>
> About it and about; but evermore
>
> Came out by the same door as in I went.

The traditional presumptions persist. The solecisms are still with us. And so are the critics. Where shall we turn, then?

Monistic or Pluralistic Control?

20. The practising arm of the profession is or should be valued, as we have said, for its expertise in providing serviceable financial information. But does that mean that it must, of its own motion, determine what is serviceable and monitor performance in the light of what it decides? No; there seems to be a better prospect from sharing those functions.

21. Take first the technical rule-making function. If we wish to have an orderly profession, common rules of practice are necessary; otherwise clients (or employers) would not know what to expect. Those rules may be devised to provide what a client expects for what he is prepared to pay. But given the corporate form of business, the profession's products may influence the interests of others than the professional and his client. The interests of third parties may only be protected from prejudicial action or information by the general law. For an orderly commerce, the parliament may not waive, and no other party may arrogate to itself, the power to determine what will be considered to be fair as between third and other parties. Hence the accounts provisions of the statutes.

22. Now, if the corpus of professional practices for non-corporate business yields serviceable information, the introduction of corporate business should make no difference. Owners (investors), managers, creditors and other parties alike are interested in the net wealth, profits, solvency, debt-dependence and asset composition of firms. But if there is any doubt about the meaning of the statutory terms, "true and fair view etc.", the doubt may be resolved in one or more of several ways - by checking the origins of the statutory prescription for amplifying detail; by checking judicial dicta that have some bearing on the words used in the statute; by checking the rules relating to the interpretation of statutes; by checking the literature (textbook and reportorial) for

372

clues to what information the commercial and financial community finds useful and necessary; by investigating what persons having some experience of financial matters find useful in their private capacities; and by proceeding from available generalized knowledge to deduce, logically and systematically, the kind of information that is pertinent to judgement and choice, and that is not obtainable otherwise than through accounting.

23.   As prelude to or in association with their edicts and prescriptions, neither professional nor governmental committees and boards have hitherto published any work of these kinds. There is no logical reason why they should not have made any such inquiries, but there are perhaps some tactical reasons, some greater wisdom in letting others do it. The interpretation to be given to a "true and fair view etc." rests on generalized and systematic knowledge, as does the elimination of the solecisms mentioned earlier. The search for that knowledge in other fields has long proceeded in independent institutions of research and learning, with the collaboration of practising professionals. In those circumstances, the complementary skills and different viewpoints of researchers and practising professionals are applied without commitment on the part of the profession until it chooses to commit itself. Meanwhile the profession would be free of association with abortive experiments and undisturbed by the controversies and debates that surround the search for new knowledge. There have been embarrassing examples over the past 20 years of attempts to force changes in practice without adequate exploration of their potential consequences. At least in prospect, the process of relying on independent researchers to gather and analyze evidence, and to experiment with rule-formulation, seems more clean-cut than the surges, stalls and reverses of the professional bodies in the recent past.

24.   Turn now to the disciplinary question. On the one hand is the disciplinary effect on business firms of the obligation to disclose the consequences of what has occurred. On the other hand is the disciplinary effect of a code of uniform practices on the performance of individual professionals. If the latter fails so does the former. To judge from the known diversity of practices, it seems to be extraordinarily difficult to sustain a uniform code where the authority for it lies in the hands of practitioners. A fabled knight may have claimed: "My

373

strength is as the strength of ten because my heart is pure". But a profession of diverse membership and different interests, confronted by a business community motivated to a large degree by individual initiative and self-interest cannot rely on pureness of heart. It can, however, rely on the stronger force of the general law. If the edicts of the profession and its standard-setting apparatus were demonstrably related to the general principles of the companies statutes, they could be defended against all attack. No stronger line need be taken than that a given practice or standard was essential to the giving of a true and fair view of results and states of affairs from time to time. The community's instrumentalities for the maintenance of law and order could then be engaged. Operation in tandem - the pursuit of excellence and the force of law- would be much more effective in disciplining members of the profession, companies and their officers, and those who would undermine the profession's aspirations, than operation in apparent conflict with or disregard for the provisions of the general law.

374

25. We have suggested a pluralistic form of professional control and discipline, a three-pronged but collaborative assault on the problems that irritate the profession, its dependents and its monitors. Independent research as a basis for technical rules, adoption by the profession of rules that are demonstrably serviceable in the light of argument and evidence, and a common front with the general law on the disciplining of practice, seem to be more promising than unilateral action by the profession. But the promise rests on the possibility of a form of accounting that would command the assent of all kinds of accountants; of businessmen, investors and creditors, and of law-makers, lawyers and regulators.

26. We believe there can be such a form of accounting. Solvency, debt-dependence, risk and profitability influence the interests of all who have a stake in the survival and success of firms, unincorporated or corporate. Up-to-date indicators of all these features are necessary to managers if firms are to take prompt steps to counter potentially adverse drifts in any of them or to take prompt advantage of any shift in prospects of gain. Those indicators are equally necessary to outsiders if they are to judge a firm's financial capacity to avert difficulties or to seek to benefit from new opportunities. The common indicators of the features mentioned are: of solvency, the current ratio; of debt-

dependence and financial flexibility, the debt to equity ratio of asset-holding risk, the asset composition; of profitability, the rate of return on net assets. Between them, these ratios make use, in different combinations, of every item in periodical financial statements. If up-to-date indicators are to be provided, every amount in a balance sheet must be an up-to-date money amount - of debts, actual amounts owed; of assets, actual amounts accessible for the payment of debts or of running costs, or for conversion to other assets if that is judged to be necessary or desirable. And if balance sheet components are to be used to calculate what is financially feasible or desirable, all of those amounts must be in units of up-to-date general purchasing power at the date of a balance sheet. These are quite general, universal and uniform conditions, yielding information that is comparable between firms and between periods.

27.   I have at different times made inquiries of all of the kinds mentioned in para. 22. Apart from some of the dicta and practices of accountants, I have never found anything inconsistent with the above prescription for a style of systematically up-to-date accounting. I interpret that as evidence that the making of judgements of the past and decisions for the future on the basis of up-to-date financial information is "in the nature of things". The propriety and serviceability of a style of accounting yielding that information is not challengeable on the ground that it is a mere matter of opinion, or that it differentially favours or prejudices any class of firm or class of users of accounts. It would therefore satisfy the equity-oriented provisions of the law on financial publicity, and should command the assent of accountants, businessmen and lawyers alike.

What, and How Much, Regulation

28.   There are no blacks and whites about who shall regulate the accountancy profession's affairs, and how. For the protection of third parties there are broad stipulations of principle in the general law. But self-regulation or self-discipline, means nothing unless it relates to a higher order of conduct than any stipulated minimum. Where the minimum is itself unclear there can be no confidence that a given style of action exceeds or falls short of it. Unless the profession itself stipulates a higher order of technical performance than the minimum implicit in the statute, others will shape its conduct. There will be

375

"other regulation" by default of self-regulation, and even in addition to
self-regulation. There will be demands within and beyond the profession
for rules on this and rules on that, and then for options of this sort
and that. Practice comes to be governed by the trivial and the
incidental rather than the fundamental. The profession will be
overregulated, and yet undisciplined. That I fear is the present state
of affairs.

29. A profession founded on generalized and systematic knowledge could,
on the other hand, be expected to be rather less rule-bound and yet well-
disciplined. Its members would know that informed judgement and choice
depend on up-to-date information, that fictions interfere with the
representation of facts, that only like quantities may properly be added
and related. These and other similar propositions - all of them "in the
nature of things" - are themselves disciplinary in a fundamental fashion.
They stand firmly in the way of the solecisms and fallacious practices
noticed in para. 18; and they cannot but yield the true and fair view of
profits and states of affairs that the Companies Acts require. If it
were understood that there are sufficient of such general principles to
yield full and serviceable accounts, all specific rules and standards
could be dispensed with. We could have a minimally regulated but a
thoroughly disciplined profession.

30. En route to that ideal situation, however, we may have to tolerate
more than minimal regulation. But whether its source and authority is
the profession itself or governmental and regulatory bodies, its success
in promoting an orderly commerce will rest on the extent to which its
specific rules are - not merely traditional, conventional or political,
in style or effect, but - firmly based on the nature of things.

376

Comments on the Proposal of the National Companies
and Securities Commission on the Establishment
of an Accounting Standards Review Board*

1.   These comments
     (a) support the proposal to establish an Accounting Standards
          Review Board (ASRB);
     (b) support the development of specific standards by the Accounting
          Standards Board (ASB) of the accounting profession;
     (c) suggest the desirability of determination and publication by
          the ASRB of the grounds on which it will recommend   standards
          for endorsement by the NCSC;
     (d) suggest the desirability of giving statutory or other official
          interpretation to "a true and fair view of profits or losses
          and state of affairs".

2.   I strongly support the establishment of an Accounting Standards
     Review Board that will be independent of the professional accounting
     bodies. For over 20 years I have been associated in one way or
     another with committees, or the work of committees, set up by the
     professional bodies with the object of developing standards. I have
     taken a continuing interest in standards proposed in Australia and
     in other countries of similar style in legal and financial matters.
     I have made numerous submissions on proposed standards to Australian
     committees, and less frequent submissions to committees in the U.K.,
     U.S.A., Canada and New Zealand. I have worked in the relevant
     division of the American Institute of Certified Public Accountants
     on two occasions over a total period of about six months. I have
     addressed the U.S. Financial Accounting Standards Board and the
     corresponding U.K. committee. As a senior official of an Australian
     professional body I was involved over a number of years in the
     consideration and endorsement of proposed standards, and in the
     reconstruction of the standard-setting arrangements. These varied
     engagements have yielded some judgements which seem to be quite

377

---

* Submission to the Australian National Companies and Securities
Commission, March 1982.

general in respect of the standard-setting arrangements in the countries with which I am familiar.

3   Merely from the order in which official standards have appeared, it can be seen that standard-setting has in all cases been **ad hoc**. The matters that have received attention seem to have depended, in some cases on the desire to set up a "programme of work", in other cases on the occurrence among practising professionals of some technical dilemma. For two reasons this has been unsatisfactory.

4.   First, there is a certain logic about tackling the design of standards of accounting for particular items that appear in accounts. The companies laws have contemplated that profit and loss accounts shall give a true and fair view of periodical profits or losses, and that balance sheets shall give a like view of the state of affairs of a company from time to time. If meanings were assigned to profit (and loss) and state of affairs, meanings that were clearly related to the uses of financial information by managers or financial supporters of companies, the setting of standards for particular items in accounts would be greatly simplified. All subsidiary standards would, of necessity, be designed to yield components of periodical accounts consistent with those meanings. Nowhere has this elementary, but systematic, procedure been adopted. Indeed, nowhere yet have profit and state of affairs been defined for the purpose of any standard.

5.   Second, the dilemmas of practising professionals are not necessarily related to the main causes of public disquiet over the quality of company accounts. The deficiencies of accounts that have emerged most clearly from litigated cases, bankruptcies and official inquiries have been the unrealistic valuation of assets, the self-serving use of favourable accounting options, and the optional dating (anticipation or deferral) of items of gain or loss. It seems reasonable to expect that public exposure of the effects of these practices on the interests of creditors and investors would induce the professional bodies to make remedial action in those directions a matter of high priority. But that has not occurred. Those practices have become so habitual that they have not been seen

by professionals as matters requiring remedy. Indeed I have not infrequently heard it said that the object of formulating statements on standards is to codify present practices – and that is all that many such statements do. That procedure, of course, will do nothing to eradicate the causes of misinformation and misdirection that are inherent in conventional practices.

6. Notwithstanding the failure of committees of professional bodies to produce serviceable standards in the past, I agree that standard setting should be left in the hands of those bodies. The primary reason for this is that professionals or their delegates might be expected to understand more fully than lay persons the ways in which particulars are interlocked in the accounting process. But since, in spite of past efforts, there is still need for improvement in standards (as the Review Board proposals of the NCSC and the Campbell Committee Report attest), the professional bodies clearly need a new sense of direction. The Accounting Standards Board (ASB) of the professional bodies may of itself adopt a more rigorous procedure and more rigorous tests of what it proposes as standards. However, whether it does so or not, the Accounting Standards Review Board (ASRB) would, in my view, have to determine the grounds on which it would judge a standard satisfactory for recommendation to the NCSC for endorsement.

379

7. To determine those grounds seems to be a matter of the highest priority. In the first place they would provide guidance to the ASB of the professional bodies, indicating what would or would not be acceptable to the ASRB, and averting expenditure of the time of both bodies on proposals that are unlikely to be endorsed. In the second place, they would provide firm tests by recourse to which the ASRB may make its judgements, and secure coherence and consistency in the standards it recommends for endorsement.

8. That the ASRB should establish those grounds at the outset, before considering any specific standard, is crucial. It seems quite proper that the proposed Board shall consist of persons of varied interests and competences. However, it is characteristic of the discussions of committees of many kinds that the specific and

personal experiences and interests of members may obtrude to a degree that is inimical to the reaching of conclusions that advance the cause for which they were established. It is almost beyond question, for example, that the products of standards committees in the past have been influenced by what is common practice (and for that reason alone, is readily acceptable), and by the expected impact of any given standard on the reported affairs of firms with which committee members are associated. As the conclusions or judgements of the ASRB will have wide and general impact, the immediate effects of any proposed standard on any particular company, and what is at present widely done or tolerated, should not interfere with what is in the best interests of the users of financial statements.

380

9. The view has been expressed in many circles that it is impossible to expect the business community (including accountants) to conform with rules or standards with which they are not in sympathy. But this overlooks the fact that periodical accounts are published for the benefit of persons on whom companies depend. The pertinence of the information to the judgements of creditors and investors outranks in importance the ease of preparation of periodical accounts. In any case, ease of preparation (a common feature of what is customary) can no longer be held to be of consequence. The proposals over the last decade for forms of "inflation accounting" have introduced quite complex modes of calculation and statement preparation. Accountants in industry and in professional practice were quite unaccustomed to these exercises. Yet, in spite of the fact that there has been no proof of the usefulness of the information these schemes would yield, and in spite of the fact that the work is **additional** to the preparation of conventional accounts, many firms have undertaken it, in some cases at great cost. I am confident that information pertinent to investors, creditors and managers alike, can be generated with greater ease and less confusion than the information generated by many existent and proposed standards. I therefore believe that the ASRB should not be dissuaded from adopting "grounds of recommendation" that cut across

present practices and standards, merely because of alleged ("practical") difficulties. There are already in the literature on accounting standards many indications of what seem to be appropriate tests of satisfactory standards; but they do need disentangling from the contradictory and the permissive propositions with which they are so often hedged.

10. I have long been of the opinion that the statutory provisions relating to the quality of periodical company accounts could, by definition in the statute, lay a firm foundation for more dependable accounting. As noted above, the professional bodies have hitherto declined to specify what is, or is to be, understood by profit or loss, state of affairs, and a true and fair view of both. By way of explanation it has been said that the professional bodies are under no obligation to make clear what the legislation does not make clear. The outcome of vagueness in the statutes has been the long series of litigated actions that have been fruitless as far as improvement in the standard of periodical accounting and reporting is concerned; and the actions that have not been brought because of the vagueness of the terms of the statute and the unlikelihood, therefore, of fruitful prosecution. In 1973 I proposed that the statutory provisions be strengthened, by definition in the acts of what was to be understood by a true and fair view of profit or loss and state of affairs. What seemed to be appropriate forms of words were given in para 8.04 of the 1978 Report of the Accounting Standards Review Committee to the NSW Attorney General. The relevant parts of that paragraph are:

> No balance sheet shall be deemed to give a true and fair view of the state of affairs of a company unless the amounts shown for the assets are the money amounts or the best available approximations to the net selling prices in the ordinary course of business of those assets in their state and condition as at the date of the balance sheet.
> No profit and loss account shall be deemed to give a true and fair view of the profit or loss of a company unless that profit or loss is so calculated as to include the effects during the year of changes in the net selling prices of assets and of changes in the general purchasing power of the unit of account.

11. It may seem that the proposed ASRB would circumvent the necessity of

381

a change in the statute. To minimize changes in the statute is, of course, the object of providing for the regulation of details by the NCSC. But the **general** expectations of the legislature should, it seems to me, be made clear in the statute, to strengthen the hands of the NCSC and the ASRB and to reduce the scope for lenient or unnecessarily generous concessions (and hence vagueness) in the standards proposed for endorsement. This view entails no disrespect for the skill or diligence of the membership of the NCSC or the ASRB. Nor does it entail any disregard for the goodwill and good intentions of those who have laboured to produce accounting standards hitherto in Australia or elsewhere. It arises simply from the known strain of standard-setting committees, in attempting to accommodate arguments arising among or beyond themselves, when the general purport of their task is insufficiently specific. Crucial principles have in the past been lost to sight in the swirling sea of fluid particulars.

12. The proposal of the NCSC in respect of the ASRB gives the Board no scope for initiatives of its own in respect of accounting standards. It may approve priorities, review standards, and recommend their endorsement if it sees fit. But even if the ASRB were to determine and disclose at the outset the grounds on which standards may be recommended for endorsement, as suggested, inclusion in the statute of general definition of the kind indicated in para 10 seems desirable. The suggested definitions are quite general in character. They say nothing about standards with respect to details. But they attempt to capture all of the elements that influence the amounts of the assets, liabilities and profits of companies from time to time; anything less would be an incomplete, and therefore misleading, accounting. The use of the phrase "best available approximations" allows some liberty in finding approximations, but at the same time places the responsibility for the quality of the accounts (and the burden of proof in dispute or litigation) on those who issue or authenticate them. The reference to "net resale prices" is unexceptionable in the context of information for the use of creditors and investors. Their interests

382

in the affairs of a company turn on its ability to meet its debts, to carry on its business, to increase its debt if necessary, to pay taxes and dividends and so on. None of these abilities can be indicated by money amounts other than the approximate amounts of the resale prices of assets; and that fact is acknowledged in a number of the presently accepted rules of valuation.

13. I am therefore of the opinion that the NCSC should consider using its best endeavours to have the terms of the statute augmented by some provisions, such as are indicated in para 10 above, giving an interpretation of what shall be understood by a true and fair view of profits and states of affairs from time to time. It may, of course, be within the power of the NCSC to provide the appropriate guidance by regulation on its own initiative. But, for the coordination of the actions of all parties (the profession's ASB, the ASRB, the NCSC) in a manner consistent with the legislation, some quite deliberate clarification of what is required in the public interest seems to be imperative.

383

14. It may be thought that to step out of line with the legislation or regulation on similar matters in other jurisdictions is not warranted. But consider the consequences of the present "line". Accounting standards developed so far, in Australia and elsewhere, are in many cases inconsistent within a given jurisdiction. In some countries, standards based on fundamentally different principles coexist. In respect of some particulars, standards have been found to be unacceptable, have been revised, and in the process have become more prolix and obscure. I am informed that one such standard (through its various stages and revisions) has cost in the vicinity of $2m so far; and it is not likely to have been the most costly. In the last decade, the standard-setting apparatus of the United States must have cost in the vicinity of $60-100 million, regardless of the time spent by professional accountants, company financial officers, analysts and others in preparing and making submissions and in carrying out procedures that were subsequently varied. The sums are enormous by reference to the modest improvement in the relevance of the information to investors and

creditors. I am unable to imagine any explanation of this other than the absence of a clear statement of what accounting information is required for a fair and informed market in securities, either in the appropriate statute or from some other official or quasi-official source.

15. I have not in these comments elaborated on the arguments and evidence which support my opinions and suggestions. Material of both kinds is at hand and can be made available if required.

384

Accounting Books Published by Garland

New Books

Ashton, Robert H., ed. *The Evolution of Behavioral Accounting Research: An Overview.* New York, 1984.

Ashton, Robert H., ed. *Some Early Contributions to the Study of Audit Judgment.* New York, 1984.

*Brief, Richard P., ed. *Corporate Financial Reporting and Analysis in the Early 1900s.* New York, 1986.

Brief, Richard P., ed. *Depreciation and Capital Maintenance.* New York, 1984.

*Brief, Richard P., ed. *Estimating the Economic Rate of Return from Accounting Data.* New York, 1986.

Brief, Richard P., ed. *Four Classics on the Theory of Double-Entry Bookkeeping.* New York, 1982.

*Chambers, R. J., and G. W. Dean, eds. *Chambers on Accounting.* New York, 1986.
Volume I: Accounting, Management and Finance.
Volume II: Accounting Practice and Education.
Volume III: Accounting Theory and Research.
Volume IV: Price Variation Accounting.
Volume V: Continuously Contemporary Accounting.

Clarke, F. L. *The Tangled Web of Price Variation Accounting: The Development of Ideas Underlying Professional Prescriptions in Six Countries.* New York, 1982.

Coopers & Lybrand. *The Early History of Coopers & Lybrand.* New York, 1984.

*Included in the Garland series Accounting Thought and Practice Through the Years.

*Craswell, Allen. *Audit Qualifications in Australia 1950 to 1979*. New York, 1986.

Dean, G. W., and M. C. Wells, eds. *The Case for Continuously Contemporary Accounting*. New York, 1984.

Dean, G. W., and M. C. Wells, eds. *Forerunners of Realizable Values Accounting in Financial Reporting*. New York, 1982.

Edey, Harold C. *Accounting Queries*. New York, 1982.

*Edwards, J. R., ed. *Legal Regulation of British Company Accounts 1836–1900*. New York, 1986.

*Edwards, J. R., ed. *Reporting Fixed Assets in Nineteenth-Century Company Accounts*. New York, 1986.

Edwards, J. R., ed. *Studies of Company Records: 1830–1974*. New York, 1984.

Fabricant, Solomon. *Studies in Social and Private Accounting*. New York, 1982.

Gaffikin, Michael, and Michael Aitken, eds. *The Development of Accounting Theory: Significant Contributors to Accounting Thought in the 20th Century*. New York, 1982.

Hawawini, Gabriel A., ed. *Bond Duration and Immunization: Early Developments and Recent Contributions*. New York, 1982.

Hawawini, Gabriel, and Pierre Michel, eds. *European Equity Markets: Risk, Return, and Efficiency*. New York, 1984.

*Hawawini, Gabriel, and Pierre A. Michel. *Mandatory Financial Information and Capital Market Equilibrium in Belgium*. New York, 1986.

*Hawkins, David F. *Corporate Financial Disclosure, 1900–1933: A Study of Management Inertia within a Rapidly Changing Environment*. New York, 1986.

*Johnson, H. Thomas. *A New Approach to Management Accounting History* New York, 1986.

*Kinney, William R., Jr., ed. *Fifty Years of Statistical Auditing*. New York, 1986.

Klemstine, Charles E., and Michael W. Maher. *Management Accounting Research: A Review and Annotated Bibliography.* New York, 1984.

*Lee, T. A., ed. *A Scottish Contribution to Accounting History.* New York, 1986.

*Lee, T. A. *Towards a Theory and Practice of Cash Flow Accounting.* New York, 1986.

Lee, Thomas A., ed. *Transactions of the Chartered Accountants Students' Societies of Edinburgh and Glasgow: A Selection of Writings, 1886–1958.* New York, 1984.

*McKinnon, Jill L. *The Historical Development and Operational Form of Corporate Reporting Regulation in Japan.* New York, 1986.

Nobes, Christopher, ed. *The Development of Double Entry: Selected Essays.* New York, 1984.

*Nobes, Christopher. *Issues in International Accounting.* New York, 1986.

*Parker, Lee D. *Developing Control Concepts in the 20th Century.* New York, 1986.

Parker, R. H. *Papers on Accounting History.* New York, 1984.

*Previts, Gary John, and Alfred R. Roberts, eds. *Federal Securities Law and Accounting 1933–1970; Selected Addresses.* New York, 1986.

*Reid, Jean Margo, ed. *Law and Accounting: Pre-1889 British Legal Cases.* New York, 1986.

Sheldahl, Terry K. *Beta Alpha Psi, from Alpha to Omega: Pursuing a Vision of Professional Education for Accountants, 1919–1945.* New York, 1982.

*Sheldahl, Terry K. *Beta Alpha Psi, from Omega to Zeta Omega: The Making of a Comprehensive Accounting Fraternity, 1946–1984.* New York, 1986.

Solomons, David. *Collected Papers on Accounting and Accounting Education.* New York, 1984.

Sprague, Charles F. *The General Principles of the Science of Accounts and the Accountancy of Investment.* New York, 1984.

Stamp, Edward. *Selected Papers on Accounting, Auditing, and Professional Problems.* New York, 1984.

*Storrar, Colin, ed. *The Accountant's Magazine—An Anthology*. New York, 1986.

Tantral, Panadda. *Accounting Literature in Non-Accounting Journals: An Annotated Bibliography*. New York, 1984.

*Vangermeersch, Richard, ed. *The Contributions of Alexander Hamilton Church to Accounting and Management*. New York, 1986.

*Vangermeersch, Richard, ed. *Financial Accounting Milestones in the Annual Reports of United States Steel Corporation—The First Seven Decades*. New York, 1986.

Whitmore, John. *Factory Accounts*. New York, 1984.

Yamey, Basil S. *Further Essays on the History of Accounting*. New York, 1982.

Zeff, Stephen A., ed. *The Accounting Postulates and Principles Controversy of the 1960s*. New York, 1982.

Zeff, Stephen A., ed. *Accounting Principles Through the Years: The Views of Professional and Academic Leaders 1938–1954*. New York, 1982.

Zeff, Stephen A., and Maurice Moonitz, eds. *Sourcebook on Accounting Principles and Auditing Procedures: 1917–1953 (in two volumes)*. New York, 1984.

Reprinted Titles

American Institute of Accountants. *Fiftieth Anniversary Celebration*. Chicago, 1963 (Garland reprint, 1982).

American Institute of Accountants. *Library Catalogue*. New York, 1937 (Garland reprint, 1982).

Arthur Andersen Company. *The First Fifty Years 1913–1963*. Chicago, 1963 (Garland reprint, 1984).

*Bevis, Herman W. *Corporate Financial Reporting in a Competitive Economy*. New York, 1965 (Garland reprint, 1986).

*Bonini, Charles P., Robert K. Jaedicke, and Harvey M. Wagner, eds. *Management Controls: New Directions in Basic Research*. New York, 1964 (Garland reprint, 1986).

Bray, F. Sewell. *Four Essays in Accounting Theory.* London, 1953. *Bound with* Institute of Chartered Accountants in England and Wales and the National Institute of Economic and Social Research. *Some Accounting Terms and Concepts.* Cambridge, 1951 (Garland reprint, 1982).

Brown, R. Gene, and Kenneth S. Johnston. *Paciolo on Accounting.* New York, 1963 (Garland reprint, 1984).

*Carey, John L., and William O. Doherty, eds. *Ethical Standards of the Accounting Profession.* New York, 1966 (Garland reprint, 1986).

Chambers, R. J. *Accounting in Disarray.* Melbourne, 1973 (Garland reprint, 1982).

Cooper, Ernest. *Fifty-seven Years in an Accountant's Office. See* Sir Russell Kettle.

Couchman, Charles B. *The Balance-Sheet.* New York, 1924 (Garland reprint, 1982).

Couper, Charles Tennant. *Report of the Trial . . . Against the Directors and Manager of the City of Glasgow Bank.* Edinburgh, 1879 (Garland reprint, 1984).

Cutforth, Arthur E. *Audits.* London, 1906 (Garland reprint, 1982).

Cutforth, Arthur E. *Methods of Amalgamation.* London, 1926 (Garland reprint, 1982).

Deinzer, Harvey T. *Development of Accounting Thought.* New York, 1965 (Garland reprint, 1984).

De Paula, F.R.M. *The Principles of Auditing.* London, 1915 (Garland reprint, 1984).

Dickerson, R. W. *Accountants and the Law of Negligence.* Toronto, 1966 (Garland reprint, 1982).

Dodson, James. *The Accountant, or, the Method of Bookkeeping Deduced from Clear Principles, and Illustrated by a Variety of Examples.* London, 1750 (Garland reprint, 1984).

Dyer, S. *A Common Sense Method of Double Entry Bookkeeping, on First Principles, as Suggested by De Morgan. Part I, Theoretical.* London, 1897 (Garland reprint, 1984).

*The Fifth International Congress on Accounting, 1938 {Kongress-Archiv 1938 des V. Internationalen Prüfungs- und Treuhand-Kongresses}. Berlin, 1938 (Garland reprint, 1986).

Finney, H. A. Consolidated Statements. New York, 1922 (Garland reprint, 1982).

Fisher, Irving. The Rate of Interest. New York, 1907 (Garland reprint, 1982).

Florence, P. Sargant. Economics of Fatigue of Unrest and the Efficiency of Labour in English and American Industry. London, 1923 (Garland reprint, 1984).

Fourth International Congress on Accounting 1933. London, 1933 (Garland reprint, 1982).

Foye, Arthur B. Haskins & Sells: Our First Seventy-Five Years. New York, 1970 (Garland reprint, 1984).

Garnsey, Sir Gilbert. Holding Companies and Their Published Accounts. London, 1923. Bound with Sir Gilbert Garnsey. Limitations of a Balance Sheet. London, 1928 (Garland reprint, 1982).

Garrett, A. A. The History of the Society of Incorporated Accountants, 1885–1957. Oxford, 1961 (Garland reprint, 1984).

Gilman, Stephen. Accounting Concepts of Profit. New York, 1939 (Garland reprint, 1982).

*Gordon, William. The Universal Accountant, and Complete Merchant . . . [Volume II]. Edinburgh, 1765 (Garland reprint, 1986).

*Green, Wilmer. History and Survey of Accountancy. Brooklyn, 1930 (Garland reprint, 1986).

Hamilton, Robert. An Introduction to Merchandise, Parts IV and V (Italian Bookkeeping and Practical Bookkeeping). Edinburgh, 1788. (Garland reprint, 1982).

Hatton, Edward. The Merchant's Magazine: or, Trades-man's Treasury. London, 1695 (Garland reprint, 1982).

Hills, George S. The Law of Accounting and Financial Statements. Boston, 1957 (Garland reprint, 1982).

*A *History of Cooper Brothers & Co. 1854 to 1954*. London, 1954 (Garland reprint, 1986).

Hofstede, Geert. *The Game of Budget Control*. Assen, 1967 (Garland reprint, 1984).

Howitt, Sir Harold. *The History of The Institute of Chartered Accountants in England and Wales 1880–1965, and of Its Founder Accountancy Bodies 1870–1880*. London, 1966 (Garland reprint, 1984).

Institute of Chartered Accountants in England and Wales and The National Institute of Economic and Social Research. *Some Accounting Terms and Concepts*. *See* F. Sewell Bray.

Institute of Chartered Accountants of Scotland. *History of the Chartered Accountants of Scotland from the Earliest Times to 1954*. Edinburgh, 1954 (Garland reprint, 1984).

International Congress on Accounting 1929. New York, 1930 (Garland reprint, 1982).

*Jaedicke, Robert K., Yuji Ijiri, and Oswald Nielsen, eds. *Research in Accounting Measurement*. American Accounting Association, 1966 (Garland reprint, 1986).

Keats, Charles. *Magnificent Masquerade*. New York, 1964 (Garland reprint, 1982).

Kettle, Sir Russell. *Deloitte & Co. 1845–1956*. Oxford, 1958. *Bound with* Ernest Cooper. *Fifty-seven Years in an Accountant's Office*. London, 1921 (Garland reprint, 1982).

Kitchen, J., and R. H. Parker. *Accounting Thought and Education: Six English Pioneers*. London, 1980 (Garland reprint, 1984).

Lacey, Kenneth. *Profit Measurement and Price Changes*. London, 1952 (Garland reprint, 1982).

Lee, Chauncey. *The American Accomptant*. Lansingburgh, 1797 (Garland reprint, 1982).

Lee, T. A., and R. H. Parker. *The Evolution of Corporate Financial Reporting*. Middlesex, 1979 (Garland reprint, 1984).

*Malcolm, Alexander. *A Treatise of Book-Keeping, or, Merchants Accounts; In *the Italian Method of Debtor and Creditor; Wherein the Fundamental Principles of That Curious and Approved Method Are Clearly and Fully Explained and Demonstrated . . . To Which Are Added, Instructions for Gentlemen of Land Estates, and Their Stewards or Factors: With Directions Also for Retailers, and Other More Private Persons.* London, 1731 (Garland reprint, 1986).

*Meij, J. L., ed. *Depreciation and Replacement Policy.* Chicago, 1961 (Garland reprint, 1986).

Newlove, George Hills. *Consolidated Balance Sheets.* New York, 1926 (Garland reprint, 1982).

*North, Roger. *The Gentleman Accomptant; or, An Essay to Unfold the Mystery of Accompts; By Way of Debtor and Creditor, Commonly Called Merchants Accompts, and Applying the Same to the Concerns of the Nobility and Gentry of England.* London, 1714 (Garland reprint, 1986).

Pryce-Jones, Janet E., and R. H. Parker. *Accounting in Scotland: A Historical Bibliography.* Edinburgh, 1976 (Garland reprint, 1984).

Robinson, H. W. *A History of Accountants in Ireland.* Dublin, 1964 (Garland reprint, 1984).

Robson, T. B. *Consolidated and Other Group Accounts.* London, 1950 (Garland reprint, 1982).

Rorem, C. Rufus. *Accounting Method.* Chicago, 1928 (Garland reprint, 1982).

*Saliers, Earl A., ed. *Accountants' Handbook.* New York, 1923 (Garland reprint, 1986).

Samuel, Horace B. *Shareholder's Money.* London, 1933 (Garland reprint, 1982).

The Securities and Exchange Commission in the Matter of McKesson & Robbins, Inc. Report on Investigation. Washington, D.C., 1940 (Garland reprint, 1982).

The Securities and Exchange Commission in the Matter of McKesson & Robbins, Inc. Testimony of Expert Witnesses. Washington, D.C., 1939 (Garland reprint, 1982).

*Shaplen, Robert. *Kreuger: Genius and Swindler.* New York, 1960 (Garland reprint, 1986).

Singer, H. W. *Standardized Accountancy in Germany. (With a new appendix.) Cambridge, 1943 (Garland reprint, 1982).*

The Sixth International Congress on Accounting. London, 1952 (Garland reprint, 1984).

*Stewart, Jas. C. (with a new introductory note by T. A. Lee). *Pioneers of a Profession: Chartered Accountants to 1879.* Edinburgh, 1977 (Garland reprint, 1986).

Thompson, Wardbaugh. *The Accomptant's Oracle: or, Key to Science, Being a Compleat Practical System of Book-keeping.* York, 1777 (Garland reprint, 1984).

*Vatter, William J. *Managerial Accounting.* New York, 1950 (Garland reprint, 1986).

*Woolf, Arthur H. *A Short History of Accountants and Accountancy.* London, 1912 (Garland reprint, 1986).

Yamey, B. S., H. C. Edey, and Hugh W. Thomson. *Accounting in England and Scotland: 1543–1800.* London, 1963 (Garland reprint, 1982).